THE PRESIDENTIALIZATION OF POLITICS

D0940854

COMPARATIVE POLITICS

Comparative Politics is a series for students and teachers of political science
that deals with contemporary issues in comparative government and politics.
As Comparative European Politics it has produced a series of high quality books since
its foundation in 1990, but now takes on a new form and new title for the new
millennium—Comparative Politics. As the process of globalization proceeds, and as
Europe becomes ever more enmeshed in world trends and events, so it is necessary to
broaden the scope of the series. The General Editors are Professor Alfio Mastropaolo,
University of Turin and Kenneth Newton, University of Southampton and
Wissenschaftszentrum Berlin. The series is published in association with the
European Consortium for Political Research.

OTHER TITLES IN THIS SERIES

Democratic Challenges, Democratic Choices
Russell J. Dalton

Democracy Transformed?
Edited by Bruce E. Cain, Russell J. Dalton, and Susan E. Scarrow

Environmental Protest in Western Europe
Edited by Christopher Rootes

Social Movements and Networks
Edited by Mario Diani and Doug McAdam

Delegation and Accountability in Parliamentary Democracies
Edited by Kaare Strøm, Wolfgang C. Müller, and Torbjörn Bergman

Losers' Consent
*Christopher J. Anderson, André Blais, Shaun Bowler,
Todd Donovan, and Ola Listhaug*

Elections, Parties, Democracy
Michael D. McDonald and Ian Budge

The Presidentialization
of Politics

A Comparative Study of
Modern Democracies

edited by

THOMAS POGUNTKE

and

PAUL WEBB

OXFORD
UNIVERSITY PRESS

This book has been printed digitally and produced in a standard specification
in order to ensure its continuing availability

OXFORD
UNIVERSITY PRESS

Great Clarendon Street, Oxford OX2 6DP

Oxford University Press is a department of the University of Oxford.
It furthers the University's objective of excellence in research, scholarship,
and education by publishing worldwide in

Oxford New York

Auckland   Cape Town   Dar es Salaam   Hong Kong   Karachi
Kuala Lumpur   Madrid   Melbourne   Mexico City   Nairobi
New Delhi   Shanghai   Taipei   Toronto
With offices in
Argentina   Austria   Brazil   Chile   Czech Republic   France   Greece
Guatemala   Hungary   Italy   Japan   South Korea   Poland   Portugal
Singapore   Switzerland   Thailand   Turkey   Ukraine   Vietnam

Oxford is a registered trade mark of Oxford University Press
in the UK and in certain other countries

Published in the United States
by Oxford University Press Inc., New York

© the several contributors 2005

The moral rights of the author have been asserted

Database right Oxford University Press (maker)

Reprinted 2009

All rights reserved. No part of this publication may be reproduced,
stored in a retrieval system, or transmitted, in any form or by any means,
without the prior permission in writing of Oxford University Press,
or as expressly permitted by law, or under terms agreed with the appropriate
reprographics rights organization. Enquiries concerning reproduction
outside the scope of the above should be sent to the Rights Department,
Oxford University Press, at the address above

You must not circulate this book in any other binding or cover
And you must impose this same condition on any acquirer

ISBN 978-0-19-921849-3

Acknowledgements and Dedication

In the course of writing this book, a number of debts have been incurred, which should be acknowledged. The seeds of the project were sewn in a Workshop of the European Consortium of Political Research staged in Copenhagen in April 2000. We are grateful for the support which the ECPR and the University of Copenhagen provided on that occasion, and to all who participated in the Workshop, regardless of whether they contributed chapters to this volume. Subsequently, the European Science Foundation provided the financial support, which enabled us to stage an invaluable project meeting in the beautiful and highly conducive surroundings of Swanborough Manor, Sussex, in April 2002. Our theoretical framework has greatly benefited from these meetings, and we are very grateful to all our collaborators for their excellent cooperation over several rounds of editing. Indeed, the entire enterprise has been an example of the positive benefits of genuinely collaborative research. For comparative political science, in particular, collaborative work is often the best way forward; the scope of a book such as this one, for instance, is inevitably beyond the knowledge of one or even two authors working alone. However, there are two further important reasons why comparative politics is likely to retain its dependence on team research: first, such an approach enables the scholar to set empirical indicators in their national political contexts, which is vital if one is to avoid the well-known traps of 'concept-stretching' and 'travelling'; second, the sheer range of knowledge and intellectual insight on which one is able to draw when working as part of a well-integrated team can be quite fantastic. In this particular instance, the personal and intellectual dynamics of the project members worked extremely well. It is for readers to judge the value of our achievement, but we are both certain that it exceeds anything we could have produced working either alone or as a duo. We understand that there are some critics who tend to denigrate the general value of edited volumes today: we strongly feel that to do so, however, is both intrinsically unjustifiable and represents a systematic bias against comparative inquiry.

In the course of working on the book, Paul Webb benefited greatly from a highly productive, if all too brief, Visiting Fellowship at the Australian National University during the final editorial phase in early 2004. He greatly appreciates the opportunity of spending that time in Canberra, and the very helpful feedback provided by various ANU faculty, visitors, and research students, including Ian McAllister, Rod Rhodes, Marian Sawer, Ian Marsh,

Barry Hindess, and Pat Seyd. Beyond this, we have presented various papers based on this project at our home universities, as well as at the universities of Essex, Sheffield, Salford and Düsseldorf. Again, a number of participants on these occasions offered particularly helpful comments, including David Farrell, Jonathan Tonge, Stephen Fielding, John Keiger, Ted Tapper, Neil Stammers, and Wolfgang C. Müller. While we are grateful for the interest shown by all these individuals in our work, sole responsibility for the contents of this book lies with us and the contributors, of course. In addition, we would like to thank the support and patience of those at Oxford University Press, especially Dominic Byatt, Claire Croft and Elizabeth Suffling, who have enabled this book to come to fruition and have helped us with the paperback edition. Finally, we would like to dedicate this book to our parents, and particularly to the memory of Heinz Poguntke.

Thomas Poguntke, Keele
Paul Webb, Sussex
July 2004

Contents

List of Figures

List of Tables

Notes on Contributors

Nicholas Aylott is Senior Lecturer (docent) in Political Science at Södertörn University College, Sweden. He previously worked at Keele University UK, and Umeå University, Sweden. His research field is comparative European politics, with special focus on Scandinavia and, thematically, political parties. He is the author of *Swedish Social Democracy and European Integration* (Ashgate 1999), and of numerous chapters and articles in such journals as *Government and Opposition, Party Politics*, and *West European Politics*.

Herman Bakvis is Professor of Public Administration at the University of Victoria in Canada. He was previously Director of the School of Public Administration at Dalhousie University. His research interests include government structure and organization, cabinet government, political parties, and intergovernmental relations. His publications include *Canadian Federalism: Performance, Effectiveness, and Legitimacy* (Oxford 2002, co-edited with G. Skogstad) and *The Hollow Crown: Countervailing Trends in Core Executives* (Macmillan 1997, co-edited with P. Weller and R.A.W. Rhodes).

Ingrid van Biezen is Reader in Comparative Politics at the University of Birmingham. She has taught at the University of Leiden and the Johns Hopkins University (Baltimore) and has held Visiting Fellowships at Yale University and the University of California, Irvine. She is the author of *Political Parties in New Democracies* (Palgrave Macmillan 2003) and has published various articles on political finance, party organization, and party membership in *Party Politics, European Journal of Political Research*, and *West European Politics*.

Mauro Calise is Professor of Political Science at the University of Naples 'Federico II', and Editor and Director of the International Political Science Association Portal for Electronic Sources (www.ipsaportal.net). He has published books and articles in several areas, including political theory, governmental elites, political parties, and conceptual analysis. His latest book is *La Terza Repubblica. Partiti contro Presidenti* (Editore Laterza 2006), and he is presently completing, with Theodore J. Lowi, *Hyperpolitics*, a book and a computer-assisted platform for the hypertextual treatment of political science concepts (www.hyperpolitics.net). He has held visiting positions at Institut d'Etudes Politique de Paris, Cornell University, and the Harvard Center for European Studies.

Ben Clift is Senior Lecturer in International Political Economy at the University of Warwick, having formerly taught at Brunel University. He is the author of *French Socialism in a Global Era: The Political Economy of the New Social Democracy in France* (Continuum Books 2003), and of various articles and book chapters on French politics and the comparative political economy of Social Democracy.

Marina Costa Lobo is a Researcher at the Social Sciences Institute of the University of Lisbon, where she directs the Master's Degree in Comparative Politics. She is co-director of the Project on Portuguese electoral behaviour and Political Attitudes, which is responsible for the Portuguese Election Study. Her main interests are electoral behaviour, political parties and Portuguese political institutions. She is the author of *Governar em Democracia*, (Lisboa:ICS, 2005), and of articles in *Electoral Studies, European Journal of Political Research*, and *South European Society and Politics*.

Sergio Fabbrini is Professor of Political Science at the University of Trento, where he directs the School of International Studies. He has also taught and lectured at the universities of California at Berkeley, Harvard (USA), Nanjing (China), Carleton (Canada), Bath (Britain), Osaka and Tokyo (Japan). He has authored or co-authored eight academic books, edited and co-edited six others, and published numerous articles in the fields of Comparative, American, Italian, and European Union politics, and Political Theory. He is currently the editor of *La Rivista Italiana di Scienza Politica* (the Italian Political Science Review).

Stefaan Fiers is Lecturer in Comparative Politics and Director of the teacher training programme in social sciences at the Catholic University of Leuven, Belgium. His main research interests include civic education and the recruitment of political elites, especially within the framework of multilevel governance. He has authored and co-authored various articles and book chapters on the recruitment of MPs and MEPs, the selection of party leaders, and the direct election of prime ministers.

Reuven Y. Hazan is Senior Lecturer in the Department of Political Science at The Hebrew University of Jerusalem. He is the author of *Reforming Parliamentary Committees: Israel in Comparative Perspective* (Ohio State University Press 2001), and the editor of *Cohesion and Discipline in Legislatures: Political Parties, Party Leadership, Parliamentary Committees and Governance* (Routledge forthcoming). His articles on electoral and political reform in Israel have appeared in a wide variety of journals, including *Comparative Political Studies, Electoral Studies, Journal of Legislative Studies, Legislative Studies Quarterly, Party Politics, Political Geography*, and *Representation*.

Richard Heffernan teaches at the Open University and has published widely on many aspects of British politics. He is the author of *New Labour and*

Thatcherism: Political Change in Britain (Palgrave 2001) and an editor of *Developments in British Politics 7* (Palgrave Macmillan 2003).

Jonathan Hopkin is Lecturer in Government at the London School of Economics. He is the author of *Party Formation and Democratic Transition in Spain* (Macmillan 1999), and has also worked on corruption and party politics, comparative party organizations, and the effects of political decentralization on parties. He has published in a range of journals, including the *European Journal of Political Research, European Urban and Regional Studies, Party Politics, Review of International Political Economy*, and *West European Politics*.

Tim Knudsen is Professor in Public Administration at the University of Copenhagen. He has published extensively on Scandinavian state-building and Danish administrative history, including 'How informal can you be? The case of Denmark' in B. Guy Peters, R.A.W. Rhodes, and Vincent Wright (eds.) *Administering the Summit: Administration of the Core Executive* (Palgrave 2000).

André Krouwel is Associate Professor of Comparative Politics in the Department of Political Science at the Vrije Universiteit in Amsterdam. He has authored or edited various books, articles, and chapters on the transformation of political parties, social movements, electoral behaviour, and democratization in Eastern Europe.

Heikki Paloheimo is Professor of Political Science and the Dean of the Faculty of Social Sciences at the University of Tampere, Finland. His research interests cover political participation, political institutions, comparative politics, and policy analysis. He has publishes extensively on these themes, including the recent publications *Vaalit ja demokratia Suomessa* (Elections and Democracy in Finland, WSOY 2005, editor), *Suomen puolueiden periaateohjelmat* (Party Manifestos of Finnish Political Parties, University of Tampere 2006, editor), and *Eduskuntavaalit 1907–2003* (General Elections in Finland 1907–2003, Edita 2007). He is a member of the editorial boards of the *European Journal of Political Research* and *Politiikka* (the quarterly Journal of the Finnish Political Science Association), Finnish representative in the *Comparative Study of Electoral Systems* (CSES), the head of the *Finnish Standing Group on Political Participation*, and has been responsible on the Finnish field work in the *Comparative Manifestos Project* (CMP). He is a regular national TV commentator on Finnish general elections, and a frequent expert witness to Finnish parliamentary committees on political institutions.

Karina Pedersen is Associate Professor in Comparative Politics at the University of Copenhagen. Her research centers on political parties, elections and representative democracy. She is the author of Party Membership Linkage: The Danish Case (University of Copenhagen), as well as several book chapters and articles published in Political Science, Party Politics, West European Politics and Scandinavian Political Studies.

Thomas Poguntke is Professor of Political Science at the University of Bochum, and Fellow at the Mannheim Centre for European Social Research, having taught previously at the universities of Stuttgart, Mannheim, Bielefeld, Keele and Birmingham. He is the series editor of the *Routledge/ECPR Studies in European Political Science* and is the author or editor of numerous publications including *Parteiorganisation im Wandel: Gesellschaftliche Verankerung und organisatorische Anpassung im Europäischen Vergleich* (Westdeutscher Verlag 2000) and *How Parties Respond: Interest Aggregation Revisited* (Routledge 2004, with Kay Lawson). His main research interests focus on New Politics, party politics, and comparative analysis of democratic regimes. He has recently lead research projects on Europarties and the Europeanization of national political parties.

Paul Webb is Professor of Politics at the University of Sussex, and has held a number of previous and visiting positions in Britain and abroad, most recently at the Australian National University. His research interests focus on representative democracy, particularly party and electoral politics. He is author or editor of numerous publications, including *The Modern British Party System* (Sage Publications, 2000), *Political Parties in Advanced Industrial Societies* (Oxford University Press, 2002, with David Farrell and Ian Holliday) and *Party Politics in New Democracues* (Oxford University Press, forthcoming, with Stephen White). He is currently co-editor of the journals *Party Politics* and *Representation*.

Steven B. Wolinetz is Professor of Political Science at Memorial University of Newfoundland. A specialist in European and Dutch politics, he is the author of numerous publications on parties and party systems, including *Parties and Party Systems in Liberal Democracies* (Routledge 1988), and editor of the International Library of Politics and Comparative Government volumes on *Political Parties* and *Party Systems* (Routledge 1998). His articles include 'The Transformation of Western European Party Systems Revisited' (*West European Politics* 1979).

The Presidentialization of Politics in Democratic Societies: A Framework for Analysis

Thomas Poguntke and Paul Webb

INTRODUCTION

The theme of the concentration of power around leaders in democratic political systems is by no means new. More than thirty years ago Farrell (1971: x) observed that 'in almost all political systems, executive dominance and the personification of this domination in a single leader is a central fact of political life'. Yet, it is hard to avoid the impression that perceptions of the personalization, and in particular, the 'presidentialization' of politics have become more widespread in recent years, regardless of formal constitutional characteristics. For instance, in the United Kingdom long-standing concerns about prime ministerial power have occasionally produced assertions of 'presidential' rule, most notably in the work of Foley (1993, 2000). Indeed, with the advent of Tony Blair's premiership such assessments became almost commonplace, especially though not exclusively among journalists (e.g. Draper 1997, 1999; Hencke 2000; Watt 2000), and similar claims have been heard in respect of Gerhard Schröder's Germany (Lütjen and Walter 2000; Traynor 1999) and even the Italy of Bettino Craxi (Fabbrini 1994) or Silvio Berlusconi (Calise 2000). Still more common, perhaps, are references to the 'presidentialization' or 'candidate-centredness' of election campaigning across the world's democratic regimes (Bowler and Farrell 1992; Mughan 2000; Wattenberg 1991).

In view of their widespread diffusion, the time is surely ripe to assess the validity of such claims. This is the primary purpose of this volume. But what exactly is the phenomenon in which we are interested? In our view, *presidentialization* denominates a process by which regimes are becoming more presidential in their actual practice without, in most cases, changing their formal structure, that is, their regime-type. This, of course, raises the question of what exactly is the actual working mode of presidential systems. There are two ways of answering this question:

1. Empirically, which is to say, by looking at existing presidential democracies. Essentially, this means looking to the US, as the prime example
of a pure presidential democracy;
2. Theoretically, that is, through an analysis of the inherent mechanics of
presidential systems. Here the focus is on the incentives and constraints
that result directly from the configuration of the essential constitutional
elements (legislature, executive, chains of accountability, methods of
election, and so on).

The latter (ideal-typical) approach is to be preferred, because it is not
confounded by the actual working mode of an existing presidential system.
Thus, our first step is to make a brief consideration of different regime types.

REGIME TYPES

Key features of presidentialism

The executive must be politically irresponsible to the legislature. The separation of powers is the classic core condition of presidentialism, which ensures
that the executive is not accountable to the legislature nor removable by it.
Rather, the president is accountable only to the electorate which furnished
his or her mandate to govern. Given that the president cannot be brought
down by the legislature, it is logical, moreover, for his or her incumbency to
be for a fixed term. Exceptionally, as in the American case, a president may
be subject to impeachment by the legislature for reasons of gross impropriety
or misconduct, but as Verney (1959) points out in his classic account of
presidentialism, this is not so much an example of political accountability
as it is of juridical control. The separation of powers doctrine works both
ways, of course, so that a president may not dissolve parliament, the members of which enjoy their own democratic mandates.

Presidential regimes have popularly elected heads of government. For a
political system to merit the presidential label in a formal sense, the president
must be the true head of government, and the most common (if not only) way
in which such status can be conferred in a democracy is for the president to be
popularly elected, either directly by the people or via an electoral college
which closely reflects the popular preferences of the electorate (Lijphart 1992:
3). As a rule, such a popular mandate is an essential precondition of a
president's democratic legitimacy and, therefore, of his or her personal
authority to govern.[1]

*Presidential regimes are characterized by unipersonal executive responsibil-
ity.* Under presidentialism, only the president is mandated to govern by the
people, and therefore, only he or she is politically accountable. This does not
mean, of course, that the executive literally comprises a single individual; the

US President, for instance, appoints the members of his cabinet, who take charge of policy in different government departments, but they are not individually responsible to the electorate (or to the legislature, given the separation of powers which operates). Only the president himself has a personal democratic mandate, which means that he has complete authority to hire and fire members of his cabinet, and they are accountable directly to him: he then carries responsibility for the entire administration.

It seems to us that these three features of a popularly elected executive, the separation of executive and legislative power, and unipersonal executive responsibility constitute the necessary and sufficient formal conditions which define presidentialism in a legal-constitutional sense. While the actual autonomy and power of a president may vary considerably within these constitutional parameters according to a variety of contingent and institutional factors, it nevertheless remains formally a presidential regime.

Parliamentarism

Under parliamentarism, the political executive emerges from the legislature whose confidence it must enjoy. This fusion of powers does not necessarily mean that the executive must actually retain the positive support of a parliamentary majority, but it does at least have to avoid a situation in which a majority forms against it on a vote of no-confidence (Strøm 1990). Thus, the executive in a parliamentary regime is formally accountable to the legislature; this represents one element of a single chain of delegation and accountability extending from voters to bureaucracy (Strøm 2000; Strøm et al. 2003). In reality, however, we know that parliamentary party discipline may be so developed that the executive enjoys a high degree of de facto control over the legislature, Bagehot's so-called 'efficient secret' of the British constitution (Bagehot 1867; see also Cox 1987). The inherent logic of the parliamentary regime compels parties of government and opposition to maintain high discipline in order to either support the government or present themselves as a credible alternative. This is not guaranteed, however, as the experiences of regimes such as the Third and Fourth French Republics, the Italian post-war republic, and modern Israel demonstrate. Party systems may provide strong countervailing incentives: in the absence of alternative majorities, parties of government may not be penalized, even if they bring down their own government. However, as the examples show, systems that continue to function against the logic of parliamentarism run into great difficulties.

Parliamentary regimes are characterized by collective executive responsibility. Under parliamentarism the executive *as a whole* emerges from (and as we have seen, is responsible to) the legislature. Even though the elevated role of the prime minister is formally recognized in some political systems, the collective character of the government represents an essential characteristic of parliamentarism.[2]

Semi-presidentialism

As Sartori (1994: 153) says, semi-presidential regimes are 'double-engine systems' characterized by dyarchic executives. That is, not only do they have popularly elected heads of state who are politically not responsible to the legislature and have a degree of real executive power, but this power must also in some way be shared with a separate prime minister, the latter being formally the head of a government which emerges from the legislature and is responsible to it (Duverger 1980; Linz 1994: 48; Sartori 1994: 131ff.; Elgie 1999: 13).[3] Thus, a semi-presidential regime mixes core elements of presidentialism and parliamentarism. Its actual working mode is directly dependent upon presence or absence of party political congruence between the president and the parliamentary majority. In periods of unified government, semi-presidential regimes resemble an extreme form of parliamentarism in that the prime minister tends to be the lieutenant of the president who ultimately controls all executive powers *and* dominates parliament through a prime minster in charge of the parliamentary part of government. In times of divided government, however, semi-presidential regimes revert to a unique mix of parliamentary and presidential elements of government and the president is reduced to that portion of executive powers which is vested directly in his or her office and hence not subject to parliamentary accountability. In effect, the chief executive office is split between a president and a prime minister (Poguntke 2000*b*: 359–61). Hence, semi-presidentialism does not simply alternate between phases of parliamentary and presidential government, as has been suggested by Lijphart (1992: 8, 1997: 127). Moreover, it is a regime type in its own right (Pasquino 1997: 129), not just a version of parliamentarism (for a different view see Strøm 2000: 266).

THE CONCEPT OF PRESIDENTIALIZATION

The preceding discussion has shown that presidential systems offer far more *executive power resources* to the leader of the executive while, at the same time, giving him or her considerable *autonomy* vis-à-vis the political parties in parliament (and vice versa). Essentially, the inherent functional logic of presidential regimes has three effects:

1. *Leadership power resources*: The logic of presidentialism provides the head of government with superior executive power resources. This emanates directly from the fact that he or she is not responsible to parliament, is usually directly legitimated and has the power to form a cabinet without significant interference from other institutions. In a nutshell, as regards the executive branch of the government, the head of the executive can govern without much outside interference.
2. *Leadership autonomy*: This is also a direct result of the separation of powers. While in office, the head of the executive is well protected against pressure from his own party. This works both ways, however. Parties in parliament are not constrained either to support the government or to present themselves as a viable opposition. Hence, while the head of the executive enjoys considerable autonomy vis-à-vis his own party, his power to lead depends directly on his electoral appeal. In other words, leadership autonomy may make for enhanced power to lead, but it is contingent upon electoral success. It is not based on organizational control of the party. In a nutshell, leadership autonomy may find expression in two different zones of action: the party organization itself, and (for governing parties) the political executive of the state.
3. *Personalization of the electoral process*: This follows directly from the natural focus on the highest elective office and implies that all aspects of the electoral process are decisively moulded by the personalities of the leading candidates.

It follows from this that the de facto presidentialization of politics can be understood as the development of (a) increasing leadership power resources and autonomy within the party and the political executive respectively, and (b) increasingly leadership-centred electoral processes. Essentially, three central arenas of democratic government are affected by theses changes, which we may refer to as three faces of presidentialization, namely *the executive face, the party face*, and *the electoral face*, respectively. Presidentialization as a process means that these three faces of presidentialization are amplified by factors other than those flowing directly from the formal constitutional structure. The central question addressed in this volume is therefore whether there are contingent and structural (as opposed to formal-constitutional) factors at work that push modern democracies towards a more presidential working mode. In exceptional cases, however, the forces of presidentialization have led to a formal ratification of changes (as temporarily in Israel).

In principle, all regime-types can move (to varying degrees) between partified and presidentialized forms of government. How closely they approach either of the opposing poles of this continuum is determined by a wide

Poguntke and Webb

range of underlying structural factors (such as changes in the social structure and the media system) and contingent factors (such as the personality of leaders). This movement is, of course, highly constrained by the formal configuration of political institutions. In other words, different regime-settings provide institutions and actors with different power resources, thus constraining correspondingly the potential space for movement. This is depicted in Fig. 1.1 by the different locations of individual regime types on the overall continuum. Pushed to its limits, the concept even allows us to distinguish between presidentialized and partified variants of presidential systems. Only 'presidentialized presidential' systems have fully realized their potential for the presidentialized form of politics.

The *horizontal dimension* distinguishes parliamentary, presidential, and semi-presidential regimes according to formal legal-constitutional criteria. The boundaries between these three categories of regime are impermeable in the sense that they are not part of a flexible continuum along which countries might gradually shift, thanks to the introduction of a little more or a little less parliamentarism or presidentialism as the case may be; for this reason, semi-presidentialism – though physically located between parliamentarism and presidentialism as in Fig. 1.1, is not simply to be understood as a vague half-way point between the two, but rather as a distinct regime-type in its own

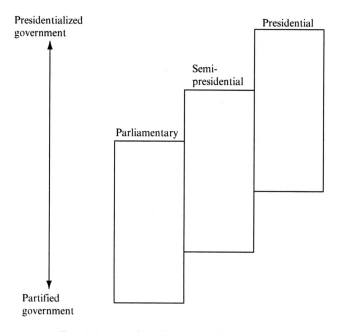

FIG. 1.1. *Presidentialization and regime type*

right. Although not all presidential regimes are identical, they must never-theless share a common set of core legal-constitutional features in order to qualify for the designation, and the same goes for parliamentary and semi-presidential regimes respectively.

The *vertical dimension* of Fig. 1.1 differs from the horizontal dimension in so far as it can be regarded as a continuum rather than a rigidly partitioned set of discrete categories. This is indicated by the double-ended arrow dis-tinguishing the 'presidentialized' northern end of the scale from the 'partified' southern end. Location on this continuum does not depend on formal legal-constitutional provisions, but rather on structural and contingent political characteristics which determine the degree of personal visibility, autonomy, and power resources which national political leaders have. By structural we mean enduring changes below the level of legal-constitutional changes such as changes in party rules or in the fabric of society, whereas contingent changes depend on the characteristics of particular political actors or specific political contexts. In effect, this dimension helps distinguish cases *within* regime boundaries; moreover, the fact that this axis can be regarded as a continuum implies that a case could migrate from the partified to the presi-dentialized end, or vice versa, as leaders become a little more or less visible, autonomous, or resourceful. What are the factors which determine location on this continuum?

Essentially, they relate to what we may think of as the *three faces of presidentialization*, each of which revolves around the tension between polit-ical parties and individual leaders. More precisely, the location on the con-tinuum is determined by the shift of *political power resources and autonomy* to the benefit of individual leaders and a concomitant loss of power and auto-nomy of collective actors like cabinets and political parties. If we conceptu-alize power as the ability to achieve a desired outcome, even against resistance (Weber 1980: 28), then autonomy is an important precondition of power in that greater autonomy means lesser likelihood of resistance. In other words, leaders who enjoy greater autonomy have a larger sphere of action in which they are protected from outside interference. To this extent they can effectively ignore other actors. Their overall power is, then, the combination of the scope of this protected area and their ability to use all their power resources to overcome potential resistance by others outside this protected area. Increased power can thus be the result of two processes:

1. A growth of the zones of autonomous control, which means that, effectively, power does not need to be exerted over others as long as desired outcomes are exclusively within such an autonomous zone.
2. A growing capacity to overcome resistance by others. This requires growing resources to overcome potential resistance, that is, to exert power over others.

The executive face

The growth of zones of autonomous control may result directly from giving the chief executive or party leader more formal powers, be it the power of appointment or the power to decide unilaterally about policy. However, the growth of zones of autonomy can also be a result of the increasing recourse to a personal mandate by the leader. In this case, elements of electoral presidentialization (see below), particularly the use of plebiscitary appeals, lead to a highly contingent growth of autonomy in that it is directly dependent upon the continued ability of the leader to substantiate the validity of his personal mandate. In other words, autonomy depends upon his continued ability to appeal successfully to relevant constituencies (be they party rank-and-file or the electorate at large). In short, in an electoralist era, parties may let their leaders 'have their way' as long as they can deliver the electoral rewards.

Exerting power outside zones of autonomous control requires resources to overcome potential resistance. Those may be the usual power resources, including formal powers, staff, and funding, but they may increasingly be connected to the capacity to set agendas and define the alternatives at stake. Increasing control over communication flows is central to this since it furnishes political leaders with enhanced potential to influence the perception of others (whether decision-makers or the public at large) as to the range of viable choices. In fact, growing involvement in international negotiation systems (either on party or government levels) tends to make this power to define the alternatives almost irresistible, because multi-lateral international agreements can rarely be re-negotiated following domestic dissent.

It follows from the preceding discussion that increased leadership power flows from the combined effect of growing autonomy and enhanced power resources. While much of this is related to structural changes such as increasing international interconnectedness, a considerable portion of it will be contingent upon the specific political context, most notably the personal appeal of a leader.

The executive and party faces of presidentialization revolve around the growing power of leaders vis-à-vis their parties. Essentially, the pertinent question is whether the exercise of power is highly personalized or primarily party-constrained ('partified' in the terminology expressed in Fig. 1.1). This question can be addressed in respect of two crucially important political arenas: the political executive of the state (for governing parties) and the political party itself (for all parties).[4] Thus, one way in which we might expect to find evidence of presidentialization of power would be through a shift in intra-executive power to the benefit of the head of government (whether this is a prime minister or a president). At the same time, executives as a whole would become increasingly independent of direct interference from 'their' parties. While partified government means governing *through* parties (Katz 1986: 42–6), presidentialized government implies governing *past* parties. As is indicated in Fig. 1.1, we would assume the logical starting and endpoints to differ substantially between regime types, because different regime types provide their leaders with different degrees of autonomy and power resources.

The party face

The second arena in which the presidentialization of power could reveal itself is the political party itself; this would involve a *shift in intra-party power to the benefit of the leader*. Were this to be the case, we would expect to find evidence of growing leadership autonomy from the dominant coalitions of power within the party. This might occur in a number of ways, including structural changes like the introduction of direct leadership elections by the party rank-and-file. As a result, party activists and factional leaders cease to be the decisive power base of party leaders; rather, claims to leadership rest on personalized mandates. This is likely to be accompanied by a shift towards plebiscitary modes of communication and mobilization which are contingent upon individual leaders' public appeal and communication skills. Increasingly, leaders seek to bypass sub-leaders and activist strata of the party and communicate directly with members (or even voters) in respect of programmatic or strategic questions. Probably most relevant in this regard is the shift towards candidate-centred electioneering (see below), since it is essentially the leader rather than the party who competes for a popular mandate; not surprisingly, therefore, the leader may expect to be accorded considerable autonomy by the party in devising his or her own policy programme.

The tendency towards personalized leadership is likely to lead to a concentration of power resources in the leader's office. However, the logic of presidentialization suggests that the bulk of these resources will not be directed towards controlling the party machinery. Instead, they will be used for enhancing the leader's personal standing through coordinated planning and public relations activities.

To be sure, it is likely that leaders who base their leadership on such (often solely) contingent claims to a personalized mandate will seek to consolidate their leadership by enhancing their control of the party machinery, not least through appropriate statutory changes which give them more direct power over the party. However, this may be a risky strategy in that it could provoke reactions by the party's middle-level strata. While they may have been prepared to accept leadership domination as long as it is contingent on (the promise of) electoral appeal, they are likely to resent the formalization of such power. Hence, while the presidentialization of internal party politics may be accompanied by growing control of the party machinery, this is not an essential characteristic of it. Rather, it is characterized by a shift towards personalized leadership which may be very strong as long as it is successful electorally, but which is likely to be vulnerable in times of impending or actual electoral defeat. In other words, we would expect party leaders to be less likely to survive electoral defeat than has been the case in the past.

What would be the effects of presidentialization on the mode of interaction between the chief executive and political parties in a formally presidential system? Essentially, it would follow the same logic as in a presidentializing parliamentary system. To the extent that the growth of executive power and the effects of electoral presidentialization have elevated the president to a paramount political figure he or she will begin to govern increasingly *past* the parties in the legislature. In other words, presidents will increasingly use the power of their popular mandate and the weight of their executive power to 'have their way' in parliament without directly attempting to control or lead parties.

The electoral face

This brings us to the third face of presidentialization, which concerns *electoral processes*. Again, it involves a shift from partified control to domination by leaders. This may be revealed in a number of closely interrelated ways. First, through a *growing emphasis on leadership appeals in election campaigning*. Again, it seems increasingly common to encounter references to the 'personalized', 'presidential', or 'candidate-centred' campaigns of certain leaders in democratic societies (for instance, Crewe and King 1994; Mughan 1993; Semetko 1996). Although such developments may well be partly contingent on the personalities and leadership styles of particular leaders, they are becoming too widespread and enduring in parliamentary regimes to be explained entirely in these terms. Second, and relatedly, we may expect such campaigning to be reflected by the media so that *media coverage of politics focuses more on leaders*. Third, we might reasonably expect such developments to resonate within the electorate: thus, evidence of the presidentialization of electoral processes could also be constituted by *the growing significance of leader effects in voting behaviour*. Note that it may be difficult to establish evidence of a systematic growth of leadership effects since they are highly dependent on contingencies such as leaders' personalities and the changing political context of elections (Bean and Mughan 1989; Kaase 1994; King 2002). For instance, the politics of a nation may alternate between polarized and consensual phases and it is reasonable to expect that leader effects would play a stronger role in the absence of highly contentious issues. That said, even a small leadership effect could make all the difference on election day. This, and the widespread *perception* of growing leadership effects may be sufficient to convince parties and their campaign planners that it is necessary to personalize campaigns. In other words, even if leadership effects are minimal, the parties may respond to their perceived relevance by consciously personalizing their campaigns.

Overall, then, it should be clear from the foregoing discussion that the 'presidentialization of democratic regimes' entails a shift away from partified democracy in terms of one, two, or all three of the dimensions that we have identified. To be sure, the rate and extent of movement along the respective faces of presidentialization may vary within (as well as between) countries. These variations reflect the impact of the different forces driving the processes of change within each of the faces (see below). However, these processes are logically connected, which means we are unlikely to find shifts in one face accompanied by complete stasis (or even counter-movement) in others.

THE DYNAMICS OF PRESIDENTIALIZATION

What are the effects of presidentialization under the conditions imposed by different political systems? One of the most widely deployed categorizations in the analysis of contemporary democracies is Arend Lijphart's distinction between majoritarian and consensual systems, by which regimes are placed on a continuum ranging between these two ideal-typical poles (Lijphart 1984). Given that our concept of presidentialization is strongly concerned with a shift from a 'partified' to a 'presidentialized' mode of operation, it is imperative to ask whether we expect the dynamics of presidentialization to differ between consensual and majoritarian systems.

Consensual democracies are defined by the fact that the ability of the government of the day to wield power is severely constrained by the existence of a number of institutionalized veto points (Kaiser 1997; Lijphart 1999). These may include judicial review, strong second chambers, coalition partners or pivotal parties in parliament (in the case of minority governments), neo-corporatist negotiation systems, independent central banks, etc. Majoritarian systems, on the contrary, furnish governments with large zones of autonomy. In other words, governments can decide a much larger range of issues without having to take other power centres into account. In all parliamentary systems, however, this autonomy is contingent upon the continued support (or tolerance) of the government by a parliamentary majority.

Under conditions of presidentialization, chief executives in majoritarian systems have more immediate power at their disposal than their counterparts in consensual regimes. While they may not differ with regard to power resources and autonomy vis-à-vis their own party, they can use their elevated position more directly, because governments in majoritarian systems generally enjoy larger zones of autonomy. Government leaders in strongly consensual systems, on the other hand, need to acquire an elevated position vis-à-vis veto players within the political system in order to achieve their goals (see Fig. 1.2). In effect, they need to extend their own and their government's zones of autonomy by reducing the ability of veto players to interfere with the objectives of the government. In doing this, they can use exactly the same resources as a chief executive in a majoritarian system (such as their personal mandate, advisory staff, and so on). However, while a chief executive in a majoritarian system uses these resources primarily to maintain his or her autonomous position vis-à-vis their own party, leaders in consensual systems primarily need to develop these resources in order to extend their autonomy vis-à-vis other actors in the political system (e.g., coalition partners, state governments, neo-corporatist actors, etc.). Their position is less threatened by their own party because they may be able to justify their decisions by referring to the constraints imposed upon them by veto players. In this sense, the very nature of consensual politics provides them with additional power resources.

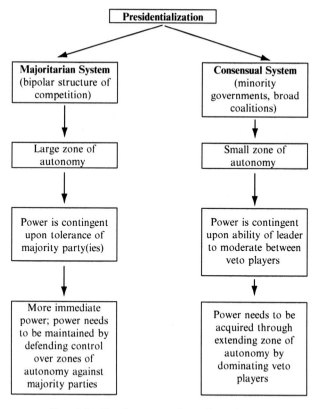

Fig. 1.2. *The dynamics of presidentialization*

In addition, under conditions of presidentialization, government leaders in consensual systems will greatly benefit from their role as chief mediators between influential political forces, because it puts them unequivocally at the centre of the political stage. Nevertheless, while the chief executive in a majoritarian system will have an elevated position by virtue of his position at the head of a single-party, or majority coalition government which dominates the legislature under conditions of bipolar competition, the leader in a consensual system needs to acquire this elevated position through performance in office. In fact, he may become prime minister as a 'party animal' and go on to acquire a 'presidentialized' stature through his role as a chief negotiator, which will then, in turn, lead to a far more presidentialized campaign in the following legislative election. If successful, he may become even more autonomous of his own party than his counterparts in majoritarian systems, because his ability to govern is less directly linked to electoral performance: while a lost majority in a majoritarian system will normally terminate the leader's governmental incumbency (and often also his control over the party), a strong leader in a consensual system may be returned to office by virtue of his continuing position as chief negotiator and arbiter of the government, even if his party has declined at the polls.

THE CAUSES OF PRESIDENTIALIZATION

In addition to contingent factors related to the political context and the personality of leaders, we would hypothesize that the following structural factors are most important for explaining shifts towards a more presidentialized mode of governance in modern democracies. The major causal flows are summarized in Fig. 1.3 (see page 16).

Internationalization of politics

It is now almost trite to observe that many of the most challenging political problems facing governments can only be dealt with via international co-operation. This is implicit in the frequently deployed concept of globalization, and examples can easily be found in policy contexts as diverse as the policing of ethnic conflict (as in the former Yugoslavia), the fight against international terrorism, the battle against environmental pollution, the establishment of effective and just asylum and immigration policies, and the control of global financial markets and patterns of transnational investment. Where such issues are dealt with via inter-governmental negotiation, this shifts power to the heads of governments and some of their key advisers or governmental colleagues. Increasingly, parliaments and even cabinets can only ratify the decisions which have been taken elsewhere. In particular, it would seem likely that the process of European integration means that a substantial part of domestic politics is now decided like international politics, which is a traditional domain of leaders and senior members of governments (as opposed to cabinets, parliaments, and parties).

Growth of the state

The growth of the state has been a long-term process which has undoubtedly led to greater bureaucratic complexity and organizational specialization. Peters et al. (2000: 8) describe this in terms of the twin processes of *institutional differentiation* ('increasing the organizational types through which government works') and *institutional pluralization* ('increasing numbers of the same type of organization'). The growing complexity and competence of the state has generated a variety of responses, some of which would seem to be relevant to the phenomenon of presidentialization, including:

- The centralization of power as the core executive seeks to coordinate the 'institutional fragments' of the state.
- The undermining of collective cabinet responsibility, as the trend towards 'sectorized' policy-making brings more bilateral contacts between relevant ministers and the head of the core executive.

Paradoxically, these processes may well go hand in hand with other initiatives designed to restructure the state by appearing to divest the executive of power, for instance, through privatizing or hiving-off responsibilities to agencies. Thus, strategies conducive to the presidentialization of politics may be compatible with the sort of 'hollowing-out' strategies which governments have sometimes pursued in order to overcome problems of 'ungovernability'. Where this happens, the core executive attempts to reduce the scope of its direct responsibility for government, while enhancing its coordinating power in the domain which it continues to regard as strategically critical. Whatever the precise approach:

there is general agreement that over the last thirty to forty years there has been a steady movement towards the reinforcement of the political core executive in most advanced industrial countries and, that within the core executive, there has been an increasing centralization of authority around the person of the chief executive – president, prime minister, or both (Peters et al. 2000: 7).

The changing structure of mass communication

Another major societal change which may be equally important in accounting for the phenomenon of presidentialization is the growing role of electronic media since the early 1960s (van Deth 1995: 59), which has fundamentally altered the nature of mass communication in modern democracies. The widespread privatization of TV has further amplified these changes. By its very nature, television tends to focus on personality rather than programme in order to reduce the complexity of political issues, and politicians frequently respond by concentrating on symbolism rather than substance and detail in order to cater for the media's inherent needs (Bowler and Farrell 1992; Farrell and Webb 2000). To be sure, it works both ways: to a degree the media require and force politicians to adapt to their logic and their format. Much of this so-called mediatization of modern politics, however, may be the result of conscious choice by politicians to *exploit* the visual media's potential for simplification and symbolism for their own ends. Thus, governmental leaders may use the potential of modern media communications techniques to bypass other executive actors in setting political agendas.

The erosion of traditional social cleavage politics

Since the 'end of ideology' debates of the early 1960s, and the associated interpretations of party transformation in the West (Bell 1960; Kirchheimer 1966; Lipset 1964), many observers have contended that traditional links between mass parties and their bases of social group support have eroded. This has found some confirmation in the work of electoral sociologists in the 1990s (Franklin et al. 1992), though it is not a view that has gone entirely unchallenged (Bartolini and Mair 1990). Yet, a large cross-national study of the organizational linkages between parties and the masses has found that even though traditional parties have striven to maintain their organizational connections to their core constituencies, these linkages have been weakened both in substance and in terms of their overall scope (not least as a result of the growth of new parties) (Poguntke 2000*a*, 2002). This has been particularly pronounced for linkage through party membership (Katz et al. 1992, Mair and van Biezen 2001). The weakening social anchorage of a party entails the increasing pluralization of its social base and carries with it a concomitant loss of social group ideology; the presentation of a coherent and integrated programmatic package to the key constituency has been the key to success in traditional cleavage politics. Yet the clear-cut orderliness of political competition based on the conflict of social group ideologies (be they class-linked, ethnic, or denominational) seems to be disappearing in modern democracies; not only have electorates become socially and ideologically more heterogeneous, but party programmes have followed suit. As a consequence, where social group identities no longer dictate voter loyalties and sharp ideological conflicts fail to provide unambiguous cues, factors such as the personal qualities of actual or prospective heads of governments may become relatively more important for the conduct of election campaigns. Simply put: if voters become 'available' as a result of loosening social ties and clear programmatic alternatives are increasingly lacking, party politicians may take refuge in a growing leadership-centredness of politics.

Fig. 1.3 specifies a number of hypothesized links between these causal factors and the dependent variables, that is, the three faces of presidentialization. It should not be assumed that these triple processes run in perfect simultaneity with each other: since our main causal factors have more immediate effects on some faces of presidentialization than on others, they might progress at different speeds and over different time-spans. That said, it is expected that once one of these processes starts it will impact on the others.

From the foregoing account, it should be clear that we would hypothesize that the internationalization of politics and the growth of the state have most immediate impact on executive presidentialization since they affect government and decision-making. The erosion of cleavage politics, however, is quite clearly a precondition of electoral presidentialization since it produces a shift in the factors influencing voter choice. The causal impact of the changing structure of mass communication is more evenly spread. Indeed, we would argue that it affects all faces of presidentialization (hence, the triple arrows leading from the changing structure of mass communication in Fig. 1.3).

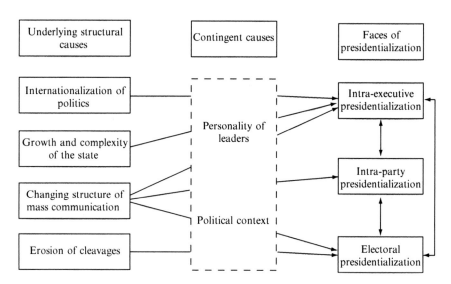

FIG. 1.3. *The major causal flows involved in explaining the presidentialization of politics*

In the preceding discussion, we drew attention to the fact that it could:

- Influence voters to focus on leaders' personal qualities in making their electoral choices.
- Be exploited by party leaders in order to bypass colleagues in setting political agendas.
- Provide a crucial power resource for chief executives to dominate their governments and govern increasingly past their parties.

Finally, we should not overlook the fact that electoral, intra-party, and intra-executive presidentialization could impact on each other. For instance, it is plausible to suggest that as individual politicians are perceived to count for more and more in the competition for electoral support, this justifies their presidentialization of election campaigns, their grip on power within the party and, should they win elective office, within the political executive of the state itself. In other words, the presidentialization of electoral processes generates greater leadership autonomy from the rest of the party, and encourages victorious party leaders to infer that their party's mandate is to a considerable extent a *personal* mandate, thus justifying their more dominant role within the executive. More succinctly, according to this interpretation, the presidentialization of electoral processes leads to the presidentialization of power. Equally, however, it is possible that causality flows in the opposite direction since structural changes like the internationalization of politics give more executive power to leaders and this, in turn, may strengthen their electoral appeal and their ability to dominate their party; that is, as executive presidentialization occurs, so the media focus more on leaders and voters then become more susceptible to leadership effects. Consequently, we have included double-ended arrows between the triple faces of presidentialization in Fig. 1.3.

LOGIC OF INQUIRY

While this book discusses the causes and constraints which condition the presidentialization of democratic politics, its first task is to decide how far the phenomenon exists as a matter of empirical observation. This requires systematic examination of a range of democratic regimes, enabling us to locate specific cases in terms of the typology outlined in Fig. 1.1, and in particular to judge if they have shifted location towards the 'northern' (presidentialized) end of the vertical axis. Analytically, each case study looks at the three faces (and individual elements) of presidentialization in turn and then summarizes individual aspects in order to arrive at an overall conclusion as to how pronounced the process of presidentialization has been in a particular country.

Since the underlying questions on which this project is based are concerned with *change*, contributors were asked to provide a sense of change from a given baseline. What is the baseline date against which change should be measured? In reality, change (where it has occurred) cannot be expected to always start from the same year, which makes this a difficult question to answer. However, some of the major causal factors which we have outlined are known to have gained relevance from approximately 1960; this would seem to be true of the development of mass access to TV, the erosion of cleavage politics and the 'internationalization' of decision-making (at least in the case of the European Community member-states). We have therefore proposed that authors take 1960 as an approximate baseline year against which to evaluate change, except where this would be plainly inappropriate (for instance, when studying countries which experienced more recent transitions to democracy, such as Spain and Portugal). While the choice of the early 1960s as a baseline for inquiring into electoral presidentialization seems relatively straightforward, given the spread of mass access to television from this time (van Deth 1995: 59), executive presidentialization is more complex. We have already alluded to the fact that the internationalization of decision-making has been given impetus by EC/EU membership, which occurs at different times for the various member-states. But for these and other countries, the advent of the UN and NATO were also of obvious significance in this regard, and they clearly pre-date 1960. In addition, the impact of the growth of the state is hard to pinpoint in terms of a precise temporal starting-point. The massive expansion of the welfare state has generally been regarded as a dominant feature of the post-1945 era in advanced industrial democracies, but the eventual impact of this in generating perceptions of governmental 'overload' did not really manifest itself until the 1970s (Birch 1984; Brittan 1977; King 1976). Thus, 1960 is only a very broad guideline, and where our country experts have seen the need to emphasize the importance of other nationally specific timelines in the presidentialization of politics in the cases about which they are writing, they have been free to do so.

CHOICE OF INDICATORS

What are the possible indicators of presidentialization? Clearly, it is not possible to suggest a list of empirical indicators that works equally well across a large number of countries. Certain measures may not travel well from one case to another, and may therefore not always be appropriate indicators of the underlying concept in which we are interested (van Deth 1998). Given the complexity of the phenomenon we are studying, particular attention needs to be given to finding functionally equivalent indicators instead of simply using identical ones. To give but one example: frequent cabinet reshuffles may indicate a strong prime ministerial position in some countries; elsewhere, however, the constitution may allow for the appointment of cabinet members not holding a seat in parliament, and this may enable strong prime ministers to appoint a comparatively large number of non-party specialists. Moreover, data constraints will mean that certain indicators are not universally available. However, we have suggested the following indicative list, which can be used to capture the phenomenon of presidentialization.

Leadership power within the executive

The objective here is for authors to provide a sense of the changing power resources and autonomy of leaders within government. How far are leaders constrained by colleagues and parties (their own and those of coalition partners) in the decisions they implement? Has there been any discernible shift over time? Institutional, procedural, and resource changes are important in this regard. Have the formal powers of the head of government been enhanced or restricted over time? Has the informal exercise of these powers altered? Have the financial resources or personnel at the disposal of the head of government developed? How far have non-constitutional factors such as change in the party system affected the exercise of leadership power in government? In addressing these issues, the following indicators—among others—seem particularly relevant:

- The growth of resources at the disposal of the chief executive.
- Trends towards an integrated communication strategy controlled by the chief executive as a means of defining policy alternatives (which is a precondition for achieving desired decisions).
- Trends towards increasingly centralized control and coordination of policy-making by the chief executive: do we find evidence that the chief executive's office seeks greater coordinating control of the policy-making process?
- Trends towards more personal polling: do we find evidence that prime ministerial offices regularly monitor the personal popularity of leaders and voter policy preferences?
- A growing tendency of chief executives to appoint non-party technocrats or to promote rapidly politicians who lack a distinctive party power base.
- A growing tendency to have more cabinet reshuffles while the prime minister remains in office.
- Prime ministers increasingly invoking a personalized mandate based on their electoral appeal, not least to control important decisions.

Leadership power within the party

Similarly, authors focus on potential changes which may indicate the development of a more personalized form of party leadership. In addition to contingent gains of leadership power resources and autonomy due to political seasons and personal qualities, there are a number of structural changes which permanently strengthen the role of leaders and make them more independent of middle-level party elites. Indicators of both contingent and structural changes may include the following:

- Rule change which give party leaders more formal powers.
- The growth of the leaders' offices in terms of funding and personnel.
- The capacity of leaders to forge programmes autonomously of their parties.
- The use of plebiscitary modes of political communication and mobilization. Do leaders seek to bypass sub-leader or activist strata of the party by communicating directly with the grass roots in respect of programmatic or strategic questions?
- Evidence of personalized mandates in the sense of people becoming leading candidates despite not being the most senior party politicians (for instance, Blair rather than Brown, Schröder rather than Lafontaine, Rutelli rather than Amato, and so on).
- The institutionalization of direct leadership elections.

Candidate-centred electoral processes

Here the authors discuss the extent to which evidence suggests a presidentialization of the electoral processes. Ideally, they should cover each of the three aspects of electoral presidentialization we mentioned earlier (campaign style, media focus, voting behaviour), though data constraints have not rendered this feasible in every case. However, all country studies have addressed at least two of our three dimensions of electoral presidentialization.

When looking at the extent to which *media coverage* has increasingly concentrated on leaders, our contributors refer to content analyses of TV and/or press coverage of election campaigns. In most cases, this involves the use of material published elsewhere (such as Norris et al. 1999), but original data sets have also been available for (re)analysis in some cases. Similarly, the analysis of *leadership focus in campaign styles* often draws on published studies of election campaigns. In addition, primary sources such as parties' election publicity, their documentation and party political broadcasts have been exploited, and interviews with campaign managers and senior politicians used by some authors to arrive at a clear image of how political parties have adapted their campaign techniques to a changing media environment. Finally, our contributors have reviewed the literature on national patterns of voting behaviour in an attempt to gauge the possible changes in *leader effects on voting behaviour*.

CONCLUSION

Our comparative study across a large number of modern democracies provides ample evidence of the extent of structurally induced presidentialization. To be sure, some of the most conspicuous examples have been driven by exceptional personalities like Margaret Thatcher, Tony Blair, Silvio Berlusconi, or Helmut Kohl. Yet, there is strong evidence of an underlying structural component in all our cases, which means that we are not simply finding unsystematic fluctuation between presidentialized and partified politics depending on contingent factors. Rather, a substantial part of these changes has resulted from long-term—and to that extent 'structural'—developments which are unlikely to be reversed in the foreseeable future.

Some readers might wonder if the themes we address are treated ahistorically. More than four decades ago, Edwin C. Hargrove observed that:

Political scientists write of the inevitability of the 'personalization of power' in modern industrial society. It is suggested that as the old politics of class and ideological conflict declines in Europe, as television becomes the chief means of political information for the public, as parties and parliaments weaken before the executive, power will increasingly become visible to people through popular leaders and these leaders will be the chief means of engaging the political interest of publics (cited in Farrell 1971: x).

The apparent prescience of these words is striking, indeed almost startling, as we read them today. It makes us wonder if those who claim evidence of the recent presidentialization of politics lack a sense of historical perspective. Perhaps they do. Nevertheless, while we may admire the insight of observers like Musgrove, it is clear that such judgements must have been impressionistic, if not to say downright speculative, at the time they were made. Bear in mind that they were articulated in the decade in which television was still emerging in many European countries as the major source of political information, and in which processes of cleavage change were less clear-cut than they have since become. We have incomparably more evidence on which to draw now in terms of our dependent and independent variables. Such developments as may have been apparent to some keen-eyed observers in the 1960s are likely to be that much more pronounced these days. This is certainly the case, for instance, in respect of media structure, socio-political cleavage formation, and the internationalization of decision-making. Thus, the time is surely ripe for the presidentialization phenomenon to be investigated in a thoroughgoing and systematic fashion.

What, then, are the likely effects of presidentialization on the quality of democratic governance? First and foremost, more power resources and autonomy for leaders means that their capacity to act has been enhanced. They find it easier now to achieve desired policy decisions, to impose their will on collective actors like cabinets or parties. This enables them to initiate substantial policy reversals without first winning over the dominant coalition within their parties. However, this does not necessarily mean that the effective steering capacity of the political centre has grown, though this may be the intention. Certainly, leaders may have more control over policy decisions than in the past, but they will not necessarily have improved their ability to achieve desired outcomes. In other words, many of the well-known problems of policy implementation could remain unaffected by trends towards a more presidentialized mode of governance.

Second, presidentialized chief executives (and party leaders) increasingly govern past their parties and, equally important, past the most important social forces which support them. Skilful use of modern mass communication has become an important resource for this strategy, and the recourse to a personalized mandate makes modern leaders simultaneously both stronger and weaker. As long as they can ride the tiger of an increasingly fickle public opinion, they can 'go it alone'; once public support begins to dwindle, however, they are left with few allies.

NOTES

1. Theoretically, it is conceivable for constitutions to prescribe a situation in which a president is not popularly elected, but is the head of the executive. In reality, however, such a figure might well struggle to enjoy legitimate authority in a democratic context.
2. The German Basic Law, for example, gives the Chancellor a more prominent position, but it also stipulates the principle of ministerial and collective responsibility (Smith 1982: 56–62). Note also that, according to Lijphart (1992: 6), there are three examples of a truly collegial executive which is not responsible to parliament: Switzerland, Cyprus (1960–3), and Uruguay (1952–67). Whether or not they should be categorized as presidential is not relevant to the logic of our argument.
3. See also Shugart and Carey (1992), who distinguish between two variants of semi-presidentialism, that is, premier-presidentialism and president-parliamentarism.
4. Though note that we are primarily concerned with actual or potential parties of government.

REFERENCES

Bagehot, W. (1867). *The English Constitution.* London: Oxford University Press.

Bartolini, S. and P. Mair (1990). *Identity, Competition and Electoral Availability: The Stabilisation of European Electorates 1885–1985.* Cambridge: Cambridge University Press.

Bean, C. and A. Mughan (1989). 'Leadership Effects in Parliamentary Elections in Australia and Britain', *American Political Science Review,* 83: 1165–79.

Bell, D. (1960). *The End of Ideology.* New York City: Collier.

Birch, A. (1984). 'Overload, Ungovernability and Deligitimation: The Theories and the British case', *British Journal of Political Science,* 14: 135–60.

Bowler, S. and D.M. Farrell (1992). *Electoral Strategies and Political Marketing.* London: Macmillan.

Brittan, S. (1977). *The Economic Consequences of Democracy.* London: Temple Smith.

Calise, M. (2000). *Il Partito Personale.* Roma: Editori Laterza.

Cox, G. W. (1987). *The Efficient Secret: The Cabinet and the Development of Political Parties in Victorian England.* Cambridge: Cambridge University Press.

Crewe, I. and A. King (1994). 'Are British Elections Becoming More "Presidential"?', in M. K. Jennings and T. E. Mann (eds.), *Elections at Home and Abroad.* Ann Arbor: University of Michigan Press, 181–206.

Duverger, M. (1980). 'A New Political System Model: Semi-Presidential Government', *European Journal of Political Research,* 8: 165–87.

Draper, D. (1997). *Blair's 100 Days.* London: Faber.

—— (1999). 'Time to Decide If You're Radical, Tony', *Observer,* 8 August.

Elgie, R. (1999). 'The Politics of Semi-Presidentialism', in R. Elgie (ed.), *Semi-Presidentialism in Europe.* Oxford: Oxford University Press.

Fabbrini, S. (1994). 'Presidentialization as Americanization? The Rise and Fall of Leader-Dominated Governmental Strategies in Western Europe in the 'Eighties', *American Studies International,* XXXII.

Farrell, B. (1971). *Chairman or Chief? The Role of the Taoiseach in Irish Government.* Dublin: Gill and Macmillan.

Farrell, D. and P. Webb (2000). 'Parties as Campaign Organizations', in R. Dalton and M. Wattenberg (eds.), *Parties Without Partisans: Political Change in Advanced Industrial Democracies.* Oxford: Oxford University Press.

Foley, M. (1993). *The Rise of the British Presidency.* Manchester: Manchester University Press.

—— (2000). *The British Presidency: Tony Blair and the Politics of Public Leadership.* Manchester: Manchester University Press.

Franklin, M., T. Mackie, and H. Valen (1992). *Electoral Change: Responses to Evolving Attitudinal and Social Structures in Western Countries.* Cambridge: Cambridge University Press.

Hencke, D. (2000). 'Special Advisers Tripled as No. 10 Staff Hits New High', *Guardian,* 2 March.

Kaase, M. (1994). 'Is there Personalization in Politics? Candidates and Voting Behavior in Germany', *International Political Science Review,* 15: 211–30.

Kaiser, A. (1997). 'Types of Democracy: From Classical to New Institutionalism', *Journal of Theoretical Politics*, 9: 419–44.

Katz, R. S. (1986). 'Party Government: A Rationalistic Conception', in F. G. Castles and R. Wildenmann (eds.), *Visions and Realities of Party Government*. Berlin/New York: Walter de Gruyter, 31–71.

—— P. Mair, L. Bardi, L. Bille, K. Deschouwer, D. Farrell, R. Koole, L. Morlino, W. C. Müller, J. Pierre, T. Poguntke, J. Sundberg, L. Svasand, H. van de Velde, P. Webb, and A. Widfeldt (1992). 'The Membership of Political Parties in European Democracies, 1960–1990', *European Journal of Political Research*, 22: 329–45.

King, A. (1976). *Why is Britain Becoming Harder to Govern?* London: BBC Publications.

—— (2002). *Leaders, Personalities and the Outcome of Democratic Elections*. Oxford: Oxford University Press.

Kirchheimer, O. (1966). 'The Transformation of West European Party Systems', in J. LaPalombara and M. Weiner (eds.), *Political Parties and Political Development*. Princeton, NJ: Princeton University Press.

Lijphart, A. (1984). *Democracies: Patterns of Majoritarian and Consensus Governments in 21 Countries*. New Haven: Yale University Press.

—— (1992). 'Introduction', in A. Lijphart (ed.), *Parliamentary versus Presidential Government*. Oxford: Oxford University Press, 1–27.

—— (1997). 'Trichotomy or Dichotomy?', *European Journal of Political Research*, 31: 125–46.

—— (1999). *Patterns of Democracy: Government Forms and Performance in Thirty-Six Countries*. New Haven/London: Yale University Press.

Linz, J. J. (1994). 'Presidential or Parliamentary Democracy: Does it Make a Difference?', in J. J. Linz and A. Valenzuela (eds.), *The Failure of Presidential Democracy*. Baltimore: Johns Hopkins University Press, 3–87.

Lipset, S. M. (1964). 'The Changing Class Structure in Contemporary European Politics', *Daedalus*, 93: 271–303.

Lütjen, T. and F. Walter (2000). 'Die präsidiale Kanzlerschaft', *Blätter für deutsche und internationale Politik*, 11: 1309–13.

Mair, P. and I. van Biezen (2001). 'Party Membership in Twenty European Democracies, 1980–2000', *Party Politics*, 7: 1.

Mughan, A. (1993). 'Party Leaders and Presidentialism in the 1992 Election: A Post-War Perspective', in D. Denver, C. Rallings, and D. Broughton (eds.), *British Elections and Parties Yearbook 1993*. New York: Harvester Wheatsheaf, 193–204.

—— (2000). *Media and the Presidentialization of Parliamentary Elections*. Basingstoke: Macmillan.

Norris, P., J. Curtice, D. Sanders, M. Scammell, and H. Semetko (1999). *On Message: Communicating The Campaign*. London: Sage.

Pasquino, G. (1997). 'Semi-Presidentialism: A Political Model at Work', *European Journal of Political Research*, 31: 128–36.

Peters, B. G., R. A. Rhodes, and V. Wright (2000). 'Staffing the Summit—the Administration of the Core Executive: Convergent Trends and National Specificities', in B. G. Peters, R. A. W. Rhodes, and V. Wright (eds.), *Administering the Summit: Administration of the Core Executive in Developed Countries*. Basingstoke: Macmillan.

Poguntke, T. (2000*a*). *Parteiorganisation im Wandel. Gesellschaftliche Verankerung und organisatorische Anpassung im europäischen Vergleich.* Wiesbaden: Westdeutscher Verlag.

—— (2000*b*). 'Präsidiale Regierungschefs: Verändern sich die parlamentarischen Demokratien?', in O. Niedermayer and B. Westle (eds.), *Demokratie und Partizipation. Festschrift für Max Kaase.* Wiesbaden: Westdeutscher Verlag, 356–71.

—— (2002). 'Parties without Firm Social Roots? Party Organisational Linkage', in K. R. Luther and F. Müller-Rommel (eds.), *Political Parties in the New Europe: Political and Analytical Challenges.* Oxford: Oxford University Press, 43–62.

Sartori, G. (1994). *Comparative Constitutional Engineering: An Inquiry into Structures, Incentives and Outcomes.* Basingstoke: Macmillan.

Semetko, H. A. (1996). 'The Media', in L. LeDuc, R. G. Niemi, and P. Norris (eds.), *Comparing Democracies: Elections and Voting in Global Perspective.* Thousand Oaks/London/New Delhi: Sage, 254–79.

Shugart, M. S. and J. M. Carey (1992). *Presidents and Assemblies: Constitutional Design and Electoral Dynamics.* Cambridge: Cambridge University Press.

Smith, G. (1982). *Democracy in Western Germany: Parties and Politics in the Federal Republic.* London: Heinemann.

Strøm, K. (1990). *Minority Government and Majority Rule.* Cambridge: Cambridge University Press.

—— (2000). 'Delegation and Accountability in Parliamentary Democracies', *European Journal of Political Research,* 37: 261–89.

—— W. C. Müller, and T. Bergman (2003). *Delegation and Accountability in Parliamentary Democracies.* Oxford: Oxford University Press.

Traynor, I. (1999). 'Schroeder Tightens Grip on Power', *Guardian,* 13 March.

van Deth, J. (1998). *Comparative Politics: The Problem of Equivalence.* London and New York: Routledge.

van Deth, J. W. (1995). 'A Macro Setting for Micro-Politics', in J. W. van Deth and E. Scarbrough (eds.), *The Impact of Values.* Oxford: Oxford University Press, 76–119.

Verney, D. (1959). *The Analysis of Political Systems.* London: Routledge and Kegan Paul.

Watt, N. (2000). 'Build Loyalty or Face Revolt, Callaghan Warns Blair', *Guardian,* 3 January.

Wattenberg, M. (1991). *The Rise of Candidate-Centred Politics: Presidential Elections in the 1980s.* Cambridge, MA: Harvard University Press.

Weber, M. (1980). *Wirtschaft und Gesellschaft: Grundriß der verstehenden Soziologie.* Tübingen: Mohr.

2

The British Prime Minister: Much More Than 'First Among Equals'

Richard Heffernan and Paul Webb

INTRODUCTION

According to the analytical framework employed in this book, two key features distinguish presidential from parliamentary regimes. First, the separation of powers between executive and legislature and second, the unipersonal nature of executive power and responsibility. Because the executive and legislative branches of government are fused in parliamentary systems, an indirectly elected prime minister heads a parliamentary executive granted office by virtue of its legislative majority. This partisan majority usually empowers a prime minister vis-à-vis a non-independent, reactive, and weak legislature, even though that legislature could remove him or her from office if it so wished. In presidential systems, where there is separation rather than fusion of powers between the executive and the legislature, the very opposite is the case. The directly elected president does not depend on the legislature for office, but is as a consequence less able to dominate an independent, proactive, and strong legislature. Parliamentary executives are collegial, while presidential executives are unipersonal. Rather than being composed of semi-autonomous political actors drawn from the legislature, each of whom could replace the prime minister as the head of government, presidential cabinets are composed of non-autonomous actors who cannot replace the president, and who invariably lack an independent political base of their own.

There are therefore differences and similarities between prime ministerial and presidential chief executives, but both require two key power resources to operate effectively: authority within the executive, and predominance over the legislature. In broad terms, the best known exemplar of presidentialism, the US, has an executive which undoubtedly possesses the first power resource, but lacks the second. By contrast, the British Prime Minister has the second, exercising this power in concert with other senior members of his executive, but has less power over the executive. However, in this chapter we argue that prime ministers have taken great steps toward extending their authority within the executive, possessing a degree of personalized power that marks a shift from a collective to a more individualized form of executive government. Widespread charges of presidentialization were levied against Margaret Thatcher when she was prime minister. Where Thatcher blazed a trail, Tony Blair has followed. This is not just a product of two ambitious individuals and their staffs, but indicates a set of cumulative structural changes enacted over time, which have built on the executive's traditional freedom of manoeuvre within the UK system of parliamentary government. These changes have enhanced the power of the prime minister. Furthermore, they have been complemented by the enhancement of leaders' traditional intra-party power, and by the personalizing of electoral processes. This suggests that many of the claims identified by the 'presidentialization' of Britain's parliamentary democracy may be more than mere journalistic hyperbole: there is some substance to the claim, at least in terms of the concept spelt out in Chapter 1. To be sure, Britain's formal regime structures remain essentially those of parliamentarism, which means that very real constraints still operate on prime ministerial power under certain circumstances: John Major's inability to control his more fractious parliamentary backbenchers after 1992 illustrates the point only too well, and even Thatcher and Blair eventually ran up against the limits of their constitutional position. Even so, there is a long-term quality to some of the relevant developments which implies that change is more than merely contingent. We examine these developments in turn, starting with the nature of prime ministerial power within the executive.

THE EXECUTIVE FACE

Changes in the UK executive have clearly weakened the decisional capacity of the cabinet, strengthening the power of cabinet committees, ad hoc ministerial committees, and most significantly, encouraging bilateral decisional processes involving the prime minister and individual ministers. In lessening the collective power of cabinet, these reforms, coupled with the creation of a Whitehall centre, have enhanced the power of a number of individual ministers, foremost among them the prime minister. It is the perception of prime ministerial power, particularly with regard to Tony Blair, that has prompted a growing public debate about the presidentialization of the UK parliamentary system.

While a 'prime minister' ultimately cannot be a 'president', any more than a dog can cross a species barrier and become a cat, debates about presidentialization in the UK obviously reflect what Elgie terms the emergence of 'more pluralistic conceptualizations of executive politics' (Elgie 1997: 217). There are 'muddy waters of the borderline between parliamentarism and presidentialism', particularly so when 'what matters most is constitutional practice, which may deviate from constitutional theory' (Lane and Errson 1999: 121). All executives, presidential or parliamentary, are collegial to some extent, even if parliamentary executives are more collegial than presidential executives. All involve a degree of delegation of power from the executive centre to the executive periphery, where actors have to share some degree of power with others, and have their freedom of manoeuvre restricted as a result. But, whatever the type of executive under consideration, if no one actor has ultimate influence, some actors have considerably more power and influence than others.

Clearly, recent changes in the functioning of British government and politics mean that the differences and distinctions between, say, the prime minister and his or her presidential counterparts, previously acute, have become blurred. Of course, the notion of presidentialization should be treated with some care. There is always the danger it may underplay the degree of collegiality found in all political regimes, particularly within parliamentary systems. Unlike a US president, no UK prime minister enjoys a 'national constituency, a fixed term of office, and an electoral and political independence from the legislature' (Foley 2000: 11). As a result, principally because they have no security of tenure in office, prime ministers are aware of a threat to their incumbency posed by senior ministerial colleagues, alternative premiers, as it were, eager to replace them should the opportunity arise. No such threat faces a US president, who cannot be unseated save for impeachment or death and can only then be replaced by the vice-president. Nonetheless, recent changes in political leadership, particularly 'the enhanced emphasis upon individual leadership, personal communications and presentational style' (ibid.: 4) demonstrate that the British Prime Minister, especially when the office is held by a well resourced and authoritative political actor, is in a very strong position to be more than simply first among equals. Indeed, in commanding authority within the executive, the British Prime Minister may well not only possess as much executive power as the US President, but in so doing will also have far more legislative power, given the ability of the UK parliamentary executive to command a weak, reactive legislature within which it usually possesses a reliable partisan majority.

Tony Blair sought to expand the powers of the prime minister, cultivating a presidential image, and aspiring to a 'command premiership' (Hennessy 1999*a*: 1; see also Foley 2000, 2002; Hennessy 1996*b*). It is incumbent upon a prime minister to manage the executive by leading it, because unlike, say, the US President, he or she cannot command it. Blair's centralized leadership of the Labour Party in opposition, 1994–7, was the model for his premiership: 'Blair's impatience with the...Shadow Cabinet meant he relied heavily on his personal aides and some supportive Shadow Ministers...They knew his mind and shared his ideas of what needed to be done. Those who were not on message were ruthlessly sidelined' (Kavanagh and Seldon 1999: 243).[1] In office, his authority enhanced by office and its administrative resources, Blair as prime minister largely dominated the government. It may remain the case that 'even with an array of institutional resources and the authority of the office a prime minister can achieve nothing on their own' (Smith 1999: 78), but Blair was his government's key agenda-setter, driving forward its programme, and made the most of his considerable popularity while it lasted among his ministers, parliamentary colleagues, the Labour Party at large, and, not least, large swathes of the electorate. That said, it is clear that this popularity was seriously eroded among each of these groups as a result of Blair's single-minded prosecution of the war in Iraq in 2003; ultimately, this inhibited and undermined his exercise of power. Note, however, that this does not necessarily undermine the presidentialization thesis as stated in this book; it is acknowledged that parliamentarism retains a variety of means by which it can inhibit prime ministerial power, and the latter will fluctuate according to contingencies such as the incumbent's political popularity.

Prime ministerial institutional and personal power resources

Executive government is to some degree fragmented and internally divided, and theories of the 'core executive' (Dunleavy and Rhodes 1990; Rhodes 1995, 1997; Smith 1999) focus on 'the complex web of institutions, networks and practices surrounding the prime minister, cabinet, cabinet committees, and their official counterparts, less formalised ministerial ... meetings, bilateral negotiations and inter-departmental committees' (Rhodes 1995: 12). Here, rightly rejecting the outdated dichotomous rivalry between prime ministerial and cabinet government theses (Crossman 1964; Jones 1965; Mackintosh 1962), a number of core executive accounts suggest that 'power does not lie anywhere in the system because it is everywhere ... all actors have resources, and outcomes need to be negotiated' (Rhodes 1995: 14). Obviously, UK government is not necessarily as centralized as traditional approaches have it, but neither is it anywhere near as fragmented or decentralized as some suggest. The executive is segmented, but not wholly pluralistic; power resources are never evenly distributed among all players. Thus, in understanding the power of the prime minister, we can see hierarchies matter, and that they are still to be found, perhaps in the plural rather than the singular, in executive government in the UK. It does not take a blinding insight to recognize that, say, the Chancellor of the Exchequer possesses a greater field of command over policy than the Secretary of State for Wales, and that the prime minister possesses a greater command still. As we shall see, however, prime ministers do not have absolute, unconditional power. But, subject to any number of variable contingencies, they do have significant conditional power, and growing structural capacity.

There are a number of models of executive governance detailing the practical influence a parliamentary chief executive may or may not have. Laver and Shepsle (1994) suggest six models of executive governance: prime ministerial, cabinet, ministerial, bureaucratic, party, and legislative. Dunleavy and Rhodes (1995) propose five: prime ministerial government, prime ministerial clique, cabinet government, ministerial government, segmented decision-making, and bureaucratic coordination. Common to both classifications is the contrast between prime ministerial and cabinet government, which were long regarded as polar antitheses within the British system. The heyday of the debate about these models was the 1960s, the central protagonists being John Mackintosh (1962), Richard Crossman (1964), and George Jones (1965). Crossman's case was stated in clear and unequivocal terms, and premised partly on the importance of leadership effects on the electorate: 'Politics is inevitably personified and simplified in the public mind, into a battle between two super-leaders—appointed for life or until they are removed by intra-party coup d'etat' (Crossman 1985: 183). That said, Crossman saw the growth of prime ministerial power as preceding the democratic era. Even before 1867, the premier's right to control patronage, to appoint and dismiss ministers, and to set the cabinet agenda and announce its decisions without recourse to formal voting assured him 'near-presidential powers'. This meant, to paraphrase Bagehot's formula, the prime minister, not the cabinet as a whole, was now the 'hyphen which joins, the buckle which fastens, the legislative part of the state to the executive part' (ibid.: 189). Later, creation of a cabinet office (in 1916), and centralization and unification of the civil service (in 1919) under Lloyd George proved to be critical steps in enhancing the structural power of the prime minister. While it is clear that prime ministerial power is never absolute and will fluctuate contingently according to the vagaries of events and personalities, these reforms clearly placed new institutional resources in the prime minister's hands, thereby facilitating his capacity to coordinate the work of the executive. While this power was enhanced yet further during the Second World War, Crossman noted that there was 'no return to normalcy' under Clement Attlee's Labour governments of 1945–51, when 'a well-organised system of centralised decision taking replaced the rather haphazard autocracy of Sir Winston (Churchill)' (ibid.: 187). By the time he himself was set to join the cabinet in 1964, Crossman felt it appropriate to conclude that 'every Cabinet minister is in a sense the prime minister's agent—his assistant', and 'in so far as ministers feel themselves to be agents of the premier, the British Cabinet has now come to resemble the American cabinet' (ibid.: 189).

George Jones' riposte to the Crossman thesis did not deny each detail of it, but emphasized the very real constraints which operated on prime ministerial power. In particular, he drew attention to the fact that while the civil service may have been formally unified under Lloyd George, it was far from mono-lithic. In reality, it was very hard for any prime minister to know all that was going on in the whole machine of government: 'to achieve anything he must work with and through his ministers' (Jones 1965: 215). Moreover, he asserted that collective responsibility and power remained meaningful. Cru-cially, perhaps, he couched this partly in terms of the supposed disadvantage to the prime minister of not having any government department of his or her own. Taken together, the prime minister's private office and the cabinet office did not constitute institutional resources comparable to those available to a departmental minister (let alone to a US president). This meant the prime minister was often excluded from the 'germination stage' of policy formula-tion, only being brought in when discussions were complete and opinions solidified.

As we shall shortly see, however, more recent analysis suggests that the emergence of a coherent Whitehall centre means there has been considerable development of the institutional resources at the disposal of the prime minister. Indeed, we would argue that the most persuasive interpretation currently abroad is that of government by prime ministerial cliques (Dun-leavy and Rhodes 1990; Rhodes and Dunleavy 1995), a form of 'shared government' where key executive actors and institutions possess power and authority, but in which the prime minister is the key player. This model provides an institutional basis for the presidentialization phenomenon. The UK does not have collective government in the sense that all executive actors have equal influence on policy making at all times. Nor does it have minis-terial government, because ministers do not alone have sole responsibility for policy under their jurisdiction. Prime ministers, although they cannot do everything and have to delegate a number of intra-executive responsibilities, are political actors of great consequence. The 'potential for influence' that prime ministers possess, together with close, senior, elected, and non-elected allies, has done much to facilitate the circumscription of less senior members of the government in cabinet (and certainly beyond the cabinet) who are unable to influence policy across the range of governmental responsibilities beyond their own departmental interests. Government departments may remain to some extent freestanding institutions, but the prime ministerial centre clearly restricts departmental autonomy (excepting that of the all-powerful Treasury), most usually by imposing financial and political con-trols. Ultimately, together with key leading ministers, the prime minister is responsible for 'green-lighting' all major policy initiatives across govern-ment. Obviously, the opportunities for prime ministerial influence are greater in certain policy sectors rather than others. For example, Tony Blair was far more able to direct defence and foreign policy in regard to, say, Iraq in 1998 and 2003, the Kosovo Crisis of 1999, and the war on terrorism (post-September 11, 2001), than he was in respect of the reform of education or health policy. That said, contra Laver and Shepsle, policy formation is not just departmental in form or origin. Any major proposal that Downing Street strongly objects to (and can avoid) will not come to pass, and ministers who lose out are, in the time honoured way, obliged to 'shut up or get out' (or pursue the matter and run the risk of being thrown out).

While prime ministers are reliant upon ministers and officials to pursue their goals, they do exercise considerable authority and power. How much power, then, does a prime minister have? Smith (1999: 28–9) suggests, 'all actors within the core executive have resources, and in order to achieve their goals they have to exchange them. The process of exchange occurs through networks and alliances which develop because of mutual dependence. Because no actor has a monopoly of resources, power cannot be located within a single site of the Core Executive. . . . Consequently, there cannot be prime ministerial government, because the prime minister will always depend on other actors'. Obviously, no simple command and obey model applies, but, if the prime minister does not possess 100 per cent of the power (indeed, no institutional actor, not even the most despotic of dictators possesses that amount), does this mean he or she cannot possess, say, 70 per cent at any given time? Or 50 per cent? How 'resource-rich'—to use Smith's term—can the prime minister be? How dependent on other actors can he or she be? How dependent on the prime minister can other actors be?

As Smith himself recognizes, the prime minister is 'in a structurally advantageous position . . . at the centre of the networks that traverse the core executive and therefore he or she has access to all areas of government . . . [is] able to define the strategic direction of government . . . choose areas of policy involvement . . . [and] has a view of government that is not available to other ministers' (Smith 1999: 77). While never being 'totally free' of other network actors (no actor or institution in any political regime ever achieves this), prime ministers exert influence by being 'less dependent' on them. To this end, they require not a 'monopoly of power', just 'sufficient power'. Thus, if it is 'impossible, and indeed fruitless, to try to identify a single site of power within the core executive', it is also impossible to suggest that power is 'everywhere'. Power, always somewhere, is found in certain places more than others; because it is not in one single place does not mean that it is diffused across many places. Because particular executive actors are far more important than others, the prime minister being a case in point, a hierarchy of power exists among unequal actors; the UK parliamentary executive is nowhere near as collegial as a number of core executive accounts suggest.

The causes of prime ministerial power lie in the ability of the prime minister to exercise a series of institutional and personal resources that complement and advance his or her formal and informal powers (Heffernan

2003). The institutional resource factors available to the prime minister include the following:

- Leadership through being the legal head of the government, and making use of the Royal prerogatives, which are theoretically unfettered, but practically limited. These include the right to lead the government; appoint and dismiss ministers; allocate and reallocate portfolios; regulate government business; create cabinet committees and appoint particular ministers to them; refashion central government; generally supervise the machinery of government; create peers; confer honours; and dissolve the parliament and call a general election.
- Organizing a *de facto* prime ministerial department, using Downing Street and the Cabinet Office to set policy agendas.
- Using the news media to set political agendas, by exploiting Downing Street as a 'bully pulpit', in the manner of the US president.
- Managing the cabinet and its committee system, with the considerable weakening of collective responsibility that results (Heffernan 2003: 356–64).

Institutional reform is especially significant, for it entails the strengthening of the prime minister's power-base in Whitehall, and has seen the establishment of a reworked 'Whitehall Centre' comprising Downing Street and the Cabinet Office. This, in effect, furnishes the prime minister with that vital resource Jones noted was absent in the 1960s, a department of his or her own. The evidence for this is reviewed by Burch and Holliday (1999: 43) who claim that:

. . . an executive office in all but name already exists. It centres on the Prime Minister's and Cabinet Offices, and has been crucially developed since the 1960s . . . there is now substantial institutional capacity in its two component Offices, and the potential for actors within them to exercise power has been enhanced . . . Quietly and without publicity, indeed in an evolutionary manner that is typically British, there has been a transformation of the centre of the state. The fact that it has not yet been labelled should not be taken to mean that it does not exist. There are times when the territory alters so much that our maps can no longer guide us and have to be changed. This is one of those times.

While concurring with others that the premiership of Margaret Thatcher was critical in the emergence of this *de facto* executive office at the heart of the British state, they nevertheless insist that a very real accumulation of functions, resources, and powers by the Prime Minister's and Cabinet Offices preceded her incumbency and has continued since. Such developments cannot be dismissed as merely contingent, therefore, although the extent to which such powers are wielded and resources exploited, will vary from premier to premier. By all accounts, Tony Blair was heavily disposed to making full use of them. What is especially interesting is the self-conscious way in which 'presidential government' was pursued by Blair and his advisers. As journalist Peter Riddell puts it:

There has been a deliberate attempt to change the way Downing Street and the Cabinet Office work to allow the Prime Minister to exercise more control over the Whitehall machine. This has not occurred out of the blue. Mr. Blair's close advisers have studied the debate over the size and scope of the Prime Minister's Office which has developed since the 1960s. (quoted in Hennessy 1998: 10)

After 1997, Blair made numerous changes to the structure of Downing Street, accompanying these with several personnel changes. By the time of the 2005 general election, the Prime Minister's Office (PMO) was run by a Chief of Staff (a choice of title that clearly evinces presidential connotations), Jonathan Powell, a career diplomat who resigned to work for Blair when Labour was still in opposition. After 1997, he was employed as a temporary civil servant and was given direct responsibility for leading and co-ordinating operations across Number 10. Geoff Mulgan, who previously ran the Strategy Unit in the Cabinet Office, headed the Policy Directorate, working alongside a career civil servant, Ivan Rogers, the Prime Minister's principal private secretary. Within this directorate a special adviser, Andrew Adonis, was the Prime Minister's Senior Policy Adviser on Education, Public Services and Constitutional Reform, while Matthew Taylor had responsibility for policy planning and strengthening links on policy between Number 10 and the Labour Party. Three other special advisers ran other parts of the Downing Street machine: Sally Morgan, the Director of Government Relations, Pat McFadden, Director of Political Operations, and David Hill, who replaced the previously all-powerful Alistair Campbell as Director of Communications, with Godric Smith and Tom Kelly continuing to head up the Press Office. There were a number of other special advisers who operated on behalf of the PM outside this structure.

In total, Burch and Holliday (1999) estimated that the PMO employed 110–20 staff in the late 1990s, a number which grew to around 150 by the end of Blair's first term as premier (Hencke 2000). While the number of special advisers within this overall total was somewhat smaller, it nevertheless grew dramatically under Blair. When John Major left Downing Street in June 1997, he enjoyed the support of just eight special advisers, but by 1999, Blair had increased this to twenty-five, a level which has remained broadly constant since then. By 2003, some twenty-seven advisers out of eighty-one who worked across all central government ministries in Whitehall were located in the PMO (Committee on Standards in Public Life 2003: Para. 9.11).

Clearly, then, Blair enjoyed the support of a substantially stronger PMO in attempting to coordinate the work of government. Key individual advisers were particularly influential; the likes of Jonathan Powell and the former official spokesperson for the prime minister, Alastair Campbell, later the Director of Communications and Strategy, have almost certainly been much more powerful actors than most ministers. Foreign policy provides a powerful illustration of the prime ministerial penchant for exploiting special advisers. Sampson (2003) argued that 'Blair has gone further than any prime minister since Churchill in overriding and by-passing the advice of the Foreign Office', by establishing his own diplomatic staff at Number 10, and promoting his own favourites, notably Sir David Manning and Sir Stephen Wall: each of these men had their own retinue of support staff, and Manning in particular was said to have become a more influential diplomat than the Permanent Secretary (nominally the top civil servant) at the Foreign Office. Moreover, Blair's control of foreign policy—which became increasingly pronounced after Robin Cook was replaced by Jack Straw as Foreign Secretary—was further enhanced by his willingness to 'politicize' the diplomatic appointments process. To the consternation of career civil servants, their road to the most senior postings no longer seemed to be via the traditional path of steady promotion through embassies abroad, but through catching the prime minister's attention. Thus, the British ambassador in Paris, Sir John Holmes, was previously Blair's principal private secretary, while the premier also chose John Sawers, his former private secretary at Number 10, as his special envoy to Iraq. In addition, Blair appointed his political ally and party fund-raiser, Lord Levy, to be a special envoy to the Middle East, with his own base in the Foreign Office. All this indicates, as Jenkins (1999) has suggested, that the prime minister's various advisers and envoys 'run Britain to a degree that no previous Downing Street team has done. They are far more than a kitchen cabinet. They are Mr Blair' (see also Kavanagh and Seldon 1999; Rawnsley 2000). However, in empowering the prime minister, his officials remain his creatures and are never autonomous of him.

Not surprisingly, perhaps, the role of these prime ministerial advisers has become increasingly controversial (White 2004). In April 2003, the independent Committee on Standards in Public Life issued a report in which it recommended clear legal definitions of the precise roles and lines of accountability concerning special advisers. It further recommended a limitation on their numbers, although it did recognize the legitimate need for the prime minister to have more advisers than other ministers (Committee on Standards in Public Life 2003: Para. 9.11). Among its main recommendations were that: The number of special advisers available to the prime minister, while greater than that at the disposal of other ministers, should be subject to a clearly defined ceiling; most special advisers should be limited to offering their political masters advice, and have no authority to direct the work of career civil servants; subject to the approval of Parliament, a small number of special advisers in the PMO should have 'executive powers'—that is, the right to 'have a role' in the line management of civil servants in the PMO and the Government Information and Communication Service; and that advisers with executive power should be directly accountable to the prime minister.

An executive order in council of 1997 had first legislated for the creation of up to three advisers with executive powers. Until Alastair Campbell's resignation in 2003, he had been one, but his successor as Director of Communications in Downing Street, David Hill, was not given such powers. At the time of writing, only Blair's Chief of Staff, Jonathan Powell, retains these privileges. To the dismay of the then Chair of the Committee on Standards in Public Life, Sir Nigel Wicks, the government rejected the recommendations limiting the number of PMO special advisers and referring the appointment of advisers with executive powers to Parliament (Hencke 2003). Subsequently, the House of Commons Public Administration Select Committee (2004) put Downing Street under further pressure on the matter by issuing a draft Civil Service Bill in which it clearly supported the recommendations of the Committee on Standards in Public Life. This controversy seems set to continue. It is interesting that, while it reveals a recognition of a prime minister's legitimate need for a special level of resourcing and advice if the strategic coordination of government is to be feasible, it nevertheless seems to insist on limits to how far this should be allowed to develop. It is hard to imagine so much concern about, say, the growing number of advisers in a formally presidential setting. Underlying this concern is a sense that an over-mighty executive office is not so appropriate in a parliamentary context.

The second key institutional structure on which British prime ministers may call is the Cabinet Office, headed by the Cabinet Secretary, currently Sir Andrew Turnbull, who is also formally head of the Home Civil Service. Its main functions are to manage the work of the civil service (under the aegis of its Office of Public Service, which alone employs some 3,300 people) and to service the cabinet and its committees (through the much smaller Cabinet Secretariat). Unsuccessful Blairite experiments to head the Cabinet Office with a 'cabinet enforcer', with Jack Cunningham, Mo Mowlam and Lord Macdonald shoehorned into the post, failed because the PMO, working in tandem with the Cabinet Secretary, had in fact become its own 'enforcer'. While Burch and Holliday (1999: 43) readily concede that the central state in Britain is fragmented, they argue that this creates a pressing and persistent need for coordination. The development of the PMO and the Cabinet Office since 1970, and the growing connectedness between them, effectively means that there now exists 'an increasingly integrated core which operates as the central point in the key policy networks of the British state'. This integrated core to key policy networks is clearly at the disposal of the prime minister and puts us in mind of Crossman's expansion of Bagehot's dictum, that the prime minister is now 'the hyphen which joins, the buckle which fastens' key elements of the governing apparatus (Crossman 1985: xx).

This executive office in Whitehall has been facilitated by and for the prime minister. It is charged with issuing prime ministerial instructions to departments, and with enabling the prime minister to respond to departmental representations. Blair's strengthening of this executive centre in Whitehall was designed to boost the prime minister and thereby presidentialize the government. Naturally, the more authoritative the prime minister, the more authoritative this Whitehall Centre; the less authoritative the prime minister, the less authoritative the Whitehall Centre. This centre no longer simply arbitrates inter-government disputes, but now prioritizes issues, manages business, and helps determine departmental priorities. A strong, proactive centre provides a prime minister with the means to intervene across Whitehall where he or she chooses, supplementing without necessarily supplanting the work of departments, directing them in certain areas, agenda-setting in others. As Peter Mandelson, a one time Cabinet Office minister, argued in 1997, this Centre's objective is to 'evaluate, develop and promote policy on the prime minister's behalf... ensur[ing] that departments' objectives and measures are made consistent with overall government strategy'.[2] In the words of one Downing Street insider, these reforms are designed to make Number 10 'the dominant department in putting forward the message of the government' (Hennessy 2000: 486). And, we might reasonably add, thereby make the prime minister the principal actor to influence what this message is. Of course, as we shall see, this Whitehall Centre, working for Downing Street, is not confined to Downing Street and the Cabinet Office: it necessarily embraces the ever-powerful Treasury, particularly when that department is headed by a powerful minister, such as by Gordon Brown.

In addition to the prime minister's institutional resource factors, there are a number of personal resource factors available to prime ministers which enhance their authority. By themselves institutional resources may not provide prime ministerial power, particularly because prime ministerial authority is associated with powers arising from party leadership and electoral–professional cadres (Mair 1994; Panebianco 1988; Shaw 1994; Webb 1992b, 2000: 208–9). By virtue of being party leaders, prime ministers can accrue political capital enabling them to exercise authority over the party and within the executive. Such political capital is provided by a number of personal power resources, and these include:

- reputation, skill, and ability;
- association with actual and anticipated political success;
- public popularity; and
- high standing in his or her party, parliamentary party, and government. (Heffernan 2003: 350–6).

It is obvious that, as prime minister with Commons majorities of 179 and 166, Tony Blair was going to be more powerful than John Major, a prime minister with a majority of −1 in early 1997. Where Blair was strong, Major was weak. Under Blair, Labour enjoyed unprecedented electoral success in 1997, 2001 and 2005, while Major led the Conservatives to electoral meltdown in 1997. While Blair generally presided over a unified party, at least until the political discord arising from the invasion of Iraq and public sector reform in 2003–4, Major led a party seriously divided over Europe and between left and right. Compared to Major, Blair basked in media approval for a long time, even if his government eventually attracted its fair share of news media opprobrium. Obviously, a 'resource-rich' prime minister will be more powerful than a 'resource-poor' one.

Clearly, in Tony Blair's case, his personal power resources generally enhanced the institutional resources available to him. A 'Blair factor' undoubtedly facilitated his less fettered prime ministerial leadership, something that, building on past reforms, strengthened the prime ministerial centre. Of course, a prime minister may or may not possess personal resources, and, when in possession of them, may use them wisely or badly, may demonstrate policy failure rather than success, have a low rather than a high party standing, be electorally popular or unpopular, and so on. The possession of personal resources is never guaranteed. They come and go, are acquired and squandered, won and lost. In short, the resources listed above are contingent (Heffernan 2003). Tony Blair finally began to exhaust his personal political resources by 2004, particularly in the wake of the war in Iraq, the Hutton inquiry, and the controversy over Iraqi Weapons of Mass Destruction. The evidence suggests that he lost the trust and esteem of many voters, party members, backbench MPs, and indeed, some former ministers, including former cabinet colleagues. However, while the structural constraints of the parliamentary constitution and the contingencies of political life are always capable of biting back, it is important to note that, regardless of the fate of Tony Blair, the underlying capacity for prime ministerial domination of the executive has undoubtedly been enhanced by his premiership.

Prime ministers, ministers and the hierarchical core executive

Of course, a prime minister's power to determine government policy either as leader, coordinator, or arbitrator is counterbalanced by constraints such as collegiality, time, knowledge, expertise, and the ever-present pressure of events. Often obliged to be as reactive as they are proactive, chief executives cannot do everything. They need to delegate authority, and have to react to economic, social, political, and electoral demands, all of which impact upon their ability to govern. Prime ministers have to work with the grain of the institutions they inherit, and the actors they are surrounded with. They can only reform where it is possible, perhaps only at the margin, not always at the centre, and not everything they want to do can be attempted or achieved. Of course this is true of presidents as well. However, British cabinet ministers, in contrast to, say, their US counterparts, have some degree of autonomy. The more senior they are, the more autonomy they enjoy, and the greater chance they have of being a check and balance on the prime minister, either as members of a prime ministerial clique or as authoritative figures in their own right. In this regard, the abandonment of Margaret Thatcher by her parliamentary party and cabinet in November 1990 places the presidentialization debate in some form of context.

According to constitutional convention, government should arrive at collective decisions with all members of the cabinet participating fully. Such collective decisions having been taken, all members of the government have the duty to defend and advance them in public. Yet, not all members do so participate. The Secretary of State for Defence has no real interest and little inclination to take an interest in the workings of, say, the Department of Health, and vice versa. Naturally, should health as an issue threaten the well-being of the government, other ministers may take an interest, particularly if they are expected to defend health policy in public. However, in contrast to Bonar Law's relaxed view of the prime minister as 'a man [sic] at the head of a big business who allows the work to be done by others . . . and gives it general supervision' (Clark 1998: 20), the prime minister is obliged to take an interest in all government business and consider the wider picture beyond narrow departmental interests. Only the Chancellor of the Exchequer's responsibilities remotely approach this, given that his or her interests embrace the government's budget and the public expenditure round, but while the Chancellor may have considerable discretion and autonomy, these matters are also discussed with the prime minister.

As with US cabinet members, British cabinet ministers are now expected to stick to their departmental brief and are given less and less opportunity to influence policy beyond their department.[3] To take but one example, when the Secretary of State for Defence, Geoff Hoon, offered a comment on economic policy at a cabinet meeting, the Chancellor of the Exchequer, Gordon Brown, is said to have told him 'it was none of his business'.[4] Membership of a cabinet committee may grant a minister some wider influence within the executive (Dunleavy 1995, 2003), but, excepting issues where collective discussion genuinely arrives at a strategic decision or a policy stance, ad hoc committees and bilateral negotiations between the most senior figures in government, specifically Tony Blair and Gordon Brown in the

post-1997 Labour governments, often pre-empt cabinet committee deliberations. This is because the executive is a set of hierarchical networks where
key ministers have more power and influence than others. A 'creeping
bilateralism' long present, is increasingly the name of the Whitehall game,
one empowering the prime minister and a clique at the expense of the
collective authority of cabinet. Ministers are often limited by their departmental function; not so the prime minister.[5]

Bilateralism is therefore a key feature of growing prime ministerial power
within the executive. The prime minister influences policy decisions because
he or she is at the centre of an interlocking network of bilateral contacts. All
roads, as it were, lead to Rome. Kavanagh and Seldon report that during his
'first 25 months in office Blair held a total of 783 meetings with individual
ministers; over the same period, Major held 272 such sessions' (Kavanagh
and Seldon 1999: 275). Blair met each cabinet minister at the beginning of the
parliamentary session to plan their departmental tasks and objectives for the
coming year; no other cabinet ministers were involved in this process, save
the Chancellor when the Treasury was involved in expenditure matters. In
addition, Blair conducted discussions with the permanent secretary of each
department to underpin the 'contract' he drew up with the departmental
minister and his officials monitored departmental progress.[6]

In the centre–periphery reality of the modern British executive, location is
everything; it determines which actor and what institution is at the centre of a
policy domain, and which are more consequential than others; those nearer
the centre naturally exert more influence. There is a number of actors in any
network, but rather than consider policy networks as simply pluralistic, it
should be emphasized that networks are hierarchical and that some actors
have more authority and power than others. Their internal hierarchies determine how actors participate and how influential they may be. It is not
the case that either the cabinet will be all-powerful or the prime minister
omnipotent.

Power dependencies among actors within governmental institutions are
not all or nothing games. Yet, while not all-powerful, the prime minister can
be more powerful as an individual than the cabinet can be as a collective
body. Tony Blair most certainly was. Yet, placing to one side prime ministerial partisans and loyalists, some ministers are able to bring significant
weight to bear on the premier. One such example is Gordon Brown as
Chancellor of the Exchequer. With but two exceptions, Anthony Barber
and Norman Lamont, all chancellors of the exchequer since 1962 have been
putative prime ministers, alternatives-in-waiting to the incumbent, should he
or she falter, and Gordon Brown is no exception (Heffernan 2003; Rawnsley
2001). He was a very powerful minister with a significant degree of independence of the prime minister. After 1997, Brown was plainly Blair's
number two in the government, and had a political base that complemented

his powerful departmental base; this combination placed him at the centre of domestic policy. Indeed, such is the range of the Treasury's policy interests, it has been suggested that Brown operated in Whitehall as if he were 'a French prime minister with Blair as a kind of Fifth Republic president' (Hennessy 2000: xx). In contrast to other executive actors, most notably John Prescott, nominally the deputy prime minister, but with little autonomy to be anything other than loyal to Blair, Brown formed an axis with Blair at the heart of the government.

Thanks to his standing in the Labour Party and his indispensability to the government, Gordon Brown could constrain Tony Blair's freedom of manoeuvre with respect to economic policy. This is because, like a prime minister, a chancellor may well enjoy his own personal power resources, which enhance the institutional power resources provided by the Treasury. As a result, because Gordon Brown had sufficient political capital generated from personal power resources, Tony Blair had to allow him considerable autonomy in regard to economic policy. For the want of such resources, previous chancellors—notably Norman Lamont in 1990–3—have not always enjoyed such autonomy. However, while such a course is fraught with political difficulties, Blair could restrain his chancellor, although the more political capital Brown had, the harder it was to pursue that option, something best illustrated by Blair–Brown spats over the issue of when (and if) Britain should finally join the European single currency (Gamble and Kelly 2002; Heffernan 2001).

That said, Blair and Brown together significantly constrained the freedom of all other executive actors in economic policy matters. For example, the 1997–8 Comprehensive Spending Review setting the government's expenditure priorities for the next three years, 'was very much a prime minister–chancellor, Treasury–No 10 Policy Unit affair, with the affected departments getting very little look in during the crucial last weeks . . . [during which] the cabinet's public expenditure committee . . . definitely did not figure as the locus of decision-taking' (Hennessy 1999a: 9). In allocating spending resources to departments for the three years from 1998, Blair and Brown 'just called in ministers and told them what they were getting. There was no appeal' (Lipsey 2000: 165). Should prime minister and chancellor agree on policy (as they generally did, differences on Euro entry notwithstanding), this type of relationship is not a problem. When they disagree, however, and their differences compound (or are inflamed by their respective camp followers), it could create enormous difficulties for the government.

Obviously, government being some form of collective endeavour, partisans and loyalists make their way up the government hierarchy in addition to party figures who might perhaps offer a possible threat to the leader. Loyalty, and to a lesser extent ability, remain the age-old means of political preferment within parliamentary government, but prime ministers also often deal with would-be potential opponents by buying them off, circumscribing them by inclusion in government. Leaders often feel compelled to apply the crude but apposite principle enunciated by Lyndon Johnson: keeping potential rivals 'inside the leadership tent pissing out', rather than having them 'outside the tent pissing in'. Clare Short's incessant campaign for Tony Blair's head once she left the government in 2003 offers a case in point. All wise prime ministers know they have often to keep their friends close, but their enemies closer.

Advancement in government is still a matter of climbing the famous greasy pole. Whether powerful or less powerful, resource-rich or resource-poor, the prime minister sits atop that particular pole, and remains the key gatekeeper determining who slithers up it and how high they climb. Understanding that there are a number of centres of power within the core executive avoids the failings of the Westminster model and incorporates many of the strengths of the core executive model. This is why Rhodes' suggestion (1999: xiv) that 'power is relational, based on dependency not domination' is accurate, but only up to a point (Heffernan 2003). Because power is not simply relational between actors, but also locational, dependent on whether actors are to be found at the centre or the periphery of core executive networks, domination can be as important as dependency.

The old Asquithian notion, then, that a prime minister may make what he or she wishes of the position they hold, remains true, but only in part. Each holder of the post can skilfully apply their formal and informal powers to extend their authority, but their capacity to do so is dependent on the personal and institutional resources they possess. These resources have then to be applied effectively, first, in the executive and second, in the legislature. However, although the prime minister occupies a very privileged position within the executive, one that at times can border temporarily on the autocratic, prime ministerial government, narrowly defined as a wholly monocratic form of government, is not possible. But, obliged to treat their executive as both obstacle and resource in the pursuit of their own agenda, prime ministers can lead from the front, and do so in concert with their clique, much as a US president works with key White House staffers and leading cabinet members.

With the possible exception of Margaret Thatcher in 1983–6 and 1987–9, Tony Blair has probably been the most executive-dominant prime minister since 1945. Gordon Brown can lay claim to being the most executive-powerful Chancellor of the Exchequer in that same period. These two factors indicate first, the reality of a creeping prime ministerial power within the UK executive and second, its realization within a stratified, concentrically circled hierarchy of government. It is such power that lies at the heart of the presidentialization argument. Actors operate in an environment of institutional constraints and uneven distribution of resources. Within these limitations a number of prime ministerial strategies for accruing power can be identified, foremost among them the creation of a coterie of advisers, officials, and some (but by no means all) ministers. To be sure, the UK political system does not automatically create a powerful prime minister. The notion that power 'does vary from prime minister to prime minister, and ... according to the political strength that a particular prime minister has at any given time' (Lawson 1994: 441) should always be very much borne in mind; resources come and go, are acquired and lost, given and taken away. But, at the very least, the past twenty-five years or so mark a definitive shift towards a greater capacity for prime ministerial influence over government and its activities. Crucially, however, in addition to their emergent intra-executive influence, UK prime ministers enjoy powers unavailable to a US president; courtesy of the majoritarian nature of the UK's parliamentary and unitary state, they lead an executive empowered with greater legislative control than most presidential counterparts.

THE PARTY FACE

Of course, in the final instance, the prime minister's dependence on party within both executive and legislature is everything. John Major observed that 'every leader is leader only with the support of his party' (Major 1999: 626), and Margaret Thatcher acknowledged that a 'prime minister who knows that his or her cabinet has withheld its support is fatally weakened' (Thatcher 1993: 851). It remains the case that British prime ministers do not enjoy the security of tenure granted to US presidents because their parties can dismiss them at a moment's notice; thus, parties are constraints as well as resources. Leaders have to use both the prospect of reward and the threat of punishment, the time-honoured carrot and stick, to manage and control their parliamentary supporters. By these means, popular, well-resourced prime ministers, in concert if needs be with certain cabinet colleagues, can dominate their parties. But, as Tony Blair became all too aware after 2003, the risk of backbench rebellion remains, something demonstrated by the tribulations of both John Major and Margaret Thatcher.

Bagehot noted that 'the principle of Parliament is obedience to leaders', and the powerful role Parliament provides to the executive is essential to an understanding of UK government. Because its legislative acts are determined by its partisan majority, Parliament, theoretically free to reject all decisions of the executive, is unwilling, rather than unable, to do so. While still responsible for scrutinizing and criticizing the decisions of the executive, the legislature is also an arena for public discussion of political issues, able to make recommendations for policies, actions, and decisions, and providing a forum for executive accountability. However, because the Commons majority invariably chooses only to endorse or at best modify proposals laid before them, the capacity to reject proposals is neutered by a partisan straitjacket. While in theory the Commons can reject legislation presented by the executive, in practice the executive has *de facto* power to enact legislation. Moreover, doctrines of ministerial responsibility tend to be honoured largely in the breach; though formally accountable for all that happens in their government departments, few ministers resign—or are compelled by the parliament to resign—over matters of policy failure or maladministration within their purview (Kingdom 1999: 462–4). Similarly, it is extremely rare for governments to be brought down by votes of no-confidence in the House of Commons; only one post-war administration, Labour in 1979, was so defeated because it lacked an overall majority. To this extent, it might seem that the government is quite autonomous of the legislature, and therefore in a position similar to a presidential executive operating under the separation of powers. However, this would be an exaggeration. Ultimately, the executive has still to govern through Parliament, and it leads rather than commands the legislature thanks to a 'law of anticipated reactions' requiring government to do only that which its majority can be persuaded (or coerced) to support.

It should further be noted that, to some extent or other, British parties claim to be avowedly democratic organizations, which accord various powers to their extra-parliamentary wings. This seems to point to the potential for yet further constraint on the leaders' freedom of manoeuvre. On the face of it, this hardly parallels the presidential model in which the leading candidate for executive office is given great latitude by his or her party to evolve an essentially personal programme of policy. Yet McKenzie (1955) famously argued that pretensions of intra-party democracy should not blind us to the fact of domination by parliamentary leaderships. Moreover, the presidentialization thesis would seem to suggest that intra-party relationships in Britain (both within parliament and outside) have further evolved to enhance the *de facto* autonomy of party leaders. Is this true? Here we examine the issue in respect of the major parties.

The Conservative Party

It should be said that the Conservative Party has made little pretence until recently of running a democratic organization, and the leader has always enjoyed considerable autonomy, at least in policy-making. The membership has never had any formal policy-making rights vis-à-vis the parliamentary leadership, although the capacity of Conservative Party conferences to exert *informal* influence on frontbench Tories should not be underestimated (Kelly 1989). In response to the heavy electoral defeat of 1997 and the recriminations of some local party members with the parliamentary party, the then leader, William Hague, initiated a radical new constitutional structure for the party.

The reforms were set out in *Fresh Future*, a document suffused with the rhetoric of participation and democratization (Conservative Party 1998: 1). The *Fresh Future* proposals were overwhelmingly endorsed by the party membership in March 1998 and provided the party, for the first time, with a unified and codified constitution. One of the most striking features of the new party constitution is the disappearance of the legal autonomy of the Constituency Associations, which are now formally subject to the authority of the central party in a number of ways concerning organization and finances, a radical departure from established tradition (Webb 2000: Ch. 7). In policy-making matters little has changed: the various internal party conferences and councils can influence but not determine policy, which leaves the leader's traditional status as the fount of all policy intact. On the other hand, the local membership organizations retain much of their longstanding independence in matters of candidate-selection. Indeed, Conservative members have been accorded new rights in the procedures to select candidates for the European Parliament, the Welsh Assembly, the Greater London Assembly, and the Mayor of London (Conservative Party 1998: 22–3).

A more striking democratization of Conservative Party procedure is apparent in the method of selecting the party leader. Prior to the *Fresh Future* reforms (and since the mid-1960s), party leaders had been elected by fellow parliamentarians: when William Hague was elected in July 1997, he required the support of an overall majority and a clear margin of at least 15 per cent over any other rival. The new constitution replaced this with a system in which the parliamentary party only has the right to act as the preliminary selectorate which, through a system of ballots, reduces to two the number of candidates; the final choice between these remaining candidates is then in the hands of the party's mass membership, who cast their votes in a one-member–one-vote postal ballot. This system was first employed in the election of Iain Duncan Smith as Hague's successor in September 2001. Though it cannot be denied that this provides for leadership election by a greatly increased suffrage, two points should be noted. First, the parliamentary elite deprived the membership of the opportunity to exercise its vote in choosing Duncan Smith's successor in 2003. This was achieved by simple virtue of the fact that only a single candidate—Michael Howard—presented himself. Howard's supporters managed to convince his potential rivals that it was in the best interest of the party to avoid a public, and possibly fractious, contest for the leadership. On the face of it, this amounted to a remarkable return to the days when Conservative leaders 'emerged' from the private negotiations of party grandees. We cannot be sure that the grass roots will always be denied their role in future leadership elections. Second, it should also be noted that the new system makes it harder to depose incumbent leaders than hitherto. Whereas a challenge to a sitting leader could previously be sparked by a contestant with the declared support of 10 per cent of the party's MPs, it can now only be triggered by an explicit vote of no confidence in the leader and such a vote can itself only be called when at least 15 per cent of MPs request it by writing to the Chair of the 1922 Committee. Of course, the deposing of Iain Duncan Smith in the autumn of 2003 demonstrates that this is not an impossible feat.

Overall, though, and notwithstanding *Fresh Future*'s bold assertion that 'the reformed Conservative Party will be an open and democratic organiza-tion...owned by its members' (Conservative Party 1998: 21), it must be reiterated that democratization does not really extend to the critical domain of policy-making within the party. While there is evidence that some in the parliamentary elite have doubts about the democratic turn represented by the new constitution, it is safe to conclude that the strategic autonomy of the Conservative Party leader—always relatively great—and his or her parlia-mentary elite remains intact.

Labour

In Labour's case, policy-making reforms since the 1980s have almost cer-tainly been motivated by the desire to enhance the strategic autonomy of the leadership. In particular, the leader's capacity to shape programmatic ap-peals and manage election campaigns has been maximized. Even though the party constitution formally attributes intra-party sovereignty to the annual conference, McKenzie (1955) showed how the parliamentary leadership has traditionally enjoyed considerable strategic freedom to devise election mani-festos and to govern relatively unimpeded by the extra-parliamentary party once in office.

Beginning with Neil Kinnock's leadership, the party leader's policy-making autonomy has been raised to new heights. This was partly apparent in the development of a new system of campaign committees and a highly influential team of advisers and officials which he gathered around himself. This process of centralized leadership control over election campaigning has undoubtedly been taken further by Blair. Kinnock also achieved a major reorientation of party policy between 1987 and 1989 by a completely innov-atory method which marginalized the National Executive and its system of sub-committees (Heffernan and Marqusee 1992; Shaw 1994: 110–11). In the wake of this, two further developments have been especially significant in respect of Labour's policy-making process. First, the role of the affiliated unions has been restricted in a number of ways, most notably during the brief leadership of John Smith (1992–4 [Webb 1995]). Second, Tony Blair pio-neered a radical recasting of the formal policy-making process after the 1997 general election through the *Partnership in Power* reforms (Labour Party Manifesto 1997). While it is certainly true that the new two-year 'rolling programme' of policy formulation which this ushered in allows for input by individual members, local branches, and their representatives, it nevertheless enshrines a powerful role for the leadership (Seyd 1999; Webb 2000: Ch. 7). In essence, the new system is designed to be iterative and consensual, so that Conference might no longer be the venue for highly publicized (or 'gladiatorial') conflicts, and it seems likely that the leadership has engineered a process by which it sets the agenda of policy debate from the outset, and maximizes its opportunities for guiding the flow of debate by hindering the articulation of public opposition, interpreting the outcome of consultation, and framing the proposals which Conference considers. This could not really be said of the previous system in which extra parliamentary actors such as the National Executive Committee played more prominent roles.

In addition to these changes, Blair occasionally resorted to exercises in plebiscitarian democracy. This was first evident in 1995, when used a ballot of individual members to approve the major and highly symbolic change to Clause IV of the party's constitution. It was deployed again to gain membership approval of the main features of the next election manifesto in 1996. Though ostensibly democratic, this model of constitutional change clearly served to bypass local party activists whom Labour's modernizers regarded as too likely to offer resistance. This process was not without its critics. For many, the plebiscitarian model of democracy has always suggested the manipulation of gullible masses by cynical elites: in this case, it might be said that, as Blair fought strongly to consolidate his leadership, it enabled the 'charismatic leader' to bypass the local activists and claim the support of the more moderate elements of the inactive membership. Regarded in this light, plebiscitarian democracy served a clear party management function.

In addition to this new plebiscitarianism, Labour has extended democratic rights to grass-root members mainly in the areas of candidate-selection without necessarily undermining the leadership's autonomy. Paradoxically, it may even have enhanced it, as Peter Mair (1994: 16) has pointed out:

... it is not the party congress or the middle-level elite, or the activists, who are being empowered, but rather the 'ordinary' members, who are at once more docile and more likely to endorse the policies (and candidates) proposed by the party leadership ... the activist layer inside the party, the traditionally more troublesome layer, becomes marginalized ... in contrast to the activists, these ordinary and often disaggregated members are not very likely to mount a serious challenge against the positions adopted by the leadership.

Finally, it should be noted that various changes have been made to procedure in order to enhance the leadership's control over the Parliamentary Labour

Party (PLP). For instance, after the 1997 election all Labour MPs were issued with pagers which could both summon them and tell them how to vote in parliamentary divisions. Backbenchers were also regularly sent faxed personalized press releases ready to be sent unchanged to their local newspapers, is another indication of the determination of New Labour to keep all its component elements 'on message' (Kingdom 1999: 395). That said, it may be that the perception that the party's leading coteries are centralizing 'control freaks' has been exaggerated, for there is no doubt that the leadership has been faced with both private criticism and public dissent from the parliamentary party since 1997 (Cowley and Stuart 2004). This pressure has grown perceptibly since 1997, with backbench unease over a range of issues including public sector reform and the war on Iraq. The growing willingness of Labour MPs to dissent from the party line in parliamentary voting (ibid.) generated a number of defeats for the government in Commons votes after the general election of 2005. Indeed, at the time of writing, it seems quite possible that this will become 'the most rebellious parliament in the post-war era' (Cowley and Stuart 2006: 1). All of this tends to re-emphasize the limits imposed by the country's parliamentary regime structures.

Overall, then, it is reasonable to conclude that, while the leadership has always enjoyed considerable autonomy within the Conservative Party, and continues to do so, the Labour leadership's freedom of manoeuvre has been enhanced since the middle of the 1980s. This has primarily been motivated by electoral imperatives, which drive the leader to seek greater strategic control over the party. While it is quite true that neither these developments, nor Britain's famous fusion of executive and legislative power, render major party leaders completely immune to the effects of intra-party factionalism or backbench rebellion (see, for instance, Norton 1975, 1978, 1980, 1994, 1998; Norton and Cowley 1996; Baker et al. 1993*a*, 1993*b*, 1999; Garry 1995; Sowemimo 1996; Taggart 1996; Webb 2000: Ch. 6), it is nevertheless the case that their general power within the parties is probably as strong as it ever has been in peace-time.

THE ELECTORAL FACE

Electoral behaviour

In general, acres of media coverage are devoted to the personalities and abilities of party leaders (Seymour-Ure 1997; Foley 2000), yet academics have remained curiously detached from this phenomenon. In part this oversight reflected a general conviction, at least in the 1970s and 1980s, that structural determinants of the vote (such as social background and ideological predisposition) counted for far more, and in part it reflected the feeling that leadership evaluations were often simply caused by prior partisanship. That is, for many voters, partisan affinities were assumed to affect the way in which they perceived the respective merits of party leaders. Until recently, therefore, few academics engaged in detailed studies of the independent impact of leaders' images. David Butler and Donald Stokes constituted a rare counter-example when they demonstrated as long ago as the 1960s that voters could be 'cross-pressured' by favouring leaders from parties other than the one they generally preferred. While it was true that partisan identity generally tended to count for more than leadership evaluations (something which is broadly confirmed at the aggregate level by the victory of parties whose leaders were personally less popular than their counterparts in 1945, 1970 and 1979), it was also notable that the incidence of electoral defection from preferred party was greater among cross-pressured voters (Butler and Stokes 1969: 462–3). It was the 1980s, however, before political scientists in Britain grew more interested in the electoral impact of leaders, and they did so chiefly because evidence of partisan dealignment after 1974 generally induced researchers to investigate the impact of short-term influences on electoral choice; like issue effects, leader effects (which plainly vary from election to election) obviously merited renewed investigation in these terms (Newton 1993: 149).

In general, the research conducted on leader effects on individual-level voting behaviour since then has, despite its methodological variety, concurred in the view that they are modest but significant (Crewe and King 1994; Graetz and McAllister 1987; Mughan 1995, 2000; Stewart and Clarke 1992; Webb 2000: Table 5.1). But how much do leader evaluations matter at the aggregate level? Bartle et al. (1997, 2001) suggest that, while the effect of leadership evaluations on *individuals* may be relatively slight compared to other factors (such as social background or evaluations of government performance), the *aggregate* impact on the electorate as a whole could still be considerable. This would be the case if the distribution of such evaluations was clearly skewed in favour of one leader over another. Thus, although a pro-Blair evaluation significantly increased the probability of an individual voting for Labour in 1997, this fact alone would have made little difference to the overall election outcome if the majority of voters had preferred John Major (or even, perhaps, if the electorate had been split equally between the two men). However, the individual-level impact coupled with Blair's clear personal advantage over Major (an 18-point lead on the eve of poll) probably helped Labour, though the overall impact appears to have been slight. Bartle and Crewe (2001: 24) argue that:

Leadership effects as a whole therefore contributed 0.0174 or 1.7 percentage points to Labour's recorded plurality of 22 percentage points. Yet again leadership effects cannot be ignored in the 1997 general election but they were hardly decisive. Had Major and Blair been evaluated equally favourably Labour's majority would have been cut from 11.9 to 11 points, altering the outcome in just four seats.

In the context of an election in which Labour achieved a 179-seat majority over all other parties, this hardly seems earth-shattering news, but one could certainly imagine scenarios in which a handful of seats might determine the overall outcome of the election; close contests such as those of 1950, 1964, and February 1974 could have turned on the impact of leadership effects of similar magnitude to those reported in 1997 (though of course it should not be assumed that leadership effects always *will* be of similar strength from one election to another).

Bartle and his colleagues make a further point about leadership effects which serves to take us into the territory of more general party reputations. That is, quite apart from the narrowly conceived leadership effects we have been exploring up to now, a leader's impact can also lie further back in the 'funnel of causality' by virtue of his or her effect on general party image. John Curtice (2003: 16) makes an essentially similar point:

[I]n a parliamentary democracy a powerful leader can be expected to demonstrate their influence by being able to shape the image of the party that they lead. If this is the case then leaders matter not because of their ability to win votes independently of their party on the basis of their personal appeal but rather because they can have a decisive impact on voters' evaluations of the parties that they lead.

In fact, Labour's general reputation improved markedly between the elections of 1992 and 1997, and we might plausibly suppose that this in no small measure reflected the impact of Tony Blair on the party. For instance, under Blair not only did Labour's reputation for competent leadership improve, but the party's images in respect of 'extremism' and internal disunity were also significantly enhanced (King 1998: 203). The question of how 'extreme' Labour was seen to be—a potentially serious issue in the context of an electorate with normally distributed core values and centripetal party competition—partly reflected Blair's determination to shift the party into centrist ideological space, but it also hinged on the leader's particular style of party management. That is, Blair quickly demonstrated his ruthlessness at imposing party discipline and continuing the work started by Neil Kinnock in marginalizing the radicals in his party. Similarly, while the importance of a party's reputation for cohesion has already been discussed, it is worth adding that such a reputation will again reflect in no small measure the managerial skills of the leaders. Thus, while John Major was often depicted as indecisive and vacillating in the face of his recalcitrant colleagues, Blair was viewed as utterly determined to impose a uniform party line. As Philip Norton has said of Major, he was essentially a 'balancer' who sought to maintain some kind of equilibrium between the various intra-party groups, but his many critics viewed such an approach as disastrous, and frequently said so in public (Norton 1998: 96). By contrast, a priority of Tony Blair's from the moment he assumed leadership of the Labour Party was party unity, '... and both the shadow cabinet and the PLP were run in a strictly controlled manner from 1994 onwards' (Seyd 1998: 66).

But have leadership effects on voters grown over time—something we would expect if the presidentialization thesis were accurate? Crewe and King have estimated that the net aggregate impact of leadership evaluations has not increased over time, but has fluctuated in a contingent manner, with 1979 representing the high point of net gains to one party derived from leader preferences (Crewe and King 1994: 139). However, their evidence only tells us about *net* effects at the aggregate level, and these are not necessarily related to *gross* effects. That is, the overall number of voters for whom leadership evaluations are important (the gross aggregate effect) may well increase over time, but if these evaluations are distributed in such a way as to (largely) cancel one another out, then the net effect may be barely visible. The distribution of such leadership preferences is bound to vary contingently over time according to events and personalities, so Crewe and King's findings are unsurprising. Of greater interest to us is measurement of *gross* aggregate-level effects and *individual-level* voter effects. The presidentialization thesis implies that parties will modify their campaign styles and structures as they come to perceive a growing *potential* for votes to be swayed by leadership evaluations. Evidence of an increase in individual-level or gross aggregate-level leadership effects is all that is necessary to confirm such potential; the *actual* net effects will vary in a contingent fashion. Mughan (2000: 49) confirms that this is indeed the case, interpreting his evidence as implying an increase in leadership effects since the 1960s and 1970s (with 1987 representing the high point). This would seem to be an important step in confirming the presidentialization thesis.

Campaign styles and media coverage

This aspect of the presidentialization thesis is closely connected with the immediately foregoing one: clearly, parties can be expected to respond to the growing potential for leadership effects on voting behaviour by making leaders a more prominent focus of their election campaigns. Is this true of modern Britain? Much academic attention has been devoted to the development of election campaigning in Britain since the 1980s (see especially Franklin 1994; Kavanagh 1995; Lees-Marshment 2001; Rosenbaum 1997; Scammell 1995, 1999), reflecting widespread interest in the evolution of campaign methods and styles. Prior to the era of mass access to television (around 1960), election campaigns were characterized by limited (and relatively late) preparation, the use of traditional party bureaucrats and volunteer activists, direct communication with electors through public meetings, rallies, and canvassing (plus indirect communication via partisan newspapers), and relatively little central coordination of campaigning across the country. Televisualization of campaigning gradually altered this traditional model, mainly by producing a far greater emphasis on indirect communication with voters via TV, but it was really only after 1979 that the modernization and professionalization of campaigning took a 'quantum leap' forward in Britain (Scammell 1995: Ch. 2). By 1987, both major parties had adopted a model of campaigning which differed from the traditional approach in a number of important respects, including a growing emphasis on the role and personal appeal of the party leader. Clearly, leadership predominance has been considerably reinforced by modern 'catch-all' electioneering, something that encourages the marketing and packaging of the party leadership, rather than the wider political party (Jones 1996; Mancini and Swanson 1996; Scammell 1995).

Neil Kinnock's leadership represents a significant turning point in presidentializing Labour's campaign style. This was revealed in two ways. First, Kinnock took pains to develop a new system of campaign committees and to gather around himself a highly influential team of advisers and officials (Webb 1992b: 269–70). In effect, the previous system which had granted the leading role to a hopelessly large and functionally undifferentiated campaign committee of fluctuating membership was abolished, and its place was taken by a new structure which allowed the leader and a small coterie of strategic advisers to devise and coordinate a carefully planned national campaign. Second, Kinnock himself took an unusually prominent place in the public campaign, inducing commentators at the time to describe Labour's 1987 campaign as 'presidential' in character (Webb 1992a). Particularly notable in this respect was the Party Election Broadcast (PEB) produced by actor/script-writer Colin Welland and director Hugh Hudson (the *Chariots of Fire* team) which was simply entitled *Kinnock*. This concentrated exclusively on the personality and qualities of Labour's leader, and— highly unusually—was even re-broadcast later in the campaign. Polls indicated an immediate and positive reaction on the part of electors, although William Miller argued that Kinnock's image improved most in unimportant areas like 'seeming energetic' or in areas where he already had a large lead, like 'being caring' or 'willing to listen' (Miller et al. 1990: 151). Labour's strategists subsequently contended that the *Kinnock* broadcast was 'not simply a biographical tract...it was using him as a vehicle—in fact, as the device—for saying something about the Labour Party' (Hewitt and Mandelson 1989: 53). Even if this were so, however, it would tend to confirm rather than contradict the presidentialization thesis since the leader would be central to the message that the party strategists seek to convey to the electorate.

As Butler and Kavanagh put it (1997: 91), 'the running of a campaign depends upon the party leader, who must be the ultimate campaign director and the central bearer of the party message'. This brings us back again to the argument proposed by commentators like Curtice and Bartle, that the pre-sidentialization of electoral processes in parliamentary systems essentially occurs through the impact of the leader on a party's overall image.

Since Kinnock, Labour's campaigning has maintained its leadership focus. PEBs have, if anything, tended to be even more oriented towards Blair than they were towards Kinnock (which is hardly surprising as the polls suggested that Blair was overwhelmingly more popular than John Major in 1997 or William Hague in 2001, thus indicating that he was potentially an important electoral asset). It is well known that officials from Labour's national head-quarters spent time during the 1990s observing the work of the US Demo-crats and attempting to draw lessons for British campaigning (Braggins et al. 1993). Bill Clinton's presidential campaign in 1992 was studied carefully and one of the central lessons which New Labour strategists felt they could adopt from this was promotion of Blair as a dynamic young leader. He figured heavily in Labour's PEBs, especially in *Tony: The Home Video,* a 'fly-on-the-wall' style film made by the director Molly Dineen. Interestingly, one PEB concluded by exhorting voters to 'Give Tony Blair your mandate': it is hard to think of a more presidential formulation than this personalized appeal. Indeed, the much heralded decision of the *Sun* newspaper to switch its allegiance from Conservative to Labour was carefully couched as an appeal to vote for 'Blair' rather than 'Labour'. This was illustrated by the front page headline announcing the change—'The Sun Backs Blair'—complete with a photograph of the Labour leader reading the newspaper. Once again in 2001, one of the party's five PEBs was dedicated to the qualities of 'the real Tony Blair' (Harrison 2001: 150). It is fascinating too to observe that even Blair's wife Cherie was a much more prolific subject for press photographers during the 1997 campaign (and subsequently) than other leading Labour politicians such as Deputy Leader John Prescott or Shadow Chancellor Gordon Brown (Scammell and Harrop 1997: 181). This was surely not true of previous party leaders' spouses, even prime ministerial ones such as Norma Major, Dennis Thatcher, Audrey Callaghan, or Mary Wilson, though Glenys Kinnock was certainly quite prominent in campaign projections such as *Kinnock: The Movie.* This rather suggests that Labour's campaign strategists see leaders and their families as a legitimate and significant marketing focus, something which is typical of presidential candidates and their (putative) 'first ladies'.

For the Conservatives, Margaret Thatcher always played very prominent campaign roles, though not necessarily more so than Kinnock or Blair for Labour. Typically, she too had entire election broadcasts devoted to her as leader, and she inevitably dominated press conferences and TV appearances. Her positive personal ratings held up throughout the 1980s although by 1987 she was attracting an unprecedented degree of attention concerning her style of government; she was closely questioned on TV about her capacity for admitting mistakes and suppressing conventions of cabinet government, while Labour tried to make the most out the personality and values which 'cut her off from ordinary people' (Webb 1992*a*). Though this hardly damaged the Conservatives at that time, it might have helped weaken Thatcher herself in the long run. The question of her style of leadership was clearly a central factor in her political demise in 1990. John Major was widely regarded as an electoral asset to his party in 1992, at least compared to Thatcher (Crewe and King 1994: 135), but was undoubtedly a net liability by 1997, as we have seen. Nevertheless, almost perversely in view of his persistently dismal personal opinion poll ratings, the Conservative campaign focused heavily on him. This reflected a conscious strategy to pursue a 'deliberately presidential race of Major versus Blair', on the premise that Blair was the 'only thing' which Labour really had going for it, but that he had been given a 'very soft ride' hitherto (Norris et al. 1999: 57). For their part, Labour's strategists were keen to take up such a challenge, confident of their man's advantage on such terrain. Butler and Kavanagh (1997: 91) noted how at times Major 'seemed to be fighting apart from his own party, as he made personal appeals to the voters to trust him on Europe, on health and on pensions'. His importance to the party's campaign was exemplified by its PEBs, three of which (out of five) were 'straight-to-camera' appeals by Major (Harrison 1997: 152). Interestingly, the 'presidential' focus was dropped for the hapless William Hague in 2001, an omission that 'spoke volumes', as Martin Harrison (2001: 151) puts it.

The dominance of the leaders in media coverage of the 1997 campaign is plain to see: Tony Blair was quoted in TV and radio news items nearly three and a half times more than the next most cited Labour politician (who was Gordon Brown), while John Major outdid his nearest colleague (Michael Heseltine) by an even greater margin in these terms: Paddy Ashdown, for the Liberal Democrats was over eleven times more likely to be quoted than his next most visible colleague, Alan Beith! (Harrison 1997: 144). The situation was very similar in 2001: Tony Blair and William Hague were quoted in TV and radio news items nearly four and a half times more than the next most cited party colleagues, Gordon Brown and Michael Portillo, respectively; Charles Kennedy, for the Liberal Democrats, was over nine times more likely to be quoted than his next most visible colleague, Simon Hughes (Harrison 2001: 140). It is interesting too to note that the voters were comparatively receptive to a leadership focus in TV coverage of the campaign: even though they were generally unhappy about the 'excessive' amount of coverage which the campaign received on TV, they were much less inclined to regard items about party leaders in such a light (Norris et al. 1999: 94). The general increase in media attention on party leaders can be dated back to the 1960s and 1970s: specifically, there is evidence to suggest that TV focus on the prime minister relative to other leading politicians leaped dramatically after 1960 (Rose 1980: 20–1), while a similar presidentialization of press coverage followed a more uneven pattern reflecting deliberate initiatives in party campaign strategies (Mughan 2000: 39).

It should be said that one continuing constraint on the presidentialization of election campaigning in Britain is the failure of the main parties to agree on a format which would allow the leaders to engage in a live TV debate. They probably came as close in 1997 as they ever have done: disagreement about the nature and scope of Liberal Democrat leader Paddy Ashdown's role in any such encounter ultimately played a big part in unhinging the delicate negotiations between party officials and broadcasters (Butler and Kavanagh 1997: 85 ff). Nevertheless, the very fact that all concerned regarded this as such a serious possibility should not be overlooked; it now seems inevitable that the question of a leaders' debate will emerge in the run-up to every general election, though it is unlikely to take place unless both major parties see the possibility of gaining an advantage. Prior to 2001, hopes that a debate would actually occur were raised when the prime minister's official spokesperson, Alistair Campbell, suggested that it might help stimulate interest in politics, but these were dashed by the perception that only the Conservative leader, William Hague could gain. One of Blair's aides is reported to have said 'we will enthusiastically support the idea [of a debate] until the moment we can extricate ourselves with dignity' (Butler and Kavanagh 2001: 28). Overall, though, there is little doubt that the party leaders figure extremely prominently in contemporary election campaigns in the UK, and that this prominence has grown with the advent of televised campaigning. Furthermore, as Mughan (2000: 120) says, leadership may be 'a more manipulable short-term electoral force than issues', which makes it unlikely that strategists will 'roll back their investment in television-based, personality-centred election campaigning'. Thus, the increasingly presidential style of election campaigning in Britain is likely to prove an enduring phenomenon.

CONCLUSION

The party leadership is increasingly at the heart of everything the electoral–professional party does, and this has become a key feature of contemporary party politics. Such predominance inevitably grants the leadership power, but only provided it is able to deliver the public goods the party wants, principally electoral popularity and policy success. Leaders invariably lead (and may squabble in so doing), and members usually follow or complain (or else exit the party). The evidence reviewed in this chapter demonstrates that party leaders play an evermore prominent role in governing and electioneering.

Specifically, we have observed three phenomena. First, election campaigns have become more candidate-centred, with parties offering leaders greater prominence in their election campaigns and the media devoting greater attention to them. This development seems to have taken place since 1960, which coincides with the spread of mass access to television in Britain, and the erosion of class politics. Second, today's major party leaders are in significant ways more strongly placed to exert intra-party power than they were in 1980, much as we might expect of electoral–professional organizations (Panebianco 1988). Third, and perhaps most important, it seems likely that the potential for prime ministerial power within the state's political executive has been enhanced due to structural changes which have generated a larger and more integrated 'executive office' under his or her control since 1970. In addition, we might add that there is individual-level evidence to suggest that leadership evaluations generally have modest direct significance for voter choice, and perhaps greater indirect significance in so far as leaders play a crucial, if unmeasurable, part in shaping overall party images. While the net effects of leader evaluations at the aggregate level will inevitably fluctuate in a contingent manner, the potential for them to be significant cannot be ignored.

We must not, of course, ever lose sight of the fact that these developments have occurred in the context of a traditionally highly partified form of parliamentarism. The impact of this institutional and historical structure continues to be felt. In particular, parliamentary parties and cabinets can, under certain circumstances, strike back at individual leaders, and occasionally even knock them clean off their elevated political perch. We do not contend that prime ministers have become completely indistinguishable from presidents, but suggest that changes have occurred across a number of political dimensions that are mutually consistent. These changes endow leaders with enhanced intra-party power resources and autonomy, provide prime ministers with greater structural resources within the political executive, and facilitate a more pronounced personalization of governmental and electoral processes. Taken together these changes mean that politics in Britain's parliamentary democracy has come to operate according to a logic which more closely echoes presidentialist politics than was hitherto the case.

NOTES

1. According to one Blair aide: 'There was never any intention of having collective cabinet government if Tony was to have the policies he wanted. As in opposition, he would have a centralised operation' (Kavanagh and Seldon 1999: 245).
2. Speech, Cabinet Office press release, 16 September 1997.

3. While private disagreements are rife, ministers tend to stick to the governmental line and resignations on grounds of policy disagreement are relatively rare. According to Dowding and Kang (1988), of 205 selected cases of ministerial resignation (as opposed to dismissal) in 1945–97, only 60 were the result of policy disagreements, compared with 65 for personal or departmental error, and 46 for personal reasons.

4. Private information.

5. According to Nigel Lawson (1994), a minister 'may well feel reluctant to spend too much of his [sic] political capital, arguing a case against the prime minister in a field which is totally outside his departmental responsibility. It is some other minister's baby and some other minister's responsibility'. Lawson suggests this suited all ministers, and recalls certain ministers who, while 'arguing very strongly for more collective decision-making in government, were at the same time busy cutting bilateral deals with the prime minister on issues within their own bailiwick'.

6. Peter Hennessy, quoted in Michael Cockerell, *Blair's Thousand Days*, BBC2, 30 January 2000.

REFERENCES

Baker, D., A. Gamble, and S. Ludlam (1993*a*). 'Conservative Splits and European Integration', *Political Quarterly*, 64/2: 420–35.

—— , A. Gamble, and S. Ludlam (1993*b*). 'Whips or Scorpions? The Maastricht Vote and the Conservative Party', *Parliamentary Affairs*, 42/2: 151–66.

—— , A. Gamble, S. Ludlam, and D. Seawright (1999). 'Backbenchers With Attitude: A Seismic Study of the Conservative Party and Dissent on Europe', in S. Bowler, D. M. Farrell, and R. S. Katz (eds.), *Party Discipline and Parliamentary Government*. Columbus: Ohio State University Press, 72–93.

Bartle, J. and I. Crewe (2001). 'The Impact of Party Leaders on Voting Behaviour in Britain: Strong Assumptions, Weak Evidence'. Unpublished paper, University of Essex.

—— —— A. King (1997). 'Was it Blair Wot Won it? Leadership Effects in the 1997 British General Election'. Paper presented to conference on *Assessing the 1997 Election*, University of Essex, September.

Braggins, J., M. McDonagh, and A. Barnard (1993). *The American Presidential Election 1992—What Can Labour Learn?* London: Labour Party.

Burch, M. and I. Holliday (1999). 'The Prime Minister's and Cabinet Offices: An Executive Office in All But Name', *Parliamentary Affairs*, 52: 32–45.

Butler, D. and D. Kavanagh (1997). *The British General Election of 1997*. Basingstoke: Macmillan.

—— —— (2001). *The British General Election of 2001*. Basingstoke: Palgrave.

—— and D. Stokes (1969). *Political Change in Britain*. Harmondsworth: Penguin.

Clark, A. (1998). *The Tories: The Conservatives and the Nation State, 1922–1997*. London: Phoenix.

Committee on Standards in Public Life (2003). *Defining the Boundaries Within the Executive: Ministers, Special Advisers and the Permanent Civil Service, Ninth Report, CM5775*. London: The Stationery Office.

Conservative Party (1998). *Fresh Future*. London: Conservative Party.

Cowley, P. and M. Stuart (2004). 'Parliament: More Bleak House than Great Expectations', *Parliamentary Affairs*, 57.

—— (2006). 'Rebelliousness in a Westminster system: Labour MPs under the Blair government' Paper presented to *Workshop of Paliamentary Scholars and Parliamentarians*, Wroxton Hall (www.revolts.co.uk).

Crewe, I. and A. King (1994). 'Did Major win? Did Kinnock lose? Leadership Effects in the 1992 Election', in A. Heath, R. Jowell, and J. Curtice (eds.), *Labour's Last Chance? The 1992 Election and Beyond*. Aldershot: Dartmouth, 125–48.

Crossman, R.H.S. (1964). 'Introduction' to W. Bagehot, *The English Constitution*, London: Watts. Reprinted in A. King (ed.) (1985). *The British Prime Minister*. London, Macmillan, 175–94.

—— (1985). 'Introduction to Bagehot's The English Constitution', in A. King (ed.), *The British Prime Minister*. London: Macmillan, 175–94, first published 1964.

Curtice, J. (2003). 'Elections as Beauty Contests: Do the Rules Matter? Paper presented at the International Conference on *Portugal: At the Polls*, Lisbon, 27–28 February.

Dowding, K. and W.-T. Kang (1988). Ministerial Resignations 1945–97', *Public Administration*, 76: 411–29.

Dunleavy, P. (1995). 'Estimating the Distribution of Positional Influence in Cabinet Committees under Major', in R.A.W. Rhodes and P. Dunleavy (eds.), *Prime Minister, Cabinet and Core Executive*. London: Macmillan.

—— (2003). 'Analysing political power', in P. Dunleavy, A. Gamble, R. Heffernan, and G. Peele (eds.), *Developments in British Politics*, 7. Basingstoke: Palgrave, 338–59.

—— and R. A. W. Rhodes (1990). 'Core Executive Studies in Britain', *Public Administration*, 68: 3–28.

Elgie, R. (1997). 'Models for Executive Politics: A Framework for the Study of Executive Power Relations in Parliamentary and Semi-Presidential Regimes', *Political Studies*, XLV: 217–31.

Franklin, B. (1994). *Packaging Politics*. London: Edward Arnold.

Foley, M. (2000). *The Rise of the British Presidency*. Manchester: Manchester University Press.

—— (2002). *John Major, Tony Blair and Conflict of Leadership: Collision Course*. Manchester: Manchester University Press.

Gamble, A. and G. Kelly (2002). 'Britain and EMU', in K. Dyson (ed.), *European States and the Euro*. Oxford: Oxford University Press, 97–119.

Garry, J. (1995). 'The British Conservative Party: Divisions over European policy', *West European Politics*, 18: 170–89.

Graetz, B. and I. McAllister (1987). 'Party Leaders and Election Outcomes in Britain, 1974–1983', *Comparative Political Studies* 19: 484–507.

Harrison, M. (1997). 'Politics on Air', in D. Butler and D. Kavanagh (eds.), *The British General Election of 1997*, Basingstoke: Macmillan, 133–55.

—— (2001). 'Politics on the air', in D. Butler and D. Kavanagh (eds.), *The British General Election of 2001*. Basingstoke: Palgrave, 132–55.

Heffernan, R. (2001) 'Beyond Euro-Scepticism: Exploring the Europeanization of the Labour Party since 1983', *Political Quarterly*, 72: 180–90.

—— (2003). 'Prime ministerial predominance? Core executive politics in the UK', *British Journal of Politics and International Relations*, 5: 347–72.

—— and M. Marqusee (1992). *Defeat from the Jaws of Victory: Inside Kinnock's Labour Party*. London: Verso.

Hencke, D. (2000). 'Special Advisers Tripled as No. 10 Staff Hits New High', *Guardian*, 2 March.

—— (2003). ' Watchdog attacks PM's rules on advisers', *Guardian*, 12 September.

Hennessy, P. (1998). 'The Blair Style of Government: An Historical Perspective and An Interim Audit', *Government & Opposition*, 33: 3–20.

—— (1999*a*). *The Blair Centre: A Question of Command and Control*. London: Public Management Foundation.

—— (1999*b*). *The Importance of Being Tony: Two Years of the Blair Style*. London: Guys and St Thomas' Hospital Trust.

—— (2000). *The Prime Minister: The Office and its Holders since 1945*. London: Allen & Unwin.

Hewitt, P. and P. Mandelson (1989). 'The Labour Campaign', in I. Crewe and M. Harrop (eds.), *Political Communications: The General Election Campaign of 1987*. Cambridge: Cambridge University Press.

Jenkins, S. (1999). 'Tony Blair's Rasputin', *The Times*, 24 February.

Jones, G. W. (1965). 'The Prime Minister's Power', *Parliamentary Affairs*, xviii: 167–85. Reprinted in A. King (ed.) (1985). *The British Prime Minister*. London, Macmillan, 195–220.

Jones, N. (1996). *Soundbites and Spin Doctors: How Politicians Manipulate the Media and Vice Versa*. London: Victor Gollancz.

Kavanagh, D. (1995). *Election Campaigning: The New Marketing of Politics*. Oxford: Basil Blackwell.

—— and A. Seldon (1999). *The Powers Behind the Prime Minister: The Hidden Influence of Number 10*. London: HarperCollins.

Kelly, R. N. (1989). *Conservative Party Conferences: The Hidden System*. Manchester: Manchester University Press.

King, A. (1998). 'Why Labour Won – at Last', in A. King, D. Denver, I. McLean, P. Norris, P. Norton, D. Sanders, and P. Seyd, *New Labour Triumphs: Britain at the Polls*. Chatham, NJ: Chatham House, 177–207.

Kingdom, J. (1999). *Government and Politics in Britain: An Introduction*. Cambridge: Polity Press.

Labour Party (1997). *Labour into Power: A Framework for Partnership*. London: Labour Party.

Lane, J. E. and S. Errson (1999). *The New Institutional Politics: Performance and Outcomes*. London: Routledge.

Laver, M. and K. Shepsle (1994). 'Cabinet Government and Government Formation in Parliamentary Democracies', in M. Laver and K. Shepsle (eds.), *Cabinet Ministers and Parliamentary Democracies*. Cambridge: Cambridge University Press.

Lawson, N. (1994). 'Cabinet Government in the Thatcher Years', *Contemporary Record*, 8: 440–52.

Lees-Marshment, J. (2001). *The Party's Just Begun*. Manchester: Manchester University Press.

Lipsey, D. (2000). *The Secret Treasury: How Britain's Economy is Really Run*. London: Viking.

Mackintosh, J. (1962). *The British Cabinet*. London: Stevens.

Mair, P. (1994). 'Party Organizations: From Civil Society to State' in R. S. Katz and P. Mair (eds.), *How Parties Organize: Change and Adaptation in Party Organizations in Western Democracies*. London: Sage, 1–22.

Major, J. (1999) *The Autobiography*. London: HarperCollins.

Mancini, P. and D. L. Swanson (1996). *Politics, Media and Modern Democracy: An International Study of Innovations in Electoral Campaigning and the Consequences*. Westport: Praeger Publishers.

McKenzie, R. T. (1955). *Political Parties*. London: Heinemann.

Miller, W., H. Clarke, M. Harrop, L. le Duc, and P. Whiteley (1990). *How Voters Change: The 1987 British Election Campaign in Perspective*. Cambridge: Cambridge University Press.

Mughan, A. (1995). 'Party Leaders and Presidentialism in the 1992 Election: A Postwar Perspective', in D. Denver, P. Norris, C. Rallings, and D. Broughton (eds.), *British Elections and Parties Yearbook 1993*. Hemel Hempstead: Harvester Wheatsheaf, 193–204.

—— (2000). *The Presidentialization of Elections in Britain*. Basingstoke: Palgrave.

Newton, K. (1993). 'Caring and Competence: the Long, Long Campaign', in A. King, I. Crewe, D. Denver, K. Newton, P. Norton, D. Sanders, and P. Seyd, *Britain at the Polls 1992*. Chatham, NJ: Chatham House, 129–70.

Norris, P., J. Curtice, D. Sanders, M. Scammell, and H. Semetko (1999). *On Message: Communicating The Campaign*. London: Sage.

Norton, P. (1975). *Dissension in the House of Commons: Intra-Party Dissent in the House of Commons Division Lobbies 1945–74*. London: Macmillan.

—— (1978). *Conservative Dissidents: Dissent Within the Parliamentary Conservative Party 1970–74*. London: Temple-Smith.

—— (1980). *Dissension in the House of Commons 1974–79*. Oxford: Oxford University Press.

—— (1994). 'The parties in parliament', in L. Robins, H. Blackmore, and R. Pyper (eds.), *Britain's Changing Party System*. London: Leicester University Press.

—— (1998). 'The Conservative Party: In office but not in power', in A. King, D. Denver, I. McLean, P. Norris, P. Norton, D. Sanders, and P. Seyd, *New Labour Triumphs: Britain at the Polls*. Chatham, NJ: Chatham House, 75–112.

—— and P. Cowley (1996). 'Are Conservative MPs revolting? Dissension by Government MPs in the British House of Commons 1976–96', *Centre for Legislative Studies Research Paper 2/96*. Hull: University of Hull.

Panebianco, A. (1988). *Political Parties: Organisation and Power*. Cambridge: Cambridge University Press.

Public Administration Select Committee (2004). *Draft Civil Service Bill*. London: The Stationery Office.

Rawnsley, A. (2000). 'How Gordon has trussed up Tony', *Observer*, 5 March.

—— (2001). *Servants of the People: The Inside Story of New Labour*. London: Penguin.

Rhodes, R. A. W. (1995). 'From Prime Ministerial Power to Core Executive', in R. A. W. Rhodes and P. Dunleavy (eds.), *Prime Minister, Cabinet and Core Executive.* London: Macmillan.

—— (1997). *Understanding Governance.* Buckingham: Open University Press.

—— (1999). 'Foreword', in M. J. Smith, *The Core Executive in Britain.* Basingstoke: Macmillan.

—— and P. Dunleavy (1995). *Prime Minister, Cabinet and Core Executive.* London: Macmillan.

Rose, R. (1980). 'British government: the job at the top', in R. Rose and E. Suleiman (eds.), *Presidents and Prime Ministers.* Washington: American Enterprise Instutute, 1–49.

Rosenbaum, M. (1997). *From Soapbox to Soundbite: Party Political Campaigning in Britain Since 1945.* Basingstoke: Macmillan.

Sampson, A. (2003). 'Hijacked by that Mob at No.10', *Observer,* 8 June.

Scammell, M. (1995). *Designer Politics: How Elections Are Won.* Basingstoke: Macmillan.

—— (1999). 'Political marketing: Lessons for political science', *Political Studies,* 47, 718–39.

—— and M. Harrop (1997). 'The press', in D. Butler and D. Kavanagh (eds.), *The British General Election of 1997,* Basingstoke: Macmillan, 156–85.

Seyd, P. (1998). 'Tony Blair and New Labour', in A. King, D. Denver, I. McLean, P. Norris, P. Norton, D. Sanders, and P. Seyd, (eds.) *New Labour Triumphs: Britain at the Polls.* Chatham, NJ: Chatham House, 49–73.

—— (1999). 'New parties, new politics? A case study of the British Labour Party', *Party Politics,* 5: 383–405.

Seymour-Ure, C. (1997). 'Newspapers: Editorial opinion in the national press', in P. Norris and N. T. Gavin (eds.), *Britain Votes 1997,* Oxford: Oxford University Press, 78–100.

Shaw, E. (1994). *The Labour Party Since 1979: Crisis and Transformation.* London: Routledge.

Smith, M. J. (1999). *The Core Executive in Britain.* Basingstoke: Macmillan.

Sowemimo, M. (1996). 'The Conservative Party and European Integration 1988–95', *Party Politics* 2: 77–97.

Stewart, M. C. and H. D. Clarke, (1992). 'The (un)importance of party leaders: leader images and party choice in the 1987 British election', *Journal of Politics,* 54: 447–70.

Taggart, P. (1996). 'Rebels, sceptics and factions: Euroscepticism in the British Conservative Party and the Swedish Social Democratic Party', *Contemporary Political Studies 1996,* 589–97.

Thatcher, M. (1993). *The Downing Street Years.* London: HarperCollins.

Webb, P. D. (1992*a*). 'Britain: The 1987 Campaign' in S. Bowler and D. Farrell (eds.), *Electoral Strategies and Political Marketing.* London: Macmillan, 43–62.

—— (1992*b*). 'Election campaigning, organisational transformation and the professionalisation of the British Labour Party', *European Journal of Political Research,* 21: 267–88.

Webb, P. D. (1995). 'Reforming the party-union link: An assessment', in D. Broughton, D. Farrell, D. Denver, and C. Rallings (eds.), *British Parties and Elections Yearbook 1994*. London: Frank Cass, 1–14.

—— (2000). *The Modern British Party System*. London: Sage.

White, M. (2004). 'No. 10 adviser to be quizzed on secret policy making role', *Guardian*, 10 February.

3

A Presidentializing Party State?
The Federal Republic of Germany

Thomas Poguntke

INTRODUCTION: CHANCELLOR DEMOCRACY, PARTY STATE, AND PRESIDENTIALIZATION

When the parliamentary council designed the institutional framework of the provisional West German state in 1948–9 under the guidance of the Allied Powers, there was little controversy about the desirability to constrain executive power. The experience of almost a century of strong and mainly disastrous executive leadership seemed to leave little alternative but to create a 'semi-sovereign state' (Katzenstein 1987) with highly constrained and dispersed executive powers. Above all, the office of the President of the Republic was to be reduced to little more than a ceremonial head of state with very few reserve powers (Smith 1982: 47–8). Almost ironically, however, the first chancellor of the Federal Republic Konrad Adenauer assumed a dominant role in the early post-war years, hence giving rise to a, at times heated, debate about the merits and dangers of *Kanzlerdemokratie* (chancellor democracy). Clearly, this debate owed much to Adenauer's specific style of incumbency (Jäger 1988) and, arguably, the pronounced scepticism among parts of the German public about the desirability of strong executive leadership. Consequently, as his successors in the 1960s provided less strong leadership, these concerns receded while unease with the paramount role of political parties in the *Parteienstaat* (party state) grew, a debate that has continued ever since (Poguntke 2001*b*; Stöss 1990, 1997). This discussion concealed another, arguably more fundamental change in the working of the first successful German democracy: a gradual shift towards a presidentialized mode of governance that was not only a result of the varying specific leadership styles of consecutive incumbents but that was also sustained by underlying structural changes in the conditions which determine the working of German democracy. It was not until the late 1990s, however, that the increasingly autocratic leadership style of Helmut Kohl and Gerhard Schröder's interpretation of his office drew attention to this phenomenon in public debate and academic analysis (Lütjen and Walter 2000; Poguntke 2000).

Parteienstaat and *Kanzlerdemokratie* are probably the most widely used labels to characterize the German system of governance. They refer to the most distinct features of the German political system, that is, the pervasive presence of political parties in all important institutions of the polity and the elevated position of the German chancellor. Normative concept and empirical reality of the *party state* go beyond models of party democracy or party government in that the German Basic Law grants political parties a privileged status in the political process and, in exchange, provides the normative foundation of extensive legal regulation of their internal organization as well as of their extensive funding by the state (von Alemann 1992; Poguntke 1994; Stöss 1997). When it comes to their actual role in the political process, these peculiarities are not very important (Pappi 2000: 345–6). No doubt, German party government, like all other parliamentary regimes, has its distinctive features, but they are not primarily related to the 'party privilege' of the Basic Law's article 21. Rather, it is the specifically German version of cooperative federalism which provides both an opportunity and a need for political parties to play a particularly pronounced role in the process of democratic government: much of the political coordination between federal government, individual *Land* governments and the federal chamber (*Bundesrat*) is facilitated through party channels (Padgett 1994*b*: 7; Pappi 2000: 346; Wewer 1999: 511). The label of *chancellor democracy* has been widely used to characterize another important feature of German politics, that is, the elevated position of the chief executive. To the extent that the term chancellor democracy has not simply been used as a synonym for a strong chancellor (Jäger 1988) or his role within the core executive (Helms 2001: 155), it has been conceptualized as comprising the following elements:

(1) prevalence of the chancellor in the cabinet;
(2) personalization of the political struggle;
(3) control of the leading party of government by the chancellor;
(4) juxtaposition of government and opposition camps;
(5) primacy of foreign policy (Niclauß 1988: 67–8).

It can hardly go unnoticed how much this concept has been inspired by Adenauer's interpretation of the office, although many have argued that it was not so much Adenauer's personal style of leadership but the specific powers of his office that have established the German chancellor's strong position (Mayntz 1980). Arguably, both perspectives tend to underestimate the essential impact of contextual factors for moulding the German chancellorship. Without the rapid concentration of the German party system, the 'plebiscitary' component of chancellor democracy, that is, the institution of the chancellor candidate, which effectively turned Bundestag elections into a decision about the chancellorship, could not have developed (Niclauß 1988: 267–82; Padgett 1994*b*: 5).

In many respects, chancellor democracy seems to be an early version of a presidentialized parliamentary system, particularly because the selection of the chief executive tends to directly involve the public at large through the nomination of chancellor candidates. There are, however, fundamental differences to the concept of presidentialization, which means that we are, evidently, not just pouring new wine into old bottles. First, in the age of globalization (and, for most European nations: Europeanization) the 'primacy of foreign policy' of chancellor democracy has been superseded by an executive bias that has become a structural condition of national politics. Inevitably, this concentrates more power resources and autonomy in the hand of the executive leader. Second, while chancellor democracy is based on tight party control, the concept of presidentialization envisages a growing distance between the chief executive (or, when in opposition, the party leader) and his or her party. In other words, just like in a truly presidential system, the leader becomes more independent from the party organization and the party in parliament. The mandate of the leader is no longer mediated through the party, as was the case in an ideal-type chancellor democracy. Instead, leaders increasingly seek a personalized mandate bypassing their parties and appealing directly to the public at large, just like Gerhard Schröder secured his position as chancellor candidate in 1998 (Niedermayer 2000: 203). Finally, while strong leaders have always been an electoral asset for political parties since the early days of mass democracy, they have become a necessity now. In other words, party leaders (or leading candidates) are no longer selected because they unite a broad or dominant coalition within their party. Instead, their ability to appeal successfully to voters has become the prime selection criterion. Nevertheless, the debate about chancellor democracy indicates that the Federal Republic's institutional framework should have made Germany's political process particularly amenable to presidentializing tendencies. In other words, we would expect to find clear evidence of a trend towards:

(a) increasing leadership power resources and autonomy within the party and the political executive respectively, and (b) increasingly leadership-centred electoral processes (p. 5, Chapter 1, this volume)

The constitutional setting

The constitutional and legal framework represents a suitable point of departure for an analysis of possible shifts in the actual mode of governance in the Federal Republic. These formal legal-constitutional rules define the boundaries between distinct regime-types (see Fig. 1.1), and movement across these boundaries is generally rare. Despite its explicitly provisional character, the constitutional fabric of West Germany's Basic Law survived even the most far-reaching of events virtually unchanged, that is, a fundamental change of its territorial scope in the wake of unification. With its weak presidency, the German political system falls unambiguously under the rubric of parliamentary regimes. On the federal level, chief executive power rests with the chancellor who has (constitutionally) considerable discretion over the selection of cabinet members who are appointed upon the chancellor's suggestion by the president. Once elected by the Bundestag, the chancellor enjoys a strong position as he or she has the right to determine the 'guidelines of policies' (*Richtlinienkompetenz*) although this right is muted by the two competing principles of collective cabinet decision-making and ministerial responsibility (von Beyme 1979; Hesse and Ellwein 1992; Rudzio 1991; Smith 1982: 56–62). While a chancellor's power to determine policies is clearly limited by the structural need to form coalition governments, the Basic Law provides the office with a special protection against parliamentary rebellion. The 'constructive vote of no-confidence' stipulates that the incumbent can only be removed by parliament through the election of a successor, and the chancellor's right to ask for a vote of confidence equips him or her with a powerful instrument for disciplining his or her own political camp because it can be used to call an early election (Niclauß 1988: 278).

The most fundamental constraint on the power of a federal chancellor to determine national policies lies with the nature of German cooperative federalism which gives Land governments an important veto position on a substantial portion of federal legislation via the Bundesrat (Benz 1999). While federal governments in the 1950s and 1960s could mainly rely on a supportive Bundesrat, a dissenting political party composition of the Bundesrat has become almost the rule since then (Wewer 1999: 511). The continuous growth of the share of national legislation that needs Bundesrat approval and the increasing number of joint responsibilities of national and Land governments (*Gemeinschaftsaufgaben*) have given rise to another interpretation of German democracy as one that should be characterized as 'negotiation democracy' where power is dispersed between different levels and arenas of governance rather than concentrated in the chief executive office (Holtmann and Voelzkow 2000*b*; Lehmbruch 2000; Mayntz 1980). This specifically German variant of consensus democracy is characterized by majoritarian traditions of federal government (a Grand Coalition is generally regarded as a means of last resort in times of crisis) combined with strong elements of segmented corporatism and strong institutional veto points (Czada 2000; Lijphart 1999: 43–57).

Patterns of government formation

Clearly, the power of a chief executive in parliamentary systems is also strongly moulded by the format of the party system and concomitant patterns of coalition formation. After a relatively short period of, first diffusion, and then imbalance in the 1950s (Smith 1982: 102), the party system consolidated into its proverbial two-and-a-half parties format which facilitated stable governments while providing feasible alternatives, furnishing the centrist FDP with a pivotal role (Poguntke 2001*b*). When the success of the Greens in the early 1980s upset this neat pattern by moving the German party system towards a two-bloc logic, the basic pattern of government formation remained unchanged. For most of its history, the Federal Republic has been governed by coalitions led by one of the two catch-all parties with a smaller coalition partner. Even German unification brought about relatively little change on the federal level because the West German parties successfully 'conquered' the East (Niedermayer 1996; Niedermayer and Stöss 1994). While party systems in the Eastern Länder increasingly follow a different pattern with a strong post-Communist Party of Democratic Socialists (PDS), the PDS has not been able to consolidate its presence in the Bundestag (von Alemann 2000; Niedermayer 2003; Neugebauer and Stöss 2003).[1] However, the apparent resilience of the German party system on the national level camouflages considerable growth in voter flexibility. Declining cleavage strength and concomitantly receding partisan attachment in the West has been complemented by a largely unattached Eastern electorate which only hesitantly develops partisan loyalty (Dalton and Bürklin 1995; Niedermayer 2001: 67–71; Scarrow 2002: 82–6).

THE EXECUTIVE FACE

The nature of executive leadership is at the core of the debate over alleged presidential tendencies of the German political process. Let us start with those aspects that have not changed at all: the formal powers of the chancellor have not been modified throughout the history of the Federal Republic. This is, however, the only constant. As soon as we move beyond a narrow focus on formal-constitutional powers, there are very substantial structural changes. As mentioned above, the need for coordination of federal and Land policies has grown substantially as a result of the extension of joint responsibilities (Mayntz 1980: 162; Schmidt 2003: 94). This represents a significant constraint even in (increasingly rare) times of supportive Bundesrat majorities as Land governments cannot be assumed to automatically support 'their' parties' federal policies (Smith 1991: 51). On the contrary, there is a constant temptation for Land governments to extract concessions from a federal government if their support in the Bundesrat is needed, even if this means undermining national party political strategies. As a result of ever more disparate economic pressures in the wake of unification, the tendency of Land governments to prioritize Land interests over party political strategies has grown stronger after 1990. In addition, the increasingly pluralistic pattern of coalition formation in the *Länder*, caused by the need to accommodate the PDS in east Germany and eruptions of populist voting, has further increased the need for negotiations between the federal majority and the Bundesrat (Czada 2000: 404).

This institutional configuration furnishes the chancellor with a key role as chief negotiator in order to get legislation approved by the Bundesrat, a role that has become structurally more prominent as the role of the Bundesrat has grown while the likelihood of supportive majorities along political party lines has decreased. What seems to severely restrain a chancellor's power makes him or her a more autonomous player under the conditions of coalition government. Quite akin to the chief executive in presidential systems, the chancellor (or his closest aides) assumes the role of a mediator between different power centres, that is, between federal and Land governments. What has been identified as 'negotiation democracy' (Holtmann and Voelzkow 2000*a*; Mayntz 1980; Scharpf 1985) describes a mode of governance that protects the chancellor from pressures of his own party (or coalition partner) because he or she can rightly claim that the preferences of crucial Land governments need to be taken into account. Of course, there may be times when such constraints are strongly resented by a chancellor who would prefer to have his or her way. Nevertheless, this does not invalidate the systematic argument that the growing power of the Bundesrat has shifted the logic of German executive leadership towards a more presidential mode. The chancellor acts increasingly less as the leader of a unified parliamentary majority. Instead, he or she needs to moderate between Bundestag and Bundesrat in order to get legislation approved.

Europeanization and the growing internationalization of politics impose a comparable logic on the chancellor's office. On the one hand, the substantial shift of powers to the EU and other supranational bodies like NATO, UN, and international regimes in charge of certain policy areas means a loss of national sovereignty and therefore of power of the chief executive (Haftendorn 1999: 256). At the same time, however, these processes have substantially altered the nature of the chancellorship (and of ministerial office). They have introduced a significant 'executive bias' into the process of national policy formulation. When the chancellor (or a government minister) comes back from a European or international summit, they are usually in no position to negotiate the results with their parliamentary majority (or the Bundesrat). What has been agreed between representatives of national governments can hardly be unravelled by national parliaments. Effectively, the internationalization of governance injects an element of *separation of powers* (that is, one of the defining element of presidentialism) into parliamentary systems by making governments more independent of the legislature. To be sure, the growing complexity and interconnectedness of international and supranational decision-making shifts substantial power to technocratic policy networks and undermines the steering capacity of the centre. This, however, applies mainly to the vast majority of non-politicized, technical issues while the growing need to reach agreement on important policies in international or supranational bodies clearly enhances the political power of the chancellor and senior cabinet members.

Similarly, the specifically German combination of majoritarian federal government with cooperative federalism and strong elements of corporatism has given rise to a tradition of policy-making through special commissions and advisory councils that put the chancellor (and to a lesser extent key cabinet members) at centre stage. As early as the late 1960s, neo-corporatist patterns of policy-making began to complement parliamentary democracy. These tripartite arrangements broke down in 1977 when the employers' associations appealed to the Constitutional Court against the co-determination reform implemented by the Social–Liberal coalition. Patterns of neo-corporatist interest intermediation continued on a less conspicuous scale and were elevated to new prominence by Chancellor Helmut Kohl in the 'Alliance for Jobs' which was launched in 1996 in an attempt to combat rising unemployment (Lehmbruch 2000; Voelzkow 2000: 186–7).

Gerhard Schröder has cultivated this tradition of a 'mediating chancellorship' by appointing a range of cross-party policy commissions with the aim to initiate policy innovation (Heinze 2000: 7–12). In order to strengthen their non-partisan appeal and to protect himself from pressures from his own majority, Schröder has tended to appoint leading opposition politicians as commission chairs. The special commission on immigration, the newly created 'Ethics Committee' and, last but not least, the re-launched (but unsuccessful) 'Alliance for Jobs' are conspicuous examples of a style of executive leadership that does not primarily rely upon support from its own ranks but seeks to forge shifting coalitions, depending on the issues at stake. The fact that both Helmut Kohl and Gerhard Schröder have tended to appoint a considerable number of cabinet ministers from outside the Bundestag parliamentary party is another indication of tendencies of chancellors to govern past the dominant coalition within their own parties even though it may be somewhat premature to identify a sustained trend on the basis of a relative small number of cases (Helms 2002: 155–6). It is indicative of this style of governance that Chancellor Schröder attempted to ignore one of the crucial systemic boundaries of German parliamentarism, namely that a government needs the support of its own majority in crucial foreign policy decisions. When it became apparent in late 2001 that the government could not count on sufficient support from its own coalition for military involvement in Afghanistan, Schröder first implied that it would not worry him if parliamentary support for his foreign policy depended on opposition votes. It was only after an increasing public debate over this issue that he decided to force his coalition to close ranks by connecting the vote on the Afghanistan mission to a vote of confidence on the government.

The preceding discussion has shown that both key cabinet members and the chancellor have benefited from structural tendencies to strengthen executive action at the expense of parliamentary, and hence ultimately party political, control. Given the constitutionally elevated position and prominent political role of the chancellor, this created the potential for a role as key coordinator of important executive action at the expense of collective cabinet decision-making, which has, in any case, never been particularly strong in German constitutional thought and executive tradition (Müller-Rommel 1997: 178; Smith 1982: 56–69). An important structural prerequisite for this has been the development of the chancellor's office (*Bundeskanzleramt*), which has, over the years, developed from a rudimentary support unit into a formidable centre of executive power with sufficient manpower to screen and coordinate governmental policy (Müller-Rommel 1994: 111, 1997: 179; Saalfeld 2003: 365; Smith 1991: 50). The office had some 120 staff during Adenauer's incumbency (1949–63) when it began to grow at an average annual rate of 4.3 per cent for the subsequent four decades, reaching about 500 staff by the late 1990s, which makes it one of the largest of its kind in Western Europe (Knoll 2004; Müller-Rommel 2000). Even though the early Brandt government's enthusiasm for central planning did not lead to convincing success (Padgett 1994b: 9), the chancellor's office maintained its pivotal role in executive decision-making, although this obviously varied with leadership styles (Helms 2002; Niclauß 1988; Padgett 1994a).

It could be argued, however, that the structural need for coalition government has tended to mitigate tendencies of strong executive leadership as coalition steering committees have represented an important party political decision-making arena in the German political process (Schreckenberger 1994). While it is true that these committees inject party political control into the process of executive decision-making by including senior party politicians like the chairs of the parliamentary and extra-parliamentary coalition parties, they are nevertheless dominated by key cabinet members and, most importantly, the chancellor (Rudzio 1991: 292–5; Saalfeld 2003: 364). In any case, the practice of deciding most important political issues in such informal rounds clearly weakens the power of the parliamentary parties supporting the government and strengthens small circles of leaders.

To be sure, the structural conditions discussed earlier create the potential for presidentialized executive leadership. Equally important, arguably, are personal and contextual political factors and, above all, the relationship between the chancellor and his or her party—a relationship that has undergone substantial structural transformation over the past decades.

Party leadership and campaign organization

One of the most important changes concerning the role and position of party leaders is directly related to the wholesale mediatization and professionalization of campaigning (see below), which has had substantial repercussions on the distribution of power within German parties. The German Social Democrats clearly set the example in their 1998 election campaign when they physically separated the campaign organization from their party headquarters. It was located in a separate building, given a distinct name, and tightly controlled by the chancellor-candidate and his closest aides (though not entirely without interference by party headquarters) (von Alemann 1999; Schmitt-Beck 2001). The initiators of this substantial departure from sacred Social Democratic organizational traditions certainly intended that this organizational innovation would assume news value itself. In other words, the very fact that the SPD ran an innovative campaign underlined the innovative image the party was trying to create.

The success of the 1998 campaign organization suggested a similar model in 2002. As in 1998, the SPD set up its campaign headquarters in a separate building located in a different part of Berlin. This time, however, spatial distance did not guarantee freedom from interference by other power centres. In 2002, the chancellor's office interfered substantially with campaign planning and organization, undermining the coherence of the campaign (von Alemann 2003: 57). In a way, the Social Democratic campaign represents an example of the presidentialization of party leadership taken one step further: if the party leader assumes chief executive office (or, in coalition government, a senior role in cabinet), it is highly likely that the party and its campaign become dominated by this particular part of the executive, given the vastly superior resources which will normally be at the disposal of a chancellor (or cabinet member) for planning and steering a campaign.

All other parties attempted to imitate the successful SPD model to a certain degree, although they did not go all the way to physically removing the campaign headquarters entirely from party headquarters. The PDS went furthest by opening a 'Wahlquartier' (campaign centre) where the campaign manager resided. However, part of the central organization remained with the federal party manager (*Bundesgeschäftsführer*) who continued to reside at party headquarters.

The Christian Democrats where confronted with a particular challenge in 2002: the chancellor-candidate of CDU and CSU was CSU leader Edmund Stoiber, whose Bavaria-based party has no headquarters in the national capital Berlin. The solution was to install a 'Stoiber Team' within the CDU headquarters in Berlin which was supposed to be in control of campaign planning and coordination and which closely cooperated with the CSU headquarters in Munich as well as with the regular staff at the Berlin CDU headquarters. Edmund Stoiber's most conspicuous (and arguably most successful) move was the recruitment of a personal media adviser, the former senior journalist Michael Spreng, who was to centralize and control his media appearance and performance. Throughout the campaign, it became obvious that he had substantial influence over decisions on policy positions and personnel which were clearly driven by the considerations of 'image engineering' for the chancellor candidate.

Mainly due to lack of financial resources, both Greens and Liberals ran their campaign from their regular headquarters without much additional staff. The pronounced personalization of their campaign strategy nonetheless had important repercussions on the way the campaign was organized. In both parties, the leading candidate exercised substantial control over campaign planning and conduct. While this was not particularly remarkable in the case of the FDP, which had previously lived through periods of substantial domination by one leader, this certainly represented a departure from previous practices for the Greens.[2]

In many ways, the 2002 campaign represents the culmination of a wider trend among German parties which is typical of developments in modern democracies where parties increasingly turn themselves into campaign organizations in response to the changed structure of mass communication and growing voter flexibility (Farrell and Webb 2000). The modernization of political campaigning implies centralized campaign planning and management. In conjunction with the increased use of external professionals and polling organizations, this centralization removes campaign planning and management from the regular process of intra-party debate and accountability. In a nutshell (although this is obviously an idealization), while election campaigns used to represent a party's political aspirations (however distorted, of course) they are now primarily driven by the professional norms of campaign managers and their counterparts in the media system (Farrell and Webb 2000: 105–6). In addition, the personalization of campaigning means that a party's front runner assumes a central role in the design of campaign strategy and contents which can hardly be subjected to internal debate. Inevitably, if the party leader is to be the central object of campaigning he or she will also want to be in control of campaign planning and management. No doubt, the modernization of campaigning leads to a marginalization of the party organization and the reduction of internal democratic accountability. Given that election campaigns represent crucial junctures at which parties (re)position themselves within the party system, this clearly strengthens leaders at the expense of intra-party democracy.

While it makes leaders more autonomous of their party, it also makes them more vulnerable. If they win, they win quite independently of their party, but if they lose, they will have few allies in defeat. The example of SPD chairman Scharping and his sudden removal by the 1995 Mannheim party congress is an obvious case in point (von Alemann 1999: 39). Similarly, Gerhard Schröder's difficulties to get his own party's approval for his neo-liberal reform programme in 2003 exemplifies the ambivalence of presidentialized party leadership. In a way, his decision to resign from party leadership in early 2004 took presidentialization to its logical conclusion. Faced with increasing resistance from his party's rank-and-file, he decided to abandon party leadership altogether and concentrate on his power resources as executive leader of a coalition government in which the SPD was the larger coalition partner. While this move made him somewhat more autonomous in his role as chief executive, his essential power resources vis-à-vis the Social Democratic party remained feeble: the Chancellor who had based his claim to leadership on his electoral appeal presided over the lowest opinion polls ratings and worst Land and Euro-election defeats for the SPD since 1949.

Bypassing the middle-level elites

The growing dominance of continuous campaigning over old-fashioned programmatic debate has been accompanied by a tendency of most German parties to resort to plebiscitary measures in order to bypass their own middle-level elites. While the Greens were the first to provide for membership referenda in their statute, it was again the Social Democrats who set the agenda when they were the first party to use a membership ballot to decide a leadership contest in 1993 (Poguntke 2002: 271). Since then, postal ballots have also been used by Christian Democratic Land parties to select their front runners, Social Democratic Land parties to select leaders and to decide on policy emphasis, and by the Liberals to settle policy disputes (Reichart-Dreyer 2002: 575; Scarrow 1999). So far, experiences have been mixed and the new statutory opportunities have not been used fully. At first, it seemed that membership ballots would have invigorating effects on rank-and-file involvement by giving ordinary party members a voice in important decisions, as the example of the successful SPD leadership contest seemed to indicate. Likewise, the Greens successfully resolved a stalemate that had plagued the party for more than a decade. After repeated attempts to relax the strict separation of office and mandate for the national executive, this issue was referred to a membership ballot held in spring 2003. The membership approved of a more flexible rule which now permits one-third of the members of the national executive to also sit as MPs. The Liberals, on the other hand, paid a substantial price for externalizing elite disputes when a government minister resigned in reaction to the outcome of the membership ballot over a civil rights issue in 1995 (Schieren 1996). Similarly, the ill-fated performance of directly elected SPD leader Rudolf Scharping cautioned the Social Democrats against further experiments with direct intra-party democracy. Ironically, Gerhard Schröder unilaterally took the experiment one step further and effectively turned the Lower Saxony Land election into a referendum over his selection as chancellor-candidate (Niedermayer 2000: 203). By appealing directly to voters, he avoided one possible pitfall of membership ballots, that is, that those who are popular with the party rank-and-file may not necessarily be the most attractive candidates for the population at large. It may be indicative from this perspective that Green Foreign Minister Joschka Fischer, who has consistently led public sympathy ratings, has never held a senior party office.

All these examples point to a growing tendency to base leadership (or claims to leadership) on a direct popular mandate (be it by voters or the party grass roots) rather than on the control of the party organization. The last telling example from this perspective was the successful leadership campaign of CDU chairperson Angela Merkel in 2000, which followed the party's leadership crisis in the wake of a massive party finance scandal. After the sudden resignation of Helmut Kohl's successor Wolfgang Schäuble, she mobilized support for her leadership challenge in so-called regional conferences open to the party's rank-and-file. This non-formalized, yet highly visible (and televised!) support allowed her to overcome reservations of the party establishment and be elected as the first female, east German and Protestant party leader of the traditionally predominantly Catholic CDU (Schmid and Steffen 2003: 82–7).

While these changes have a structural component in that they are either related to persistent changes in mass communication or rules, the full realization of their potential is highly dependent on the qualities and talents of individual leaders. In contrast, structural changes with immediate consequences on the power resources of party leaders have not played a comparable role. None of the old parties has significantly revised formal rights and powers of their leaders, nor have we seen fundamental shifts in terms of intra-party resource allocation (Poguntke 2002: 267–8) even though there has been a reduction in the CDU central office staff as a result of losses in public funding in the wake of the party finance scandal of the late 1990s (Schmid and Steffen 2003: 74). As is often the case, the Greens are the exception—this time, however, because they chose to become 'normal'. A series of organizational reforms has turned the formerly participatory party into an almost conventional party with a leadership structure that is very similar to that of all other German parties (Poguntke 2001*a*). Ironically, this may have reduced the party's potential for presidentializing tendencies. After all, creating leadership structures with real power may limit the scope for 'virtual' party leaders to appeal to the wider public in order to lead the party.

While there are unambiguous indications of structurally sustained trends towards more personalized party leadership in Germany, it is worth emphasizing that party ideology has represented an important countervailing force within the Greens and the PDS where shifting coalitions of party activists have frequently reasserted their influence using party ideology as a resource in internal power struggles. In a similar vein, federalism has represented a significant constraint against thoroughgoing presidentialization of both the CDU and the SPD. Land party chairmen and Land prime ministers remain powerful actors who cannot be easily bypassed by even the most successful national party leader. In fact, Helmut Kohl's impressive reign over the CDU was as much based on his ability to forge coalitions within his party as it was based on his appeal to ordinary party members and the electorate at large (Schmid 1999).

THE ELECTORAL FACE

Like in all other modern democracies, the German structure of mass communication has undergone substantial transformations that have thoroughly changed the environmental conditions for political action in general and campaigning in particular. Shortly after television was launched in the 1950s it assumed a leading role as a source of political information (Niedermayer 2001: 135–47). Unsurprisingly, the controlling bodies of public TV stations were frequently turned into party political battlegrounds. Nevertheless, party political leanings in some of the regional TV stations that make up the first channel tended to cancel each other out, and the nation-wide second programme (launched in 1961) was controlled by a board that was broadly representative of relevant political and social interests thereby ensuring fairly neutral political coverage (Humphreys 1990: 165–7). Naturally, TV quickly assumed central importance in political communication strategies (Hetterich 2000: 203–13), although it offered only limited opportunities during election campaigns: free air time for political party broadcasts is strictly limited and available to all parties on a broadly proportional basis while additional air time cannot be bought. This did not change fundamentally with the advent of private TV stations in the late 1980s, which follow the same logic when allocating (limited) paid air time for political party broadcasts (Hetterich 2000: 85–7; Holtz-Bacha 2000*b*: 63–76). While private TV did not substantially widen the scope for direct political advertising, it profoundly transformed the overall structure of mass communication by changing the nature of competition between TV stations. Competition has become fierce since then and, as a result, a certain degree of trivialization of political coverage has crept in. 'Infotainment' and 'talk show politics' seem to have taken over while more analytical political programmes are increasingly marginalized, even in the programmes of the public stations (Hetterich 2000: 374; Holtz-Bacha 2000*a*, 2002: 49). Arguably, the concomitant increase of personalization of political and quasi-political coverage should have worked in favour of trends towards a presidentialization of the electoral process.

Electoral presidentialization is essentially Janus-faced. On the one hand, we need to look at media coverage, that is, we need to establish whether or not the media concentrate more on leaders than in the past. Naturally, the prime focus will be on election campaigns as they epitomize more general changes in the structure of public communication. On the other hand, parties may succumb more or less enthusiastically to the pressures of their communicative environment when devising their campaigns. In other words, party strategists may chose to ride the tiger of personalization or they may continue to strive for more substantive, programmatic debates. In addition to their own ideological convictions, their decision is clearly influenced by their perception of the true effects of such changes. Increasingly leadership-centred campaign strategies are often regarded as evidence of a growing *leadership effect* when it comes to opinion formation in general and voting behaviour in particular. Clearly, this assumption is essentially flawed as it may simply be the perception of party strategists—and not real electoral gains—which may induce parties to change their campaign strategies. Nevertheless, the political effects are real in that the decision to embark on a leadership-centred campaign inevitably shifts the balance of power inside political parties in favour of the party leader and his team of campaign specialists while the party's rank-and-file is increasingly sidelined.

Media coverage

The preceding brief discussion has indicated that the changing nature of media coverage represents an environmental change for political parties which offers them opportunities to respond without determining a particular path of action (Harmel and Janda 1992; Panebianco 1988). How exactly has media coverage changed in the Federal Republic?

Personalization is as old as politics, of course, and it would be misleading to claim that the mass media of the 1950s and 1960s did not devote a great deal of attention to the most senior politicians in party and government. On the contrary, we have already mentioned that the paramount stature of Konrad Adenauer gave rise to debates about chancellor democracy. Consequently, a longitudinal analysis of newspaper campaign coverage shows only a modest increase in the attention given to the chancellor candidates of the two main contenders CDU/CSU and SPD since 1980. In addition, the greatest newspaper focus on the leading candidates was in 1961 (Wilke and Reinemann 2001: 301–2). However, while the emphasis of the media on leaders may not have changed that much, the quality of the coverage has. First and foremost, it is the visualization of mass communication through the victory of television that has fundamentally transformed the nature of the message that reaches the public. The image has become an important part of the message; some even say it is the message. Inevitably, this induces the personalization of political controversies or debates. The very format of TV (in contrast to much of the print media) puts a premium on reducing complex problems to a confrontation between the main protagonists. Consequently, there is a widespread consensus among analysts that German politics has seen a growth in the personalization of media coverage (Holtz-Bacha 2002: 48–9; Keil 2003: 23).

A conspicuous example of the reduction of the political to its 'show element' has been the media hype about who was to reap a longer applause for his speech to the CDU party congress in late 2001, CDU chairperson Angela Merkel or her contender for chancellor candidature, CSU chairman Edmund Stoiber (Brettschneider 2001: 359–60). If anything, the trend towards personalization of media campaign coverage has continued in the 2002 Bundestag elections. When the CDU and the CSU agreed on Edmund Stoiber as chancellor candidate, it was Chancellor Schröder who aptly defined the mode of the impending campaign by stating it would amount to choice between 'him or me'—and the media coverage followed suit.

Changing campaign strategies

There can be little doubt that all relevant German parties have increasingly modernized their campaign techniques. This means that media communication has become more important at the expense of more traditional campaign techniques like mass rallies or working through the membership organization (Oellerking 1988; Wortmann 1989). And, as a probably inevitable corollary of the 'mediatization of campaigning', they have also become more personalized (Niedermayer 2000: 195; Schoenbach 1996; Semetko and Schönbach 1999; Swanson and Mancini 1996). Again, one objection would be that there are early examples of highly personalized campaigns in German electoral history. In the 1950s, the CDU relied heavily on the appeal of Konrad Adenauer and the legendary 'Willy wählen' campaign of 1972 was certainly a conspicuous case of a highly personalized campaign. However, while those campaigns were contingent upon the availability of a particularly suitable candidate, personalization has now become an integral part of a highly professionalized campaign strategy which increasingly relegates substantive messages to a secondary place (Niedermayer 2000: 195). Clearly, the changing structure of mass communication has made it more imperative to attempt to find media savvy candidates (Schoenbach 1996: 95). Longitudinal analyses of party campaign advertisements in leading German newspapers show that both large parties have increasingly emphasized their leading candidates or party leaders since the 1980s (Keil 2003: 342–3). Analyses of TV spots show a comparatively high level of emphasis on leading candidates without a change over time, which confirms the point made earlier about the inherent personalizing nature of TV. Fluctuations over time also reflect the quality of chancellor candidates and the political contexts (Holtz-Bacha 2000*b*: 183–93, 233–5). Given the format of German party competition, it is unsurprising that the main contenders for power have adapted faster to the logic of personalization than the smaller German parties. The extent to which election communication has come to resemble commercial advertising was epitomized by the 1994 Christian Democratic campaign which featured a massive poster of Chancellor Helmut Kohl without a party label or any other message. Clearly, the image was the message in the 1994 campaign when personalization reached unprecedented levels (Hetterich 2000: 373–4; Niedermayer 2000: 198), a trend that continued four years later (Hetterich 2000: 404–7). The 1994 campaign is, however, also a cogent example of the inherent dangers and limitations of a highly personalized campaign strategy in that the party becomes hostage to its front runner's talents as a media performer. When it became apparent that the 1994 SPD chancellor-candidate Rudolf Scharping did not live up to the challenge, there was relatively little the party could do to limit the damage.

To be sure, it is important to guard against the dangers of making hasty generalizations on the basis of one or two possibly exceptional election campaigns. After all, the Christian and the Social Democrats have always been prone to personalization, not least because they are competing for the chancellorship and the institution of nominating a chancellor candidate before the election has become a regular feature of German electoral politics. Furthermore, this is not likely to be an uninterrupted development as a highly personalized campaign depends on the availability of a suitable candidate. Parties may not always find a gifted media performer and may therefore attempt to 'hide' him or her in a larger leadership team, thereby de-emphasizing the presidentialized nature of their campaign. However, the fact that a party like the Greens took a conscious decision to focus its campaign strategy on its leading personnel certainly testifies to the strength of the perceived or real adaptive pressures towards personalization. After all, the party has rejected both professionalized and personalized politics from the outset, and its original organizational concept of grass-root democracy was the very antithesis of leadership-centredness (Kitschelt 1988; Poguntke

1987; Raschke 1993). While the party's 'unofficial party leader' Joschka Fischer had already played a very prominent role in previous election campaigns (particularly in 1998), the decision to officially nominate Fischer as a front runner (*Spitzenkandidat*) for the 2002 campaign was a significant departure from the founding myths of the party. Given that the Greens obviously need no chancellor-candidate, the option to select a team of leaders instead of concentrating on an individual was clearly on the cards. The fact that the party decided to go all the way towards personalization for the first time in its history clearly indicates how strong the perceived competitive pressures were—indirect yet unambiguous evidence of how much German election campaigns have become personalized.

In the event, the Greens stuck unashamedly to their departure from formerly sacred principles and ran a TV campaign which focused almost exclusively on Joschka Fischer. One of the party's central campaign slogans read: 'Second vote is Joschka vote', thereby targeting SPD voters who might be prepared to split their ticket in order to guarantee the survival of the red–green coalition. The Liberals provided an even stronger (and somewhat bizarre) indication of the perceived pressures to adapt to the format of increasingly personalized campaigning in 2002. For the first time in their history, and obviously without the slightest prospect of success, they nominated their party leader Guido Westerwelle as chancellor-candidate. The intention was obvious: the existence of an official chancellor-candidate would force the media to include the FDP (and its leader) in their campaign coverage on an equal footing. The effort was in vain: Guido Westerwelle was excluded from both televised debates between Schröder and Stoiber and the Liberals scored a dismal result. It goes almost without saying that both large parties focused their 2002 campaign almost exclusively on their chancellor-candidates. As mentioned above, Chancellor Schröder had set the stage by announcing that this was to be a personal contest, and Edmund Stoiber followed suit by trying hard to steer clear of substantive policy positions. Except for the PDS, who lost their media star Gregor Gysi over the air miles affair, German parties took campaign personalization to new heights in the 2002 campaign. Whether this paid electorally is, of course, another matter to which we will now turn.

Leadership effects

In conjunction with the inescapable visualization of public communication, the assumption that the qualities of leaders play an increasing role in individual voting decisions has led to a growing personalization of election campaigns. Yet, this may be a good example of perceptions rather than facts having real political consequences. There is little controversy in the literature that processes of social pluralization, even individualization (Beck 1986) have resulted in declining cleavage voting. In other words, more voters have become 'available' as their voting decision is no longer predetermined by integration into a social milieu and/or by party identification (Falter and Schoen 1999: 466; Feist and Hoffmann 1999; Forschungsgruppe Wahlen 1998; Jung and Roth 1998). It seems therefore likely that the influence of candidate and/or issue effects on voting behaviour have grown (Falter and Schoen 1999: 468; Klein and Ohr 2001: 126). Yet, longitudinal analyses are inconclusive. There is no unambiguous evidence that leadership effects have significantly increased over time. Rather, the impact of candidates on voting decisions seems to vary with the political issues at stake and, not surprisingly, with the quality of the candidates (Brettschneider 2001: 387–8, 2002). While these findings seem to refute the thesis of an inevitable trend towards stronger leadership effects, they can be read another way. After all, if much depends on the issues and the candidates of the day, parties may choose to de-emphasize issues and focus on their candidates in order to maximize leadership effects in an increasingly complex and contradictory political world. In other words: to the extent that campaign strategies based on coherent programmes appear to be less promising, party strategists may choose to embark on a strategy of personalization. The fact that candidate effects have conspicuously risen in 1998 may be an indication of change and a longitudinal perspective may disguise more than it reveals (Brettschneider 2001: 373; Brettschneider and Gabriel 2002: 152).

CONCLUSION

The nature of the chancellorship is at the centre of the concept of presidentialization. It is therefore consistent to start the conclusion by summarizing those changes and changed opportunities that have directly affected the chancellorship. Constitutional rights and powers represent a suitable point of departure, and it has been mentioned already that the Basic Law provides the German chancellor with a range of powers that situate the German political system somewhat closer towards the 'presidentialized pole' of the continuum (see Fig. 1.1). On the other hand, German chancellors have always been constrained by the need to maintain a coalition (save for brief exceptional spells). In fact, even in the only case of an overall majority, CDU/CSU Chancellor Konrad Adenauer chose to invite the FDP into an oversized coalition. In addition, German chancellors have become increasingly constrained by the growing role of the Bundesrat under the conditions of the specifically German variant of cooperative federalism. However, what seems to be a cause of weakness has increasingly come to represent an important power resource of German chancellors: the need to build consensus among diverse veto players has provided German chancellors with an increasingly prominent role as chief negotiators, allowing them to govern increasingly past their parties.

There is strong evidence that many of the other structural factors favouring this drift towards a more presidentialized mode of governance have also become stronger over the history of the Federal Republic: the mediatization of politics has given chancellors a more elevated role in the political process; not only will they find it easier to claim a personal mandate (rather than one that is derived from their party), but they can now make use of the powerful machinery of the chancellor's office in order to screen individual ministries and coordinate government policies. Above all, European integration in conjunction with a general internationalization of politics have made them more autonomous of party political control although, at the same time, they have lost real power as a result of a substantial transfer of sovereignty.

Similarly, there is a growing gap between the image of an ever more powerful chancellor and the fact that his increasingly elevated role is not necessarily substantiated by an enhanced steering capacity. In fact, and ironically, much of his visibility flows from the peculiarity of German cooperative federalism which gives the chancellor high visibility as chief negotiator between the federal and Land governments. However, this comes at a price: veto players in the Bundesrat are harder to overcome than veto positions within a coalition government where all players tend to share a common interest in the survival of the government. In other words, compared to some colleagues in consensual systems of a more conventional variant, the German chancellor may find it harder to substantially expand his zones of autonomy. Clearly, his actions have become more autonomous from his own party (and his coalition) but if power is the ability to achieve desired outcomes, then the increased power of the German chancellor is relative in that the desired outcomes shift as a result of negotiations with Land governments. In fact, the growing structural opportunities for presidentialized governance in combination with the specific constraints of German cooperative federalism makes German chancellors resemble chief executives in truly presidential systems: they, too, combine high visibility and strong leadership in international affairs with a sometimes very constrained yet autonomous role in domestic politics.

The consistent growth of structural opportunities for presidentialization over the past decades does not necessarily mean that there will be a linear trend towards a growing presidentialization of German governance. While there can be little doubt that these features have become much more visible since the early 1990s, the importance of political contingencies and, above all, of the skill of political leaders in exploiting these opportunities must not be forgotten. First, we need to remember that German politics in the 1990s was dominated by the imposing stature of Helmut Kohl whose success over unifying Germany had elevated him to monumental heights. Second, his successor Gerhard Schröder could take advantage of an unprecedented range of coalition options which allowed him to reach out to the opposition parties and include all but the PDS in his variant of 'negotiation democracy'. The future may hold less dominant leaders, and while Rudolf Scharping's failure may have been inevitable given the requirements of modern presidentialized politics, his ill-fated 1994 campaign and his subsequent ousting by the SPD party congress reminds us of the persistent underlying logic of German parliamentarism. German leaders rise from their parties, even if they enjoy a quasi-plebiscitarian legitimation. Party members may not always choose the candidate who is most suited for a presidentialized campaign or style of government. More crucially, however, parties and their parliamentary groups still have the power to remove their leaders, and sometimes they do.

NOTE

1. This may change if the merger between the PDS (which changed its name into Left Party before the 2005 Bundesbeg elections) and the pro-welfare state protest party WASG turns out to be successful.
2. The previous account and the section on campaign strategy below have benefited from a series of interviews in July and September 2002 that were supported by a British Academy grant (No. SG 32843). The author is indebted to the following interviewees: Ms Wawzyniak, PDS election manager (Leiterin Wahlquartier PDS); Matthias Machnig, SPD campaign manager (Bundesgeschäftsführer SPD, Leiter der, Kampa'); Reinhard Bütikofer, general secretary Bündnis 90/Grüne (politischer Geschäftsführer); Dr. Willi Hausmann, CDU party manager; Hans-Jürgen Beerfeltz, FDP party manager (Bundesgeschäftsführer); Franziska Pagel (personal assistant to Beerfeltz); Oliver Röseler, Stoiber-Team, CSU; Peter Radunski, former CDU campaign manager.

REFERENCES

Alemann, U. von (1992). 'Parteien und Gesellschaft in der Bundesrepublik', in A. Mintzel and H. Oberreuter (eds.), *Parteien in der Bundesrepublik Deutschland.* Opladen: Leske + Budrich, 89–130.
—— (1999). 'Der Wahlsieg der SPD von 1998: Politische Achsenverschiebung oder glücklicher Ausreißer?', in O. Niedermayer (ed.), *Die Parteien nach der Bundestagswahl 1998.* Opladen: Leske + Budrich, 37–62.
—— (2000). *Das Parteiensystem der Bundesrepublik Deutschland.* Opladen: Leske + Budrich.
—— (2003). 'Der Zittersieg der SPD: Mit einem blauen Auge davon gekommen', in O. Niedermayer (ed.), *Die Parteien nach der Bundestagswahl 2002.* Opladen: Leske + Budrich, 43–69.

Beck, U. (1986). *Risikogesellschaft. Auf dem Weg in eine andere Moderne.* Frankfurt/ Main: Suhrkamp.

Benz, A. (1999). 'Der deutsche Föderalismus', in T. Ellwein and E. Holtmann (eds.), *50 Jahre Bundesrepublik Deutschland. Rahmenbedingungen, Entwicklungen, Perspektiven (PVS Sonderheft 30)*. Opladen/Wiesbaden: Westdeutscher Verlag, 135–53.

Beyme, K. von (1979). *Das politische System der Bundesrepublik Deutschland. Eine Einführung.* München: Piper.

Brettschneider, F. (2001). 'Candidate-Voting. Die Bedeutung von Spitzenkandidaten für das Wählerverhalten in Deutschland, Groabritannien und den USA von 1960 bis 1998', in H.-D. Klingemann and M. Kaase (eds.), *Wahlen und Wähler. Analysen aus Anlass der Bundestagwahl 1998*. Wiesbaden: Westdeutscher Verlag, 351–400.

—— (2002). *Spitzenkandidaten und Wahlerfolg.* Wiesbaden: Westdeutscher Verlag.

—— and O. W. Gabriel (2002). 'The Nonpersonalization of Voting Behaviour in Germany', in A. King (ed.), *Leaders' Personalities and the Outcome of Democratic Elections*. Oxford: Oxford University Press, 127–57.

Czada, R. (2000). 'Konkordanz, Korporatismus und Politikverflechtung: Dimensionen der Verhandlungsdemokratie', in E. Holtmann and H. Voelzkow (eds.), *Zwischen Wettbewerbs- und Verhandlungsdemokratie*. Wiesbaden: Westdeutscher Verlag, 23–49.

Dalton, R. J. and W. Bürklin (1995). 'The Two German Electorates: The Social Bases of the Vote in 1990 and 1994', *German Politics and Society, 13*.

Falter, J. and H. Schoen (1999). 'Wahlen und Wählerverhalten', in T. Ellwein and E. Holtmann (eds.), *50 Jahre Bundesrepublik Deutschland. Rahmenbedingungen, Entwicklungen, Perspektiven (PVS Sonderheft 30)*. Opladen/Wiesbaden: Westdeutscher Verlag, 454–70.

Farrell, D. M. and P. Webb (2000). 'Political Parties as Campaign Organizations', in R. J. Dalton and M. P. Wattenberg (eds.), *Parties without Partisans. Political Change in Advanced Industrial Democracies*. Oxford: Oxford University Press, 102–28.

Feist, U. and H.-J. Hoffmann (1999). 'Die Bundestagswahlanalyse 1998: Wahl des Wechsels', *Zeitschrift für Parlamentsfragen, 30*, 215–51.

Forschungsgruppe Wahlen (1998). *Bundestagswahl 1998. Eine Analyse der Wahl vom 27. September 1998.* Mannheim: mimeo.

Haftendorn, H. (1999). 'Kontinuität und Wandel des außenpolitischen Entscheidungsprozesses in der Bundesrepublik Deutschland', in T. Ellwein and E. Holtmann (eds.), *50 Jahre Bundesrepublik Deutschland. Rahmenbedingungen, Entwicklungen, Perspektiven (PVS Sonderheft 30)*. Opladen/Wiesbaden: Westdeutscher Verlag, 247–57.

Harmel, R. and K. Janda (1992). *An Integrated Theory of Party Goals and Party Change*, Paper prepared for delivery at the 1992 Annual Meeting of the American Political Science Association, 3–6 September.

Heinze, R. G. (2000). *Die Berliner Räterepublik.* Wiesbaden: Westdeutscher Verlag.

Helms, L. (2001). 'Gerhard Schröder und die Entwicklung der deutschen Kanzlerschaft', *Zeitschrift für Politikwissenschaft, 4*, 1497–517.

—— (2002). '"Chief Executives" and their Parties: The Case of Germany', *German Politics, 11*, 146–64.

Hesse, J. and T. Ellwein (1992). *Das Regierungssystem der Bundesrepublik Deutschland*. Opladen: Westdeutscher Verlag.

Hetterich, V. (2000). *Von Adenauer zu Schröder – Der Kampf um Stimmen. Eine Längsschnittanalyse der Wahlkampagnen von CDU und SPD bei den Bundestagswahlen 1949 bis 1998*. Opladen: Leske + Budrich.

Holtmann, E. and H. Voelzkow (2000*a*). 'Das Regierungssystem der Bundesrepublik zwischen Wettbewerbs- und Verhandlungsdemokratie', in E. Holtmann and H. Voelzkow (eds.), *Zwischen Wettbewerbs- und Verhandlungsdemokratie*. Wiesbaden: Westdeutscher Verlag, 9–21.

—— —— (ed.) (2000*b*). *Zwischen Wettbewerbs- und Verhandlungsdemokratie*. Wiesbaden: Westdeutscher Verlag.

Holtz-Bacha, C. (2000*a*). 'Entertainisierung der Politik', *Zeitschrift für Parlamentsfragen*, 31, 156–66.

—— (2000*b*). *Wahlwerbung als politische Kultur*. Wiesbaden: Westdeutscher Verlag.

—— (2002). 'Parteien und Massenmedien im Wahlkampf', in U. v. Alemann and S. Marschall (eds.), *Parteien in der Mediendemokratie*. Wiesbaden: Westdeutscher Verlag, 42–56.

Humphreys, P. J. (1990). *Media and Media Policy in West Germany*. New York/Oxford/Munich: Berg.

Jäger, W. (1988). 'Von der Kanzlerdemokratie zur Koordinationsdemokratie', *Zeitschrift für Parlamentsfragen*, 35, 15–32.

Jung, M. and D. Roth (1998). 'Wer zu spät geht, den bestraft das Leben', *Aus Politik und Zeitgeschichte*, 3–18.

Katzenstein, P. (1987). *Policy and Politics in West Germany. The Growth of a Semisovereign State*. Philadelphia: Temple University Press.

Keil, S. I. (2003). *Wahlkampfkommunikation in Wahlanzeigen und Wahlprogrammen*. Frankfurt u.a.: Peter Lang.

Kitschelt, H. (1988). 'Organization and Strategy of Belgian and West German Ecology Parties. A New Dynamic of Party Politics in Western Parties', *Comparative Politics*, 20, 127–54.

Klein, M. and D. Ohr (2001). 'Die Wahrnehmung der politischen und persönlichen Eigenschaften von Helmut Kohl und Gerhard Schröder und ihr Einfluß auf die Wahlentscheidung bei der Bundestagswahl 1998', in H.-D. Klingemann, and M. Kaase (eds.), *Wahlen und Wähler. Analysen aus Anlaß der Bundestagwahl 1998*. Wiesbaden: Westdeutscher Verlag, 91–132.

Knoll, T. (2004). *Das Bonner Bundeskanzleramt von 1949–1999*. Wiesbaden: VS Verlag für Sozialwissenschaften.

Lehmbruch, G. (2000). *Parteienwettbewerb im Bundesstaat*, 3rd edn. Wiesbaden: Westdeutscher Verlag.

Lijphart, A. (1999). *Patterns of Democracy. Government Forms and Performance in Thirty-Six Countries*. New Haven/London: Yale University Press.

Lütjen, T. and F. Walter (2000). 'Die präsidiale Kanzlerschaft', *Blätter für deutsche und internationale Politik*, 1309–13.

Mayntz, R. (1980). 'Executive Leadership in Germany: Dispersion of Power or "Kanzlerdemokratie"?', in R. Rose and E. N. Suleiman (eds.), *Presidents and*

Prime Ministers. Washington, D.C.: American Enterprise Institute for Public Policy Research, 139–70.

Müller-Rommel, F. (1994). 'The Chancellor and his Staff', in S. Padgett (ed.), *Adenauer to Kohl. The Development of the German Chancellorship.* London: Hurst & Co, 106–26.

—— (1997). 'Federal Republic of Germany: A System of Chancellor Government', in J. Blondel and F. Müller-Rommel (eds.), *Cabinets in Western Europe.* London: Macmillan, 171–91.

—— (2000). 'Management of Politics in the German Chancellor's Office', in B. G. Peters, R. A. W. Rhodes, and V. Wright (eds.), *Administering the Summit. Administration of the Core Executive in Developed Countries.* Basingstoke: Macmillan.

Neugebauer, G. and R. Stöss (2003). 'Die PDS in Not', in O. Niedermayer (ed.), *Die Parteien nach der Bundestagswahl 2002.* Opladen: Leske + Budrich, 125–58.

Niclauß, K. (1988). *Kanzlerdemokratie. Bonner Regierungspraxis von Konrad Adenauer bis Helmut Kohl.* Stuttgart: Kohlhammer.

Niedermayer, O. (1996). *Intermediäre Strukturen in Ostdeutschland.* Opladen: Leske + Budrich.

—— (2000). 'Modernisierung von Wahlkämpfen als Funktionsentleerung der Parteibasis', in O. Niedermayer and B. Westle (eds.), *Partizipation und Demokratie. Festschrift für Max Kaase.* Wiesbaden: Westdeutscher Verlag, 192–210.

—— (2001). *Bürger und Politik. Politische Orientierungen und Verhaltensweisen der Deutschen. Eine Einführung.* Wiesbaden: Westdeutscher Verlag.

—— (2003). 'Die Entwicklung des deutschen Parteiensystems bis nach der Bundestagswahl 2002', in O. Niedermayer (ed.), *Die Parteien nach der Bundestagswahl 2002.* Opladen: Leske + Budrich, 9–41.

Niedermayer, O. and R. Stöss (1994). *Parteien und Wähler im Umbruch. Parteiensystem und Wählerverhalten in der ehemaligen DDR und den neuen Bundesländern.* Opladen: Westdeutscher Verlag.

Oellerking, C. (1988). *Marketingstrategien für Parteien.* Frankfurt am Main: Peter Lang.

Padgett, S. (ed.) (1994a). *Adenauer to Kohl. The Development of the German Chancellorship.* London: Hurst and Co.

—— (1994b). 'Introduction: Chancellors and the Chancellorship', in S. Padgett (ed.), *Adenauer to Kohl. The Development of the German Chancellorship.* London: Hurst & Co, 1–18.

Panebianco, A. (1988). *Political Parties: Organization and Power.* Cambridge u.a.: Cambridge University Press.

Pappi, F. U. (2000). 'Wahlen und öffentliche Meinung im deutschen Parteienstaat', in O. Niedermayer and B. Westle (eds.), *Demokratie und Partizipation. Festschrift für Max Kaase.* Wiesbaden: Westdeutscher Verlag, 341–55.

Poguntke, T. (1987). 'The Organization of a Participatory Party—The German Greens', *European Journal of Political Research,* 15, 609–33.

—— (1994). 'Parties in a Legalistic Culture: The Case of Germany', in R. S. Katz and P. Mair (eds.), *How Parties Organize. Change and Adaptation in Party Organizations in Western Democracies.* London: Sage, 185–215.

—— (2000). 'Präsidiale Regierungschefs: Verändern sich die parlamentarischen Demokratien?', in O. Niedermayer and B. Westle (eds.), *Demokratie und Partizipation. Festschrift für Max Kaase.* Wiesbaden: Westdeutscher Verlag, 356–71.

—— (2001*a*). *From Nuclear Building Sites to Cabinet: The Career of the German Green Party.* Keele: Keele European Parties Research Unit (KEPRU), Working Paper No. 6.

—— (2001*b*). 'The German Party System: Eternal Crisis?', in S. Padgett and T. Poguntke (eds.), *Continuity and Change in German Politics. Festschrift for Gordon Smith (first published as special issue of German Politics, Vol. 10, No. 2).* London: Frank Cass, 37–50.

—— (2002). 'Parteiorganisationen in der Bundesrepublik Deutschland: Einheit in der Vielfalt?', in O. W. Gabriel, O. Niedermayer, and R. Stöss (eds.), *Parteiendemokratie in der Bundesrepublik Deutschland,* Wiesbaden: Westdeutscher Verlag, 253–763.

Raschke, J. (1993). *Die Grünen. Wie sie wurden, was sie sind,* Köln: Bund Verlag.

Reichart-Dreyer, I. (2002). 'Parteireform', in O. W. Gabriel, O. Niedermayer, and R. Stöss (eds.), *Parteiendemokratie,* Wiesbaden: Westdeutscher Verlag, 570–91.

Rudzio, W. (1991). *Das politische System der Bundesrepublik Deutschland,* 3rd edn. Opladen: Leske + Budrich.

Saalfeld, T. (2003). 'Germany: Multiple Veto Points, Informal Coordination, and Problems of Hidden Action', in K. Strom, W. C. Müller, and T. Bergmann (eds.), *Delegation and Accountability in Parliamentary Democrcacies.* Oxford: Oxford University Press, 347–75.

Scarrow, S. (1999). 'Parties and the Expansion of Direct Democracy: Who Benefits?', *Party Politics,* 5, 343–67.

Scarrow, S. E. (2002). 'Party Decline in the Parties State? The Changing Environment of German Politics', in P. D. Webb, D. M. Farrell, and I. Holliday (eds.), *Political Parties in Advanced Industrial Democracies,* Oxford: Oxford University Press, 77–106.

Scharpf, F. W. (1985). 'Die Politikverflechtungsfalle. Europäische Integration und deutscher Föderalismus in Vergleich', *Politische Vierteljahresschrift,* 26, 323–56.

Schieren, S. (1996). 'Parteiinterne Mitgliederbefragungen: Ausstieg aus der Professionalität ? Die Beispiele der SPD auf Bundesebene und in Bremen sowie der Bundes-F.D.P.', *Zeitschrift für Parlamentsfragen,* 27, 214–29.

Schmid, J. (1999). 'Die CDU/CSU nach dem September 1998: Von der Wende zum Ende?', in O. Niedermayer (ed.), *Die Parteien nach der Bundestagswahl 1998.* Opladen: Leske + Budrich, 63–81.

—— and C. Steffen (2003). 'Stark aufgeholt und doch nicht gewonnen: CDU/CSU nach der Wahl', in O. Niedermayer (ed.), *Die Parteien nach der Bundestagswahl 2002,* Opladen: Leske + Budrich, 71–87.

Schmidt, M. G. (2003). *Political Institutions in the Federal Republic of Germany,* Oxford: Oxford University Press.

Schmitt-Beck, R. (2001). 'Ein Sieg der "Kampa"? Politische Symbolik in der Wahlkampagne der SPD und ihre Resonanz in der Wählerschaft', in H.-D. Klingemann and M. Kaase (eds.), *Wahlen und Wähler. Analysen aus Anlaß der Bundestagwahl 1998.* Wiesbaden: Westdeutscher Verlag, 133–62.

Schoenbach, K. (1996). 'The "Americanization" of German Election Campaigns: Any Impact on the Voters?', in D. L. Swanson and P. Mancini (eds.), *Politics, Media, and Modern Democracy*. Westport/London: Praeger, 91–104.

Schreckenberger, W. (1994). 'Informelle Verfahren der Entscheidungsvorbereitung zwischen der Bundesregierung und den Mehrheitsfraktionen: Koalitionsgespräche und Koalitionsrunden', *Zeitschrift für Parlamentsfragen*, 25, 329–46.

Semetko, H. A. and K. Schönbach (1999). 'Parties, Leaders and Issues in the News', *German Politics*, 8, 72–87.

Smith, G. (1982). *Democracy in Western Germany: Parties and Politics in the Federal Republic*. London: Heinemann.

—— (1991). 'The Resources of a German Chancellor', *West European Politics*, 14, 48–61.

Stöss, R. (1990). 'Parteikritik und Parteiverdrossenheit', *Aus Politik und Zeitgeschichte*, 15–24.

—— (1997). 'Parteienstaat oder Parteiendemokratie?', in O. W. Gabriel, O. Niedermayer, and R. Stöss (eds.), *Parteiendemokratie in Deutschland*. Bonn: Bundeszentrale für politische Bildung, 11–39.

Swanson, D. and P. Mancini (1996). 'Patterns of Modern Electoral Campaigning and their Consequences', in D. L. Swanson and P. Mancini (eds.), *Politics, Media, and Modern Democracy*. Westport/London: Praeger, 247–78.

Voelzkow, H. (2000). 'Korporatismus in Deutschland: Chancen, Risiken, Perspektiven', in E. Holtmann (ed.), *Zwischen Wettbewerbs- und Verhandlungsdemokratie*. Wiesbaden: Westdeutscher Verlag, 185–212.

Wewer, G. (1999). 'Regieren in Bund und Ländern (1948–1998)', in T. Ellwein and E. Holtmann (eds.), *50 Jahre Bundesrepublik Deutschland. Rahmenbedingungen, Entwicklungen, Perspektiven (PVS Sonderheft 30)*. Opladen/Wiesbaden: Westdeutscher Verlag, 496–519.

Wilke, J. and C. Reinemann (2001). 'Do the Candidates Matter? Long-Term Trends of Campaign Coverage—A Study of the German Press since 1949', *European Journal of Communication*, 16, 291–314.

Wortmann, M. (1989). *Political Marketing. A Modern Party Strategy*. Ph.D. thesis. European University Institute, Florence, Italy.

4

Presidentialization, Italian Style

Mauro Calise

INTRODUCTION

Italy represents, in most respects, an ideal-type for the presidentialization of the political system. All the main features of the presidentialization process have been present over the past twenty years. This has been the case in respect of all three 'faces' of presidentialization: the role of individual leaders has been greatly enhanced vis-à-vis their parties, while they have simultaneously gained a stronger hold over the executive branch of the state through the growing autonomy of the prime minister's office and the exercise of an increasingly monocratic form of rule. Presidentialization has also deeply affected the electoral process, with relevant changes occurring in each of its dimensions: campaign style, media focus, and voting behaviour have all come to reflect an increasingly personalized form of leadership.

Among the major causes of presidentialization (see Chapter 1), two—the internationalization of politics and the growth of the state—refer to general trends common to most industrial democracies, and Italy has certainly not been excluded from their effects. Thus, the presidentialization of the Italian political system must be seen, at least in part, as a response to the growing demands laid upon the political executive by the changing role of the state, both domestically and internationally. However, in order to account for the momentous and rapid nature of change in Italy, one needs to focus primarily upon the critical role played by the other two factors: the erosion of traditional social cleavage politics and the mediatization of politics.

The general understanding of the erosion of social cleavage politics is that parties have lost their grip on their traditional social and political constituencies. In the case of Italy, the process culminated in a dramatic crisis leading to the breakdown of the party system in the elections of 1994 (Diamanti and Mannheimer 1994). Each of Italy's three main parties underwent profound changes. The Socialists all but disappeared, while the Christian Democrats, who had ruled the country for the entire post-war period, split into several minor parties. The former Communist party was the only one to survive while maintaining a substantial degree of unity, although, following the fall of the Berlin Wall, its ideological cohesiveness was deeply undermined.

Explanations of the breakdown of the Italian party system, once considered the most stable and immutable among Western democracies, have mainly centred on the widespread exposure of political corruption within the country's political elite. As such excesses were widely and legitimately considered a consequence of the enduring dominance of the Christian Democratic Party, the fall of the Berlin Wall suddenly created viable alternatives. Thus, several actors—from the reformed ex-Communist party to the radical anti-centralist Northern League—were eager to compete for government, with an aggressive judicial branch as their formidable ally.

Political corruption and ideological renewal were not the only factors leading to the transformation of the Italian party system. As long-term data show, the decline of the major parties was well underway at both electoral and organizational levels (Bardi and Morlino 1994). However, this only serves to reinforce the conclusion that, by the early 1990s, a severe crisis of the established parties had created a political vacuum that enormously enhanced the opportunities for—and drives towards—the presidentialization of Italian politics.

In order to better understand the relationship between the crisis of traditional parties and the rise of presidentialization, one needs to focus on the role played by the media in the transition from the First to the Second Republic (as the pre- and post-1994 political systems became known). The mediatization of politics—as we shall see—largely coincided with the development of modern communication techniques in electoral campaigning. In addition, however, the national and local media played an instrumental role in the transition by becoming the most outspoken sponsors of institutional reform of the party system.

The proactive role of the media in the Italian crisis largely coincided with their unprecedented autonomy. In the land of *partitocrazia* (as the First Republic's party-dominated political system was often referred to) the media had traditionally been heavily dependent—both culturally and financially—on the party nomenclature. Political communication mainly worked as a horizontal channel, conveying messages among the party elites rather than between the government and the citizenry (Mancini 1990). This situation started to change with the growth of a (truly) independent press and the expansion of private television networks. Yet, changes only became evident with the collapse of the party system. After being, for so many decades, carefully geared to the machinery of political patronage and power, the media system suddenly found itself in a condition of quasi-independence. The collapse of the party system did not just leave the media without their traditional (party) filters, it also suddenly imposed upon both television and the press an urgent need to fill the void in political communication, by developing a new agenda. This agenda revolved around the institutional reform of the political system and the new creed of direct democracy.

The 1990s will be remembered in Italian politics as the decade of direct election (Fedele 1994). Now that the parties were widely regarded as having failed in their role as intermediaries between the people and the governing institutions, many advocated the direct intervention of citizens to take on the decision-making function. The creed of direct democracy enjoyed whole-hearted academic support, as well as massive media coverage and promotion. Yet, the decisive factor in its success was the institutional weapon that was used to spread it throughout the country: the referendum. The referendum brought the idea of direct democracy to each and every household, fostering a handy functional substitute for the declining parties (Calise 1993). Political participation could now be perceived as a much easier undertaking, with almost instantaneous results.

The main object of referendum campaigns in the 1990s was the replace-ment of proportional representation by a majoritarian electoral law (Chi-menti 1999). The way it was presented to the people, a majoritarian electoral law would enable them to directly choose the winning party or a coalition. Leaving aside the issue of how sound the scientific foundations of this supposition might have been (Calise 1998), the majoritarian platform strongly reinforced the view that the people would henceforward directly decide on political outcomes: first through the referendum, soon after, through the new electoral law. In fact, when the new law was passed in the wake of a sweeping referendum victory, the country stepped into its first majoritarian electoral battle with one very clear expectation in the public mind: the result of the election would no longer be a loose and flexible parliamentary majority, but a government—and a head of the govern-ment—directly chosen by the people. Through the Trojan horse of major-itarian democracy, the presidentialization of the political system gained momentum and legitimacy.

The media played a decisive role in legitimizing the presidentialization process, though in a largely unconscious way, through their unanimous backing of the referendum movement and the majoritarian platform. The reform of the electoral law rapidly became the primary issue on the media's political agenda, for at least two reasons:

- First, it neatly fit the need for a public discourse focusing on innovation and discontinuity with a discredited past. The collapse of the old party system was presented as due in large part to the obsolete system of proportional representation, which left the party elites to construct and dismantle governments at will. By contrast, the new majoritarian law promised to generate two, and only two, competing parties, so that victory at the polls would coincide with governmental responsibility.

The decision to form the government would be taken directly by the people (Pasquino 1992).

- Second, the majoritarian platform represented an easy message to convey. The notion that, by means of a mere new electoral law, the whole political system could be reformed and made more democratic was very appealing. The fact that some political scientists knew better (Sartori 1986), carried little weight with the media—hardly surprising in view of the fact that other members of the discipline joined the majoritarian crusade with the enthusiasm of neophytes (Barbera 1991; Fusaro 1991). The simplicity and power of their case ensured that the media became the apologists of the new system.

In spite of the fact that the constitution remained a strictly parliamentary one, the presidentializing impact of the majoritarian ideology was immediate and enduring. Soon after the victory of the centre-right coalition in 1994, Berlusconi outspokenly referred to himself as an elected premier, a stance shared by a majority of the press. The centre-left coalition at first tried to defend some of the prerogatives of parliamentary democracy, hoping that the President of the Republic would forbid a TV tycoon and his new party (Forza Italia) from entering the Palazzo Chigi. Yet, it was soon compelled to adjust to the new rules of the game. In the elections of 1996, the centre-left Ulivo coalition unanimously backed Romano Prodi as its candidate for the premiership. When Berlusconi ran for re-election as the centre-right nominee, Italy entered its first full-fledged 'presidential' contest, with the leader's personality and appeal becoming a crucial factor in the voters' decision-making (Venturino 2000).

While the collapse of the traditional parties and the media's campaign for institutional reform precipitated the presidentialization of party and electoral politics in Italy during the 1990s, it is important to note that a parallel process had already been under way in the executive arena for more than two decades.

THE EXECUTIVE FACE OF PRESIDENTIALIZATION

A stronger executive

An important feature of the Italian road to presidentialization is the strengthening of the executive branch. The representation of Italian government as an inherently weak and unstable entity has deep historical roots in the pre-fascist era and sound empirical evidence for the first thirty-five years of its republican life. This may help explain why it has survived as a stereotype long after things started to change. The transformation of the Italian executive has been massive as well as steady over the past twenty years.

Its early stages were first identified and outlined in a seminal study by Sabino Cassese (1980), who was able to foresee the momentous changes which were set to take place. These changes can be sub-divided into two main categories: normative and organizational.[1]

The former are 'normative' in the sense that they embody the idea that legislative activity by the council of ministers (that is, the cabinet[2]), and by individual ministries, is legitimate and should be expanded. Collective governmental law-making has developed through three main channels:

1. The increased use of so-called *emergency bills*, that is, laws which the government is constitutionally empowered to enact without parliament's approval, on the grounds of exceptional urgency. Since the early 1980s, emergency bills have become more and more numerous, to the point of becoming the predominant part of the total legislation passed. Formally, emergency bills needed to be approved by parliament within 60 days of their enactment by the government. Yet it became customary for the government to reiterate a bill shortly before its expiry date up to six or seven times (!), a practice which has in effect transformed emergency bills into ordinary laws. In other cases, emergency bills could be employed to accomplish certain (often expenditure-related) aims rapidly. Once such expenditures were made, parliament could exercise the option of voting the bill down, but this would have little practical effect.

2. The expansion of *delegated legislation*, or detailed measures directly enacted by the government on the basis of broad guideline laws already approved by parliament. Most EU regulatory activity has been handled through such measures (Menè 1993; Calandra 2002), as well as some of the most important reforms of the last decade, including those of the pension system and the overall reorganization of the ministries (Criscitiello 1999). This approach to law-making has been particularly favoured by Berlusconi's centre-right government. Indeed, the showdown between Berlusconi and the unions in the autumn of 1994, leading to mass demonstrations and a general strike, was caused by the government's determination to modify a key article of the Workers' Statute through delegated legislation.

3. The growing control of the government over the *legislative agenda*. Thanks to drastic changes in the rules regulating the parliamentary agenda, both on the floor and in committees, the government has become able to promote its own bills far more effectively. The ratio of laws originating in parliament and laws initiated by the government has consequently shifted dramatically towards the latter.

Along with these changes which concern the collective decision-making power of the government, account should also be taken of an increase in *secondary normative power*, that is, the regulatory power enjoyed by government departments through their administrative prerogatives; these detailed rule-making powers inhere both in individual ministers and in the cabinet as a collective body (Calandra 2002: 100; Lupo 2003). The domain of such power has grown, largely as a result of the deregulation process, which has sought to eliminate the rigidity and confusion of parliamentary legislation, while expanding the scope of ministerial responsibility and intervention.

It is difficult to imagine such an impressive expansion of normative power by the government without a parallel improvement in the organizational resources available to it. The literature on the Italian council of ministers of the 1970s reveals the disastrous condition of its secretariat at that time. Most laws would be discussed and approved by the cabinet without the formal texts being available, let alone previously circulated to ministers. They were nicknamed 'cover laws', as the only thing available to ministers were folders bearing the titles of the proposed legislation: empty dossiers (Rodotà 1977). This may not be surprising if one considers that the government only gained a home of its own in 1961, with its relocation from the Ministry of the Interior to its present residence at the Palazzo Chigi. At that time, only fifty individuals serviced the Presidency of the Council (in effect, the prime minister's office).

From the time of the Giannini Report on the reform of public administration (1979), the reorganization of the premiership became the object of intensive research and reflection, culminating in the enactment of a new law in August 1988. Attempts at such reorganization dated back to 1901, but the 1988 reform was saluted as a historical landmark, which thoroughly redefined the tasks of the prime minister's office, as well as its financial and administrative resources. Those involved in drafting and promoting this institutional re-design included several of the most prominent Italian jurists, some of whom were also politically active: Andrea Manzella became General Secretary of the Presidency of the Council of Ministers; Sabino Cassese and Franco Bassanini served as Ministers for the Public Function[3]; while Giuliano Amato became Prime Minister in 1992 and 2000.

Since the passing of the new law, several further reforms have reinforced the position of the executive, the most recent approved by the D'Alema government in July 1999, before being enacted by the Berlusconi government in 2002. While the efficiency of Palazzo Chigi may still lag behind that of other countries, the improvements in its decision-making and policy-steering capacities are unprecedented (Lanzillotta 2003). It is little wonder, then, that the focus of political competition has shifted from control of parliament to governmental leadership. During the golden age of Italian *partitocrazia,* Palazzo Chigi had remained in the shadow of the much more powerful major party headquarters. Now the time had come to turn the power structure—and struggle—on its head.

Prime Ministerial Dominance

The coming of prime ministerial dominance in Italian politics is by far the strongest indicator of presidentialization. To a large extent, it is closely dependent on the strengthening of the executive as a whole vis-à-vis parliament. Indeed, in many respects, it can be said to have been the driving force behind the whole process. From the early 1980s, prime ministers took the lead in the process of reorganizing and strengthening the executive branch. Bettino Craxi, the long-standing general secretary of the Socialist Party, played a highly visible role in this game, by advocating a formal constitutional transition to a presidential regime. Although not all would have gone as far as this, other prime ministers were also very active in pursuing the expansion and reorganization of executive power. Importantly, they all came from the 'lay' establishment, outside the Christian Democratic party. Indeed, one may well say that prime ministerial dominance would never have emerged without the historical discontinuity in the political and cultural control of the Palazzo Chigi, which commenced with the Spadolini premiership in 1981. Craxi, a strong personality, powerfully consolidated this historical break, while successors such as Carlo Azeglio Ciampi (a former governor of the Bank of Italy) and Giuliano Amato (a constitutional law professor) brought to the leadership of the executive the prestige of their considerable professional reputations. The stage was set for the coming of the modern Italian premiership with the election in 1996 of Romano Prodi, a manager and former president of IRI.[4]

Although the complex process of executive reorganization is still on-going, it is interesting to note that, from the outset, the Italian reformers took as their cue the British model.[5] Since the early committee work coordinated by Giuliano Amato in 1981 to the more recent bilateral seminars held at Palazzo Chigi during the Prodi premiership, the British premiership has served as a guideline for innovation. The office of the president of the council of ministers has been equipped with a general secretariat, with the role of the general secretary clearly distinguished from that of the deputy minister in charge of coordinating the work of the cabinet. For the first time, too, there is recognition of, and provision for, the creation of a personal staff for the prime minister, with full financial and organizational autonomy. Policy advisers and political communications experts have thus at last entered the rooms once accessible only to career politicians.

The General Secretariat has become a powerful coordinating centre for all the activities of the prime minister's office. The general secretary oversees the budgetary policy and personnel organization of the PM's office and, more importantly, has been empowered since 2000 to promote all necessary adjustments to the internal functioning of the office. This creates the possibility of autonomous adaptation of the organizational structure of the PM's office, without any further need to seek parliament's approval. It comes as no surprise that Berlusconi was quick to use such enhanced self-regulating power in order to create, within the PM's office, a 'Communication Centre' for the electronic handling of classified documents, while greatly expanding the functions and size of the premier's press office.[6]

Because they occupy a pivotal position that requires technical, political, and administrative skills, general secretaries have been selected from a close circle of 'political experts', mainly with judicial or economic backgrounds, as in the cases of Paolo de Ioanna (in the D'Alema Cabinet) and Linda Lanzillotta (Amato's Cabinet). The professional requisites change if we move to the more overtly political tasks performed by the under-secretaries to the prime minister. They share a very close fiduciary relationship with the prime minister, and are his *alter ego* in handling the most delicate affairs. While they are governmental appointees, only one of them has the special privilege of quasi-ministerial status, which permits him to take part in the cabinet meetings, where he serves as an important instrument of liaison between individual ministers and premier.

Besides concentrating on providing the prime minister with an efficient administrative machinery, organizational reform has changed the overall structure of the office. Over the course of time, the Presidency of the Council had developed into a large, but heterogeneous, super-ministry. The result was that the premiership was overloaded with activities having very little or nothing to do with its core political mission. They included, among others, the departments for social affairs, metropolitan areas, tourism, and civil protection, as well as a plethora of other administrative units. By dismantling this unwieldy apparatus, which had a combined workforce of 4,500, the prime minister's office has been able to concentrate upon performing its key political mission: legislative initiative and policy coordination (Pajno and Torchia 2000). Thus, the prime minister's office is now organized around a limited number of departments, which all share a very direct relationship with the overall functioning and coordination of the state apparatus. This is a good example of the phenomenon referred to in Chapter 1, whereby core executives seek to reduce the scope of their direct responsibilities, while enhancing their coordinating power in the domain which they regard as strategically critical.

The office of the prime minister still retains under its aegis a few departments with ministerial status; these enjoy substantial political autonomy while still taking full advantage of the premiership's special organizational position. The Department for the Public Function, under Minister Franco Bassanini, who served in the centre-left cabinets of Prodi, D'Alema, and Amato, became the vehicle of an extensive programme of legislative reform affecting central and local public administration. Similarly, the Department for Institutional Reform has, during the past decade, been at the centre of recurring attempts to revise the constitution in a semi-presidential direction and was eventually chosen by Umberto Bossi, leader of Lega Nord, as his stronghold to push the centre-right coalition towards a federalist reorganization of the Italian state.

In light of such widespread and substantial change, it is only fair to conclude that Italy has witnessed the emergence of a presidentialized political executive, albeit still formally under a parliamentary regime. From being scarcely even *primus inter pares*, with the status of little more than a mediator among the parties (and factions) that comprised his government, the prime minister has now evolved into by far the most prominent political figure in the nation. Yet this unquestionable institutional primacy has inevitably disrupted the pre-existing power balance. This became first evident during the tussle between Ciriaco De Mita (Christian Democrat) and Bettino Craxi (Socialist) for the premiership in 1986–7. Where hitherto the post could have been traded for a number of ministerial portfolios, by the mid-1980s the competition for control of Palazzo Chigi already offered very little scope for such compromise. Neither political party—or leader—was prepared to forego the premiership, a confrontation that eventually resulted in the breakdown of a thirty-year-old coalition, and of the party system as a whole.

Indeed, it may well be said that the premiership controversy strongly contributed to the crisis of *partitocrazia*. When the *Tangentopoli* typhoon hit the political establishment, it became evident that the coalitional equilibrium had been deeply eroded by the emergence of such a powerful premiership. Parties found themselves losing their ability to control the governmental process from above at the very moment when the exposure of widespread corruption precipitated them into a dramatic crisis. In any case, it is hardly surprising that the presidentialization of the Italian executive should reverberate within the very organizational structures of the parties themselves, old and new alike.

THE PARTY FACE: THE PERSONAL PARTY

In Chapter 1, it is argued that there is a trade-off between partified and presidentialized forms of politics. Parties embody the organizational principle of collective action and their natural tendency is to resist the emergence of strong, monocratic forms of leadership. Powerful confirmation of this analytical framework is provided by the transformation of the American presidential system. As long as American parties kept their firm organizational grip on the electoral process, US presidents remained weak institutional actors. Lord Bryce (1910) once famously explained 'why great men are not chosen as Presidents': throughout the nineteenth century, real governmental power remained firmly in party hands; it was only with the decline of party machines during the Progressive Era that the political conditions were created for the rise of the modern presidency. US presidential history is clearly divided into two constitutional epochs, with FDR as the watershed (Pious 1979; see also Fabbrini's chapter in this volume). In fact, its formal presidential prerequisites notwithstanding, Woodrow Wilson would refer to the American government of his time as 'congressional government'. And one may conclude that American presidentialism only became truly presidentialized with the advent of the 'imperial presidency' of the post-FDR era (Lowi 1985; Schlesinger 1973).

The Italian transition from the First to the (so-called) Second Republic may well be considered a similar example of change from partified to presidentialized polity. As we have seen, the main factors behind this transformation are the decline of the major political parties and the strengthening of the political executive. When we consider this process at the level of intra-party organizational change, the main result is a major shift in power to the benefit of the leader. Such a development had been anticipated as early as the mid-1980s, with the rise of Bettino Craxi as the general secretary of the Socialist Party *and* the prime minister of Italy. Both offices were thus unified in the same person. Until then, the unchallenged rule of the Christian Democratic Party (the DC) had been based on a strict division of labour between the party leadership and the prime minister's office. With the party secretary playing the role of chief political strategist and the prime minister frequently at the mercy of his own coalition, there was little doubt that Piazza del Gesù (the location of the DC's headquarters) was of greater importance than the Palazzo Chigi. The separation of the two roles between different individuals testified to the ruling party's determination to keep the prime minister's office from gaining strength and autonomy.

The advent of Craxi changed the rules of the game, and in a most effective way. His premiership (1983–7) turned out to be the longest in the troubled history of post-war Italian cabinets, thus forcing the Christian Democrats to follow suit. The eventual ousting of Craxi was followed by the premiership of Ciriaco De Mita, who was also able to retain the post of DC General Secretary. However, it proved a short-lived innovation, as the party reacted fiercely and swiftly to terminate De Mita's experiment. This might have seemed like a reassertion of partified politics, but ultimately it only served to accelerate the process of party decline, for the Tangentopoli earthquake found a party leadership profoundly weakened by internal feuding.

Bettino Craxi's personalization of party and executive leadership resonated with the media, and set the stage for the rise of his close friend, media tycoon Silvio Berlusconi, as the new playmaker of Italian politics (Hine 1986; Merkel 1987). The relationship between Berlusconi and his party, *Forza Italia*, presents an extreme case of presidentialization of party control. The party was founded by Berlusconi, largely as a by-product of his corporate empire, using his huge financial means as well as his sophisticated television network to create the party's central structure, which was mainly staffed with leading executives from Berlusconi's companies, such as Publitalia and Fininvest (Poli 2001). Besides being, to a substantial extent, the private property of its founder, Forza Italia was also highly dependent upon Berlusconi in a political sense, as it focused, from the very beginning, exclusively on promoting Berlusconi's ascent to the prime ministerial office. This implied that Berlusconi would keep absolute control over both the communication and organizational aspects of the party, creating an indistinguishable identity between the party and the man (Poli 2001). In essence, *Forza Italia* was conceived and developed as Berlusconi's *personal party* (Calise 2000).

Yet, in establishing and consolidating his personal party, Berlusconi was also facilitated by three systemic factors. At the institutional level, the strengthening of the political executive had created an appropriate environment for the rapid ascent of a party whose main objective was the 'presidential' victory of its leader: a monocratic party could have no better institutional incentive than a monocratic premiership. At the political level, the sudden collapse of all major governmental parties created an exceptional vacuum and an opportunity for the rise of a new party. What is more, achieving a national impact with his personal party was made considerably easier for Berlusconi by the fact that he faced no strong competitors within the centre-right camp. Indeed, the ideological platform of *Forza Italia* largely reproduced the pre-existing orientations of the former Christian Democrats, a feature that has been confirmed in more recent elections (ITANES 2001). Finally, Berlusconi's presidential campaign style was perfectly suited to the new brand of electioneering that emerged as a consequence of the new law establishing the direct elections of mayors in 1993 (see below).

This helps to explain why the 'new model army' of the personal party did not remain Berlusconi's exclusive prototype, but was quickly expropriated by the centre-left camp. Needless to say, the format—and strength—of the personal parties developed by the Ulivo leaders differed in various respects from Berlusconi's exact model. Lacking the huge financial and communication resources (as well as the professional skills) of the founder of Forza Italia, the Ulivo's leaders tried to maximize the only relevant organizational asset that was available in the troubled waters of changing Italian politics: the prime minister's extraordinary media visibility and institutional leverage.

As a result, both Lamberto Dini (who served as Prime Minister—after a coalition crisis brought down the first Berlusconi government—from January 1995 to May 1996) and Romano Prodi (who became Prime Minister after the 1996 elections) managed to create personal parties as spin-offs of their premierships. While Dini's party never went beyond the scope—and influence—of a notable's party, Prodi's *Democratici* became very important within the centre-left coalition, their main purpose being to counterbalance the hegemony of the former Communist *Democratici di Sinistra* (DS). The *Democratici*'s role was further enhanced through merger, in 2001, with a centre-left faction of the former Christian Democrats, the *Partito Popolare*, to form the new *Margherita* party. Ironically, the Margherita gained a significant number of parliamentary seats, in spite of the disastrous defeat which the Ulivo coalition suffered in the general elections held that June. The Ulivo's leader in 2001 was also the Margherita's founder, Francesco Rutelli: while a personalized campaign enabled his own party to do well, the overall coalition was nevertheless in disarray.

THE ELECTORAL FACE

Much of the popularity of presidential-style electoral contests sprang from the successful implementation of directly elected mayors in 1993 (Fabbrini 2000). The new electoral law not only provided for the direct election of mayors, but also for greatly expanded executive powers at city hall. This reform provoked the first outright experience of candidate-centred campaigning in post-war Italy. In 1993, all the major Italian cities, from Milan and Turin (spring) to Naples, Venice, Genoa, and Rome (autumn) witnessed a general shift—away from party competition towards a highly personalized form of campaign organization and presentation (Marrone 1996). At local level, personalization also found a very hospitable environment because it was not so heavily dependent on the role of media. For the new politics of mayoral government and electioneering, personalization simply stood, to a large extent, for a more direct, face-to-face relationship between leaders and supporters (Legnante 1999; Mazzoleni 2004).[7]

Following the first direct elections of mayors, Silvio Berlusconi's entry into the political arena had a huge impact. From the small-scale efforts of the candidates for local office, the personalization of elections was suddenly transformed into a massive nationwide undertaking. As a man who personally owned a media empire—including the three main private television networks in the country (Italia Uno, Retequattro, and Canale Cinque)— and was himself highly adept in the language and logic of television, Silvio Berlusconi would soon set a standard for personal campaigning with no comparable precedents in modern mass democracies, and a very difficult one to match.

Berlusconi's personal campaigning has utilized all the major means of communication. While television has obviously taken primary place, and a vital one strategically, *Forza Italia*'s campaigning has also emphasized the party leader's role and personality through more traditional media, such as newspapers and posters. During the 2001 national campaign, the country was flooded with copies of a 150-page booklet, describing the candidate's extraordinary road to success. *Una Storia Italiana* was sent to every household, at an estimated cost of €6 million. Meanwhile, for several months before the official commencement of the election campaign, the major advertising locations in the largest Italian cities were occupied by gigantic posters of Berlusconi's smiling face and the main slogans of the coalition he headed, the *Polo della Libertà*. National and local newspapers offered little diversity, since *Forza Italia*'s parliamentary candidates were formally prohibited from displaying photographs of themselves, in order to permit their leader a total image monopoly (Poli 2001). Nevertheless, TV undoubtedly remained the most important channel of communication in establishing the new personalized format of national campaigning which so rapidly brought Silvio Berlusconi electoral success—and prime ministerial office.

Three features of Berlusconi's political communication strategy deserve particular attention:

- the distribution of pre-recorded campaign videos directly to voters;
- his ubiquitous TV presence; and
- the personalization of campaign issues.

The first of these is a technique that was imported from Ross Perot's presidential campaigns in the USA. These videos included a list of Berlusconi's campaign agenda items, shown on a coloured board, and backed by quantitative data which purported to support his case. A typical feature of his campaign was to cite polling evidence showing that a majority of Italians agreed with him about various political issues. This generated a bitter controversy as to the reliability of the figures that Berlusconi quoted, the more so as the sources were seldom cited, but tended to coincide with the findings of survey research companies closely associated with Berlusconi's business empire. However, criticisms levelled by various opinion research and academic experts seemed to carry little weight with most voters.

If the use of pre-recorded videos was a clear departure from previous practice, the domination of TV time by the prime ministerial candidates in 2001 was not unprecedented, and cannot be considered a peculiarly Italian feature. Yet, it is still impressive how this rapidly became a dominant feature of what formally remained a competition between two rather loose coalitions, each comprising a number of very heterogeneous parties. In the 2001 elections, Berlusconi and Rutelli, the two prime ministerial candidates, enjoyed over 400 minutes each on the three public television channels (RAI 1, 2, and 3), which was more than four times the average accorded to the seven other leaders from allied parties. Yet, even this level of coverage paled into insignificance compared to the exposure accorded to Berlusconi on his own Mediaset channels—a whopping 1,427 minutes, as against 887 minutes for his main rival, Rutelli. Of the other party leaders, only Alleanza Nazionale's Gianfranco Fini—Forza Italia's main coalition ally—surpassed

200 minutes, barely one-seventh of Berlusconi's score. No other leader received more than 40 minutes air time on the Mediaset channels.[8]

But perhaps the most striking feature of recent campaign strategy has been the personalization of issues and platforms. The 2001 election campaign was, in essence, about the question of whether to vote for or against Berlusconi. In what is perhaps the most rigorous empirical analysis of televised electoral communication, Legnante and Sani argue that most salient campaign issues were 'inextricably interwoven' with the candidates' personal roles and qualities (2002: 47). Berlusconi's own strategy of personalizing his campaign dictated his adversaries' main weapon against him: the centre-left's main campaign theme was the risk of Berlusconi becoming, because of his financial wealth and media empire, an authoritarian prime minister.

It is not easy to assess the effect of this strategy of 'dramatizing mobilization'. When considered in terms of the impact on voting behaviour, it seems that the strategy made a substantial impact, as anti-Berlusconi sentiment was found to be the main factor motivating a vote for the centre-left (Mannheimer 2001). However, in embracing the outright personalization of the campaign, this strategy was considered by many to belittle the programmatic virtues of the centre-left. By failing to stress the governmental record of economic and social achievement since 1996, the *Ulivo* may have lost sight of its main electoral asset. All the more so in view of the fact that the strategy of personalizing its campaign led to the nomination, in the summer of 2000, of Francesco Rutelli, the mayor of Rome, as the prime ministerial candidate for the general election that was forthcoming in spring 2001. This choice was made at the expense of Giuliano Amato, an internationally renowned figure and at that time the incumbent prime minister. According to the polls, Rutelli had the stronger personal appeal. As a result, the whole electoral communication strategy hinged on Rutelli's personal qualities, in a manifest attempt to replicate Berlusconi's own success story. The disastrous outcome of an overwhelming and unprecedented parliamentary majority for Berlusconi (Pasquino 2002), would show that polling is not an easy political weapon to handle—at least for the strategists of the centre-left.

CONCLUSION

In presenting Italy as an exemplar of presidentialization, we have stressed the fact that the process has long been underway on all major analytical dimensions. The severe crisis of traditional parties undermined their parliamentary environment, while generating the internal organizational transformations which resulted in the emergence of a strongly presidentialized party type, the personal party. At the same time, the mediatization of electoral competition achieved its apogee with the rise of media tycoon Silvio Berlusconi, the dominant political figure of the past decade in Italy. Yet, in order to fully appreciate the pervasive and enduring nature of change, one needs to look into the sweeping institutional reforms that have paved the way for presidentialization of politics in the country: the strengthening of the political executive and the introduction of a majoritarian electoral law.

While the extraordinary expansion of leadership power in national government can be traced back over twenty years or more, and may be considered a long overdue development which enables Italy to catch up with most other comparable countries, the new electoral law was mainly a response to the breakdown of the party system. The movement for a new electoral law had been active throughout the previous decade (Segni 1994), but it had been hostage to the well-known paradox of institutional reforms: No major change can be introduced to the (main) rules of the game as long as these changes need the approval of the very political actors they are likely to jeopardize (Sartori 1994; Sundquist 1992). Yet, with the collapse of all of the major ruling parties, the way was cleared for the electoral reform movement, aided by strong support within the mass media, to achieve its goal by way of the referendum.

The combination of the new electoral law, a strengthened executive, and a heavily mediatized political arena produced a majoritarian form of politics quite different from the one the reformers had envisaged. While the referendum movement had aimed for a Westminster model of two strong and cohesive programmatic parties, the actual result was two very loose coalitions of parties constructed around the unifying factor of a highly personalized leadership. The road to British parliamentarism got sidetracked onto the path of American-style presidentialism.

This trend towards presidentialization, however, does not necessarily mean that a regime change has definitively occurred. If we look at the quasi-direct election of the prime minister, the chronicle of the last decade has proved quite controversial. In the wake of the first two presidentialized elections (1994 and 1996), parliamentary politics has been eager to step back in. Both the first Berlusconi cabinet and the Prodi cabinet were voted down by parliamentary votes, and were succeeded by new prime ministers who assumed office without recourse to new elections. In the first case, this occurred as a result of a change in the parliamentary majority, while in the second case, Massimo D'Alema replaced Romano Prodi, a succession within the centre-left coalition. Yet, in both cases the overthrow was met with outright hostility from the press, a sign that the transition to a new system, while far from complete, had gained widespread legitimacy. This sentiment had been nurtured through the referendum crusades and, probably to an even greater extent, through the changes wrought in local politics.

As we have seen, it may well be that the main turning point was represented by the victorious mayoral campaigns of 1993, with the winning candidates from the centre-left soon becoming the apostles of a 'new politics' based on clear personal institutional responsibility and a closer personal relationship with the electorate. The systemic influence of the mayoral reform also eventually extended to the election of regional governors, who became directly elected from April 2000. In the light of the popularity of these reforms, and with some of the most prominent mayors also running for election as heads of regional government, the term presidentialization quickly became the catchword which characterized the new scenario. Yet, the personalized political strategy deployed by Prime Minister Massimo D'Alema for these regional elections proved ineffectual. The forecasts of his polling advisers, who anticipated a sweeping victory for the centre-left coalition, encouraged D'Alema to take a very assertive role in the campaign, transforming an important yet limited mid-term administrative election into a personal showdown with Berlusconi. But they proved misleading, and electoral defeat led to the unexpected resignation of D'Alema.

In the end, as in any major transition, the institutional picture remains one of conflicting forces or, more optimistically, checks and balances. The national parliamentary elections of 2001, which saw the return to power of Silvio Berlusconi with a sweeping majority, seemed to strongly reinforce the trends towards presidentialization. This is clearly true at the electoral level, as we have seen, in respect of campaign strategy and management, media coverage, and electoral behaviour. But, if anything, it has proved even truer in the running of the cabinet, where Berlusconi felt strong enough to dismiss two of his most prominent ministers (those for the interior and foreign affairs), an unprecedented move in the history of Italian government. As a consequence, he himself served as foreign minister for several months.

Yet, by stressing the importance of Silvio Berlusconi for the presidentialization of Italian politics, one is bound to wonder about the consequences of Berlusconi's eventual demise. That the process was well under way in the country prior to Berlusconi's ascent to power, suggests that it may endure, in at least some respects. And the effects of institutional changes and mediatization are likely to reinforce the long-term nature of the phenomenon too. Yet, there is no doubt that Berlusconi has had an extraordinary personal impact in elevating presidentialization to its current level in Italy. Through the creation of his personal party he has introduced a short-cut between party politics and presidential politics, and inspired a degree of imitation well beyond the boundaries of Forza Italia. Whether this consequence of the collapse of *partitocrazia* leaves a lasting legacy remains to be seen.

NOTES

1. For an in-depth analysis of the expansion of executive power in Italy, see Calise 1997 and 2006.
2. Note that the formal Italian title of the Cabinet is the Council of Minsters ('Consiglio dei Ministeri'), while the title of the prime minister is actually the President of the Council of Ministers. In order to avoid confusion with the President of the Republic (the formal head of state in Italy), and to ease comparison with other parliamentary regimes, this chapter will refer to the President of the Council as Prime Minister or Premier, and the Council of Ministers as the Government or Cabinet.
3. 'Minister for the Public Function' loosely translates as 'Minister for the Civil Service', in Anglo-Saxon terms.
4. IRI was the Istituto per la Ricostruzione Industriale, a major public corporation which held mixed assets across the industrial and financial sectors.
5. For a detailed reconstruction of both normative and organizational aspects of change, see Criscitiello 1999.
6. See President of Council of Ministers' decrees of 12 December 2001 and 23 July 2002.
7. At the local level, organized face-to-face encounters may indeed prove to be a successful substitute for indirect political communication through the mass media. At a recent seminar, Mario De Biase, the mayor of Salerno—a mid-sized southern city—declared that, during his victorious campaign, he had only spoken at half a dozen public meetings, while personally taking part in more than 500 small encounters, totalling over 10,000 personal contacts with his electors. It is perhaps worth noting that this mayor holds a degree in Sociology.
8. These figures refer to the entire two-month campaign period, for all broadcast programmes, as measured by the *Osservatorio di Pavia* (Legnante and Sani 2002: 58–9).

REFERENCES

Barbera, A. (1991). *Una riforma per la repubblica*. Rome: Editore Riuniti.
Bardi, L. and L. Morlino (1994). 'Italy: Tracing the Roots of the Great Transformation', in R. Katz and P. Mair (eds.), *How Parties Organize: Change and Adaptation in Party Organizations in Western Democracies*. London: Sage, 242–77.
Bryce, J. (1910). *The American Commonwealth*, Volumes 1 and 2. London: Macmillan (originally published 1888).
Calandra, P. (2002). *Il governo della Repubblica*. Bologna: Il Mulino.
Calise, M. (1993). 'Remaking the Italian Party System: How Lijphart Got it Wrong by Saying it Right', *West European Politics*, 16: 545–60.
—— (1997). 'Il Governo', in F. Barbagallo (ed.), *Storia dell'Italia Repubblicana*, Vol. III. Torino: Einaudi.
—— (1998). *La costituzione silenziosa*. Roma: Laterza.
—— (2000). *Il partito personale*. Roma: Laterza.
—— (2006) *La Terza Repubblica. Partiti contro Presidenti*. Roma: Laterza.

Cassese, S. (1980). 'Is There a Government in Italy? Politics and Administration at the Top', in R. Rose and E. Suleiman (eds.), *Presidents and Prime Ministers*. Washington: American Enterprise Institute for Public Policy Research.

Chimenti, A. (1999). *Storia dei referendum. Dal divorzio alla riforma elettorale*. Roma: Laterza.

Criscitiello, A. (1999). 'La riforma di Palazzo Chigi: come cambia l'organizzazione della Presidenza del Consiglio', *Quaderni di Scienza Politica*, VI: 489–509.

Diamanti, I. and R. Mannheimer (1994). *Milano a Roma. Guida all'Italia elettorale del 1994*. Roma: Donzelli.

Fabbrini, S. (2000). *The Presidentialization of Italian Local Government*. Paper presented at the 28th Joint Sessions of ECPR Workshops, Copenhagen, 14–19 April.

Fedele, M. (1994). *Democrazia referendaria*. Roma: Laterza.

Fusaro, C. (1991). *Guida alle riforme istituzionali*. Soveria Mannelli: Rubettino.

Hine, D. (1986). 'Il terzo anno di presidenza Craxi: radici e limiti di un record', in P. Corbetta and R. Leonardi (eds.), *Politica in Italia. Edizione 1986*. Bologna: Il Mulino.

ITANES (2001). *Perchè ha vinto il centro-destra?* Bologna: Il Mulino.

Lanzillotta, L. (2003). 'La riforma della Presidenza del Consiglio dei Ministri', *Quaderno dell'Associazione per gli studi e le ricerche parlamentari*, 13: 165–76.

Legnante, G. (1999). 'Personalizzazione della politica e comportamento elettorale. Con una ricerca sulle elezioni comunali', *Quaderni di Scienza Politica*, VI: 395–487.

—— and G. Sani (2002). 'La campagna piu lunga', in S. Bartolini and R. D'Alimonte (eds.), *Maggioritario finalmente? La transizione elettorale 1994–2001*. Bologna: Il Mulino.

Lowi, T. J. (1985). *The Personal President: Power Invested, Promise Unfulfilled*. Ithaca: Cornell University Press.

Lupo, N. (2003). *Dalla legge al regolamento*. Bologna: Il Mulino.

Mancini, P. (1990). 'Tra di noi. Sulla funzione negoziale della comunicazione politica', *Il Mulino*, XL: 2.

Mannheimer, R. (2001). 'Le elezioni del 2001 e la "mobilitazione drammatizzante"', *Rivista Italiana di Scienza Politica*, XXX: 543–60.

Marrone, T. (1996). *Il sindaco*. Milano: Rizzoli.

Mazzoleni, G. (ed.) (2004). 'Il Grande Comunicatore. Dieci anni di Berlusconi sulla ribalta politica', *Comunicazione Politica*, 1, Special Issue.

Mené, A. (1993). Cronache Costituzionali 1990–91, *Rivista Trimestrale di Diritto Pubblico*, No. 3.

Merkel, W. (1987). *Prima e dopo Craxi*. Padova: Liviana.

Pajno, A. and L. Torchia (2000). *La riforma del governo*. Bologna: Il Mulino.

Pasquino, G. (1992). *Come eleggere il governo*. Milano: Anabasi.

—— (2002). *Dall'Ulivo al governo Berlusconi. Le elezioni del 13 maggio 2001 e il sistema politico italiano*. Bologna: Il Mulino.

Pious, R. (1979). *The American Presidency*. New York: Basic Books.

Poli, E. (2001). *Forza Italia. Strutture, leadership e radicamento territoriale*. Bologna: Il Mulino.

Rodotà, S. (1977). 'La circolazione delle informazioni nell'apparato di governo', in S. Ristuccia (ed.), *L'istituzione governo. Analisi e prospettive*. Milano: Comunità.

Sartori, G. (1986). 'The Influence of Electoral Systems: Faulty Laws or Faulty Method?', in B. Grofman and A. Lijphart (eds.), *Electoral Laws and their Political Consequences*. New York: Agathon Press.

—— (1994). *Comparative Constitutional Engineering*. London: Macmillan.

Schlesinger, A. M. (1973). *The Imperial Presidency*. Boston: Houghton-Mifflin.

Segni, M. (1994). *La rivoluzione interrotta. Diario di quattro anni che hanno cambiato l'Italia*. Milan: Rizzoli.

Sundquist, J. L. (1992). *Constitutional Reform and Effective Government*. Washington: Brookings.

Venturino, F. (2000). 'La personalizzazione della politica italiana. Il ruolo dei leader nelle elezioni del 1996', *Rivista Italiana di Scienza Politica*, XXX: 294–327.

5

The Presidentialization of Spanish Democracy: Sources of Prime Ministerial Power in Post-Franco Spain

Ingrid van Biezen and Jonathan Hopkin

INTRODUCTION

Spain is a good example of a formally parliamentary regime subject to presidentializing pressures. Although the degree of presidentialization has varied over the post-Franco period, prime ministers have mostly been powerful figures, and election campaigns have been heavily concentrated on the rivalry between prime ministerial candidates. This chapter will examine the foundations of this presidentialization, focusing on three broad areas: the formal constitutional framework and other institutional features stemming from the nature of the Spanish transition to democracy, the internal dynamics of Spanish political parties, and the dynamics of electoral competition. It will assess the different levels of presidentialization at different points in time in order to disentangle the relative importance of these factors in bolstering prime ministerial power resources and autonomy in the Spanish political system.

THE INSTITUTIONAL CONTEXT: TRANSITION AND THE 1978 CONSTITUTION

Spain is a young democracy, and the present parliamentary monarchy was established by the transition to democracy after Franco's death in 1975, which culminated in a new constitution in 1978. The nature of executive power in democratic Spain can only be properly understood in terms of the dynamics of this democratization process. Two features of this transition are particularly important.

First, the transition was itself influenced by historical legacies. The lessons drawn from the failure of Spain's first democratic regime, the Second

Republic (1931–6), were consistently invoked during the transition to democracy. Key transition leaders took the view that Spain's bloody Civil War (1936–9) was the result of the weak and fractious nature of the Second Republic. The 1931 constitution had provided for an uneasy sharing of executive power between the offices of president and prime minister, which contributed to this weakness (Heywood 1995: 89). The new democracy, it was argued, should have a strong executive capable of governing authoritatively.

Second, Spain's transition to democracy avoided a clear break with the Franco regime. The process began with a Political Reform Law passed by the Francoist institutions themselves, and at all points in the process a pretence of constitutional continuity was maintained. As a result, the institutional features of the Franco regime inevitably influenced the nature of the post-Franco democracy. The decision not to purge the Spanish public administration, and institutions such as the army and the judiciary, of Francoist appointees ensured elements of the governing culture of the dictatorship would persist (Bar 1997: 116). Needless to say, the Franco dictatorship had concentrated political power around the executive and around the figure of the *Caudillo* himself, and so institutional continuities would tend to reinforce the power of the executive, and in particular the prime minister.

The transition to democracy was achieved through consensus and negotiation among the major political forces. This had important consequences. Paradoxically, consensus weakened parliament: because of the difficulty of the compromises the parties had to make, and the need to ensure the acquiescence of extra-parliamentary forces (such as the army, the church, and big business), the real action took place behind the scenes (Herrero de Miñón 1993). This set a precedent which has proved difficult to shake off: as we will show later in this chapter, parliamentary parties have tended (with some exceptions) to be subordinated to their leaderships, and parliament as a whole has rarely challenged the dominant position of the prime minister and executive.

The constitutional settlement of 1978 entrenched executive power, even though the original parliamentary draft had advocated a much more balanced system (Herrero de Miñón 1993: 126). The PSOE (Spanish Socialist Party) and the PCE (Spanish Communist Party) were initially predisposed to a strongly parliamentary constitutional settlement, but Adolfo Suárez (appointed prime minister by King Juan Carlos in July 1976) insisted on a more 'presidential' approach, supported by the conservative *Alianza Popular* (AP—Popular Alliance). Above and beyond his natural preference to concentrate power around himself, his main concerns were to convince hard-line sectors of the military and the Francoist political class that democracy could be compatible with strong and authoritative government, and to ensure the government had sufficient means to manage and control the transition process itself. The Socialists in particular could sense the possible future benefits to them of such an arrangement.

The 1978 constitution therefore adopted the so-called 'Chancellorship' model of the Federal Republic of Germany, with the explicit objective of ensuring executive dominance over parliament, and prime ministerial dominance within the executive (Heywood 1991, 1995). The prime minister (*presidente del gobierno*) is invested personally with the confidence of parliament in a vote of investiture, and only then chooses a cabinet (*consejo de ministros*). This reinforces the prime minister's power within the cabinet itself, as only he or she can claim this special legitimacy (Aragón 2002: 43–4; Heywood 1991: 98–9). The prime ministerial position is further strengthened by the 'constructive motion of censure', whereby the parliament can only censure the government through a majority vote for an alternative candidate for the prime minister's office (ibid.). Finally, the parliamentary standing orders established in 1977 were designed to maximize the government's authority over parliament (ibid.; see also Maurer 1999: 41). The government has the dominant role in initiating legislation, and wide powers to issue decree-laws, as well as far superior material means for drawing up legislation (Heywood 1999: 105).

The 'Chancellorship' model adopted by the 1978 constitution therefore does more than simply strengthen the executive at the expense of parliament. It also creates the conditions for the presidentialization of the political system by concentrating executive authority around the prime minister's office. The prime minister directs the action of the government, names the ministers and allocates responsibilities between them, and coordinates the activities of the different ministers (Articles 98–100), as well as having the power to dissolve parliament (Article 115) and sack ministers (Article 100). These powers enhance prime ministerial authority and autonomy within the government (Heywood 1999; Heywood and Molina 2000).

The electoral law is also crucial in determining the level of presidentialization. The current Spanish electoral system is one of proportional representation with a series of 'correctives' which were designed to make the outcome as majoritarian as possible (Gunther et al. 1986; Montero et al. 1992). These correctives included the d'Hondt system of calculation, which tends to favour larger parties, and a low average district magnitude, as well as a 3 per cent threshold at district level. This system was designed to secure two objectives: to limit the fragmentation of the party system, and to secure strong governments (if possible, single-party governments). It has been largely successful in achieving these objectives. Although the number of parties with parliamentary representation has been comparatively high in Spain (twelve in 1977–9, eleven in the parliament elected in 2000), the level of parliamentary fragmentation has been relatively low, largely because almost all the smaller parties in parliament have been regionalist forces incapable of

TABLE 5.1. *Governments, prime ministers and parliamentary support in Spain 1977–2000*

Dates	Prime Minister	Parliamentary Support	Supporting Parties
1977–79	Suárez (UCD)	47.1 (Minority)	UCD (+ various)
1979–81	Suárez (UCD)	48.0 (Minority)	UCD (+ various)
1981–2	Calvo Sotelo (UCD)	48.0 (Minority)	UCD (+ various)
1982–6	González (PSOE)	57.7	PSOE
1986–9	González (PSOE)	52.6	PSOE
1989–93	González (PSOE)	50	PSOE
1993–6	González (PSOE)	45.4 (Minority)	PSOE (+ CiU)
1996–2000	Aznar (PP)	44.6 (Minority)	PP (+ CiU, PNV)
2000–2004	Aznar (PP)	52.3	PP
2004–	Zapatero (PSOE)	42.6 (Minority)	PSOE (+various)

Notes: All figures are percentages of seats held by governing party. 'Minority' refers to minority government status.

challenging the two main parties at the national level (Holliday 2002: Table 9.1). Spain has effectively maintained a moderate bipolar—one might say an adulterated two-party—system ever since the restoration of democracy in 1977, despite the vote share of the two main parties oscillating between only 63.7 per cent and 78.6 per cent of votes cast. This makes government formation a far more straightforward task than in some other multiparty systems. As Table 5.1 shows, there has not yet been a case of formal coalition government under Spanish democracy, and for fifteen out of the last twenty-nine, Spain has had a single-party government with an absolute majority of parliamentary support (and single-party minority governments for the remainder).

With the help of a relatively majoritarian electoral law, prime ministers in Spain have therefore been able to claim a democratic mandate to form governments, strengthening their position vis-à-vis parliament and laying the foundations for the presidentialization of the Spanish system of government.

THE PARTY FACE: LEADERS AND THEIR PARTIES

The nature of party organization in Spain is a major contributor to the personalization of politics. The image of the party leaders has come to assume a prominent role in campaigning (see below) and politics more broadly tends to be highly personalized. However, at least on the face of it, Spanish parties seem quite decentralized. In the space of just a couple of decades, Spain has evolved from the unitary and highly centralized state it was under Franco towards an almost federal state structure, with the 1978 constitution explicitly recognizing the right of regional autonomy. All Spanish parties have adapted their organizational structures to the federal structure of government, although the parties of the left have tended to grant more formal autonomy to their regional organizations than those of the right. In recent years, however, even the conservative *Partido Popular* has adapted its organization to the rapidly federalized state structure, now defining itself as a 'regionalized organization'.

Despite this formal decentralization, in practice Spanish parties are highly centralized organizations. The formal autonomy granted to the regional echelons of the party is often at the same time curtailed by statutes, with provisions in the national party rules that ensure that decisions made by the lower strata are bound to the confines established by the national party programme and constitution. In many cases, moreover, the autonomy of the lower echelons is effectively negated by stipulating that their decisions, on financial matters, or the selection of candidates for sub-national public office, for example, actually require the approval of the national party leadership.

Similarly, candidate selection procedures for national office are highly centralized, and have been ever since the first democratic elections (de Esteban and Guerra 1985). The candidates for the *Partido Popular* are normally selected from the centre with very little influence from below. Even if the selection process formally occurs according to a bottom-up procedure, as in *Izquierda Unida* (United Left) the ultimate authority over the candidates and their rank-order on the party lists rests with the national leadership. Equally, in the PSOE the selection process starts off at the local branch and concludes at the Federal Committee, which not only has formal veto powers over the proposals of the lower strata, but may also add names to the lists. As Méndez (1998: 195) observes in this context, the preliminary lists emanating from the local branch have to pass so many stages that the final result can be completely different from the initial proposals, and there is no room for disagreement or appeal.

Hence, the picture that emerges here is that, rather than operating in relatively autonomous decision-making spheres, the national and lower organizational strata of Spanish parties are in fact highly interdependent. The parties are hierarchical and top-down organizations with strong oligarchic tendencies, concentrating power at the highest echelons of the party in the hands of a small elite (Gillespie 1989: 323–4). Paradoxically, this tight hierarchical structure can also act as a constraint on presidentialization, in that party leaders have to win organizational control of the party in order to dominate. However, the main trend in the Spanish democracy has been towards centralization and the institutionalization of personalized leadership, as the following analysis of the major parties shows.

The Partido Popular: Concentration of powers and the personalization of leadership

The clearest case of a party with high levels of centralization and personalization is the *Partido Popular* (PP), the successor party to the *Alianza Popular* founded during the transition period. 'Presidentialism', as Cotarelo and López Nieto (1988) observe, was already an essential characteristic of *Alianza Popular* and was reinforced with the party's 'refoundation' as *Partido Popular* in 1989 (García-Guereta 2001). The predominance of the leader in the party's early years was in part the result of the informal and highly personalized networks surrounding the party president. Clientelism and personal ties with the party president were important in establishing the territorial structures of the party, and personalist features tended to dominate internal party conflicts. This hindered the institutionalization of the party and brought an excessive dependence on its charismatic leader and founding father, Manuel Fraga, which continued until his resignation (Montero 1989: 516).

The presidential structure of the PP is codified in the party statutes through the institutionalization of a personal leadership and extensive formal authorities assigned to the party president. The statutes institutionalize the party presidency as a separate party office which occupies a privileged position within the party as a whole and is granted important prerogatives. The authority of the party president, moreover, has tended to increase over time: for instance the president chairs all the national party decision-making bodies and has a decisive vote. In 1993, in addition, the party leader acquired the *ex officio* leadership of the parliamentary groups in the lower and upper chamber as well as the European Parliament, extending his reach over both parliamentary and extra-parliamentary arenas of party activity, even at the supranational level. The party president can personally appoint additional members to the executive committee (that is, over and above those elected by the party congress) and, most tellingly, has the exclusive authority to choose the members of the smaller, inner core, permanent executive. The subordination of the executive committee to the party president is furthermore explicitly recognized by authorizing him to discharge and replace those members who are elected by the party congress.

As in most Spanish parties, the members of the executive committee are elected by the party congress through a closed (and blocked) list according to a simple majority system. In practice, this leaves the composition of the executive committee to a large extent down to the party leader. Typically, only one list for the future executive committee is submitted for ratification to the party congress (although after Fraga's resignation in 1986 a bitter leadership contest pitted two candidates head to head at the 1987 party congress, for the first [and so far only] time in the party's history). The election of the executive is merged with the election of the presidency (with the exception of a brief period between 1986 and 1989), making the choice of executive members a vote of confidence in the presidency. Not only does this discourage dissent, it also means that it is the party president who is invested personally with a mandate from the party congress, at the expense of the authority of the executive.

In many respects, the *Partido Popular* can be seen to resemble the former *Unión de Centro Democrático* (UCD), which also had a highly centralized and presidential party structure, in which Suárez and his close allies controlled virtually all facets of the party organization. The party president was attributed substantial powers in manufacturing the electoral lists, for example, and was also responsible for the coordination of the party in government and parliament, to the latter of which he was the *ex officio* president. The party presidency was also responsible for the supervision of the party apparatus, which in practice gave him control over party expenditure, and the functioning of the lower organizational echelons, which were directly subordinated to the central authority (Hopkin 1999: 84–93; Huneeus 1985: 234).

The Socialist Party: Oligarchic constraints on party presidentialization

Rather than a presidentialized party, the PSOE has traditionally been an oligarchic organization, although with a predominant party leader. In contrast to the *Partido Popular* or *Izquierda Unida*, the PSOE has not institutionalized the party presidency, maintaining instead a formally collegial executive. However, the Socialist Party leader is both by statute and political practice much more than a *primus inter pares*. Felipe González, party leader for most of the democratic era, dominated the party, although this was as much down to his personal charisma as to formal prerogatives (Colomé 1998). Indeed, his predominance was such that it enabled him to make the party embrace positions it had previously opposed, such as when González persuaded the party to abandon its anti-NATO stance almost overnight in 1986. Throughout virtually the entire post-Franco period, González maintained a firm control over the party until his unexpected resignation in 1997, leaving the party in disarray and creating a leadership vacuum that culminated in the clashing 'dual leadership' after the 1998 party primaries. The PSOE under González can be seen as an example of a personal leadership based on a personal mandate which he derived from considerable and long-standing electoral success. However, the less fortunate experiences of his successors demonstrate that the party structures of the PSOE continue to act as an important constraint on intra-party presidentialization.

In addition to the widely used practice of a majoritarian election through a closed list (as in the PP), until 1994 the executive committee of the Socialist Party was elected by a so-called collective vote. This meant that the heads of the provincial delegations, rather than individual delegates, cast a block vote, and provincial delegations often pooled their votes so that a single block vote could be cast by the regional leadership. At the extraordinary party congress in 1979, for example, Vice-Secretary-General Guerra thus controlled the whole region of Andalucia, representing 25 per cent of the total congress, with one single vote.[1] This procedure effectively filtered out the representation of critical minority groups, highlighting the high degree of internal centralization of the party organization and the hegemony of the internal party oligarchy over the entire organization. Control over the party organization, however, remained contingent upon the cohesion of the dominant coalition.

The first signs of a rupture in the dominant coalition emerged in the early 1990s and intensified after the resignation of Guerra as deputy prime minister in 1991, following his brother's alleged involvement in a corruption scandal. As a result of the departure of Guerra and some of his followers—the *guerristas*—from the cabinet, the government became more coherent and uniform and, as Puhle (2001: 290) asserts, 'it also became even more "presidentialist" and isolated from the party.' In addition to the outcome resulting from a schism in the dominant coalition, the shift towards higher levels of presidentialization can be seen from the modification of the party's internal electoral system and particularly the voting procedures for the election of the party leader: in 1998, the PSOE introduced primary elections to select its candidate for prime ministership.

Their election through primaries gives party leaders a direct and personal mandate from the party rank-and-file, and thus potentially enhances their autonomy vis-à-vis the party apparatus. As in most other western parties, however, the direct involvement of the PSOE membership did not permit candidate selection to escape the control of the party elites entirely (Hopkin 2001). In this sense, therefore, the nature of the party organization continues to act as a constraint on presidentialization. As will be argued below, parties should also be seen as the pivotal political institutions in the parliamentary arena, even though the leaders' dominance of their parties is a key factor in ensuring that prime ministers are able to control their parliamentary support bases.

Executive strength, parliamentary group subordination, and prime ministerial power

Spanish parties are primarily elitist organizations, with the locus of power to be found within the extra-parliamentary executives (van Biezen 2003: ch. 7).

This contrasts with the patterns observed for the longer established democracies in the West European democracies (Katz and Mair 1995), where the party in public office has become increasingly predominant vis-à-vis the party central office and the membership organization. The Spanish scenario of a national executive exercising a remarkable degree of control over the parliamentary groups is a characteristic shared with recently established democracies more generally (see also van Biezen 2000).

The subservience of the parliamentary party vis-à-vis the party central office can be seen in all the Spanish parties, in a number of respects. First of all, the party central offices tend to have an advantage over the party in public office in terms of human and financial resources. Second, formal provisions in the party statutes explicitly limit the autonomy of the parliamentary groups in deciding on the distribution of its material and financial resources or the employment and dismissal of parliamentary party staff, for example, by stipulating that these require the approval of the party executive. Political decisions are taken at the party headquarters and parliamentarians are constrained by a severe party discipline. For PSOE parliamentarians, failing to observe the compulsory voting discipline is formal grounds for expulsion from the party. Similarly, the PP has enshrined this principle in its party statutes as the so-called *criterio de dependencia*. This contrasts with the higher degree of parliamentary group autonomy found in many established democracies in Western Europe.

This leadership predominance does not imply, however, that leaders are entirely autonomous of party organizations. Instead, the Spanish party system continues to exhibit substantial elements of what Poguntke and Webb (in this volume) identify as 'partified control'. In other words, and following King's (1976) classification of executive–legislative relations, the typical mode of interaction between government ministers and MPs in Spain would be the inter-party mode, that is, one in which ministers and MPs belonging to the governing party interact with MPs from opposition parties. This particular mode of parliamentary functioning serves to underline that political parties are the key institutions within the parliamentary arena and highlights the fact that primary loyalty of ministers and MPs is towards the party. In the relationship between government ministers and MPs, and given the general subservience of the parliamentary party to the extra-parliamentary executive, coupled with the constitutionally crafted executive dominance over parliament, it is the party in government which has a clear predominance over the party in parliament. This serves to further strengthen the already substantial sources of prime ministerial power. At the same time, however, the strong role of extra-parliamentary parties constrains tendencies towards the personalization of power implied by the term 'presidentialization'.

THE EXECUTIVE FACE

Party leaders' domination of their parties has generally coincided with prime ministers' domination of their executives, for a number of reasons. As outlined above, the powers the constitution gives to the prime minister are significant. The prime minister is invested by the vote of the parliamentary majority before choosing the members of the council of ministers. Given that the investiture process revolves around a debate of the government's programme to the Congress of Deputies, ministers find themselves bound to a particular set of policy aims before they are even appointed (Aragón 2002: 44; Bar 1997: 124).

Spanish prime ministers have also been able to strengthen their position within the executive in other ways, for instance, through the concentration of powers and resources around the prime minister's office in the Palace of the Moncloa. The minister of the presidency, directly responding to the prime minister, has particular responsibility for coordinating parliamentary bills, chairing cabinet committees (*comisiones delegadas del gobierno*) and for overseeing the work of central state representatives in the seventeen regional governments (*comunidades autónomas*) (Bar 1997: 119–22). The post of deputy prime minister for economic affairs (*vicepresidente económico*) has, for much of the post-Franco period, operated from the Moncloa complex, indicating the prime minister's close monitoring of economic policy (Heywood and Molina 2000). The sheer size of the Moncloa complex, with 1,500 employees in the mid-1990s, gives a clear indication of the material and human resources available to the prime minister. These resources are a source of prime ministerial autonomy not only from parliament, but also from the rest of the government, contributing to the presidentialization of the system as a whole (ibid.). The gradual expansion of the Moncloa complex has enhanced the 'presidential' nature of the Spanish executive over the quarter century of democratic government.

This quasi-presidential dominance is enhanced by the length of tenure of prime ministers in the post-Franco period: between 1977 and 2006 the keys to the Moncloa changed hands only four times (see Table 5.1). If we exclude the brief period of office of Leopoldo Calvo Sotelo (1981–2), each of the other four incumbents have had sufficiently long tenures to 'personalize' the prime minister's office. This is most notable in the case of Felipe González, whose dominance of Spanish politics during his fourteen years in office spawned the term *felipismo*, but the same dynamics have been observable in the cases of Suárez and Aznar. However, prime ministerial autonomy has fluctuated considerably over this period, and individual leaders have faced constraints on their ability to presidentialize their office. This variation over time, analysed in the remainder of this section, offers some indication of the conditions under which presidentialization takes place.

The Union of the Democratic Centre (1977–82): Prime ministerial
dominance and the parliamentary backlash

The UCD, the party formed by Prime Minister Adolfo Suárez to direct the transition to democracy, governed Spain for five years until the Socialist Party's landslide victory in 1982. Suárez was initially extraordinarily dominant: his electoral popularity, the prime minister's control over the highly centralized and largely unaccountable set of state institutions inherited from the dictatorship, and his pivotal role in the negotiations leading up to the constitutional settlement of 1978, all contributed to presidentializing the prime ministerial office (Hopkin 1999: chs. 2–3). For instance, the constituent negotiations with the Socialist and regionalist opposition had essentially bypassed both the parliamentary party and most of the executive, being controlled directly by the prime minister through his closest ally Fernando Abril (Hopkin 1999: ch. 3).

The fact that this apparent presidentialization unravelled so swiftly in the 1979–81 period confirms that Suárez's strong position was contingent on a variety of short-term political factors (Hopkin 1999: chs. 4–5; Gunther and Hopkin 2002). In 1977–9, most legislation was pacted with the opposition forces, so the UCD's minority position had little effect, but after 1979 the Socialists adopted a more combative approach, leaving Suárez constantly short of parliamentary support. The government's weaknesses undermined Suárez's popularity and the party factions least close to Suárez became increasingly critical to the point of challenging the prime minister's authority quite openly in an extraordinary meeting held in secret outside Madrid (the so-called *Casa de la Pradera*). One of the main bones of contention was Suárez's extensive delegation of powers to unelected advisers based in the Moncloa palace (the so-called *fontaneros* or 'plumbers'), whose policy responsibilities undermined the position of the government ministers.

The decline of personal authority within the executive in this period is clearly indicated by a series of unplanned and difficult cabinet reshuffles in which Suárez was forced to include his main party rivals inside the executive (Hopkin 1999: ch. 4; Huneeus 1985). Suárez's last government before his resignation, formed in September 1980, consisted of twenty-six ministers, compared to an average government size of just seventeen ministers for the rest of the 1977–2000 period (Linz et al. 2002: 82). Although the UCD's internal statutes placed Suárez in a cast-iron position, internal opposition in the parliamentary party forced him into resignation in 1981, and his replacement, Leopoldo Calvo Sotelo, failed to resolve the party's internal divisions (Hopkin 1999: ch. 6). The experience of the UCD, which concluded with electoral humiliation, demonstrates neatly that party cohesion is a precondition for presidentialization in the Spanish case, and that this cohesion cannot be taken for granted, even in apparently highly centralized party organizations.

The rise and fall of 'Felipismo': Socialists in power 1982–96

With the Socialists' electoral victory in 1982 the balance shifted abruptly. Not only was the new prime minister firmly in command of his party to an extent that had never been true for his predecessors, the Socialists also had a comfortable parliamentary majority which made Felipe González's first government more or less immune to parliamentary blackmail. González centralized decision-making mechanisms in order to ensure cohesion in executive–parliamentary group relations (Capo Giol et al. 1990: 107–10; López Garrido 1985). This had the effect of crushing internal opposition, and ensuring that even the most controversial policies—for instance the government's 'U-turn' on NATO membership in 1986, which was opposed by large swathes of the party grass roots—did not threaten the authority of the prime minister. The sustainability of this strategy was heavily dependent on the electoral appeal of the party leader, and his ability to control internal party structures through his deputy Alfonso Guerra.

The relative cohesiveness of the González governments is confirmed by a much lower ministerial turnover than in the UCD period, and the relatively smaller size of the government (Linz et al. 2002: 82–3). The González–Guerra partnership was key to this. As prime minister and deputy prime minister, González and Guerra were until 1991 (when Guerra resigned) the only members of the government who were simultaneously members of the PSOE executive committee. This placed other ministers in a markedly weaker position, since the prime minister and his deputy could invoke the authority of the extra-parliamentary party machinery to suppress any dissent within the government.

However, as the Socialists' parliamentary majority declined over time, González's dominant position within the government declined too, and in his third and fourth governments (the latter a minority administration dependent on external support) ministerial turnover accelerated (Heywood 1995: 93). There are two key factors behind González's declining authority in the later part of his period in office. First, the Socialists' electoral decline signalled a decline in the party leader's electoral position at the same time as it weakened the government's parliamentary position (it was one seat short of a majority). This meant that González could no longer invoke his own electoral appeal in internal conflicts. Second, closely related to these developments, the party's internal cohesion was undermined by a corruption scandal which forced Alfonso Guerra out of the government, opening up a gap between government and the party organization. A further wave of corruption scandals weakened González's authority in the country, encouraging internal opponents to come out into the open.

However, even under the pressure of a hostile public opinion and difficult parliamentary arithmetic, González still maintained considerable authority within his government and the party as a whole, indicating the degree to which his power as party and government leader rested on his own personal charisma and appeal. One indication of this is that even when Guerra began to act as an internal opponent to González within the party (after 1991), the prime minister was still able to exclude Guerra's own allies from the government, appointing his own supporters, and even a number of 'independents' from outside the Socialist Party (Amodia 1994: 189). In the 1993–6 parliament, González's position was under challenge both in the parliamentary and the intra-party arenas, yet he was still effectively able to manage and control his Cabinet. González is therefore a far better example of presidentialization than Suárez, in that his position as party leader and prime minister rested in large part on his own personal charisma and his historic role as leader of the Socialist Party throughout the intense period of the transition to democracy (Heywood 1995: 95).

Presidentialization or party control? Aznar in government 1996–2004

It is perhaps early to draw many conclusions on the post-1996 period, given the lack of primary research on intra-government dynamics available for this period. The Socialists' electoral defeat in 1996 ushered in a new prime minister, PP leader José María Aznar, but the essential dynamics of executive–legislative relations changed little, as the new government was again a minority administration forced to rely on political rivals (the Basque and Catalan nationalists) for parliamentary support. Aznar's position was stronger than González's had been in the preceding parliament, because the last Socialist government had been subject to intense media criticism and judicial investigations which placed it on the defensive. However, all parliamentary activity was subject to a nationalist veto that was potentially more threatening to the PP, which was unpopular in the Basque Country and Catalonia.

Aznar's position was immeasurably strengthened by his second electoral victory in 2000, which gave the PP an absolute majority. With the high level of internal party cohesion he achieved, the parliamentary arithmetic once more pushed towards a high degree of government control over the policy process. What is notable about this period is that, despite lacking the personal charisma of Felipe González or Suárez in his first government, Aznar was able to control both government and party very effectively, and there were few serious challenges to his authority. There are two possible explanations for Aznar's dominant position. The first is that, after two decades of electoral failure, Aznar brought his party to government, and his own contribution to this electoral success was recognized by internal party rivals. Moreover, the weakness of the Socialist party in opposition gave Aznar a relatively 'easy ride', and his position as prime minister remained solid, discouraging any internal challenges until the election defeat of March 2004. The second explanation is that, unlike González, Aznar's authority rested essentially on his institutional position as party leader, and tended to integrate representatives of all the party interest groups inside his governments. Even with an absolute majority, Aznar's exercise of presidential power was 'partified' rather than personalized, all the more so since he was publicly committed to leaving office at the end of his second term as prime minister (a promise made in the early 1990s, as González was facing criticism for being 'out of touch' after such a long tenure in office). Aznar's well-trailed departure from office in fact made the presidentialization of his premiership difficult, and enhanced the institutional and party-based elements of his authority.

THE ELECTORAL FACE:
THE PERSONALIZATION OF CAMPAIGNING

The nature of electoral campaigning itself has also pushed Spain in the direction of presidentialization. From the very beginning of the transition period, electoral politics in Spain has been highly personalized (Pasquino 2001; Rospir 1996: 163), and in particular, personalized around the figures of the two main party leaders. There are a number of reasons for this. First of all, the weakness of party organizations in the early stages of the transition was such that party leaders monopolized the public image of their parties. In part due to the consensual nature of the transition, Spanish parties had difficulty mobilizing grass-root supporters, and for a long time Spain had the weakest membership organizations of any European democracy (Mair and van Biezen 2001; Montero 1981). In these circumstances a high degree of personalization was inevitable.

A second factor was the strategic advantage that this personalization brought to the incumbent Prime Minister Adolfo Suárez. Suárez favoured a strongly 'presidential' approach to electoral campaigning for a number of reasons. His party, the UCD, was internally divided, and focusing on the party leader helped hide these divisions. Moreover, Suárez was able to capitalize on his successful stewardship of the transition process to enhance his own image as a political leader. Suárez also controlled important campaigning resources: as a former Director General of Spanish State Television (RTVE), he had a good understanding of the use of modern media for the promotion of political leaders, and a network of close contacts within RTVE, as well as the power to appoint the director (Hopkin 1999: 47). As prime minister, Suárez set the tone of the political campaign, and his decision to personalize the UCD's campaign around himself encouraged the opposition parties to do likewise. The Socialists adopted a similar approach, emphasizing the youthful image of their leader González. The other main opposition parties—the Communists and the conservative Popular Alliance—had less telegenic candidates, and suffered as a result. The success of Suárez's and González's highly personalized campaigns in 1977 therefore established a precedent: all the major parties began to focus on leadership image.

Party leadership was all the more important because of the low degree of ideological and political awareness of the Spanish electorate during the transition period. The majority of voters failed to identify strongly with any political party and tended to bunch around the centre of the left–right ideological scale (Linz 1980). This was an ideal context for electoral competition around personalities rather than ideological or programmatic issues. The UCD exploited this successfully in 1977, and repeated this success in 1979, using even more sophisticated and 'Americanized' campaigning techniques in this second electoral campaign (García Morillo 1979). The party organized spectacular but politically vacuous rallies, enlisted 'apolitical' media personalities to express support for the party, and generally adopted a 'show business' style campaign, including the famous *chicas UCD*, young women wearing T-shirts decorated with the party symbol (ibid.). A key moment of the 1979 campaign was a dramatic televised appeal by Suárez on the evening before the vote, with no right of reply, urging Spaniards to reject the risks of Socialism and vote for UCD. The importance of personalized leadership in these inter-party battles is confirmed by survey data. Voters in the transition period were very aware of the different party leaders, and electoral research suggested that evaluations of party leaders were a significant factor in determining the vote (Gunther et al. 1986: ch. 8; Sani 1986).

This emphasis on highly personalized leadership, channelled through the modern mass media, continued in the period of Socialist dominance: González was equally keen to exploit his popular image for electoral purposes (Amodia 1990, 1994), and the Socialist administration was equally reluctant to relinquish its political control of the state television network (Heywood 1995: 172). As well as confirming the bias towards the incumbent party, RTVE broadcasting in the Socialist period contributed decisively to the presidentialization of electoral campaigning, focusing attention on national party leaders even during regional and local electoral campaigns (Gunther et al. 2000: 82–3, note 42). The opposition *Alianza Popular/Partido Popular*, first under Fraga, and then under the youthful leadership of Aznar, placed similar emphasis on leadership image (Pasquino 2001: 195).

This leader-oriented style of political competition culminated in the adoption in 1993 of televised debates between the two main party leaders during the election campaign (Heywood 1995: 172; Rospir 1996: 164–5). Studies have shown that the second of the 1993 debates, in which González gave a bravura performance to reverse his 'defeat' by Aznar in the first debate, had a significant impact on the vote (Gunther et al. 2000: 68–9; Wert 1994). By encouraging voters to see the election as a choice between two leaders, these televised debates suggest a high level of presidentialization. Aznar's refusal to accept such a debate in the 1996 campaign put an end to that particular experiment, and Spanish legislative elections have not entirely lost their 'parliamentary' character, in part due to the involvement of minority nationalist parties in the governmental majorities between 1993 and 2000. But media coverage of politics has continued to accentuate the role of party leaders at the expense of other representatives of the main political forces. Even Aznar's refusal to participate in a leadership debate in 1996 is consistent with a leader-oriented strategy. In 1993, the PP leader needed to develop and strengthen his image, whereas in 1996 he needed to protect the image he had achieved; in both cases, the importance of leadership for the party's electoral fortunes was clear.

In part, of course, this is the consequence of the conscious strategies of the party leaders themselves. The PP's political strategy in the first half of the 1990s was clearly oriented towards undermining Felipe González's image with accusations of corruption and dishonesty, while presenting the modest tax inspector José María Aznar as an unspectacular but honest alternative. Aznar personalized the political debate by directly inviting González to resign—'váyase Señor González' (Aguilar 2000: 190). In turn, González himself, recognizing the dangers of a resurgent PP, took personal charge of the Socialists' 1993 election campaign, relegating the rest of the party leadership to a secondary role (Pérez-Díaz 1996: 92). While in 1989, González had addressed only nine party rallies during the election campaign, in 1993 he addressed twenty-one (Amodia 1994: 184), mounting 'the most highly personalized campaign since 1977' (ibid.).

These choices can only be fully understood in terms of the nature of party organization in post-Franco Spain, since presidentialization is a function of the inability or refusal of party organizations to fulfill their traditional role of supporting and constraining their leaders. Like most other West European parties, Spanish parties lack the human and financial resources to engage in labour-intensive and long-term mobilization of social support, and focus instead on rather short-term and capital-intensive means of attracting voters. Moreover, party identification and interest in politics (Pasquino 2001: 208–9) remain rather low in Spain, which means that a large proportion of votes are at least potentially 'up for grabs', accentuating the importance of electoral campaigns. These campaigns, given the organizational limitations mentioned above, tend to imply a heavy use of television, which is amenable to a high degree of personalization of the political battle. The institutional and organizational context of political communication therefore favours presidentialization.

The personalized nature of inter-party competition in Spain has varied relatively little over the democratic period, despite significant changes in the Spanish media since the 1970s. Most importantly, the television market has been liberalized. In the 1970s, the state television company, RTVE, was the only provider of television programming, and as a legacy of the dictatorship remained under tight government control throughout the transition period (Roldán Ros 1985: 265). Although the UCD came under a significant degree of pressure from the Socialist opposition to reform RTVE, things changed little in the initial period of Socialist dominance, as the new government came to realize the advantages of the existing arrangements (Hooper 1986: ch. 11). Only in 1990 were three new private channels allowed to begin transmitting. The expansion of the television market was matched by a steady increase in TV viewing in Spain (Gunther et al. 2000: 58), which by the 1990s made Spaniards the most assiduous TV watchers in Europe after the British. However, there does not seem to be any relationship between the changes in the media environment and the degree of personalization of electoral politics, which has remained broadly constant throughout the post-Franco period. To this extent, Spanish parties' adoption of a 'catch-all' model of party organization and party competition, through which leaders are able to reach beyond traditional cleavage boundaries on the basis of a very personalized appeal (Pasquino 2001: 194–5), seems to offer the best explanation of the presidentialization of electoral politics.

CONCLUSIONS: HOW AND WHY PRESIDENTIALIZATION VARIES

This chapter has argued that there are clear tendencies towards presidentialization in the Spanish political system, but also countervailing factors which to some extent redress the balance. Institutional arrangements strengthen the position of party leaders and the head of the executive, and these arrangements have remained more or less constant throughout the period analysed here. Features of party competition, in particular the nature of party organization, also tend to militate in favour of the presidentialization of Spanish democracy. However, party competition does not always work in favour of leadership autonomy, and the nature of party organization, as the previous section has argued, in some ways acts as a constraint on presidentialization. Moreover, these factors do not move neatly in any clear direction over time. Spanish democracy can therefore be described as a hybrid: parliamentarism with some features of presidentialism (Aragón 2002).

The empirical record assessed in this chapter confirms this mixed picture. First of all, we would conclude that there is no clear evidence of a gradual presidentialization of Spanish democracy over the post-Franco period. Instead, the new Spanish democracy was presidentialized from the very beginning, and the difficulties of establishing mass party organizations in what was in many ways already a post-industrial society ensured that this presidentialized style of government would persist. As a result, the status and autonomy of prime ministers have fluctuated over time with no clear pattern or direction, affected by contingent factors. Second, we suggest that the kinds of structural changes which could promote a greater degree of presidentialization do not point unequivocally in any one direction in the Spanish case. There has been an expansion of mass communications in post-Franco Spain, but modern media were already well established in the 1970s, and party leaders have used these media fairly effectively from the first democratic elections in 1977. Electoral politics in Spain is very personalized, but has been from the beginning of the transition. Party organizations have been informally, and to some extent formally, very centralized from the outset, but if anything, have become more institutionalized over time and more able to impose constraints on their leaders.

In short, presidentialization has varied considerably throughout a period in which the main structural factors addressed in this book have either remained constant or moved in contradictory directions. This suggests that the key to explaining the degree of presidentialization of Spanish democracy lies in intra- and inter-party dynamics, and in the characteristics of leaders themselves. Electoral strength, the personal appeal of the governing party's leader, and leadership control over the governing party organization, are key factors in presidentialization. Charismatic leaders have personalized their office more than less charismatic ones, electorally strong parties have conceded more powers to their leaders than electorally struggling ones. In conclusion, the variations in the exercise of presidential authority in Spain appear to us to rest on contingent rather than structural factors. Spain has strongly 'presidential' tendencies, but its constitutional arrangements can also accommodate the reassertion of parliamentary power. In this sense, it has become quite a flexible institutional arrangement where political authority can shift in line with the unpredictable evolution of party politics.

NOTE

1. Given Andalucia voted first (the vote followed alphabetical order), Guerra was able to set the tone for the vote of the whole provincial organization (Gillespie 1989: 350).

REFERENCES

Aguilar, M. A. (2000). 'Los medios de comunicación', in J. Tusell (ed.), *El Gobierno de Aznar. Balance de una gestión 1996–2000*. Barcelona: Crítica, 181–208.

Amodia, J. (1990). 'Personalities and Slogans: The Spanish Election of October 1989', *West European Politics*, 13: 293–8.

—— (1994). 'A Victory Against All the Odds: The Declining Fortunes of the Spanish Socialist Party', in R. Gillespie (ed.), *Mediterranean Politics*, 171–90.

Aragón, M. (2002). 'Un parlamentarismo presidencialista?' *Claves de Razón Práctica*, 123: 42–9.

Bar, A. (1997). 'Spain: A Prime Ministerial Government', in J. Blondel and F. Müller-Rommel (eds.), *Cabinets in Western Europe*, 2nd edn. Basingstoke: Macmillan, 116–35.

van Biezen, I. (2000). 'On the Internal Balance of Party Power: Party Organizations in New Democracies', *Party Politics*, 6: 395–417.

—— (2003). *Political Parties in New Democracies: Party Organization in Southern and East-Central Europe*. Basingstoke: Palgrave Macmillan.

Capo Giol, J., R. Cotarelo, D. López Garrido, and J. Subirats (1990). 'By Consociationalism to a Majoritarian Parliamentary System: The Rise and Decline of the Spanish Cortes', in U. Liebert and M. Cotta (eds.), *Parliament and Democratic Consolidation in Southern Europe*. London: Pinter, 92–130.

Colomé, G. (1998). 'The PSOE: The Establishment of a Governmental Party', in P. Ignazi and C. Ysmal (eds.), *The Organization of Political Parties in Southern Europe*. London: Praeger, 270–80.

Cotarelo, R. G. and L. López Nieto (1988). 'Spanish Conservatism, 1976–1987', *West European Politics*, 11: 80–95.

de Esteban, J. and L. López Guerra (1985). 'Electoral Rules and Candidate Selection', in H. R. Penniman and M.-L. Eusebio (eds.), *Spain at the Polls: 1977, 1979 and 1982*. Durham: Duke University Press, 48–72.

García-Guereta, (2001). *Factores Externos e Internos en la Transformación de los Partidos Políticos: el Caso de AP-PP*. Madrid: Centro de Estudios Avanzados en Ciencias Sociales.

García Morillo, J. (1979). 'El desarrollo de la campaña', in J. de Esteban and L. López Guerra (eds.), *Las elecciones legislativas del 1 de marzo de 1979*. Madrid: CIS, 189–291.

Gillespie, R. (1989). *The Spanish Socialist Party: A History of Factionalism*. Oxford: Clarendon Press.

Gunther, R. and J. Hopkin (2002). 'A Crisis of Institutionalization: The Collapse of the UCD in Spain', in R. Gunther, J. R. Montero, and J. Linz (eds.), *Political Parties: Old Concepts and New Challenges*. Oxford: Oxford University Press, 191–232.

—— , J. R. Montero, and J. I. Wert (2000). 'The Media and Politics in Spain: From Dictatorship to Democracy', in R. Gunther and A. Mughan (eds.), *Democracy and the Media: A Comparative Perspective*. Cambridge: Cambridge University Press, 28–84.

—— G. Sani, and G. Shabad (1986). *Spain After Franco. The Making of a Competitive Party System*. Berkeley: University of California Press.

Herrero de Miñón, M. (1993). *Memorias de estío*. Madrid: Temas de Hoy.

Heywood, P. (1991). 'Governing a New Democracy: The Power of the Prime Minister in Spain', *West European Politics*, 14: 97–115.

—— (1995). *The Government and Politics of Spain*. London: Macmillan.

—— (1999). 'Power Diffusion or Concentration? In Search of the Spanish Policy Process', *West European Politics*, 21: 103–23.

—— and I. Molina (2000). 'A Quasi-Presidential Premiership: Administering the Executive Summit in Spain', in B. G. Peters, R. Rhodes, and V. Wright (eds.), *Administering the Summit: Administration of the Core Executive in Developed Countries*. London: Palgrave.

Holliday, I (2002). 'Spain: Building a Parties State in a New Democracy' in P. Webb, D. M. Farrell, and I. Holliday (eds.), *Political Parties in Advanced Industrial Democracies*. Oxford: Oxford University Press.

Hooper, J. (1986). *The Spaniards*. London: Penguin.

Hopkin, J. (1999). *Party Formation and Democratic Transition in Spain: the Creation and Collapse of the Union of the Democratic Centre*. London: Macmillan.

—— (2001). 'Bringing the Members Back In? Democratising Candidate Selection in Britain and Spain', *Party Politics*, 7: 343–61.

Huneeus, C. (1985). *La Unión de Centro Democrático y la Transición a la Democracia en España*. Madrid: Centro de Investigaciones Sociológicas.

Katz, R. S. and P. Mair (1995). 'Changing Models of Party Organization: The Emergence of the Cartel Party', *Party Politics*, 1: 5–28.

King, A. (1976). 'Modes of Executive-Legislative Relations: Great Britain, France and West Germany', *Legislative Studies Quarterly*, 1: 11–36.

Linz, J. (1980). 'The New Spanish Party System', in R. Rose (ed.), *Electoral Participation: A Comparative Analysis*. London: Sage, 101–89.

—— and M. Jérez (with S. Corzo) (2002). 'Ministers and Regimes in Spain: From the First to the Second Restoration (1874–2002)', *South European Society and Politics*, 7: 41–116.

López Garrido, D. (1985). 'Gobierno y Parlamento: Dos Modelos de Relaciones Internas (UCD y PSOE)', in *El Gobierno en la Constitución Española y en los Estatutos de Autonomía*. Barcelona: Diputación de Barcelona, 231–43.

Mair, P. and I. van Biezen (2001). 'Party Membership in Twenty European Democracies, 1980–2000', *Party Politics*, 7: 5–22.

Maurer, L. (1999). 'Parliamentary Influence in a New Democracy: The Spanish Congress', *Journal of Legislative Studies*, 5: 24–45.

Méndez, M. (1998). *Organising for Victory . . . and Defeat? The Organisational Strategy of the Spanish Workers' Socialist Party (1975–1996)*. Ph.D. thesis, European University Institute, Florence.

Montero, J. R. (1981). 'Partidos y Participación Política: Algunas Notas sobre la Afiliación Política en la Etapa Inicial de la Transición Española', *Revista de Estudios Políticos*, 23: 33–72.

—— (1989). 'Los Fracasos Políticos y Electorales de la Derecha Española: Alianza Popular, 1976–1987', in J. F. Tezanos, R. Cotarelo, and A. de Blas (eds.), *La Transición Democrática Española*. Madrid: Sistema, 495–542.

—— F. Llera, and M. Torcal (1992). 'Sistemas electorales en España: una recapitulación', *Revista Española de Investigaciones Sociológicas*, 58: 7–56.

Pasquino, G. (2001). 'The New Campaign Politics in Southern Europe', in N. Diamandouros and R. Gunther (eds.), *Parties, Politics, and Democracy in the New Southern Europe*. Baltimore: Johns Hopkins University Press, 183–223.

Pérez-Díaz, V. (1996). *España puesta a prueba 1976–96*. Madrid: Alianza.

Puhle, H.-J. (2001). 'Mobilizers and Late Modernizers: Socialist Parties in the New Southern Europe', in N. Diamandouros and R. Gunther (eds.), *Parties, Politics, and Democracy in the New Southern Europe*. Baltimore: Johns Hopkins University Press, 268–328.

Roldán Ros, J. (1985). 'The Media and the Elections', in H. Penniman and M.-L. Eusebio (eds.), *Spain at the Polls, 1977, 1979 and 1982*. Durham: Duke University Press, 253–73.

Rospir, J. (1996). 'Political Communication and Electoral Campaigns in the Young Spanish Democracy', in D. Swanson and P. Mancini (eds.), *Politics, Media and Modern Democracy*. Westport, CT: Praeger, 155–69.

Sani, G. (1986). 'Los Desplazamientos del Electorado: Anatomía del Cambio', in J. J. Linz and J. R. Montero (eds.), *Crisis y Cambio: Electores y Partidos en la España de los Años Ochenta*. Madrid: Centro de Estudios Constitucionales, 1–26.

Wert, J. I. (1994). 'Perspectivas de Reforma del Régimen Electoral: Campañas, Medios de Comunicación y Encuestas Electorales', in J. R. Montero, R. Gunther, J. I. Wert, J. Santamaría, and M. Abad (eds.), *La Reforma del Régimen Electoral*. Madrid: Centro de Estudios Constitucionales.

6

The Low Countries: From 'Prime Minister' to President-Minister

Stefaan Fiers and André Krouwel

INTRODUCTION: THE PRESIDENTIALIZATION OF CONSENSUS DEMOCRACIES?

Ever since Lijphart characterized the Dutch political system as a 'consociational democracy', this concept has become widely used to characterize several European countries, including Austria, Belgium, and Switzerland (Daalder 1987; Lijphart 1968, 1977, 1994, 1999; Luther and Deschouwer 1999). Historically, heterogeneous societies in both Belgium and the Netherlands resulted in consociational democracies characterized by broad multiparty coalitions, numerous other power-sharing devices, and fragile checks and balances in order to ensure due influence for all relevant minority groups (Lijphart 1968; Luther and Deschouwer, 1999). In Belgium, moreover, the division between French-speaking and Dutch-speaking parties, and the process of federalization fragmented the political landscape further and resulted in a political system with numerous devices of power dispersion.

The overarching logic of consensus democracies, that is, power-sharing between various political groups, would seem to represent an obstacle to a process of presidentialization. However, one of the main characteristics of parties' internal life in a consociational system is the need for strong leadership, as 'elites must be able to make the most appropriate strategic choices without being constantly challenged about these choices' (Deschouwer 1994: 80). So, within the last two decades, (parliamentary) party leaders and prime ministers alike both in Belgium[1] and the Netherlands have acquired more prominent and powerful positions, shifting these consensus democracies in the direction of 'presidentialized' parliamentary systems.[2] This process of presidentialization gained momentum in the Netherlands a decade earlier than it did in Belgium. During the 1970s, Joop Den Uyl (PvdA) and Dries Van Agt (CDA) exploited an already rudimentary tradition of strong Dutch prime ministers (van den Berg 1990), while Ruud Lubbers (CDA) and Wim Kok (PvdA) carved out an even more dominant role during the 1980s and

1990s. In the Belgian 'partitocracy', this presidentialization only became obvious in the 1980s, when Prime Minister Wilfried Martens (CVP) broke the almost absolute power of the extra-parliamentary party leaders. His successors, Jean-Luc Dehaene (CVP) and Guy Verhofstadt (VLD), could clearly show themselves to be 'strong' prime ministers, with pronounced styles of governing.

It is important to point out that these developments have taken place despite there having been virtually no significant changes in the prime ministers' constitutional rights or formal political prerogatives. At face value, the systemic features and institutional formats of both countries even provide clear constraints on tendencies towards presidentialization. First, the roles and competencies of the prime minister are not constitutionally defined. In Belgium, it took until 1970, before the existence of a prime minister was recognized in the constitution, despite the fact that the title of 'Prime Minister' was introduced in 1918 (Plavsic 1988),[3] while the Dutch prime minister was given constitutional status only in 1983 (Rehwinkel 1991). Second, the constitutional position in both countries is that prime ministers are only *primus inter pares*, first among equals, which implies that formally they are no more powerful than their fellow ministers. Prime ministers have no specific legal resources at their disposal by which to assert their authority. According to former Belgian Prime Minister Dehaene, they thus have to derive their authority primarily from their own personality and experience (Dehaene 2000).

Clearly, then, the recent increase in authority of Dutch and Belgian prime ministers has occurred virtually in the absence of constitutional modification (Andeweg 1988, 1990, 1997; Eyskens 1983). The only exception is a recent change to the Belgian constitution, which served to strengthen the position of the prime minister there. In 1993 a constructive vote of no-confidence was introduced, meaning that parliament could only bring down a government when a majority, involving at least four parties, agreed on a new prime minister. This is a radical departure from the days when the fate of the prime minister was in the hands of the extra-parliamentary leaders of the coalition parties who often threatened to bring down the government in order to influence governments' policy.

Beyond the fact of their weakly defined constitutional role, it is difficult for prime ministers in the Low Countries to dominate the political arena on their own. First of all, they are not directly elected by voters, and are formally appointed by their national monarchs. In reality, prime ministers are selected in a (frequently) lengthy process of government formation involving complex intra- and inter-party negotiations. Since 1919, only seven out of sixty-one Belgian governments have been single-party formations, of which only three lasted for more than three months. The only three Dutch single-party governments in the post-war era have all been interim cabinets after the downfall of coalitions (Woldendorp et al. 2000). Typically, governments in the Low Countries are broad multiparty coalitions committing themselves to extensive agreements (De Winter et al. 2000; Timmermans 1994; Timmermans and Andeweg 2000) which limit the premier's freedom of action (Eyskens 1983).[4] On top of that, in both countries each coalition party provides a vice-prime minister and the government rules as a collective body by consensus (Andeweg 1990). This means that it is relatively difficult for one politician to dominate the executive arena since a variety of leading politicians from all of the major parties are usually involved in the nomination of ministerial recruits and the decision-making process.

Nevertheless, in spite of the various constraints which apply, prime ministers have managed to become more predominant in the Low Countries in recent decades. Even though their power resources and zones of autonomy seem relatively limited, the consensual nature of the policy process and the specific style of intra-cabinet decision-making provide them with an opportunity structure in which it is possible to extend their zones of autonomy through skilful performance over time.

THE EXECUTIVE FACE

The emergence of modern national political parties led to an extensive fusion of executive and legislative powers in Belgium and the Netherlands. This strengthened the position of the cabinet versus parliament, and subsequently of the prime minister within the executive (Raalte 1954). In Belgium, the formal separation between executive and legislative powers became stricter through the constitutional changes of 1993. Yet, this was counterbalanced by the process of federalization and the introduction of a constructive vote of no-confidence that strengthened the position of the prime minister. In both countries prime ministers also became more powerful vis-à-vis their party organizations and they increased their autonomy within the executive.

Limited control over ministerial recruitment...

Prime ministers in the Netherlands and Belgium have 'little or no influence on the composition of their own cabinet' (Andeweg 1991: 116; Dewachter 1995). In Belgium, up until 1999, the bargaining process at federal level was further complicated by the concurrent process of government formation at the regional level.[5] Although cases of cross-party obstruction to ministerial appointments have been reported (as was the case in the Netherlands in the 1960s when ARP-leader Biesheuvel refused to govern with certain nominees of the Catholic People's Party), ministerial recruitment is clearly the prerogative of the parliamentary and extra-parliamentary party leaderships. This means that the Belgian and Dutch prime ministers, unlike their French and British colleagues, cannot decide on cabinet reshuffles or dismiss ministers at will, not even those from their own party (Andeweg 1988, 1991).[6] In Belgium this role as 'kingmaker' is primarily the privilege of a small group of extra-parliamentary party leaders who select ministerial candidates single-handedly (Dewachter 1995; Fiers 1998). The prerogative of nomination is therefore one of the most powerful assets of these party politicians, because it provides the opportunity to decide upon the careers of both friends and foes within their party. However, Prime Ministers Dehaene and Verhofstadt have played more prominent roles in the few cabinet reshuffles that have taken place over the last decade.

Despite this limited control over cabinet composition, prime ministers in the Low Countries have become more predominant because of an important change concerning their route to power. Recruitment of the prime minister has shifted from the coalition negotiations to the intra-party leadership selection process for parliamentary elections. Before the early 1970s, Dutch parties tended to have multiple leaderships[7] and the prime minister was only proposed during coalition negotiations. Dutch Christian Democrats were even wont to recruit their prime ministers from the parliamentary back-benches. Since 1971—for all parties—there has been a shift from multiple leaderships (between six and thirteen individuals for each party) to a single leader (Toonen 1992: 91). Nowadays the 'national leader' (*lijsttrekker*) of the largest party entering government in the Netherlands becomes the prime minister almost automatically (Rehwinkel 1991: 33; Van den Berg 1990: 98). As a result, parliamentary elections have now turned into popular elections to decide the prime minister, while intra-party leadership elections have become the functional equivalent of prime ministerial primaries. The PvdA has recently introduced direct elections for the *lijsttrekker* and other parties are moving in the same direction.[8] Their popular mandates through general elections and their often substantial (prime) ministerial experience enhance the status of prime ministers (Andeweg 1991: 123).

Likewise, the road to power in Belgium usually runs through the official party leadership.[9] Formally, it is the king who selects the prime minister by appointing a *formateur* after the elections, but the monarch's choice is normally limited to the leader of the largest party in parliament, or the party which has made the most significant electoral gain. Moreover, since the 1993 constitutional change, another factor works in favour of the official party leaders, as they (or the incumbent prime minister) head the electoral lists for the Senate. These nationwide lists are regarded as a kind of semi-direct election for the prime ministerial position. Whoever wins this 'clash of titans' will have the opportunity to make the first move in the post-election game of coalition building.

... Yet increasing decision-making autonomy

We have suggested that there have been only minor extensions of formal prerogatives of Belgian and Dutch prime ministers (Van den Berg 1990). Nevertheless, over time, prime ministers in both countries have enhanced their autonomy in matters of cabinet decision-making primarily because of the increasing need for policy coordination and intra-executive brokerage. Slowly, but surely, there has been an abandonment of the pure *primus inter pares* position of prime ministers (Schagen 1995), allowing them to take up a more predominant role in policy development and coordination. This has been caused by at least two, and in Belgium three, factors.

The first is that Belgian and Dutch prime ministers are not usually in charge of a ministerial department or specific policy area and can thus focus almost exclusively on policy coordination.[10] The Dutch prime minister heads the small department of 'General Affairs', responsible for policy oversight and coordination, as well as press relations (Andeweg 1991: 118). As Rose says (1982: 43), this leaves the prime ministers 'in a unique position... to see government as a whole'. Moreover, the need for coordination has increased with a rise in the number of cabinet ministers and the process of European integration.

In Belgium the need for coordination became even more pressing as the federalization process generated some seven policy levels after 1970.[11] Constitutional changes in 1993 provided yet greater autonomy for the regions, since then the federal prime minister's coordinating role has been combined with an increasingly outspoken role as arbiter. When conflicts arise between regional governments, the regional minister-presidents often turn to the federal prime minister to mediate, a tendency exacerbated by the fact that the regional governments have very few direct lines of communication between each other. Furthermore, federalization strengthens the federal prime minister by downgrading the influence of departmental ministers relative to him. During the prolonged course of the federalization process, nearly all federal ministries (except for Defence and Finance) have either been split up or lost at least some competences in favour of regional governments. This has inevitably diminished the influence of federal ministers, while the prime minister's powers remain untouched. As a result, the premier enjoys both a strategic and psychological advantage over his cabinet colleagues.

On top of these advantages, King (1994: 161) identifies a second factor strengthening prime ministers, which he coins 'summitry'. A more presidential profile has been achieved in the media, as a result of 'the increasing tendency for prime ministers from different countries to meet and do business with one another, especially under the aegis of the European Community'. Since the prime ministers of both Belgium and the Netherlands are mentioned in the Single European Act of 1979, their positions have been strengthened (especially vis-à-vis their respective ministers of Foreign Affairs). While foreign policy has primarily been the prerogative of the minister of foreign affairs (especially in the Netherlands, where ministers have been careful not to encroach upon each other's policy areas), the prime minister is nowadays increasingly involved in foreign affairs and often acts as the main national spokesperson at summit meetings (Andeweg 1991: 126). Increasing visibility is an important spin-off effect of this development. Voters see their prime minister on European Councils or NATO summits interacting with world leaders like the British prime minister, the German chancellor, and even the president of the United States. Andeweg (1997: 238) observes that summitry has even been used as an argument in favour of the direct election of the prime minister, in order 'to put the Dutch prime minister on a par with his colleagues in the European Council'. Clearly, the prestige acquired via summitry can be used as a power resource within the domestic political sphere. An illustration of this is provided by Jean-Luc Dehaene. As a result of the credibility Dehaene built through almost being selected as President of the European Commission at the Corfu Summit in 1994, his domestic popularity climbed to an unprecedented level. This was manifest in a remarkable change of attitude towards his person and his government by both the press and his own CVP party (De Ridder 1996). Equally, however, Dehaene demonstrates how a politician's domestic position can be undermined by the perception that he might not be suited to the demands of international summitry. In 1988, King Baudouin of Belgium refused to name the new coalition's *formateur* Dehaene as prime minister, for fear that his unconventional style would harm the country's image. As one commentator put it at the time, the royal entourage sensed that Dehaene 'would not be representative enough for the country, given the leading role of Belgium in the European and international context. Dehaene never showed any interest in international problems, and did not seem to feel at ease on summits. Other sources even go further, and talk about his image, his language, and his unconventional performance...' (De Ridder 1989, *our translation*).

A third fact, peculiar to the Belgian case, is that Brussels hosts the headquarters of many international organizations, which places the Belgian federal prime minister in a particularly advantageous position, as he meets his foreign counterparts more often than any other European prime minister. After six months in office, Prime Minister Verhofstadt expressed surprise that he had spent half of his time on foreign policy (*De Standaard*, 1 December 1999). Furthermore, summitry is an important asset for the federal Belgian prime minister vis-à-vis the minister-presidents of regional governments, because the latter still have, with few exceptions, no formal access to EU meetings. In short, the role of Belgian and Dutch prime ministers in international summitry, and the media attention they attract thereby, has provided them with a status that exceeds that of all other national political actors.

That said, prime ministers in the Low Countries exert most power over policy-making through the capacity to set their cabinets' agendas. According to Jean-Luc Dehaene, 'the prime minister is the chef in the cabinet's kitchen: he chooses the menu, decides on what goes into the refrigerator, puts the pots in the oven, and decides on the baking-time' (Dehaene 2000: 26, *our translation*). In this process, he has frequent contact with the vice-premiers of all coalition parties in the inner-cabinet (*kerncabinet*). This power of agenda-setting is reinforced by the centralization of decision-making. This is reflected in the growing use of the *kerncabinet*, since the mid-1970s, as the forum for both conflict-prevention and conflict-resolution (Claes 2000). Thus, in 2000, for instance, it met nearly twice as often as the larger Council of Ministers (that is, sixty-four times compared to thirty-eight times).

Dutch prime ministers have also increased their influence over the decision-making process as a result of more frequent cabinet meetings and changing inner-cabinet procedures in recent decades. The Dutch Standing Orders in Council provide the prime minister with some power to decide the frequency of meetings, the timing of issues on the agenda and a decisive voice in matters of conflict between ministers (Andeweg 1991: 117–18; Broeksteeg et al. 2004; Rehwinkel 1991: 16–22; van den Berg 1990: 99). From a comparative perspective the Dutch cabinet has always met exceptionally often, and this frequency has actually grown in the last fifty years. On an average the number of full cabinet meetings increased from seventy-five times a year in the late 1940s to more than 125 times a year into the 1970s. Recently the number of full cabinet meetings has declined somewhat (Andeweg 1990), but they still take place at least once a week. Looked at one way, this could be seen as evidence of the high number of opportunities for collective decision-making. In reality, however, this would be misleading, for, the frequency of the prime minister's bilateral meetings with individual (or subsets of) ministers has also increased, as has the number of meetings with the parliamentary leaders of government parties. This reflects the fact that decision-making within the Dutch cabinet is in fact highly departmentalized, with ministers regarding themselves as representatives of their respective ministries rather than their parties (Andeweg 1990: 26). In addition, the 'non-intervention principle' within Dutch cabinets means that ministers only participate in deliberations when their departmental interests are at stake, thereby rendering collective decision-making within the council of ministers a myth. The Dutch prime minister and the minister of finance are usually the only two cabinet members participating in the discussion of each item on the agenda (Andeweg 1990: 27). Brokerage in the decision-making process has therefore increasingly been vested in the prime minister or has been devolved to various formal and informal 'meetings of sub-councils of ministers'

(Andeweg 1990: 18), or to bilateral negotiations between the prime minister and particular ministers. The full council of ministers only ratifies (and legitimizes) decisions made by individual ministers or sub-councils, whose membership is decided by the prime minister on an ad hoc basis.

Over time, the increasing frequency of inner-cabinet gatherings and bilateral decision-making, combined with the exclusive focus on coordination of government policy, has given the prime ministers of both Belgium and the Netherlands more room for manoeuvre than their formal position as *primus inter pares* would suggest. Indeed, this is highlighted by Dutch plans to formalize the predominance of their prime minister constitutionally by installing him as chair of the National Security Council, and by providing him with a substantially higher wage than his cabinet colleagues.

Professionalization and expansion of the prime ministerial office

Autonomy in decision-making for Dutch and Belgian premiers has also been strengthened by enlargement and professionalization of the prime ministerial office. For a long time, the prime minister's office has been controversial in Belgian politics, because it was regarded as an unnecessary intermediary between the premier and the civil service. Information on the number and nature of civil servants in ministerial offices has been characterized by a degree of secrecy and non-transparency (Van Hassel 1988), but it is believed that their number rose from 750 in 1960, to 1,867 by 1973, and an estimated 3,500 by 1991 (Hondeghem 1996). More recent estimates per minister range from several dozen to 200 staff (De Winter et al. 2000). Notwithstanding the introduction in 1995 of legislation designed to limit the number of people employed in ministerial offices, and Prime Minister Verhofstadt's 1999 pledge to get rid of these personal *cabinets* of advisers, they are still very influential in policy-design.

It is easier to find hard data on the size of ministerial offices in the Netherlands, as the prime minister's office is integrated into the Department of General Affairs. A minimum of ten of its staff (of which there are approximately 350 at present) can be considered policy advisers with extensive access to the prime minister himself (Andeweg 1991: 118; Margés 1989: 207). Each adviser monitors one or more departments and reports to the prime minister weekly. Recent Dutch prime ministers, particularly Kok and Balkenende, have augmented their teams of advisers with party political confidantes and media experts, who cover developments within the parliamentary and extra-parliamentary parties. These agents further increase the informational advantage of Dutch premiers over their ministerial colleagues.

Growing longevity in office of prime ministers
relative to other executive Actors

In both Belgium and the Netherlands, the duration of governments, and thus of prime ministers in office, has increased. Despite government instability in Belgium in the 1940s, 1950s, and 1970s, there is an overall linear and positive trend in government survival. The average duration of Belgian cabinets rose steadily from ten months in the 1970s, to more than twenty months in the 1980s, and over thirty months in the 1990s. The introduction of the constructive vote of no-confidence has been particularly significant in explaining this development. However, greater average longevity of government has been accompanied by more frequent reshuffling of ministerial personnel. While, for instance, the mere two changes in the 1968–71 cabinet were due to the sudden death of ministers in office, eleven of the original seventeen ministers in Dehaene's first cabinet (1992–5) left the cabinet prematurely. None of the substitutions had been caused by the death of a member of the cabinet. Instead all were due to voluntary or forced retirement of ministers. Thus, while prime ministers have generally been enjoying more extended periods of governmental incumbency, their cabinet colleagues have not. This reflects a 'decline in the collective character of government and a concomitant gain in the individual element, that is, a growing supremacy of the prime minister' (Poguntke 2000). In contrast to Belgium, government stability has always been relatively high in the Netherlands. Nevertheless, it has also grown over time, from an average of thirty months in the 1940s and 1950s to more than thirty-five months in the 1990s. The only periods with lower rates of government survival were the 1960s and early 1970s and the first government of the new millennium, which survived for just eighty-four days. In general, the growing longevity of cabinets in the Low Countries provides Dutch and Belgian prime ministers with more authority over, and decisional autonomy from, other cabinet members and civil servants.

THE PARTY FACE

Three mutually reinforcing processes can explain the increasing control and autonomy of leaderships within parties in Belgium and the Netherlands: the centralization of candidate selection procedures, an accumulation of human and financial resources at leadership level, and the professionalization and specialization of decision-making, which make it increasingly difficult for individual politicians to develop and promote policy alternatives. In addition, in the late 1990s all Belgian and some Dutch parties introduced one of the key elements of presidentialized politics: the direct election of their leaders by rank-and-file members, providing personal mandates to lead and decide on party policy.

The accumulation of power and resources within leader's offices

Before going into detail, it is crucial to point out an important difference between Belgian and Dutch parties in respect of the party face. In the Netherlands, parties have generally accrued material and human capital at the parliamentary level, while Belgian party elites have accumulated their resources at the extra-parliamentary level. By and large, this reflects the way in which already existing power structures have been reinforced by resources from the state (Krouwel 2004). Belgian parties derive a small proportion of their income from membership fees (maximum 10 per cent) and depend primarily on extensive public funding, which constitutes up to 94 per cent of the revenues of the Vlaams Blok (Noppe 2002, 2003). Still, it is important to note that the collection of membership fees was organized by the national party headquarters since the mid-1980s, and that only a part of this sum is redistributed to the local party branches. In former days, the collection of membership fees at local level, which afterwards had to be transferred to the national party organization, constituted an important lever for rebellious local party branches in their battle for autonomy.

As Belgian political parties were under no obligation to publicize their financial accounts prior to 1989, it is impossible to assess the long-term evolution of party budgets with confidence (Deschouwer 1994). However, it seems likely that the parties have gained substantially in financial terms, as illustrated by the PS's income of 2001, which totalled €8,997 million (Noppe 2002); this compares with a figure of €2,168 million in 1990 (Vos 1992). Parties in the Netherlands, on the contrary, are still largely financially dependent on membership contributions due to the low level of direct state support: around 73 per cent to 80 per cent of their income comes from membership fees (Koole 1996: 179; Krouwel 1996, 1999). Still, here, we also witness the development towards political parties as professional campaign machines instead of membership organizations. In the Netherlands, substantial subsidies are given to various types of party activities, such as research, development aid, and youth participation (see Koole 1992), and although these funds are earmarked for specific activities, financial resources and staff are frequently pooled for campaigning purposes.

The distribution of personnel reflects the general pattern of financial resourcing in the two countries: Dutch extra-parliamentary party organizations are generally much smaller in staff than their parliamentary counterparts, while in Belgium the contrary is the case. Early introduction of generous state subsidies for parliamentary parties has resulted in well-resourced and professional parliamentary party organizations in the Netherlands (Katz and Mair 1992; Krouwel 1999, 2004). Direct subsidies to parliamentary parties were introduced in 1964, while assistance for individual MPs was followed in 1968. Belgian MPs gained the right to hire one publicly funded assistant each in 1971. In addition, the two largest parties employed thirty-three (PS) and forty-two (CVP) parliamentary professionals across the various assemblies in the federal state by 2000.[12]

Our overall conclusion is that an increasing quantity of financial and human resources has come under the direct control of the party leaderships and they use these resources for personalized electoral campaign activities (as we shall see below). As a result of direct state subsidies to extra-parliamentary organizations, this development is stronger in Belgium than in the Netherlands. Nevertheless, in view of Dutch developments at the parliamentary level, we can reasonably state that increasing professionalism and capital accumulation at the top party level are common to both countries. This has coincided with the declining importance of party memberships as sources of funding and personnel. In conjunction with directly elected leaders, these developments have increased the decisional autonomy of the party leadership.

Increasing formal power and policy autonomy for party leaders

Party leaders have also increased their grip over internal decision-making processes by other means. Selection procedures for the national party chairperson and parliamentary candidates have been centralized, as have those for drafting party manifestos and the proceedings of national congresses. Once again, the crucial difference is that power has shifted from the extra-parliamentary organization to party representatives in parliament and government in the Netherlands, while the extra-parliamentary party leadership is now dominant in selecting leaders and formulating policy in Belgium (Dewachter 1995; De Winter 1996; Fiers 1998; Katz and Mair 1994). This power shift has taken place even though the party rules define Belgian party leaders' roles only vaguely and attribute virtually no real power to them (Maes 1990). At most, they describe how party leaders are entitled to arbitrate in conflicts and, in the past, the number of members of the party executive they could appoint single-handedly. Even so, Belgian extra-parliamentary party organizations have developed several control mechanisms over their representatives in parliament and government as a result of the development of an *oligopolistic partitocracy* in Belgium, a process which started as early as 1918 (Dewachter and De Winter 1981). As former CVP leader Frank Swaelen (1981–8) testifies: 'Public opinion and the media regard the party leader as *the* oracle of the party and they expect him to declare the definite truth on no matter what issue. They expect him to say: "So be it! This is the party's point of view"' (F. Swaelen, cited in Fiers 1998: 246, *our translation*). Consequently, Belgian parliamentary party groups merely serve as extremely cohesive voting machines (Depauw 2000; De Winter and Dumont 2000). Analysis of party statutes does not reveal crucial formal changes of party leaders' powers in recent decades (Fiers 1998), but the increased number and changing role of media appearances since the end of the 1980s have certainly had an effect on the image of the party leader as the sole spokesperson of the party.

In the Netherlands, power has shifted from the extra-parliamentary organization to the leadership of the parliamentary party and the representatives in government. Andeweg (2000) argues that this shift was caused by the more rapid professionalization of the parliamentary face of the party and the fusion of the policy coordination function between the parliamentary party and government ministers. This reflects the increasing specialization of MPs and the growing importance of parliamentary committees. Some MPs are partisan, some are policy advocates, others are pure specialists, while only a few are 'real parliamentarians' that seek to scrutinize and control the executive. Andeweg (2000) concludes that the Netherlands is en route to become a 'fractiocracy'. The blurring of the distinction between legislature and executive is often referred to as a type of monism, in which political power is concentrated within the parliamentary party leadership and the contingent of ministers in the cabinet. All depends on whether the electoral party leader (*lijsttrekker*) opts for a position in government as prime minister/vice-prime minister or for a role as leader of the parliamentary party.

In sum, the trend towards specialization in policy-making and the subsequent ever-increasing need for policy coordination by leaders of the 'three faces of the party' has augmented the policy autonomy of party elites in both countries. A small group of party leaders, including the prime minister, is able to dominate the policy decisions of their parties, particularly since the elite has become more powerful in internal party decision-making procedures and exerts substantial control over the careers of MPs.

The increased policy autonomy of party leaders can be identified clearly by examining decision-making processes during party conventions. Open conflict over policy and the party programme causes a party to look divided and weak, which can have serious electoral repercussions. Therefore, party conventions have been transformed into carefully orchestrated media events where dissent by the rank-and-file is downplayed in order to create an image of a unified, united organization capable of governing. The national leadership controls the agenda of debate, ensuring that congresses remain 'little more than a forum for the expression of approval' (von Beyme 1985: 235). In Belgium, party conferences mainly serve ideological and electoral purposes (Deschouwer 1994: 87); despite their official status as the highest party body, they are seldom genuinely open forums for policy decisions. The national executives maintain strict control over the agenda and decision-making procedures. Motions are monitored (and sometimes rejected) and their acceptability is evaluated before they are put to the conference (Krouwel 1999). A notable exception among the major parties was the Flemish Liberal party after its reinvention in 1992, but only so long as it remained in opposition.[13] In addition, new, smaller, and more participatory left-wing and environmental parties have adopted more open procedures which permit members to participate in debates. Nevertheless, within most traditional parties—especially when in government—policy decisions remain the prerogative of a core group of national leaders (Laver and Hunt 1992: 84).

Centralized control in matters of candidate-selection

Policy autonomy of the core party leaders (including the prime minister) is high, not only because they determine the agenda at national party conferences, but also because they exert substantial control over the (pre)selection of parliamentary candidates and the national executive. If leaders can determine the composition of the parliamentary party they can compel MPs to accept the policy preferences of the leadership. Both in the Netherlands and particularly in Belgium, selection procedures for MPs have become progressively more centralized over the post-war period. During the 1960s, most Belgian parties held closed primaries (among party members), yet, this tradition was gradually abandoned by the party leadership (De Winter 1988: 42). Instead of the traditional poll, the party executive makes up a so-called 'model list' which needs a two-thirds majority to be rejected. Deschouwer (1994: 96) therefore concludes that 'it is the leadership which has the final word'.

A similar process of centralization has occurred in the major Dutch parties (VVD, PvdA, and CDA) and, to a lesser extent, in the formerly ultra-democratic D66. In many local branches the lists of candidates are not even discussed, and when they are on the agenda only a limited number of party members participate in the decision-making (Hillebrand 1992). Some observers have argued that candidate-selection procedures were decentralized during a wave of democratization in the late 1960s and early 1970s (Koole 1994: 294). However, more recent developments show extensive central control over the selection of parliamentary candidates (Krouwel 1999). In most parties the national leadership 'pre-selects' all the candidates and put them on a so-called 'model list', which party members are subsequently asked to ratify, although D66 and recently the PvdA selected their parliamentary leader through a membership ballot.

Overall, parliamentary candidate-selection in the Low Countries is mainly a prerogative of the national party executive with only formal ratification by active (local) party members. Most parties shy away from giving members, let alone voters, a direct voice in the selection of parliamentary candidates. The practice of primaries and membership ballots has given way to more central control. Regional or local elites usually nominate candidates while party members are at best asked for their approval of these pre-selected candidates. Even when members are given this opportunity, they usually avail of it in very low numbers (Gallagher 1988: 246). Where candidate-selection does take place at the local level, national executives generally maintain tight supervision and control: thus, they generally retain the power of veto as a final safeguard. What seems to be occurring is a move towards a more direct election of the parliamentary party leader by the membership, who then becomes the leader of a core elite within the party that selects the other MPs, some of which move into ministerial position after the election.

Control over party leadership selection

As with parliamentary candidate-selection, the selection of party leaders in Belgium and the Netherlands is primarily an oligarchic process. Party members are, at most, allowed to rubber-stamp decisions at the national party congress or in a postal ballot after they have been taken by the party national leadership. In this respect the selection of an extra-parliamentary party leader is merely a 'horizontal power game' rather than a 'vertical power game' (Müller and Meth-Cohn 1991: 56); the real choice of the party leader remains with the inner-party selectorate (Punnett: 1992). In both countries, the national party leadership (meaning a core group of leaders from the national executive, the parliamentary party and government ministers) has typically maintained firm control over the pre-selection procedure. Despite factionalism in almost all parties, overt challenges to incumbent leaders are rare and party leadership elections in Belgium and the Netherlands are seldom open and competitive. With the notable exception of the VLD in Belgium, where, on a few occasions, members had a choice between several candidates, all other parties usually only present a single candidate to their members (Fiers 1998; Maes 1990). Even the recent introduction (after 1993) in all Belgian parties of party leadership elections by OMOV (one-member–one-vote), combined with a system of open candidacies, barely affected the modest influence of party members. The real choice of the party leader is hardly ever left in the hands of the rank-and-file members.

That said, the introduction of OMOV has had an important consequence for the party leader's position vis-à-vis his fellow party officials.

The personalized mandate enhances the legitimacy of extra-parliamentary party leaders (especially when derived from a high turnout[14]) and lends additional weight to their policy preferences. Backed by their rank-and-file supporters, party leaders find themselves in a much stronger position vis-à-vis other party notables. In a way, and despite the basic idea of democratization, direct leadership elections have thus further strengthened the already powerful position of the party leader within his or her party.

In the Netherlands, where party leaders are far less powerful than their Belgian counterparts, the national executives nevertheless maintain strict control over the pre-selection of prospective extra-parliamentary party leaders. Normally, their choice is confirmed by the national party congress. Since the 1960s there have been few open challenges to the executives' choices: on the rare occasions they have manifested themselves, it has usually been within the PvdA. In the PvdA and new parties, such as D66, more open elections were held in the 1960s and 1970s. Nevertheless, most executives maintained or increased their control over the selection of the extra-parliamentary leadership. Since the merger of the three Christian Democratic parties into the CDA during the 1970s, there have been only sporadic instances where members have even been offered a choice. National executives have usually coopted new party leaders, although recently Christian Democratic party members have been offered a choice between two pre-selected candidates who do not compete on policy. This procedure is also commonplace within the right-wing VVD. Recent electoral defeats of the major parties and declining membership levels have resulted in adoption of OMOV practices within the PvdA. This method of direct election of the party leader is now also debated, but not yet adopted, by other parties.

Centralized control of party congresses, leadership and candidate-selection procedures reinforces the policy autonomy of core groups of party leaders. Within such groups, the prime minister is usually a key player with substantial veto power and most resources and information. Since he is also best informed about the policy preferences of other parties and their ministers, as a result of their coordinating role within cabinet, prime ministers in both countries have been able to increase their policy autonomy significantly in recent decades. These developments have, especially in the Netherlands, transformed relationships within the executive, and between the executive and legislature. Government policy is increasingly identified with the prime minister. More often now than before the prime minister is called to the parliament to defend government policy, and other party leaders debate government policies with the prime minister rather than with the ministers responsible for specific portfolios. In short, politics in the Low Countries is generally oligarchic, but within these small core groups, prime ministers have become more powerful. In combination with more human and financial resources being pooled at the top party level, there are clear trends towards the presidentialization of political parties in the Low Countries.

THE ELECTORAL FACE

Voting behaviour in Belgium and the Netherlands was strikingly stable and predictable until the mid-1960s as religious affiliation and social class largely determined party choice. From the 1960s onwards, confessional parties in both countries began to lose their electoral appeal in a process that became known as de-pillarization (Lijphart 1968). The erosion of ideological and institutional certainties that accompanied de-pillarization left all traditional political parties with shallow claims for popular legitimacy, while depriving citizens of their most important cues for voting behaviour. The result has been a declining party identification and loyalty, and greater electoral volatility, especially from the mid-1980s (Deschouwer 2002; Krouwel 1999). As we shall see, parties have responded to this trend by focusing increasingly on the qualities of their leaders in an attempt to attract floating voters, thereby strengthening party elites, particularly the prime minister.

As a direct result of the de-pillarization process, and reinforced by its growing commercialization, Belgian and Dutch parties lost control of the media. Party-affiliated newspapers disappeared (as in the case of the Flemish socialist *Volksgazet* in 1978), or became components of commercial corporations with only loose ties to the political party world (as in the cases of the original Flemish Catholic *De Standaard* in 1976 and the Dutch *Volkskrant* and *Trouw*). In addition, the emergence of commercial broadcasting companies (in 1959 in the Netherlands and 1989 in Flanders) had substantial effects on the political content of television (Witte and Craeybeckx 1997: 426–8). It is true that some potential for party-controlled patronage in public sector television (for instance, via nominations for seats on the boards of the broadcasting corporations VRT and RTBf in Belgium and NOS in the Netherlands) remained. Arguably, party political influence over the media evolved from direct control—which went as far as control over the content of the programmes—into indirect influence by means of patronage. But even this must be set in the context of competition from independent commercial channels (Deschouwer 2002).

In such an environment, election campaigns have become increasingly professional in the Low Countries, despite the fact that Dutch campaign expenditures look moderate compared to those typical in many other advanced industrial countries (Koole 1992: 369–71; van Praag 1995: 235). However, Dutch and Belgian parties have access to considerable non-monetary resources, including free access to the media, patronage appointments, and the use of state bureaucracies, all of which are exploited during electoral

campaigns without being reported in official campaign expenditure statements (Krouwel 1999). Furthermore, election campaigns have been centralized significantly as leaders have extended their control over external
communications (van Praag 1995: 233). In Belgium, control of election
campaigns remains firmly in the hands of extra-parliamentary party leaderships, even though the influence of commercial advertising and consultancy
has grown since the 1990s. Recent campaigns in both countries have become
more capital-intensive and, as we shall see, increasingly oriented towards
party leaders or prospective prime ministers (*lijsttrekker*). This has been
accompanied by changes in press coverage of campaigns and in voting
behaviour.

Press coverage: More limelight for the dutch prime minister

Undoubtedly there has been a substantial increase in media coverage of
prime ministers in Belgium and the Netherlands. There are several reasons
for this. First, it should be understood that there is the long tradition of
governments being named after their prime ministers,[15] which enables the
latter to personify the entire government (within the broad constraints of
consensus democracy). All references to government policy thus mention the
name of this individual. The resulting name-recognition among voters is
substantial; surveys show a level of name-recognition of between 92 per
cent and 98 per cent for the Dutch prime minister (Holsteyn and Irwin
1998: 143), and 93 per cent to 95 per cent for the Belgian prime minister
(Maddens and Dewachter 1995, 1998). Second, in both the Netherlands and
Belgium the prime minister traditionally meets the press on Friday, after the
council of ministers. Depending on the problems and legislative proposals
that have been discussed, the Belgian prime minister might be accompanied
by a couple of ministers, but in general he faces the press on his own. This is
always the case in the Netherlands. Moreover, the Dutch prime minister now
gets 15 minutes of broadcasting time on the Friday evening TV news to
comment upon and explain the most important decisions taken by the
council of ministers during the week. Significantly, this system has been
copied by Flemish public television since January 2002. Finally, the new
phenomenon of spin-doctoring has also infected Dutch and Belgian politics.
Prime Ministers Kok, Balkenende, and Verhofstadt have followed Tony
Blair's example and employed full time press officers and special marketing
advisers.

Overall, the media focus on the prime minister is greater in the Netherlands. As suggested above, this can be explained by the less pronounced
political position of the Belgian prime minister, at least until the 1990s. In the
1980s, the Belgian prime minister participated no more than six times per

year in the most important weekly political debating programme on Flemish public television; in effect, the prime minister only represented the government in one-third of cases, leaving the floor to junior or departmental ministers on other occasions.[16] The figures for the francophone public television RTBf are very similar, with the prime minister's share of government representation on such broadcasts ranging from a low of 6 per cent (in 1989) to a maximum of 25 per cent in 1985 (an election year). This clearly indicates that the Belgian prime minister did not assume the role of government spokesperson as frequently as his Dutch counterpart.

Despite this, there is still a discernible trend towards personalization of politics in the Belgian media. In an influential though small tri-monthly opinion poll by the journal *La Libre Belgique*,[17] respondents are asked for which party they would vote if elections were held the following day, and 'which politician they would like to assume a more important role in politics in the coming months' (*our translation*). Since it goes back to 1992, it is, more than any other poll, a good instrument for measuring popular support of individual politicians over time. Its results are carefully analysed by politicians, media advisers, and political analysts alike. In the federal elections of May 2003, the number of surveys mushroomed remarkably, with almost every newspaper and television channel commissioning one of their own. It is interesting to note that the prime minister hardly ever comes first in the ranking for popularity, even though all prime ministers score higher in popularity than before assuming office (Nuytemans 2002).

The Dutch media focus much more on the prime minister than their Belgian counterparts. Kleinnijenhuis et al. (1995, 1998, 2003) have shown that 50 per cent of political news coverage mentions the name of a politician and journalists personalize politics to a large degree. Leading politicians such as prime ministers, cabinet ministers, electoral leaders, and parliamentary party leaders receive a disproportionate amount of media attention. Overall, between seven and ten politicians dominate political news coverage and the media usually limit their focus to two or three politicians per party. As a result, there is an almost total neglect of the opposition in Dutch news coverage; the main opposition leaders receive around 7 per cent of all TV coverage of politics (see also Oegema et al. 2001).

Election campaigns are increasingly presented as a horse race between the leaders of the largest parties. For example, during the Dutch campaign of 1994, 25 per cent of political news coverage in the press and on TV showed photos of the two prospective prime ministers (Kok and Brinkman); overall, the two men received 23 per cent of all TV news coverage. Furthermore, televised debates between leaders have amplified the 'horse race' character of media coverage. This is reflected in the way in which viewers are polled and newspapers and television report who has 'won the debate' in the eyes of the electorate. In the 1998 campaign, media attention on the incumbent prime minister exceeded that of all other politicians by a factor of 20, and was three times higher than that of other senior ministers. Television focused particularly heavily on the incumbent Prime Minister Wim Kok: he was the subject of 16 per cent of all broadcasts, and personally attracted 10 per cent of total media coverage (Kleinnijenhuis 1998). This disproportionate concentration on the incumbent premier by the media has been coined the 'prime minister's bonus'.

Thus, parliamentary elections in the Netherlands seem to have been transformed into a 'presidential race' for the position of prime minister; in this sense, the elections of 2002 and 2003 culminated in the direct election of the prime minister. In the former instance, the populist outsider Pim Fortuyn entered the race by straightforwardly asking Dutch voters to make him prime minister. In TV debates the leaders of the traditional parties looked bleak and indecisive compared to the eloquent and colourful Fortuyn. When he was able to attract one-third of the vote in the Rotterdam local elections preceding the national poll, the mass media focused even more heavily on this political entrepreneur, primarily discussing his personality and the (negative) reactions of the established political elite. Personalization of politics reached an all-time high when 65 per cent of all media coverage focused on individual politicians in the weeks prior to the national elections (Kleinnijenhuis et al. 2003). The twist on this particular occasion was that attention was focused principally on an anti-establishment outsider without any formal political position, nor any real party to speak of. Despite this, he was seen as a serious contender for the premiership. When Fortuyn was assassinated a week before the elections all political campaigning ground to a halt. As the coalition government that emerged from this election only lasted some eighty days, new elections were held in 2003. Notwithstanding the absence of Fortuyn from the hustings on this occasion, the later weeks of the campaign were once again completely dominated by a horse race between the incumbent Prime Minister Balkenende and his challenger from the PvdA, Wouter Bos.

Personalization of voting behaviour: Preference votes and 'personal appeal'

Leadership effects on voting behaviour are another important indicator of electoral presidentialization. A higher share of preference votes for party leaders can be regarded as an indicator of their growing personal appeal. The Belgian data, which goes back to the first elections after the First World War, show a remarkable increase of the proportion of voters who use a preference vote. While in 1919 just 10 per cent did so for Senate and 18 per cent for House elections, the corresponding figures for 2003—66.5 per cent and 68.0 per cent respectively—were new records (Wauters 2003). This represented the culmination of a process of gradual evolution, starting with the first person-alized electoral campaigns in 1958.[18] Interestingly, the steepest rise in the number of preference votes cast is very recent: in 1991 only 41 per cent of the electorate expressed a preference vote for the Senate and 48 per cent for the House. This remarkable increase over the last decade can be explained by three factors. Besides the growing awareness among voters that preferen-tial voting is the only way in which the fixed-order of candidates on party lists can be changed,[19] and the possibility of expressing multiple preference votes from 1994 onwards,[20] the changes in the composition of the Senate have had the clearest effect. In 1995, a re-districting exercise introduced the election of (a reduced number of) senators by two nationwide electorates—one French-speaking and one Dutch-speaking. This served to increase the visibility of candidates, with the result that elections for the Senate turned into a 'clash of titans' with all parties presenting their top candidates as prospective prime ministers. Paradoxically, elections for the politically less influential Senate became transformed into a kind of semi-direct election for the prime minis-ter. This explains why the number of voters expressing preference votes for the Senate exceeds that for the House.

Not surprisingly, the share of preference votes won by party leaders and prospective prime ministers has also increased. Looking at the share of preference votes that is given to the various heads of list compared to the total number of preference votes for their respective parties, a clear picture of personalization emerges. In the 2003 election, 80.1 per cent of VLD voters who used a preference vote gave their personal support to the incumbent Prime Minister Verhofstadt, while in 1999 some 82.6 per cent of the CVP electorate voted personally for the then Prime Minister Dehaene.[21] Prior to 1995, when MPs were elected in smaller electoral districts, prime ministers attracted far fewer preference votes.

In the Netherlands a similar personalization of voting behaviour can be identified, even though hard data on preference voting are lacking. Holsteyn (2000), for example, has shown that voting on the basis of socio-economic status, group interests, religion, and party identification (all indicative of a pillarized society) is declining in importance, whereas voting on the basis of programmes, issues, and personalities has increased. In particular, the pro-portion of voters who vote according to leadership qualities has increased from 2 per cent in 1971 to around 12 per cent in the late 1990s. Similarly, Kleinnijenhuis et al. (1998: 116) reported that 15 per cent of Dutch voters based their party choice primarily on the evaluation of party leaders in the 1998 election, while another 38 per cent were partly influenced by such considerations.

Clearly, the personal appeal of leaders has become increasingly important in the Low Countries, particularly as the main parties lose their strong links with sociologically defined voter groups and their programmatic differences shrink. Human capital, in the shape of politicians who can connect with the electorate, particularly via the mass media, becomes crucial for the electoral fortunes of political parties. This has transformed parliamentary elections in both countries into more presidential contests as the position of prime minister becomes the ultimate focus for the media, the parties, and the voters.

Leadership Focus in campaigns: Familiar Faces as electoral assets

However, increasing personalization of politics only becomes presidentiali- zation when leaders become the main focus of the electoral campaign at the expense of policies, issues, and parties. As a concomitant, we might expect to find evidence of an increase in campaign expenditures on individual candi- date campaigns.

Personalized campaigns are not entirely new phenomena in Belgian and Dutch politics. In the Netherlands, emphasis on the leadership qualities of prime ministers was already visible from the late nineteenth century onwards (Toonen 1992: 85). Prime Ministers such as Colijn (ARP) and Drees (PvdA) conducted highly personalized campaigns in 1937 and 1956 respect- ively. The PvdA focused their campaign entirely on Drees, often without a visible party name or logo. However, the increasing influence of television and the emergence of a more independent and commercial media landscape marked a watershed in the early 1960s. From that time, Dutch voters witnessed televised election debates between party leaders, including the incumbent prime minister. Prime ministerial incumbency became even more important for parties after the introduction of a weekly interview with the prime minister (mentioned earlier) generated a considerable 'bonus' in terms of media exposure. This exposure undoubtedly impacted on voting behaviour.[22] Parties recognized this and have increasingly come to focus on the personality and qualities of 'their' prime ministerial candidate. In 1977 the PvdA campaigned with the slogan 'Choose the prime minister', referring to their leader Den Uyl who subsequently won a landslide victory. The Christian Democrats, who provided most Dutch prime ministers, made equally personalized appeals. Thus, in 1986 the CDA campaigned with the slogan 'Let Lubbers finish the job'. During the 1990s the PvdA profited heavily from the reputation of their leader and prime minister, Wim Kok, as it became clear that the party was less popular than the man (Wiersema 1998). Neither of the Liberal parties (VVD and D66) has ever provided a prime minister, yet they also tend to focus heavily on the qualities of their leaders in their campaigns and the VVD habitually presents its *lijsttrekker* as a prospective prime minister. In sum, despite the use of list-PR (which compels voters to make a *party* choice, first and foremost) and the prevalence of broad coalition governments, the personal qualities of prime ministerial candidates play an increasingly important role in Dutch national elections. Party leaders have become the dominant focal point of national elections, for all that they are, nominal parliamentary elections.

In Belgium the first clearly personalized election campaign dates back to 1958. This election was fought primarily over the choice between the so-called 'key plan' of Gaston Eyskens (CVP) and the continuation of the government of incumbent Prime Minister Van Acker (SP). For the first time the (then unitary) Christian Democrats and Socialists tied their election campaigns to their candidates for the premiership. Still, it will be another decade before any politician ran an 'Americanized' campaign. In 1968 the incumbent Prime Minister Vanden Boeynants got involved in a severe dispute with his own PSC, set up his own list and ran a highly personalized campaign. He sent some of his collaborators to the United States to learn and adopt some of the campaign techniques that were used in presidential campaigns there (De Ridder 1999). Ever since, election campaigns have been predominantly characterized by a battle between an incumbent prime minister and rival party leaders, each of whom is portrayed as a prospective premier. In 1974, the CVP campaigned with the slogan that the country needed its leader 'Tindemans more than ever!' Interestingly, dual electoral leadership campaigns do not work: The CVP's experiment in 1978 of placing both party leader (Martens) and prime minister (Tindemans) in the limelight was criticized afterwards by the latter because 'only one product or person can be sold at a time, not two' (Van Dyck 1981, *our translation*). From 1985 onwards, the CVP would always centre its election campaign on its incumbent prime minister: Wilfried Martens in 1985, 1987, and 1991; Jean-Luc Dehaene in 1995 and 1999. When in opposition (2003), the campaign revolved around party leader Stefaan De Clerck. This emphasis on the prime ministerial candidate is sometimes very explicit. In 1985, for instance, the CVP devoted 43 per cent of its TV advertising time to the accomplishments of Prime Minister Martens. The remaining 57 per cent was divided between the party programme and the presentation of other leading politicians (Van den Bruel 1986). A similar pattern characterized the SP campaign, where party leader Van Miert was the only politician who featured in adverts and took up 49 per cent of the party's total air-time. Indeed, as early as 1965, analysis revealed how television campaigning advantaged 'national' figures and disadvantaged local candidates (Van der Biesen 1965).

Leadership-centred campaign strategies also leave their imprint on patterns of campaign expenditure. While each political party in Belgium was allowed to spend a maximum of €1.1 million on general campaigning by the end of the 1990s, the total sum of candidate spending had risen to no less than €17.35 million. This is in the context of a rise in total campaign expenditure from €5.41 million in 1974 to €26.80 million in 1999 (Biondi et al. 2000).[23] Additionally, each party is allowed to identify six so-called national figures eligible for extra-party funding of their individual campaigns. This is likely to have an effect on the number of preference votes gained (Maddens et al. 2006) and, consequently, strengthen the position of these individuals within their respective parties.

In sum, Belgian and Dutch leaders and their qualities have increasingly become the key campaign assets. Prime ministers, in particular, draw very substantial media attention and their international exposure is exploited by parties in the quest for electoral support. Election campaigns have become focused on the leaders of the larger parties and thus elections for parliament are being transformed into contests for prime ministerial office. Party programmes, government policies, and political parties have been relegated to a secondary role (Bowler and Farrell 1992; Farrell and Webb 2000).

CONCLUSIONS

Despite different institutional developments in the Low Countries over recent decades, the position of their prime minister has been strengthened significantly. This evolution has depended hardly at all on constitutional changes; indeed, prime ministers remain poorly defined in a constitutional sense in both countries. Clearly, there have been no formal regime changes from parliamentarism to presidentialism, even though more recent institutional changes such as the federalization of Belgium might suggest that the position of the prime minister has been weakened. That is, as a result of the division of competencies between the various levels of policy-making, it could have been much harder for the Belgian prime minister to speak 'on behalf of the nation', because he now had to share media attention with five other regional minister-presidents. In reality, however, his role as coordinator of government policies, combined with growing status as arbiter in conflicts between regional governments, has served to place him at the very heart of politics in the country.

Although no such radical institutional change has taken place in the Netherlands, a similar trend can nevertheless be discerned. In former days, the prime minister used to be a kind of arbiter within a cabinet in which individual ministers enjoyed substantial policy autonomy. Owing to the budgetary discipline imposed by the European Union, this role as arbiter has been taken over partly by the minister for finance. Also the prime minister spends an increasing amount of time playing the role of national policy coordinator and figurehead of the whole nation in international forums. Most notably, this development can be identified in foreign affairs, where former Prime Minister Wim Kok worked hard to assert the prime ministerial prerogative, even at the cost of frequent conflict with his ministers of foreign affairs.

Furthermore, several other developments have helped produce a kind of presidentialization within the limits of the Low Countries' well-known variety of consensus democracy. First of all, recent developments have resulted in a greater personalization of governmental decision-making, at least in terms of presentation and media coverage of politics. The collective identity of the council of ministers has been undermined by frequent interventions of prime ministers in specific policy areas and a stronger *de facto* emphasis on the individual responsibility of each member of the council. The personalization of politics is also visible in the increasing focus on party leaders and prime ministerial candidates during national and even local election campaigns. Today, few parties conduct issue-oriented campaigns. To attract increasingly volatile voters, they prefer to highlight personality and the qualities of individual politicians, most notably the managerial skills of their prime ministerial candidates. Finally, popular perception of the importance of the position of prime minister has risen significantly as a result of greater media exposure and the internationalization of politics (via the effect of summitry). In a fierce competition for scoops and appealing one-liners, the mass media focus heavily on the prime ministerial candidates of the major parties. Incumbent prime ministers, speaking as representatives of their party and as heads of government, enjoy significantly more media exposure than their main contenders, particularly those in opposition. Skilful use of the media by the Dutch and the Belgian prime ministers, supported by teams of spin-doctors and professional campaigners, turns this advantage into a real 'prime ministerial bonus'. At the same time, the status and position of leaders within their own parties have also been strengthened by a process of centralization. Resources and power have accumulated around the extra-parliamentary elites in Belgium and around the party in government and the parliamentary elites in the Netherlands. Control over the party agendas and over the (pre)selection of parliamentary candidates has given leaders room for manoeuvre needed to compete for the most important political job in the system—the prime ministership. Indeed, parliamentary elections have been transformed into contests for the position of prime minister, especially in the Netherlands. This was best exemplified by the Dutch parliamentary elections of 2002, in which a total outsider without any significant party organization emerged as a front-runner for prime ministerial power.

However, while similar trends can be observed in both countries, it seems that they have had a much more profound effect in the Netherlands. Due to the linguistic cleavage and federal structure, the Belgian political system remains more balanced. Coalitions consist of at least four parties, each of which is given a vice-prime minister. These individuals act as brokers between the government and their own parties and meet frequently with the prime minister in the *kerncabinet*. It is the *kerncabinet* which sets out the lines for the policy at the federal level, preventing the prime minister from playing *cavalier seul*. In the Netherlands the power-sharing elements are largely cultural in essence, and are increasingly under pressure from a wide range of factors pushing the system in a more presidentialized direction.

NOTES

1. Unless otherwise stated, the focus of interest in the Belgian case is the federal level of government. Developments in regional politics will be discussed only in so far as they contradict those occurring at the federal level.
2. Thus, for instance, Van den Berg concludes (1990: 120) that the office of the position of the Dutch prime minister has developed from a relatively 'invisible' chairmanship to a role verging on personal leadership of cabinet and policy-making.
3. The change in 1970 simply consisted of the statement that the prime minister could be excluded from the parity provision governing the number of French-speaking and Flemish ministers.
4. Coalition agreement documents in Belgium range between 3,150 and 43,500 words, averaging 14,183 words, while in the Netherlands they range between 3,100 and 36,000 words, at an average of 14,579 words (De Winter et al. 2000; Timmermans and Andeweg 2000).
5. Until 1999 both formation processes took place simultaneously, and as fewer parties were involved in the formation talks at regional level, these negotiations resulted more rapidly in agreement. Since none of the major parties before 2004 was willing to form asymmetric coalitions (in which the coalitions at the federal level do not match those in the regions), the regional government coalitions strongly influenced developments at federal level. This was most notably the case in 1988, 1992, and 1999.
6. Cabinet reshuffles are almost exclusively the prerogatives of the party leader of the extra-parliamentary party. Recent examples are the decisions of PS leader Di Rupo regarding his party's ministers in Spring 2000, of PRL leader Ducarme after the local elections of October 2000, and of VLD party leader De Gucht on several occasions in 2003 and 2004.
7. The true leader was the leader of the parliamentary party (*'fractievoorzitter'*), while the national leader (*'lijsttrekker'*) was the spearhead of the electoral campaign and the party chairman was the organizational manager of the party. Quite often the *'lijsttrekker'* was a different person from the *'fractievoorzitter'*.
8. While direct membership elections for the Dutch extra-parliamentary party leaders have also been introduced by several parties, they remain relatively marginal political figures.
9. Notable exceptions to this rule are Prime Ministers Harmel (1965–6), Eyskens (1968–72), Tindemans (1974–8), and Dehaene (1992–9), who were not formally elected or appointed as *partijvoorzitter* before assuming the office of prime minister.

10. There have been some exceptions to this rule of prime ministers 'without portfolio' in Belgium, including Lefèvre (1961–5), Harmel (1965–6), and Vanden Boeynants, who combined the prime ministerial office with responsibility for Scientific Policy from 1966 to 1968, and for Defence from 1978 to 1979.

11. Besides the federal level, there are three regional levels (Flanders, Wallonia, and Brussels) and three Community levels (the Flemish Community, the French Community, and the German-speaking Community).

12. Note that these figures do not include purely clerical or secretarial staff.

13. During this period (1992–9) VLD party conferences were open: all party members were invited to participate and had the right to intervene. It thus happened more than once that the party leadership found itself in a minority position and had to change its policy objectives. However, after the VLD joined government in 1999, only one highly contested party conference was held (in February 2004 on voting rights for immigrants at local level).

14. Recent participation rates vary between a mere 20.7 per cent (CVP in 1999) and 65 per cent in highly contested elections (PSC in 1996; Volksunie in 2000).

15. On rare occasions, a cabinet is named after both the prime minister and the deputy prime minister. This was the case, for instance, with the cabinet Eyskens-Merlot, which was continued as the Eyskens-Cools cabinet after the death of J J. Merlot (1968–71), or the Dutch Drees-Schermerhorn government. Similarly, the fifth government of Martens in Belgium is often referred to as the Martens-Gol cabinet (1981–5). Usually this happens when coalition parties want to stress the importance of their deputy prime minister, and the political circumstances of the time allow it.

16. Research based on data collected for the period 1983–90 in Res Publica's *Political Yearbook of Belgium*, editions 1984 to 1991.

17. The survey is based on a sample of 1000 Dutch-speaking and French-speaking respondents and the results are published every third Monday of March, June, September, and December.

18. Between 1919 and 1958 the total number of preference votes increased only gradually by 10 percentage points (Wauters 2003).

19. Between 1919 and 1995 only thirty candidates were able to win seats on the basis of the number of preference votes won. This represents a mere 0.64 per cent of the total number of seats (4,507) won during the period (Dewachter 1967; Fiers 2000).

20. As a result, the average number of preference votes per ballot increased to 2.73 for the Senate in 2003 (Wauters 2003).

21. In 2003, five other politicians figured on more than half of the preference ballots of their parties, with a range of support varying from 53.8 per cent for Mieke Vogels of Agalev to 79.4 per cent for the popular Socialist leader Steve Stevaert (Wauters 2003).

22. Estimates of the exact strength of this impact range between 5 per cent and 25 per cent of the variance in voter choice, according to the individuals and parties concerned (Bank 1989: 38–9; De Nederlandse Kiezer 1956: 10).

23. At 1999 prices, campaign expenditures in 1974 totalled €15.47 million.

REFERENCES

Andeweg, R. B. (1988). 'Centrifugal Forces and Collective Decision-Making: The Case of the Dutch Cabinet', *European Journal of Political Research*, 16: 125–51.
—— (1990). *Ministers en ministerraad*. Den Haag: Sdu Uitgeverij.
—— (1991). 'The Dutch Prime Minister: Not Just Chairman, Not Yet Chief?', *West-European Politics*, 14: 116–32.
—— (1997). 'Institutional Reform in Dutch Politics: Elected Prime Minister, Personalised PR, and Popular Veto in Comparative Perspective', *Acta Politica*, 32: 277–357.
—— (2000). 'Fractiocracy? Limits to the Ascendancy of the Parliamentary Party Group in Dutch Politics', in R. Koole and K. Heidar (eds.), *Parliamentary Party Groups in European Democracies*. London: Routledge.
Bank, J. Th. M. (1989). 'Televisie in de politieke cultuur van de jaren '60', in J. Th. J van den Berg et al. (eds.), *Tussen Nieuwspoort en Binnenhof. De jaren 60 als breuklijn in de naoorlogse ontwikkelingen in politiek en journalistiek*. Den Haag: Sdu Uitgeverij.
Biondi, P., W. Dewachter, S. Fiers, and B. Wauters (2000). 'Political Belgium 1980–2000: A Concise Statistical Overview', *Res Publica*, 42: 119–63.
Bowler, S. and D. Farrell (1992). *Electoral Strategies and Political Marketing*. New York: St. Martins.
Broeksteeg, J., J. Knippenberg, and L. Verhey (2004). De minister-president in vergelijkend perspectief, Onderzoeksrapport Universiteit Maastricht, Uitgave Ministerie van Binnenlandse Zaken.
Claes, W. (2000). 'Vice-Premiers en kernkabinetten. Een evaluatie van deze innovaties', *Res Publica*, 42: 33–44.
Daalder, H. (1987). *Party Systems in Denmark, Austria, Switzerland, The Netherlands and Belgium*. London: Frances Pinter.
Dehaene, J. L. (2000). 'De (on)macht van de Eerste Minister. Een a-wetenschappelijke ervaringsbenadering', *Res Publica*, 42: 23–32.
Depauw, S. (2000). *Cohesie in de parlementsfracties van de regeringsmeerderheid. Een vergelijkend onderzoek in België, Frankrijk en het Verenigd Koninkrijk*. Unpublished Ph.D. thesis. Catholic University of Leuven.
De Ridder, H. (1989). *Sire geef me 100 dagen*. Leuven: Davidsfonds.
—— (1996). *Jean-Luc Dehaene... met commentaar*. Tielt: Lannoo.
—— (1999). *Vijftig jaar stemmenmakerij*. Gent: Scoop.
Deschouwer, K (1994). 'The Decline of Consociationalism and the Reluctant Modernization of Belgian Mass Parties', in R. Katz, and P. Mair (eds.), *How Parties Organize*. London: Sage.
—— (2002). 'The Colour Purple: The End of Predictable Politics in the Low Countries' in P. Webb, D. Farrell, and I. Holliday (eds.), *Political Parties in Advanced Industrial Societies*. Oxford: Oxford University Press, 151–80.
Dewachter, W. (1967). *De wetgevende verkiezingen als proces van machtsverwerving in het Belgische politieke bestel*. Antwerpen: Standaard Wetenschappelijke Uitgeverij.
—— (1995). *Besluitvorming in politiek België*. Leuven: Acco.
—— and L. De Winter (1981). *Over particratie*. Leuven: KULeuven.

De Nederlandse Kiezer (1956). *De Nederlandse Kiezer. Een onderzoek naar zijn gedragingen en opvattingen*, Den Haag: Sdu Uitgeverij.

De Winter, L. (1988). 'Belgium: Democracy or Oligarchy?', in M. Gallagher and M. Marsh, *Candidate Selection in Comparative Perspective: The Secret Garden of Politics*. London: Sage.

—— (1996). 'Party Encroachment on the Executive and Legislative Branch in the Belgian Polity', *Res Publica*, 38: 325–52.

—— and P. Dumont (2000). 'PPGs in Belgium: Subjects of Partitocratic Dominion', in K. Heidar and R. Koole (eds.), *Parliamentary Party Groups in European Democracies*. London: Routledge.

—— A. Timmermans, and P. Dumont (2000). 'Belgium: On Government Agreements, Evangelists, Followers, and Heretics', in W. C. Müller and K. Strøm (eds.), *Coalition Governments in Western Europe*. Oxford: Oxford University Press.

Eyskens, G. (1983). 'De functie van eerste minister in België, in de periode 1945–1975', *Res Publica*, 25: 533–52.

Farrell, D. and P. Webb (2000). 'Political Parties as Campaign Organisations', in R. Dalton and M. Wattenberg (eds.), *Parties Without Partisans*. Oxford: Oxford University Press.

Fiers, S. (1998). *Partijvoorzitters in België, of 'Le parti, c'est moi'?*. Leuven: KULeuven.

—— (2000). *Vijftig jaar volksvertegenwoordiging. De circulatie onder de Belgische parlementsleden 1946–1995*. Brussels: Koninklijke Vlaamse Academie van België voor Wetenschappen en Kunsten.

Gallagher, M. (1988). 'Conclusion', in M. Gallagher and M. Marsh (eds.). *Candidate Selection in Comparative Perspective: The Secret Garden of Politics*. London: Sage.

Hillebrand, R. (1992). *De antichambre van het parlement. Kandidaatstelling in Nederlandse politieke partijen*. Leiden: DSWO Press.

Holsteyn, J. van (2000). 'De kiezer verklaart', in J. Thomassen, K. Aarts, and H. Van der Kolk (eds.), *Politieke veranderingen in Nederland 1971–1998. Kiezers en de smalle marges van de politiek*. Den Haag: SDUitgeverij.

—— and G. A. Irwin (1998). *De wilde frisheid van limoenen. Studiën over politici in de ogen van de kiezers*. Leiden: DSWO Press.

Hondeghem, A. (1996). 'De politieke en ambtelijke component in het openbaar bestuur', in R. Maes and K. Jochmans, *Inleiding tot de Bestuurskunde*. Brussels: STOHO.

Katz, R. S. and P. Mair (1992). *Party Organizations in Western Democracies 1960–1990: A Data Handbook*. London: Sage.

—— —— (1994). *How Parties Organize*. London: Sage.

King, A. (1994). 'Chief Executives in Western Europe', in I. Budge and D. McKay (eds.), *Developing Democracy*. London: Sage.

Kleinnijenhuis, J., D. Oegema, J. A. de Ridder, and H. Bos (1995). *Democratie op drift. Een evaluatie van de verkiezingscampagne van 1994*. Amsterdam: VU Uitgeverij.

—— —— —— and P. C. Ruigrok (1998). *Paarse polarisatie. De slag om de kiezer in de media*. Alphen aan den Rijn: Samsom.

Kleinnijenhuis, J., D. Oegema, J. A. de Ridder, A. van Hoof, and R. Vliegenthart (2003). *De puinhopen in het nieuws. De rol van de media bij de Tweede-Kamerverkiezingen van 2002.* Alphen aan den Rijn: Kluwer.

Koole, R. (1992). *De opkomst van de moderne kaderpartij. Veranderende partijorganisatie in Nederland 1960–1990.* Utrecht: Aula.

—— (1994). 'The Vulnerability of the Modern Cadre Party in the Netherlands', in R. S. Katz and P. Mair (eds.), *How Parties Organize.* London: Sage.

—— (1996). 'Ledenpartijen of staatspartijen. Financiën van Nederlandse politieke partijen in vergelijkend en historisch perspectief', in DNPP, *Jaarboek 1995,* Groningen.

Krouwel, A. (1996). 'Partijverandering in Nederland: de teloorgang van de traditionele politieke partijen', in DNPP, *Jaarboek 1995,* Groningen.

—— (1999). *The Catch-All Party in Western Europe 1945–1990: A Study in Arrested Development.* Ph.D. thesis, Vrije Universiteit Amsterdam.

—— (2004). *Partisan States: Legal Regulation of Political Parties in France, Germany, The Netherlands and the United Kingdom.* Nijmegen: Wolf Legal Publishers.

Laver, M. and W. B. Hunt (1992). *Policy and Party Competition.* New York: Routledge.

Lijphart, A. (1968). *The Politics of Accommodation: Pluralism and Democracy in the Netherlands.* Berkeley: University of California Press.

—— (1977). *Democracy in Plural Societies: A Comparative Exploration.* New Haven: Yale University Press.

—— (1994). *Electoral Systems and Party Systems: A Study of Twenty-Seven Democracies 1945–1990.* Oxford: Oxford University Press.

—— (1999). *Patterns of Democracy: Government Forms and Performance in Thirty-Six Countries.* New Haven: Yale University Press.

Luther, K. R. and K. Deschouwer (1999). *Party Elites in Divided Societies.* London: Routledge.

Maddens, B. and W. Dewachter (1995). 'Politieke kennis', in M. Swyngedouw and J. Billiet (eds.), *Kiezen is verliezen. Onderzoek naar de politieke opvattingen van Vlamingen.* Leuven: Acco.

—— —— (1998). 'Politieke belangstelling, kennis en onderlegdheid', in M. Swyngedouw and J. Billiet (eds.), *De (on)redelijke kiezer. Opvattingen naar de politieke opvattingen van Vlamingen. Verkiezingen van 21 mei 1995.* Leuven: Acco.

—— B. Wauters, J. Noppe and S. Fiers (2006). 'Effects of Campaign Spending in an Open List PR-System. The 2003 Legislative Elections in Flanders/Belgium, in *West European Politics,* 29: p. 161–168.

Maes, M. (1990). 'De formele aanstelling van de partijvoorzitters in België, 1946–1990', *Res Publica,* 32: 3–62.

Margés, H. (1989). 'Lubbers en zijn ambtenaren', in A. Joustra and E. van Venetie (eds.), *Ruud Lubbers. Manager in de Politiek.* Baarn: Sesam.

Müller, W. C. and D. Meth-Cohn (1991). 'The Selection of Party Chairman in Austria: A Study in Intra-party Decision-making', in *European Journal of Political Research,* 20: 39–65.

Noppe, J. (2002). 'Morphologie des partis politiques francophones en 2000 et 2001', *Res Publica,* 44: 473–516.

—— (2003). 'Morfologie van de Vlaamse politieke partijen in 2001 en 2002', *Res Publica,* 45: 507–72.

Nuytemans, M. (2002). *Het vertrouwen in de regering. Verklaringen voor het verschil in vertrouwen tussen de regeringen Dehaene I en Verhofstadt I*, Antwerp: unpublished.

Oegema, D., J. de Ridder, and J. Kleinnijenhuis (2001). *Politicians and the semantic gatekeepers. Subtle but meaningful differences in media coverage of Dutch politicians during the 1998 election campaign*, Paper presented at ICA Conference, Washington DC.

Plavsic, W. (1988). *Monsieur le Premier Ministre*. Brussels: Didier Hatier.

Poguntke, T. (2000). *The Presidentialization of Parliamentary Democracies: A Contradiction in Terms?* Paper presented at the 28th Joint Sessions of workshops of ECPR (Copenhagen).

Punnett, R. (1992). *Selecting the Party Leader: Britain in Comparative Perspective*. London: Harvester Wheatsheaf.

Raalte, E. van (1954). *De ontwikkeling van het minister-presidentschap in Nederland, België, Frankrijk, Engeland en enige andere landen. Een studie van vergelijkend staatsrecht*, Leiden Universitaire Pers.

Rehwinkel, J. P. (1991). *De minister-president. Eerste onder gelijken of gelijke onder eersten?*, Zwolle: Tjeenk Willink.

Rose, R. (1982). 'British Government: The Job at the Top', in R. Rose and E. Suleiman (eds.), *Presidents and Prime Ministers*. Washington DC: American Enterprise Institute for Public Policy Research.

Schagen, J. A. van (1995). 'De minister-president: van primus inter-pares tot regeringsleider', in J. B. J. M. ten Berge et al. (eds.), *De Grondwet als voorwerp van aanhoudende zorg* (Burkens-bundel). Zwolle: Tjeenk Willink.

Timmermans, A. (1994). 'Cabinet Ministers and Policy-making in Belgium: The Impact of Coalitional Constraints', in M. Laver and K. A. Shepsle (eds.), *Cabinet Ministers and Parliamentary Government*. Cambridge: Cambridge University Press.

—— and R. B. Andeweg (2000). 'The Netherlands: Still the Politics of Accommodation?', in W. Müller and K. Strøm (eds.), *Coalition Governments in Western Europe*. Oxford: Oxford University Press.

Toonen, S. (1992). *Op zoek naar charisma: Nederlandse politieke partijen en hun lijsttrekkers 1963–1986*. Amsterdam: Vrije Universiteit.

Van den Berg, J. Th. J. (1990). 'De Minister President. Aanjager van noodzakelijk beleid', in R. B. Andeweg (ed.), *Ministers en Ministerraad*. Den Haag: Sdu Uitgeverij.

Van den Bruel, Ch. (1986). *De verkiezingscampagne n.a.v. de parlementsverkiezingen van 13 oktober 1985, met een detailanalyse van de politieke tribunes op televisie*. Leuven: unpublished.

Van der Biesen, W. (1965). *TV en politieke voorlichting. De reacties van het Vlaamse publiek op de TV verkiezingscampagne 1965*. Mechelen: Sint-Franciscus Uitgeverij.

Van Dyck, F. (1981). *De organisatie van de verkiezingscampagne van de CVP*. Leuven: unpublished.

Van Hassel, H. (1988). 'Het kabinetssyndroom in historisch perspectief', *Tijdschrift Gemeentekrediet van België,* 42: 11–36.

van Praag, P. (1995). 'Hoe 'Amerikaans' is de Nederlandse verkiezingscampagne?', in K. Brants and P. van Praag (eds.), *Verkoop van de politiek: de verkiezingscampagne van 1994*. Amsterdam: Het Spinhuis.

von Beyme, K. (1985). *Political Parties in Western Democracies*. Aldershot: Gower.

Vos, M. (1992). 'Morphologie des partis francophones en 1990 et 1991', *Res Publica*, 34: 453–93.

Wauters, B. (2003). 'Het gebruik van voorkeurstemmen bij de federale parlements-verkiezingen van 18 mei 2003', *Res Publica*, 45: 401–28.

Wiersma, J. M. (1998). 'Sterk en sociaal: de twee-in-een campagne van de PvdA', in P. Kramer, T. van der Maas, and L. Ornstein (eds.), *Stemmen in stromenland: de verkiezingen van 1998 nader bekeken*. Den Haag: Sdu Uitgeverij.

Witte, E. and J. Craeybeckx (1997). *Politieke geschiedenis van België*. Antwerpen: Standaard Uitgeverij.

Woldendorp, J., H. Keman, and I. Budge (2000). *Party government in 48 democracies (1945–1998): Composition, Duration, Personnel*. Dordrecht: Kluwer.

Party Acronyms

The Netherlands:

ARP – *Anti-Revolutionaire Partij* – Anti-Revolutionary Party (joined CDA in 1980)

CDA – *Christen-Democratisch Appel* – Christian Democrats (1980–)

D66 – *Democraten 66* – Democrats '66 (left-liberal party) (1966–)

PvdA – *Partij van de Arbeid* – Labour Party (1946–)

VVD – *Volkspartij voor Vrijheid en Democratie* – People's Party for Freedom and Democracy (conservative-liberal party) (1948–)

Belgium:

Agalev – *Anders Gaan Leven* – Flemish Greens (1982–2003, then reformed into *Groen!*)

CVP – *Christelijke Volkspartij* – Flemish Christian-People's Party (1968–2001, then reformed into *CD&V*)

PRL – *Parti Réformateur Libéral* – Francophone Party of Liberal Reform (1979–2002, then reformed into *MR*)

PS – *Parti Socialiste* – Francophone Socialist Party (1978–)

PSC – *Parti Social Chrétien* – Francophone Christian – Democrats (1968–2002, then reformed into *cdH*)

SP – *Socialistische Partij* – Flemish Socialist Party (1980–2001, then reformed into *SP.A*)

VLD – *Vlaamse Liberalen en Democraten* – Flemish Liberal Party (1992–)

Vlaams Blok – Flemish Bloc, (rightwing populist party) (1978–2004, then reformed into *Vlaams Belang*)

Volksunie – People's Union (Flemish nationalists) (1954–2001, dissolved in *Spirit* (left-liberals) and *N-VA* (Flemish nationalists))

7

Denmark: Presidentialization in a Consensual Democracy

Karina Pedersen and Tim Knudsen

INTRODUCTION

When the two Danish prime ministerial candidates in the general election campaigns of 1998, 2001 and 2005 met in televised debates, the parallel with US presidential election campaigns seemed stark. The voters' clear choice lay between two candidates for the office of prime minister and their attendant governments. The media were quick to label these elections 'presidential'. But are such similarities deep-seated or merely superficial? The purpose of this chapter is to assess just how pronounced the process of presidentialization is in the Danish case.

Denmark has a multiparty system with approximately ten parties represented in parliament. However, in spite of the relatively high number of parties the Danish political system is not strongly polarized. Danish political culture is not characterized by ideological posturing, but has often been described as pragmatic and consensus-seeking (Elder et al. 1987; Henningsen 1980; Pedersen 1987). Indeed, consensus-seeking is a necessity, given that no political party has held a majority since 1909. There is a long-standing tradition of comparatively effective minority and coalition cabinets. Since October 1945 Denmark has had twenty-one governments, as defined by party composition (whereby changes of the prime minister are not counted as a change of government), eleven of which were coalitions. Furthermore, all seven governments since 1982 in Denmark have been coalition governments. Among these, the Social Democratic-led four-party coalition of 1993–4 is notable for its dependence on a fragile single-vote majority in parliament. However, there is political stability within this context of apparent instability insofar as there is a core of ministers that often continues from coalition to coalition. The most stable of all posts in the cabinet is that of prime minister; from 1975 to 2006 Denmark had only four prime ministers.

The Danish system of government follows the logic of 'negative parliamentarism', according to which a ruling government survives as long as the prime minister is not ousted by a vote of no-confidence supported by a parliamentary majority (cf. the chapter on Finland in this volume). Informally, this has been the case since 1901, though it was only legally codified in 1953. However, votes of no-confidence have only been passed on three occasions, in 1909, 1947, and 1975, and unsuccessful attempts have been extremely rare.

Danish parties tend not to formulate detailed political manifestos prior to elections, and governmental platforms rarely extend beyond a few pages. This reflects the consensual nature of the political system. It maximizes flexibility, and requires trust and willingness to compromise between coalition partners. Leadership in cabinet involves the creation of team spirit and the avoidance of conflict as much as top-down command. That said, it should also be stressed that the team spirit is most important among leaders of the governing parties and one or two other core members of the cabinet. As long as *they* stand united it is easier to discipline less important ministers.

Ministers do not form a cabinet in the British sense, as there is a greater emphasis on each minister's individual responsibility to parliament than on collective accountability. Thus, individual ministers can be subjected to parliamentary votes of confidence. In practice these virtually never take place, although ministers have occasionally resigned 'voluntarily' after criticism from parliament has led them to anticipate a vote of no-confidence. Five times since the 1850s individual ministers have been put before the Court of Impeachment.

The prime minister has important powers vis-à-vis parliament. He may dissolve parliament and call a general election at his own discretion, and exert much influence on the parliamentary agenda, even though the latter is formally decided by parliament. These powers are important, though ultimately the prime minister cannot lose sight of the fact that he needs the support of several other political parties in order to get things done. 'Leadership' in the Danish context requires flexibility and compromise rather than confrontation. There is a need for compromise within governing parties and, on occasion, between governing parties and elements of the opposition. This seems to be an unpromising setting for the presidentialization of politics; rather, it emphasizes the partified nature of the governing process.

When discussing presidentialization it is important to bear in mind that not all Danish party leaders are potential prime ministers. Since the introduction of democracy only the four old parties—the Social Democratic Party, the Conservative People's Party, the Liberal Party, and the Social Liberal Party—have produced prime ministers. In the last decade only the leaders of the Liberals and the Social Democrats have been realistic candidates for the premiership. When assessing the presidentialization thesis, therefore, it is important to distinguish between 'prime ministerial' parties and other parties, as this enables us to consider whether it relates only to the former or has a broader systemic impact.

THE EXECUTIVE FACE OF PRESIDENTIALIZATION

The strengthening of the executive vis-à-vis the legislature is a common theme in comparative politics. In the Danish case there is no doubt that executive power has been enhanced through the growing importance of delegated legislation over the decades, but this must be seen in the context of frequent minority government. This leaves non-governing parties in a relatively strong position to exert influence on day-to-day administration, rendering difficult overall judgements about the relationship between parliament and government. In addressing the specific issue of prime ministerial power resources and autonomy, we draw on four factors which have been identified as influencing the strength of prime ministers:

• the ability to hire or fire ministers;
• influence in cabinet committees;
• the range of patronage; and
• the level of policy advice (Weller 1985).

The right to hire and fire ministers is an old power which has steadily grown in importance. Ministerial terms of office have become more short-lived. In part, this is because of the greater incidence of reshuffles, and in part because prime ministers since 1964 have been more inclined to exploit their right to dissolve parliament. The average duration of ministerial terms of office has roughly halved by comparison to the period 1920–40. The increasing turnover of ministerial incumbents has been especially marked since the early 1970s. However, there are some exceptions to this trend. These are the core ministers, first and foremost the prime minister, plus the minister of finance and the minister of foreign affairs. This suggests that core and periphery layers of Danish government have in reality become more distinguishable (Knudsen 2000*b*). We may reasonably speak of a centralization of the cabinet around the 'core' ministers and especially around the prime minister. This core has the upper hand in the formation of the government's general strategy, while other ministers are easier to discipline given that they know they can be fired. The prime minister at the time of writing (Anders Fogh Rasmussen) has, in the view of many observers, also been able to neutralize his coalition partners to an unprecendented degree in the formation of policy (Taudorf 2003).

Genuine cabinet reshuffles were not routine prior to 1973, although ministerial turnover was already prevalent in the 1960s, due to the more frequent incidence of general elections from that time. In 1973 seven ministers were reshuffled. Then, in 1986 Prime Minister Poul Schlüter reshuffled his Cabinet on an unprecedented scale, introducing nine new faces to ministerial posts. Between 1993 and 2001 Poul Nyrup Rasmussen reshuffled his ministerial pack on no less than twelve occasions. In all but two of these instances, the reshuffles were brought about by general elections or changes in the party composition of coalition governments. However, there is not much doubt that the desire to renew the government's image with fresh faces often motivated these reshuffles, even after general elections. In contrast, Thorvald Stauning, Prime Minister from 1929 to 1942, altered his list of peacetime ministers (1929–40) on only four occasions. Significantly, the present prime minister declared publicly, at the outset of his premiership, that ministers not doing their jobs in a 'satisfactory' manner would be sacked. This kind of public declaration is without precedent. The very possibility of a reshuffle may in itself create discipline within cabinets and thereby enhance the position of the prime minister. It should be added, however, that changes of ministers from parties other than that of the prime minister need to be negotiated with the leaders of these parties, though this does not prevent such changes from happening.

Danish prime ministers also have a legal duty to monitor individual ministers. This was originally established by the Court of Impeachment in 1910. This requirement had no practical consequence until the 1990s, when the Conservative prime minister from 1982 to 1993, Poul Schlüter, was compelled to resign before impeachment became a reality. He had been criticized for not fulfilling his obligation to monitor a minister who was accused, and later found guilty of, illegal administration. Schlüter's successor, Poul Nyrup Rasmussen, was far more active in intervening in his ministers' affairs. The tendency for premiers to be more activist in this monitoring role nowadays further implies that they exert greater 'hands-on' control over their cabinets.

The second indicator of intra-executive presidentialization is the prime minister's influence on cabinet committees. Ministers gather each week at full cabinet meetings chaired by the prime minister, but many important issues are not really discussed at these meetings as individual ministers do not like to interfere in each other's affairs: to try to deprive other ministers of their autonomy is to risk being deprived of one's own. Cabinet meetings are therefore not the most important mechanism in coordinating the work of governments. Denmark is no different from a number of other countries in this respect, though the importance of cabinet meetings as means of conflict-resolution is probably less than in most cases. The expectation is that conflicts between ministers will be settled prior to full cabinet meetings. On the rare occasions this does not happen, the prime minister takes the final decision; cabinet votes, as a means of resolving conflict, are last thought to have occurred in 1924. The most important function of full cabinet meetings nowadays is to perform a final check on government initiatives before bills are presented in parliament. In addition, ministers' memoranda to parliament, ministers' replies to parliament, and bills and proposals from other parties or private members of parliament are among the most important matters discussed in cabinet (Knudsen 2000*a*, 2000*b*; Nielsen 1996; Wolf 1996).

In the past, cabinet meetings had a much more important role. In the 1930s more than 100 meetings were held each year, whereas the annual number is now less than forty. Under the present government, they often only last for no more than an hour (Taudorf 2003). Today, the cabinet is often the last ritual link in a chain of decisions. In its place, a system of cabinet committees has become prominent since the Second World War, a trend common to a number of other countries (Andeweg 1997: 69). Cabinet committees will usually be the venues for important strategic discussions of policy initiatives. Such initiatives will be coordinated 'top-down' through a series of core government consultations, which set out the framework to be filled in by line ministries. In some cases detailed negotiations are conducted (or at least supervised) by the ministry of finance and the prime minister's office (PMO) in order to control politically sensitive issues (Knudsen 2000*a*). The right to shape this committee system and to choose where to participate within it, are important means by which the prime minister can exert control over government, although negotiations over committee composition can constitute a part of the coalition-building process. The most important committees in Denmark are the Coordinating Committee (formed in 1982), the Cabinet Committee on Economic Affairs (formed in 1947), and the European Summit Committee (formed in 1975). The most important ministers meet in these committees, joined by less important ministers on an ad hoc basis. It is much easier to discipline an individual minister in these meetings than at cabinet meetings where all ministers are present (Knudsen 2000*b*). The number of committees was reduced in 2001 to six by the present prime minister. He is a member of five and the chairman of four of these. This level of prime ministerial dominance within the cabinet committee system is without precedent.

An interesting trend in the prime minister's own membership of cabinet committees can be observed. The Social Democratic Prime Minister from 1993 to 2001, Poul Nyrup Rasmussen, became increasingly involved in committees related to international affairs. Throughout his time in office, Nyrup Rasmussen was chairman or member of seven committees, of which four were exclusively dedicated to international affairs—including Danish membership of the EU. By contrast, his predecessor was a member of only one committee related to international affairs. The growing importance of regular EU summits is one of the reasons why the prime minister has generally become much more visible in the media as the personification of the Danish state, while the minister of foreign affairs increasingly plays second fiddle. One indication of the growing importance of the Danish premier's role in international affairs is the increasing frequency of foreign travel which his official website reports: On sixty days of the year 2000 he travelled, or participated in international conferences, which was a new record. Subsequently, in 2002, his successor Anders Fogh Rasmussen travelled on a total of sixty-nine days. This is interesting because, since 1870 Denmark has considered herself to be a 'small state', with few pretensions to playing a leading role in international affairs, and premiers have consequently restricted themselves largely to the domain of domestic politics. Several of them, including Anker Jørgensen (Prime Minister from 1972 to 1974 and from 1975 to 1982), only had a rudimentary knowledge of English and other foreign languages. The new trend reflects the fact that presidents and prime ministers are much more heavily involved in foreign affairs than hitherto because of the EU and other forms of supranational cooperation. This development seems likely to have strengthened the prime minister within the cabinet, though it does not necessarily strengthen him in relation to the electorate. Opinion polls suggested that Nyrup Rasmussen was regarded as having handled the 'war on terrorism' well after September 11, 2001; accordingly, he called a general election in November 2001, but he and his party suffered defeat. The voters seemed more interested in domestic politics.

Presidentialization in Denmark has its limitations, especially in respect of prime ministerial rights of patronage. Indeed, the most striking characteristic of the Danish civil service is that patronage as such does not exist. In principle, each ministry is autonomous in establishing its own pattern of employment, a state of affairs which follows logically from the emphasis on individual ministerial responsibility. Denmark resembles Germany and the Netherlands in this respect, rather than countries like the United Kingdom or Sweden, where the prime minister enjoys considerable power over appointments. That said, the reality is not entirely straightforward. Danish prime ministers have significant influence over individual ministers' decisions concerning the appointment and dismissal of senior civil servants. Since 1977, there has been a small appointments committee within the cabinet, which affords the inner core of ministers influence over these decisions. The operation of this committee is somewhat obscure, but it appears to serve as a reminder to individual ministers not simply to accede to the requests of their civil servants in making appointments. Moreover, since the mid-1970s top civil servants have been removed from office more frequently. Consequently there have been more opportunities for prime ministerial intervention over these appointments (Børsen 2003).

What of the final aspect of prime ministerial power, the level of policy advice which he or she may enjoy? Here, we also find evidence of constraints operating on the Danish prime minister. Denmark permits an unusually restricted number of political appointments in government. There are no junior ministers, state secretaries, or coteries of political advisers. All but a few appointments are non-partisan and purely meritocratic. However, since 1998 ministers have been allowed to appoint 'specific advisers'. These advisers can only be employed on a short-term basis and are supposed to have a 'specific' relationship—either political or personal in nature—with the minister involved. The conveniently vague concept of 'specific adviser' facilitated the smooth introduction of a limited number of political appointees and expert advisers. Such individuals can only be appointed to positions within a minister's personal secretariat. Thus far, only a dozen or so media consultants have been appointed to such positions. Hence, Danish ministers are still largely left to depend on advice from career civil servants, although for election campaigns, they will normally seek advice from party specialists.

Until 1964, the PMO was very small and organizationally not suited to meet the requirements of giving policy advice or parliamentary analysis. However, organizational reforms in 1964 and 1980 greatly enhanced the level of service and advice enjoyed by the prime minister, especially in foreign affairs. As a result, the prime minister's ability to steer the cabinet and to set the parliamentary agenda has been dramatically improved. Further reforms were introduced in 1994, which strengthened the hierarchy within the PMO, enlarged its staff from twenty-three to thirty, and enabled it to recruit younger civil servants from line ministries on a temporary basis. In addition, the prime minister has a private secretariat, which has also been strengthened, while the handling of the media has been upgraded and centralized.

These changes have not always produced straightforwardly positive results for the prime minister. This was especially evident in the case of Poul Nyrup Rasmussen. The 'old guard' within the PMO reacted with hostility to their new boss, partly because he gradually phased them out, and partly because he twice informed the press about the removal of a permanent secretary before the permanent secretary himself was informed. Moreover, suspicion was generated by a media which created an exaggerated impression of a new 'super ministry' staffed with young party affiliates of the prime minister. Further, there have also been a number of instances in which the PMO has had severe problems over political communications, notably in international affairs. In November 2001, a change of government brought a new prime minister, Anders Fogh Rasmussen, who introduced a new system of centralized control of media relations. The most important media advisers met weekly under the leadership of Fogh Rasmussen's personal adviser to develop joint media strategies. This implies a new, if moderate, degree of centralization and coordination of media relations in the hands of the prime minister and his personal media adviser.

To sum up, the historical institutional background of the Danish prime minister means that he (or she) has strong powers in relation to hiring and firing ministers, the (re-)distribution of portfolios, and the cabinet committee system. However, prime ministers are constrained by a necessary respect for their coalition partners. These constraints are not new, but their importance has grown due to the increasing frequency of coalition governments. Furthermore, the prime minister is comparatively weak when we look at the power to control appointments below ministerial level, and when we consider the level of expert advice available. Neither does the Danish prime minister (unlike his Swedish counterpart, for example) have an apparatus for formulating administrative policy; for historical reasons, that lies with the minister of finance (which still has to face the fact that every other ministry is formally independent in internal organizational and personnel matters). In general, the comparatively small size of the PMO means that the prime minister has to be very careful in his relations with the minister of finance and minister of foreign affairs. These actors, and their ministries, are important to the tasks of coordinating the work of government and handling international affairs. In essence, then, the weak point of the Danish prime minister is the relative under-capacity of the PMO.

That said, if we look at *trends* since 1960 we see a more general strengthening of the prime minister. Prime ministers themselves enjoy growing longevity in office compared to other ministers. They have used their right to hire and fire other ministers—with the exception of the ministers of finance and foreign affairs—more often. Cabinet reshuffles have become more prevalent, and the organization of governmental work in ministerial meetings and committees, including the Appointments Committee, has changed in ways that have improved the prime minister's potential for control over political and organizational processes. The PMO has gradually been strengthened to enhance the level of advice and service available to him. And finally, the prime minister has gained an increasingly important role in European and international affairs since the early 1990s. This has afforded him a stronger hand within the cabinet, and vis-à-vis the legislature. Perhaps the most remarkable sign of this change is the (symbolic) Danish participation in the war against Iraq in 2003. It was decided only by a small parliamentary majority, and represented a dramatic break with the traditions of Danish foreign policy, which have long centred on the UN and the need for consensus at home. This was, in reality, first and foremost the decision of the prime minister personally, abetted by a somewhat more reluctant foreign minister. The new developments seem to be caused largely by two factors: First, the need to discipline individual ministers and their ministries in the context of a highly ambitious welfare state; and second, the twin and allied processes of Europeanization and globalization.

THE PARTY FACE OF PRESIDENTIALIZATION

To what extent have leaders in Denmark become more powerful within their own parties since 1960? In addressing this question, we will draw on three indicators:

- the manner of their own election;
- the influence they exert over processes of candidate-selection;
- the financial and personnel resources at their disposal within the party.

A number of leadership positions are found within Danish parties (Bille 1997: 379–86). The leader of the party organization is *the* leader in the case of the Socialist People's Party, the Social Democratic Party, the Centre-Democrats, the Liberal Party, and the Danish People's Party, and has primarily been so in the case of the Christian People's Party. These leaders are elected by the members at their parties' annual conferences, and are therefore able to claim a personal mandate from the grass-root activists. In the Social Liberal Party and the Conservative People's Party the party leaders have primarily been the leaders of the parliamentary groups, and are elected by their respective parties' MPs. The Red-Green Alliance does not have a party leader but is led by a collective leadership body.

Though formally elected by their members or parliamentarians, some party leaders have a more personal mandate than others. Personal mandates are in particular claimed by party founders, such as Pia Kjærsgaard of the Danish People's Party, Mogens Glistrup of the Progress Party, and Erhard Jakobsen of the Centre-Democrats. The latter was succeeded by his daughter, Mimi Jakobsen, who 'inherited' the leadership and the personal mandate. Party leaders elected in contested elections, rather than at elections where they are the only candidates, may more legitimately claim a popular personal mandate than in situations where the party elite effectively chooses the one and only candidate. Overall, there is a modest trend towards contested party leadership elections. The Socialist People's Party has always had genuinely competitive party leadership elections, but they have tended to be more sporadic among the other parties: for instance, the Liberal Party experienced one in 1984, the Social Democrats in 1992, and the Christian People's Party in both 1979 and 1990 (Bille 1994: 143). On all other occasions there has been only one candidate for the leadership, and therefore only notionally an 'election'. Party leaders may also claim a more personal mandate, and thereby a higher degree of autonomy, when chosen in a plebiscitary consultation of the membership. Across Western Europe, there is evidence of a trend towards a greater role for party members through the introduction of leadership elections conducted by postal ballot (Scarrow et al. 2000: 142). In Denmark, however, this applies only to the Social Democrats, and only on occasions when no candidate gets 75 per cent of the votes cast at the national congress; in fact, this procedure has yet to be implemented.

The second indicator of leadership power in the party relates to the process of candidate-selection. Always a source of potential conflict within parties, this area of activity tends to be heavily regulated by the party statutes. Disputes may arise when the national party leadership seeks the selection of specific candidates against the wishes of local constituency organizations, particularly in 'safe' constituencies; similarly, conflicts can occur between different party factions over their preferred candidates. Rules regarding candidate-selection in Danish parties have been fairly stable since 1960 (Bille 1997: 119). Generally, local party organizations are autonomous when selecting candidates, although approval by the national party organization is required by the Social Democrats, the Socialist People's Party, and the Christian People's Party. Local or regional party organizations are sovereign in these matters in most other Danish parties.

The major innovation in respect of candidate-selection in Denmark (as elsewhere in Western Europe) has been the increased use of membership ballots since 1960. No Danish party used this procedure in 1960, whereas by 2000, postal ballots were mandatory for the Social Democrats, the Socialist People's Party, the Centre-Democrats, and the Red-Green Alliance, while they were optional for the Liberal Party and the Social Liberals. Thus, the party selectorates have become more inclusive in Denmark (Bille 2001; Rahat and Hazan 2001). On the face of it, this might seem to run against the grain of a 'presidentialized' party, but this is not necessarily true. Even though party leaders have not formally been empowered in the process of candidate-selection, the use of postal ballots effectively by-passes the middle-level elites and party activists. This increases the autonomy of the party leadership because the middle-level elites and activists are generally in a better position to constrain the leadership than the ordinary party members; through channels of communication such as the media, party leaders can directly appeal to all their members. When the power of the activists is curbed, the capacity of the leadership to manoeuvre freely is enhanced. In a nutshell, postal ballots tend to strengthen, rather than weaken, the autonomy and power resources of the party leadership, thereby 'presidentializing' the party arena.

The final aspect of leaders' intra-party power concerns the resources at their disposal. Have these increased? Party central offices tend to be small, but are effectively under the control of the leadership. In general, party staff in Denmark has grown since 1960, especially within the parliamentary organizations (Bille 1997: 205). Since party leaders normally assume a prominent position in their parliamentary groups, we can infer that this has enhanced the resources at their disposal. It has, among other things, enabled them to bring a new professionalism to the party organizations, in terms of people with political, financial, or media expertise. Similarly, the parties' financial resources have increased considerably since 1960 (Bille 1997: 339–45). This was the case even before the introduction of public subsidies to party organizations in 1987, but state funding—which rose particularly sharply after 1995—has really boosted this process. What is more, party leaderships have particularly benefited from this development, thanks to the degree of control they tend to exert over party finances.

Overall, the evidence suggests that the presidentialization of the intra-party arena is somewhat limited in Denmark. There is a modest trend towards more personalized mandates for party leaders, and the latter have also benefited from greater capacity to influence candidate-selection processes, and are better resourced. But the leaders remain constrained by party statutes to a significant degree.

THE ELECTORAL FACE OF PRESIDENTIALIZATION

The electoral face of presidentialization draws us into discussion of three issues:

- have the media focused increasingly on party leaders during election campaigns?
- have Danish parties emphasized the appeal of party leaders more now than in the past?
- is there evidence of a growing leadership effect on voting behaviour?

The Danish media environment has undergone substantial change. The 'four-newspaper-system' where each of the four old parties owned a newspaper or had a newspaper affiliated to it in most parts of the country disintegrated following the Second World War (Pedersen 1987: 38). The number of newspapers declined and those which remained were de-party-politicized. Furthermore, the introduction of television in the 1950s fundamentally transformed the media environment. Television is now the most important medium, not only as a channel of information for Danish voters, but also as an instrument of agenda-setting (Siune 1992). Subsequently, the introduction of computers, cable and satellite television, and the internet has further changed the media context (Farrell 1996).

The growing role of the electronic media is significant, for it naturally tends to focus on personality and sound bites, and thereby sets different conditions for political actors to operate in. The internet, for example, facilitates a weekly newsletter and other kinds of personalized communication from party leaders to voters. Most Danish parties—even those without genuine prime ministerial candidates—have chosen to create party leaders' newsletters; this direct form of communication between leaders and grass-root followers—members as well as voters—exemplifies the kind of elite-mass relationship on which presidentialization is founded.

Danish parties are legally prevented from advertising on nationwide television, and they therefore depend on broadcasters for their coverage. All parties represented in parliament are entitled to equal broadcast time on state-regulated channels of communication, a principle derived from the constitution (Jensen 1989). However, the principle of equal representation does not apply to news coverage, where journalistic criteria apply, and neither does it apply so strictly to the second national broadcasting channel. Party leader debates on the first television channel have been a regular feature of election campaigns since the establishment of nationwide television in the 1950s. Each party has the right to a prime-time broadcast slot during the campaign, and all party leaders participate in the televised debate, which traditionally takes place on the evening before election day. Over the past three decades, political parties' control over these debates has receded, while the broadcasting station and its journalists have increased their influence. Analysis has shown that campaign coverage gives priority to party leaders, to controversial issues, and to parties that are particularly interesting in a given election campaign because of their position on certain salient issues. Television broadcasters also seek to achieve a balance in their coverage of governing and opposition parties. Overall this indicates that there are limits to the extent to which television can focus on party leaders alone, but this nevertheless happens more now than before. Thus, the coverage of election campaigns by television has become somewhat more presidential.

The national elections of 1998, 2001 and 2005 were widely described as 'presidential' even before they had started. There is a danger that the media's approach to the campaigns might have made this a self-fulfilling prophecy (Nielsen 1999: 20). Much media attention was thereby devoted to the format of the campaign, while content and messages tended to attract less attention. Moreover, since the media designated them 'presidentialized' elections and focused on leaders, the parties needed to adjust to this fact in their campaigns. This, in turn, may have influenced the voters. This process may be facilitated in elections where there is a clear division between government and opposition, each with a clear candidate for prime ministerial office. In such instances, competition is bipolar, a phenomenon which is characteristic of presidential elections (as well as of parliamentary elections in the Westminster model). In fact, this scenario is common in the Danish context. Of the last sixteen national elections, eleven (including those of 1998, 2001 and 2005) have had two prime ministerial candidates (cf. Borre 1999: 109). However, not every election in Denmark is so straightforwardly bipolar. The multiparty system calls for consensual politics with coalition governments and cooperation across the political spectrum, and implies that it is not the case in every election that there are only two candidates for prime minister. When there are more than two prime ministerial candidates, the election campaign will not take on the dynamics of a presidential system to quite the same extent, and the media will focus on more than the party leaders.

The focus of the media on leaders forces political parties to adapt their campaigns accordingly. This brings us to the second indicator of electoral presidentialization: party campaign strategies. The changing context provides challenges as well as possibilities for parties in the way they conduct election campaigns. In the three most recent campaigns, Danish parties drew inspiration from both the USA and the United Kingdom on how to conduct campaigns, but the national context does impose certain limitations on how far this can go. First, the money available to Danish parties is limited compared to other West European parties, even though the introduction of state funding in 1987 enabled parties to undertake more capital intensive campaigning. Second, access to the mass media is regulated and political commercials are banned from national radio and national, as well as local, television. Third, the electoral system affects the way in which parties campaign. Parties cannot focus exclusively on the party leader's personality, as they need to enhance the general party image so that candidates across the country get votes. Voters can only vote for parties or candidates within one of seventeen electoral districts. It may of course be argued that party leaders are important to the general party image, in as much as the latter is enhanced through focus on the former. But other party candidates still need to be promoted.

On the other hand, many of these constraints apply to other parliamentary democracies in Europe, and the erosion of traditional cleavage politics and increased electoral volatility imply that parties may be obliged to appeal to voters on the basis of personal qualities instead of ideological packages. The potential for fundamental policy differences is particularly limited by the process of globalization in a small, open economy like Denmark's. Thus, Danish parties largely agree on welfare issues, though they may give priority to different improvements in social policy.

There are no systematic longitudinal studies of Danish parties' election campaigns but anecdotal evidence points towards a weak tendency towards an increasing emphasis on their leaders. Analyses of election campaigns in 1990 and 1998 suggest that the campaign focus on party leaders has not increased substantially in this period (Andersen and Pedersen 1999; Bille et al. 1992). Most, but not all, parties focused on their leaders throughout this period. In 1990 the Social Democrats presented their party leader as the natural prime ministerial candidate. He debated only with the incumbent prime minister and attempted to appear 'statesmanlike'. The incumbent prime minister at that time was Conservative, and his party ran a leader-focused campaign, the key theme of which was 'Schlüter again—who else?' The Liberals also focused on leader image in their campaign (Bille et al. 1992:

73–6). In 1998, the Liberals found it hard to distinguish between the leader and the party, while for the Centre-Democrats, the leader was 'the one pulling it all', and the Socialist People's Party depended on their leader to the extent that they posted his name 'in neon lights' (Andersen and Pedersen 1999). In both 1998, 2001 and 2005 many parties did not advertise in national newspapers without including pictures of their party leaders. The major parties sent their leaders on bus tours around the country to talk at schools, town square meetings, and the like, the purpose of which was not merely for as many voters as possible to 'shake hands with' the party leader, but primarily to provide photo opportunities. Overall, these developments indicate a pronounced emphasis on leadership throughout the 1990s, but there is no direct evidence as to how far this contrasts with earlier elections.

To a degree, the various parties reveal differing attitudes towards the presidentialization of campaigning because of their rather divergent internal political cultures. Some have always focused on their party leaders, and have sought charismatic individuals who will serve this purpose: this has been particularly pronounced in the case of the Centre-Democrats, the Progress Party, and the Danish People's Party. Others, however, have tended to refrain from personalizing politics, not least for ideological reasons: the Red-Green Alliance is the prime example here, although the Socialist People's Party was also resistant for a long time.

The picture is harder to characterize in simple terms for most other cases. Analyses of the 1990 and 1998 campaigns show that parties find it difficult to focus their campaigns on their leader if he or she is not supported by a large majority within the party. This applied, for example, to the Christian People's Party before 1990 when the party elected a new young party leader, and for the Conservatives in 1998, after a period of frequent changes in the party leadership. Another obstacle to personalization is prior (negative) experience, as illustrated by the Social Liberals who lost support in the election of 1988 after running a leader-oriented campaign. Thereafter, they decided to focus on the parliamentary group more generally, and particularly on those who served as members of the government (Bille et al. 1992: 74). The internal balance of power within a party can also act to constrain the presidentialization of campaigning, as can evidence that a particular leader lacks appeal for the electorate.

The third aspect of electoral presidentialization concerns the effect of party leaders on the electorate. There are few studies of leadership effects on Danish voting behaviour, but there is some evidence upon which to draw. The extent to which prime ministerial candidates directly determine voter choices has been analysed for national elections held in 1971, 1994, and 1998, and shows that in four out of six cases (that is, two major party leaders at each of the three elections) sympathy for the leader had a significant effect. The effects were modest, however, in that they never amounted to more than one-sixth of the effect of general party sympathy (Borre 1999: 112–13). In a nutshell, this does not support the proposition that leadership effects on voting behaviour have grown in Danish electoral politics. That said, this analysis only takes into account the direct effect of voter attitudes towards party leaders (ibid.: 113). What this type of research cannot easily do is gauge the extent to which party leaders influence voters' attitudes towards their parties as a whole. Leaders are in some cases associated with their parties to such an extent that the two become virtually indistinguishable; this leaves us uncertain as to where the party effect finishes and the leader effect starts.

On the basis of these—admittedly somewhat meagre—results, it is tempting to agree with the view of one of Denmark's most experienced electoral analysts, who argues that there is little evidence to suggest that electoral behaviour in the country is becoming more presidential (ibid.: 110). Nevertheless, the contemporary media seem determined to adopt a 'presidential' focus in their coverage, while the evidence on party campaigning is not clear-cut; most parties—both those with and those without prime ministerial candidates—seek to emphasize the appeal of the party leader, but it is not certain that this is universally true, nor that it holds to a substantially increasing degree.

CONCLUSION

Presidential trends are apparent, if limited, in both the electoral and party faces of politics in Denmark. In the latter, there is a discernible strengthening of party leaders in respect of the resources available to them and their potential to influence the candidate-nomination process; however, these tendencies remain limited and have not been formalized in party statutes. There is also some presidentialization of the electoral process, especially in relation to media coverage. Perceiving the way in which the media seeks to personalize its coverage of politics, the parties have sought to accommodate this in their campaign strategies. Thus, parties focus on their leaders, probably a little more than earlier—but the extent to which the leaders' personal qualities determine voter choice remains limited.

The presidentialization process seems stronger in the governmental arena. This is apparent in the growing longevity of prime ministers in executive office vis-à-vis other ministers (excepting the ministers of finance and foreign affairs), and in the increasing frequency with which the premiers reshuffle their cabinets. It is also evident in the growing use of cabinet committees for executive coordination, the gradual, if modest, growth of the PMO, and the new system by which media relations are coordinated by the prime minister's staff. Last, but not least, the Europeanization of politics has imposed a more visible and active role on the prime minister in international affairs, which has strengthened the premier's hand within the cabinet, at the particular expense of the foreign minister.

Nevertheless, even within the governing arena, constraints operate on presidentialization. For one thing, the prime minister does not enjoy any formal rights of patronage; for another, anything looking like an attempt to create a super-ministry out of the PMO has met with criticism from line ministries and the media. Most significantly, though, prime ministerial power in Denmark is still kept in check by consensus politics. The tradition of minority and multiparty government makes this a necessity, and consensus culture does not generally call for strong personalized leadership. Thus, even though structural causes of presidentialization such as the growth of the state, the development of a modern mass media, the erosion of cleavages, and the Europeanization of politics, all exist in the Danish case, the logic and reality of consensus politics means that domestic politics is still not heavily presidentialized.

REFERENCES

Andersen, P. W. and K. Pedersen (1999). 'De danske partier og folketingsvalgkampen i 1998', *Politica*, 21: 297–312.

Andeweg, R. (1997). 'Collegiality and Collectivity: Cabinets, Cabinet Committees, and Cabinet Ministers', in P. Weller, H. Bakvis, and R. A. W. Rhodes (eds.), *The Hollow Crown*. Basingstoke: Macmillan, 58–83.

Bille, L. (1994). 'Denmark: The Decline of the Membership Party?', in R. S. Katz and P. Mair (eds.), *How Parties Organize*. London: Sage, 134–57.

—— (1997). *Partier i forandring*. Odense: Odense Universitetsforlag.

—— (2001). 'Democratizing a Democratic Procedure: Myth or Reality?: Candidate Selection in Western European Parties, 1960–1990', *Party Politics*, 7: 363–80.

—— J. Elklit, and M. V. Jakobsen (1992). 'Denmark: The 1990 Campaign', in S. Bowler and D. Farrell (eds.), *Electoral Strategies and Political Marketing*. Basingstoke: Macmillan, 63–81.

Borre, O. (1999). 'Partiernes og ledernes popularitet', in J. Andersen, O. Borre, J. G. Andersen, and H. J. Nielsen (eds.), *Vælgere med Omtanke—en analyse af folketingsvalget 1998*. Århus: Systime, 107–14.

Børsen (2003). *Ældre embedsmænd sætter karrieren*, 7–9 March.

Elder, N., A. H. Thomas, and D. Arter (1987). *The Consensual Democracies?*. Oxford: Basil Blackwell.

Farrell, D. M. (1996). 'Campaign Strategies and Tactics', in L. LeDuc, R. G. Niemi, and P. Norris (eds.), *Comparing Democracies: Elections and Voting in Global Perspective*. London: Sage, 160–83.

Henningsen, B. (1980). *Politik eller kaos*. København: Berlingskes Forlag.

Jensen, T. (1989). 'Politiske udsendelser i Danmarks Radio før valg og folkeafstemninger', *Ugeskrift for Retsvæsen*, 129–39.

Knudsen, T. (2000*a*). 'How Informal Can You Be?', in B. G. Peters, R. A. W. Rhodes, and V. Wright (eds.), *Administering the Summit: Administration of the Core Executive*. Basingstoke: Macmillan, 153–76.

—— (2000*b*). *Regering og embedsmænd: Om magt og demokrati i staten*. Århus: Systime.

Nielsen, C. (1996). *The Prime Minister's Office and How the Danish Government Operates in Outline*, personal note, 7 October.

Nielsen, H. J. (1999). 'Op til valget', in J. Andersen, O. Borre, J. G. Andersen, and H. J. Nielsen (eds.), *Vælgere med Omtanke—en analyse af folketingsvalget 1998*. Århus: Systime, 17–28.

Pedersen, M. N. (1987). 'The Danish "Working Multiparty System": Breakdown or Adaptation', in H. Daalder (ed.), *Party Systems in Denmark, Austria, Switzerland, the Netherlands, and Belgium*. London: Pinter, 1–60.

Rahat, G. and R. Y. Hazan (2001). 'Candidate Selection Methods: An Analytical Framework', *Party Politics*, 7: 297–322.

Scarrow, S. E., P. Webb, and D. M. Farrell (2000). 'From Social Integration to Electoral Contestation: The Changing Distribution of Power within Political Parties', in R. J. Dalton and M. P. Wattenberg (eds.), *Parties without Partisans: Political Change in Advanced Industrial Democracies*. Oxford: Oxford University Press, 128–53.

Siune, K. (1992). 'Mass Media and Their Agenda-Setting Function', in P. Gundelach and K. Siune (eds.), *From Voters to Participants*. Århus: Politica, 148–65.

Taudorf, B. (2003). 'Prime Ministerial Predominance: A Comparative Study of the Power Resources of the British and the Danish Prime Ministers'. Unpublished Master thesis, Department of Political Science, University of Copenhagen.

Weller, P. (1985). *First Among Equals: Prime Ministers in Westminster Systems*. Sydney: Allen and Unwin.

Wolf, A. (1996). *Structuring the Management of Policy Making in Coalition Governments: The Case of Denmark*. Unpublished paper, January.

8

'President Persson'—How Did Sweden Get Him?

Nicholas Aylott[1]

INTRODUCTION

By any formal, constitutional measure, Sweden is a parliamentary democracy. The political executive, the government, emerges from the legislature (Riksdagen), and is responsible to it. Second, the executive is collegial. There are no direct, popular elections to individual executive positions at any level of Swedish government. Lijphart (1999: 119), for one, classifies Sweden as a pure parliamentary regime. Moreover, Swedish parliamentarism has deep roots. A proto-parliament developed as a counterweight to royal power during the Middle Ages, with four chambers or 'estates' representing the nobility, the clergy, the emerging urban bourgeoisie, and—in an early indication of the country's egalitarian, participatory political culture—the peasantry. A new constitutional law was adopted in 1719–20, and this heralded a period in which the estates enjoyed political dominance, an 'age of liberty'.

True, a type of separation of powers existed then and after the constitutional reform of 1866, with political authority divided between crown and parliament (Larsson 1999: 324). As late as 1914, in the 'courtyard crisis', the king could resist the cornerstone of parliamentary government, namely, the executive's responsibility to the legislature (Petersson 1994: 25).[2] But the new constitution adopted in 1974 entirely separated the head of state, the monarch, from the head of government, the prime minister.[3] It also placed a unicameral parliament unambiguously at the centre of the constitutional power structure. In fact, by the 1990s the constitution was widely seen as having promoted a sort of super-parliamentarism. Minority governments have increasingly become the norm in Sweden, and, according to Lijphart (1999: 136), 'minority cabinets are by their nature at the mercy of the legislature in parliamentary systems'. Lijphart's view seemed verified by the fall of a Social Democratic government in February 1990. It had made its emergency economic package an issue of confidence, and the government lost the vote. It duly resigned. It quickly became clear, though, that there was no tenable basis for an alternative administration, given the balance of parliamentary forces. Within a week the same Social Democratic prime minister was back in office, minus his finance minister, and the country seemed no nearer to tackling its crisis (Lindbeck et al. 1994: 171; Petersson 1994: 95).

Yet within a few years this argument had been turned on its head. Political commentators complained that, far from being beholden to the whim of the legislature, the prime minister, Göran Persson, was actually too powerful. *Dagens Nyheter* (2002), the biggest-selling broadsheet, frequently presented such a view, arguing, for instance, that 'instead of ultra-parliamentarism we have ended up with a type of presidentialism'. A respected political journalist, Björn Elmbrant (2002), broadcast a much-discussed series of radio articles entitled 'President Persson—hur fick vi honom?' (How did we get him?). Away from the corridors of power, meanwhile, a comparable development had already been identified in electoral politics. The director of the Swedish Institute for North American Studies at Uppsala University observed:

In contrast to the US, Sweden is a parliamentary democracy, built around a multi-party system and proportional elections. The US has a presidential system with two dominant parties, whose candidates are chosen according to majoritarian principles ... Our political system has long had a collectivist character, in which party representatives would rather talk in terms of 'we' than 'I'. In the US, individual politicians take centre stage, and the media's fixation with personality has over the years been very strong.... Many of these differences seem now to be diminishing or disappearing. (Åsard 2000)

Given its unambivalently parliamentary constitution, how can these assertions about Swedish politics be explained? Is there more to its 'presidentialization' than journalists sniping at a prime minister's domineering personality? This chapter argues that, in fact, there is more than a little substance to the idea of an informal Swedish presidency, but that some of the conditions that created it may not be structural—that is, they may diminish in significance according to prevailing political circumstances.

Examining presidentialization

One way of understanding the nature of power in different political regime-types is through the powerful yet essentially simple concept of principals and agents (Strøm 2000: 266–70). The principal is a political actor that wants something done; the agent is the actor to which the principal delegates the task. In all systems of representative democracy, a chain of principals and agents, and thus a chain of delegation and accountability, can be modelled. In parliamentary systems, the basic principals, the *electors*, delegate certain powers to their *parliamentary representatives*, who delegate in turn to a *prime minister*, who delegates to *individual ministers*, who delegate to the people who actually administer the implementation of public policy, *civil servants*. In presidential systems, by contrast, electors delegate power directly to a single-person, non-collegial executive—the president. But they also delegate to a separate, competing agent, or even two of them—namely, the legislature, which may comprise two chambers. There is, then, more than one chain of delegation and accountability in a presidential system.

However, delegation in a parliamentary system is also not quite as straightforward as it might first appear, thanks to the role of one additional set of actors: political parties (see also Kiewiet and McCubbins 1991). They help principals at each stage of the chain of delegation to overcome agency problems—in other words, they reduce the agent's scope for pursuing its own interests above those of the principal. Indeed, parties are so important to this process that they should, according to Müller (2000: 317–19), constitute a distinct 'track' through which delegation and accountability pass. A prime minister, for instance, is not just accountable to parliamentarians, who are accountable to voters (the constitutional channel). She is also, as a *party leader*,[4] accountable to her *party organization*, which is accountable to its *activists*, themselves drawn from the ranks of more passive party *members* (the party track). The leader of a party in a parliamentary system is, therefore, much more accountable to her party than a presidential candidate is to her party in a presidential system. The latter, once nominated, is largely free of control from the party. If elected, her mandate comes directly from the electorate, and her party cannot remove her from office.[5]

Of course, envisaging regime-types in these principal–agent terms does involve considerable simplification.[6] But envisaging a political chief executive in a parliamentary system as an agent of two principals, parliament and party, suits our purposes here, because it illuminates the nature of the phenomenon, presidentialization, that interests us. We may assume, then, that *de facto* presidentialization in the sense set out in this book's introductory chapter occurs when the head of government, the prime minister, slips the controls that her supposed principals, the country's parliamentarians and her party, have placed on her, and she instead acquires a 'personal mandate' to hold her office, rather than one bestowed on her by dint of her being party leader. Rather than remaining practically accountable to these two actors, as the chain of delegation in a parliamentary system would suggest, the prime ministerial agent has established, albeit informally, a direct accountability relationship with the ultimate principals in each track, the voters and the party rank-and-file—precisely the sort of accountability that formally characterizes a presidential system. As Poguntke and Webb (this volume) argue, this sort of personal mandate may—somewhat counter-intuitively—even be more readily acquired in a consensual system than in a majoritarian one, as the prime minister claims the licence to broker deals in the crowded thicket of veto players. Arguably, this process of presidentialization is driven by changes at the elite level, including the growing internationalization of governance and the overall growth of state activity. However, it is also facilitated by wider social changes, particularly as regards mass communication and the way voters relate to political parties. This explains why the overall process is increasingly centred on political leaders, irrespective of their being credible contenders for prime ministerial office.

The questions now are: has this process occurred in Sweden and, if so, to what extent and with what degree of durability? In seeking answers, the rest of this chapter is divided into three main sections, which address the various 'faces' of presidentialization (see Chapter 1). The first is the executive face. Here we look at the means by which parliament can hold the executive to account, the cabinet can hold the prime minister to account, and the effectiveness of these means in practice. The second is the party face, and accordingly we turn to examine power within the parties. The third face of presidentialization is the electoral one. Here we examine the extent to which electoral campaigns have become focused on individuals, either at the media's or the political parties' instigation, and whether this has influenced voting. Finally, we draw overall conclusions about presidentialization in Sweden.

THE EXECUTIVE FACE

The prime minister's material power resources

Long after the wartime national government, Sweden's chief executive was still not much more than first among equals. But, under the 1974 constitution, the prime minister, like a president, has the constitutional right to choose the rest of the cabinet, which then takes decisions as a collegial body. Moreover, the resources available to the prime minister for coordination have grown considerably (see Larsson 1986: 182ff). When Tage Erlander, prime minister for a record twenty-three years, assumed the position in 1946, his staff comprised—famously—just one caretaker and a part-time secretary. Erlander apparently held a general antipathy to building up prime ministerial resources, which he feared might drag him into day-to-day management and conflict. But when, in 1963, he was left ill-informed as a spy scandal broke, this approach changed. Since then, the accumulation of the chief executive's resources has been concentrated in the newly established Prime Minister's Office (*statsrådsberedningen*). This comprises both career civil servants and politically appointed special advisers. Headed by the prime minister, its next-most senior figures are a 'minister for coordination' and one or more under-secretaries of state (politically appointed bureaucrats).

In the mid-1980s, Larsson (1986: 194), in his exhaustive study of the Swedish cabinet, could still claim that the Prime Minister's Office was primarily for internal government coordination, rather than for promoting the prime minister as a party politician. But a reform in 1997 enhanced the role of the Prime Minister's Office in the budgetary process, at the expense of the traditionally powerful finance ministry (Elder and Page 2000: 146). Furthermore, Göran Persson felt able and inclined to replace with his own people fifteen of the twenty political advisers in the Prime Minister's Office when he became prime minister in 1996 (ibid.: 138). By some accounts, it accrued still more power as Persson continued as prime minister. During 2003 the government's major initiatives in three crucial policy fields—promoting economic growth, reducing sickness in the workforce, and reforming social security—all emanated from the Prime Minister's Office.[7] In 2002 it employed sixty-three staff, up from forty-six in 1994 (Regeringskansliet 2003: 144).

Above all, one major institutional and political reform has, almost all observers agree, given the government greater licence to act than hitherto: namely, EU membership, which Sweden took up in 1995. The Union's democratic deficit is well known (cf. Bergman and Damgaard 2000). Sweden, like the other member states, has seen the power of its executive increase under this system, and that of its parliament decline. Some attempt has been made to offset this problem through the establishment of a parliamentary Committee on EU Affairs to scrutinize ministers' behaviour in EU negotiations. But, although the committee was modelled partly on the famously powerful Danish equivalent, most observers suggest that it has not proved to be as effective a constraint on the executive (Bergman 1997; Lindgren 2000). There may also be subtler ways in which EU membership has promoted presidentialization in Sweden, through its serving to insulate the prime minister from the control of parliament. Elmbrant (2002: part 2) points to a specific policy initiative, the sanctions that EU members implemented against the new right-wing Austrian government in early 2000. This, he argues, was the result of 'mobile-phone diplomacy'—EU prime ministers communicating directly with each other, and initiating policy without reference to bureaucrats or cabinets, let alone parliaments.

Block politics, the pivotal party, and negative parliamentarism

While these power resources and the developing European political arena have certainly boosted the prime minister's standing, domestic political circumstances may be just as germane to our topic. The dynamics of competition in the party system, the constitutional rules that apply to government formation and maintenance, and the internal life of the parties are all vital to our understanding of presidentialization in Sweden.

In Lijphart's (1999: 131–4) comparative framework, the strength of the executive vis-à-vis the legislature is indicated by cabinet duration. Of thirty-six countries for which an 'index of executive dominance' is calculated, Sweden lands just above mid-table, a long way behind Britain, the country that is, for Lijphart, the 'exemplar of cabinet dominance'. As Fig. 8.1 shows, the trend in Sweden is towards smaller minority governments, whether comprised of single parties or coalitions. The absence of majority bases for governments has, by necessity, cemented the Swedish tradition of consensualism in policy-making. Proposals for legislation usually emanate from the cabinet. They are sent to the appropriate parliamentary committee, which then requests a commission to investigate the prospective law's consequences. The commissions include MPs as well as outside experts and advisers (Arter 1990: 126). Opposition parties are thus incorporated into policy-making at a comparatively early stage, even before the commission's thoughts are sent for referral to interested bodies outside parliament, such as local authorities.

This does indeed look like the antithesis of 'executive dominance'. Yet the government's capacity to ram its legislative preferences through parliament is not the appropriate indicator in our discussion of presidentialization. After all, real presidents often have to bargain tortuously with other branches of government in order to enact legislation. What matters to us is whether the modern Swedish prime minister has gained greater autonomy to act without constant deference to other political actors.

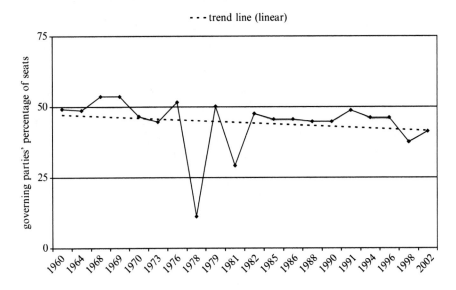

FIG. 8.1. *Trend in Swedish governments' parliamentary bases*

The ultimate way in which his autonomy might be constrained is, of course, if parliament exercises its constitutional right to bring down the government. Certainly, the formal right to do so is present in Sweden. Under the rules incorporated into the constitution in the early 1970s, a new prime minister requires a parliamentary vote of investiture; he can be removed by a parliamentary vote of no confidence; and a government can fall if it loses a vote that it has declared a formal test of confidence (Bergman 2003: 601–3). But these mechanisms, in practice, have become weak means of parliamentary control. This is essentially because there have been precious few 'partisan veto players' (Tsebelis 1995: 302–3) in parliament with the strategic power to bring down a government and—even more importantly—the inclination to exploit that power. And the reason for *that* is an interaction between, on one hand, the constellation of party preferences among the electorate, particularly bloc identity; and, on the other, the basic rule of government formation and maintenance.

The Swedish party system has become more fragmented in recent decades. Sweden's five 'old' parties, which for many years comprised the range of parliamentary representation, have been supplemented by two newer ones. Thus, from 1994 there have been seven parliamentary parties, divided into two competing and (with some exceptions) reasonably coherent blocs. On the left, the 'socialist bloc' consists of the system's dominant party, the Social Democrats; the former Communists, now called the Left Party; and, with what might be called associate membership, the Greens. On the right, the 'non-socialist' or 'bourgeois' bloc features the Centre Party, with its agrarian roots; the Liberals, the Christian Democrats and the conservative Moderates.

The Social Democratic vote has declined. The party won an average of 47 per cent in parliamentary elections in the 1960s, and was even able to form a single-party majority government in 1968–70. By the 1990s this average had fallen to 39.8 per cent. Yet the Social Democrats could still dominate government office, thanks to their frequently maintaining control of the 'median legislator' in parliament—that is, the position at the middle of the left-to-right spectrum. Such a position has been crucial because of the continuing relevance of the two blocs to the Swedish party system. In other words, despite their firm anchor in the socialist bloc, the Social Democrats have been the only party capable of forging coalitions—usually legislative coalitions, occasionally executive ones, recently something in between (Bergman and Aylott 2003)—with parties in both blocs. In addition, the rules of government formation, 'negative parliamentarism' (Bergman 1993), have meant that formal, executive coalitions involving the Social Democrats have been rare, and unknown since 1957. Negative parliamentarism means, essentially, that a prime minister does not require the active backing of a parliamentary majority in order to be seen to enjoy the confidence of the parliament. Instead, all that he requires is that an absolute majority does *not* support a vote of no confidence against him or his government. Thus, abstention is interpreted as passive support for prime ministerial candidates in votes of investiture, and for sitting prime ministers in votes of confidence and no confidence.

The reason that negative parliamentarism, *inter alia*, allows a Social Democratic prime minister to keep government dominated by a single party (his own) is because it improves his bargaining position vis-à-vis the leaderships of cautiously supportive parliamentary parties. He can say to them, in effect: tolerate my single-party government, or actively vote against it and thus allow in the opposition—which, because of the traditional antagonism between the two blocs, your party memberships would probably not like.[8] This, in fact, is pretty much what has happened in Sweden in recent years. The Greens, who gained the prized median-legislator position in parliament in both the 1998 and 2002 elections, nevertheless joined the Left Party on both occasions in agreeing to prop up a purely Social Democratic government. The Greens did this largely because of their members' likely suspicion of any coalition between them and the bourgeois parties.[9] In this way, the Social Democrats have combined exclusive power with strategic flexibility. When the government has found itself at odds with its support parties, as over European policy or security doctrine, it has simply attained parliamentary majorities by cooperating with opposition parties that, on those questions, were of like mind.

Indeed, according to Lewin (1996, 1998), the framers of Swedish constitutional arrangements consciously rejected the Westminster model of single-party majority governments, in favour of something much closer to Lijphart's (1999) consensual ideal-type: rule, not by the majority, but through 'representativeness'—that is, through bargaining that involves as many as possible of the parliamentary parties. In this model, the likeliest governing party was not necessarily the largest one, but the one that 'could play the role of pivot, putting together voting majorities from its position in the political middle with support sometimes from the left and sometimes from the right' (Lewin 1998: 197).[10] With the continuing strategic power of the Social Democrats in the party system, plus the effects of negative parliamentarism, the tradition of minority, consensual government has grown stronger in Sweden. The pivot—usually, the Social Democratic prime minister—has certainly not been all-powerful. But it has become harder to imagine that parliament, through assembling an active majority against him, could dislodge him between elections. In that, he has come to resemble a more presidential figure.

Two additional features of the constitution may have accentuated this trend. First, even if there is an early election (as the cabinet, with few formal restrictions, can decide), the next scheduled election must also be held. This makes it less likely that the parliament would try to induce such a development. Second, under the new constitution, a minister with a parliamentary seat must nominate a stand-in MP while she serves in government. This resembles a presidential separation of powers, and the informal, personal, everyday connections between ministers and MPs that often characterize parliamentary systems have been reduced (Ruin 2004).

THE PARTY FACE

In the Swedish context, even if the prime minister exploits his party's pivotal position to enhance his freedom from parliamentary control, he would still lack a genuinely presidential source of power if he remained formally and practically constrained by his party from pursuing his own interests and preferences, as distinct from those of the party. Do Swedish parties have the scope for such control?

The internal structures of Sweden's major parties look similar today. A congress, elected by local party branches, is the sovereign body, and it delegates its power to smaller executive bodies. Yet despite this model of apparently democratic internal procedures, it has been widely observed that, as elsewhere in Europe, party elites have grown increasingly dominant.

Certainly, as far as the usually governing party, the Social Democrats, is concerned, the leadership does hold a strong position, even if, particularly since its years of opposition in 1976–82, the party's MPs have insisted on closer collaboration with both their steering committee and the party's government ministers at an early stage of policy formulation (Arter 1990: 135; Sannerstedt and Sjölin 1992: 115). According to Hagevi's (2000: 156) research, this underpins coordination between the parliamentary group and the party leadership, whether the party is in government or opposition. Both MPs and the party leadership, he argues, 'behave like members of the same team'. Once a decision has been taken within the parliamentary group, voting discipline is very strong, as it is in all Swedish parties, and has become stronger since unicameralism was adopted. One reason is that the leaderships of the extra-parliamentary organizations and parliamentary groups are well integrated.[11] Together with other members of the parliamentary group's steering committee (*förtroenderåd*), which is elected by the MPs, the party leader appoints individuals to positions on cross-party parliamentary standing committees and intra-group policy committees. This naturally encourages loyalty among those who are elected to the parliament.

When in government office, party leaders have the right to nominate their MPs or individuals outside parliament to ministerial posts, and there is evidence that Social Democratic prime ministers, at least, have felt increasingly free of party influence in exercising this right. In the early 1990s, Ruin

(1991: 64) could report that the number of ministers chosen from the ranks of Social Democratic MPs had 'sharply declined. Not even half of those appointed since [1982] have had such experience.' What we might call the 'departification' of the cabinet has continued. Göran Persson's preference for ministers without a real base in the party has been noted; he has even publicly lamented the lack of ministerial talent available within the labour movement (Elmbrant 2002: part 3). Bo Rothstein, a political scientist, has remarked on the growing proportion of ministers and others in the chancery[12] who are neither elected politicians nor expert bureaucrats, but something in between—what he calls 'policrats' (*polikrater*) (*Svenska Dagbladet,* 16 November 2002). Without any base of support within the governing party, nor an independent authority based on their expertise, a 'policrat' has no principal other than the prime minister (see also Ruin 2004). This, of course, resembles the relationship between ministers and chief executive in a presidential system.[13]

The ability to appoint ministers with only a weak anchor in the party inevitably gives a prime minister a large asset in his management of relations with the party organization. So too has the changing role of the party congress, which has become as much a means of conveying the party's message to the wider electorate as a mechanism for democratic steering of the party by its membership (Pierre and Widfeldt 1994: 344–6). Indeed, two frequently discussed changes in Swedish Social Democracy—increasingly pragmatic policy and increasingly elite-led policy—may not be unconnected (Elmbrant 2002: part. 4).[14] Such trends have surely been accentuated by the advent of state subsidies for political parties, introduced in Sweden in 1965. Subsidies have allowed the different levels of the parties to live increasingly independent lives—one of the characteristics of Katz and Mair's (1995: 21) semi-state 'cartel party'. With the capital resources to spend on modern, targeted election campaigning, a party leadership is less reliant on the human resources of a mass membership to convey its message through traditional techniques, such as organizing meetings and door-to-door canvassing.

Another sign of the increasing autonomy enjoyed by party leaderships is the declining institutional linkage between certain parties and the social and economic organizations that originally provided their foundations (Wörlund and Hansson 2001). The Christian Democrats have loosened their ties to the free churches; the Centre has ended its formal association with the farmers' unions; and, above all, the Social Democrats have significantly reformed their connection with the trade unions. It is hard to overstate the influence that organized labour has had on Sweden's dominant party, both intellectually and organizationally, since it was formed in 1889. The link was epitomized by the system of near-automatic party membership for many trade union members. In a country with the highest density of union membership in the world (around 80 per cent), this system of collective membership long provided 75 per cent to 80 per cent of Social Democratic members. Total party membership reached a staggering 1.23 million, or around 15 per cent of the Swedish population, in 1983 (Widfeldt 1999: 112).

The ties between the two wings of the labour movement have certainly not disappeared. They remain, both formal and informal, at all levels of the party. Moreover, the logic of the exchange relationship between the Social Democrats and the trade unions endures: each side has something to offer to the other. The unions provide crucial capital and human resources for the party before an election, as well as a direct channel to a large proportion of the Swedish electorate (Aylott 2003). No Swedish prime minister, least of all a Social Democratic one, can ignore the power of organized labour.[15] Yet the relationship is undoubtedly much looser than it was. This growing distance was marked most visibly by the decision of the 1987 party congress to phase out collective membership by 1991.

The effects on prime ministerial autonomy of this looser relationship should not be exaggerated. Few governing parties in Europe listen as attentively to an external interest group as the Swedish Social Democrats do to the main union confederation, LO, and its member unions. Nevertheless, if the points of comparison are restricted to Sweden, it is clear that a Social Democratic prime minister in 2003 was less constrained by the power of organized labour, exercised through his party, than his counterpart was thirty years previously. The days when LO could persuade Social Democrats to adopt a policy as radical—and as electorally damaging—as the wage-earner funds, as it did in the 1970s (Pontusson 1992: 186–237), have gone. In that limited sense, then, a Social Democratic prime minister has become more presidential.

THE ELECTORAL FACE

As we saw earlier, Åsard (2000) sees American politics as essentially about individuals, whereas Swedish politics has been about parties. Although explicit reference to them only appeared in the Swedish constitution in 1969, parties have indeed been the basic actors in Swedish democracy. Some explanations for this are cultural and historical. The 'people's movements' that emerged in the nineteenth century created political fronts that were at the sharp end of the struggle for democracy, and this led to a strong tradition of party membership and activity. The modern electoral system, with its twenty-nine multi-member constituencies that return an average of ten deputies each to the parliament, is also designed with parties very much in mind. The parties thus retain their monopoly of the supply of candidates to elective public office (Bergman 2003: 599).

The party procedures for selecting candidates have adapted and conformed to this historical and institutional framework. Members cannot join a party directly at the national level, but must instead do so through a local branch; and it has long been the branches that nominate both (a) candidates to a party list in a given constituency, and (b) delegates to the regional party conferences that decide the list and its order. Party leaderships have no formal role in candidate-selection, and seldom intervene informally in the process. It is this practice that underpins the collectivist, party-dominated character of Swedish representative democracy that Åsard identified in the quotation near the beginning of this chapter. Party identity and interests are impressed upon aspiring political leaders. While semi-outsiders may be whisked into the cabinet from beyond the party's structures,[16] the party's leader and all others within its executive organs must have worked their way up from its base, building support as they progressed.

Might this be changing? If prime ministers are on the way to establishing a direct, presidential-style accountability with the electorate, without effective mediation by a party or the parliament, we would expect this to be reflected in voting behaviour. In our examination of presidential trends in this, the electoral face, we look for psephological evidence. First, however, we ask whether the media's coverage of campaigning has reflected such developments, and whether the campaign styles of the parties have moved away from the emphasis on collective messages and identities.

Parties, leaders, media focus and parties campaign strategies

Swedish newspapers, national and local, used to have clear party affiliations, to the extent that they 'functioned as passive megaphones for the respective parties' (Esaiasson 1991: 271). Though they still display overt sympathies on their leader pages, they also now tend to stress their independence from political parties. The newspapers that the parties themselves used to publish have almost all now been discontinued. Above all, and in common with other developed countries, from the early 1960s television became the main medium for communication between politicians and electors, displacing public meetings and workplace events from the primary position that they enjoyed in the 1930s, though without ending their importance for election campaigns (ibid.: 264–8).

Alongside the rise of television, Swedish journalists increasingly have rejected the passive conveying of the parties' propaganda, in favour of questioning the parties' representatives more independently and aggressively. Indeed, according to some critical observers, since the 1968 election, when the parties lost their right to produce their own campaign broadcasts, the media have increasingly sought to set the political agenda, to the detriment of the information that the voters can obtain about the parties' intentions (Esaiasson and Håkansson 2002). Whether or not that is the case, the media's expanding role does seem to have coincided with a greater concentration on party leaders. One study examined the proportion of three broadsheet newspapers' campaign coverage that was devoted to the parties or their representatives in the last ten days before an election. In 1960, 16 per cent of it had the party leader as the main actor. By 1991 that figure had risen to 35 per cent—and that was a decline from a peak of 38 per cent in 1988 (Bennulf and Hedberg 1993: 116). The television debate between the parliamentary leaders that precedes an election these days draws around 70 per cent of the population, although the radio equivalent in the 1950s won a similar audience (Asp and Esaiasson 1996: 79–84).

Certainly, campaigning has become more demanding for politicians, party leaders above all. According to Esaisson's (1990: 324) research, Swedish party leaders each made, on average, twenty-seven campaign appearances of various kinds in 1960. By 1985 the figure had risen to ninety-six. Moreover, politicians are, of course, well aware of the potential for efficient and effective communication that the broadcast media offer. In 1960, 89 per cent of the party leaders' campaign appearances were devoted to public meetings and speeches. A decade later, that proportion had fallen to 59 per cent, and by 1988 it was 41 per cent. This was not because the numbers of such meetings had fallen in absolute terms (they had actually risen), but because the proportion of campaign events held specifically for the media, including press conferences, had greatly expanded, from 12 per cent in 1960 to 30 per cent in 1988 (Esaiasson 1990: 324–5, 1991: 274).

Apart from these general trends, case studies show how media strategy forms an essential component of modern party leaders' political role. Certainly, it played a part in Persson's extraordinary transformation from bumbling liability (who had become prime minister in spring 1996 only because other candidates for the Social Democratic leadership either declined or were ruled out by scandal) to international statesman. In 2001 the Social Democrats' sister parties in Sweden's Scandinavian neighbours, Denmark and Norway, suffered their worst electoral defeats since the 1920s. Yet, by then, Persson towered over Swedish politics. He was comfortably the country's most respected and trusted political leader (*Dagens Nyheter,* 15 March 2002). The economy's improvement surely played a part in this metamorphosis. So too did Sweden's presidency of the EU's Council of Ministers during the first half of 2001, which put Persson very much in the limelight. Perhaps still more importantly, his media profile in the aftermath of the terrorist attacks on America in September 2001 did him no harm. But he had also grown into the role. He had become confident enough to give frank personal interviews to newspapers (for instance, *Svenska Dagbladet,* 15 March 2001) about his experiences, including his contemplation of resignation during his difficult early years as prime minister, and turning in warm, relaxed performances on television chat shows.[17]

Not too much about the structural trends in political reporting and party strategies should be read into one case of image transformation, particularly one that arguably was brought about by an unusual combination of favourable circumstances. But the general data do suggest that the media, particularly television, now dominate political communication; that the media, led by television, focus more on party leaders; and that the parties have responded by increasing the emphasis that they place in their campaign strategies on their leaders. These might be seen as presidential developments. The next logical question is whether they have influenced voting behaviour.

Presidentialized voting?

For the 1998 election, the electoral system was reformed. The voter was given the opportunity to mark a preference for an individual candidate on a party's list, and, if that candidate won at least 8 per cent of her party's votes, she was automatically thrust to the top of the list. In the event, a reasonable number of voters, 29.9 per cent, used the new mechanism. This was enough to propel eighty candidates up their respective lists, and to bring a dozen of them into parliament who would otherwise have been placed too low to have been elected. This led the parties to take recognition by the wider electorate more seriously in candidate-selection in 2002. A few celebrities found their way onto party lists. Might it be that Swedish electoral politics is becoming significantly less party-orientated and more candidate-orientated, both at constituency and national levels?

Partly because of the newspapers' drift away from party loyalty, and the proliferation of impartial television news coverage, the flow of political information in Sweden, as elsewhere, has become much freer. Voters, as the consumers of this information market, have had more power to shape its content and focus, and it is quite plausible that they may prefer to see and read coverage of individuals rather than organizations. With class identities fading (Oskarsson 1994: 208–9), organizational attachment to parties declining, voting behaviour becoming more promiscuous, and radical political alternatives losing credibility, the parties have come to look more like each other. Personality may be one of the few remaining ways for voters to distinguish the parties reliably, and voters may consequently elevate leadership among the criteria that they use to determine their party choice.

Leaders are, it seems, ever more often blamed or praised for influencing the fortunes of their parties. The Liberals' successes in the mid-1980s were so strongly associated with their leader, Bengt Westerberg, that his 'effect' became part of the political lexicon. The big gains made by the Left and the Christian Democrats in the 1998 election were frequently attributed to their leaders' qualities, and the losses suffered by the Centre, Liberals, and Social Democrats were put down to their leaders' deficiencies. In 2002, apart from Persson's starring role for the Social Democrats, the 'Maud effect' (after the party leader, Maud Olofsson) was at least part of the commonly offered explanation for the Centre's first electoral upturn since 1973, while it was the Moderate leader's turn to have his party's feeble performance pinned on his own failings. Decline and division were then widely seen as the unavoidable fate of the Left when, in January 2003, the party lost its leader, Gudrun Schyman, its 'vote-magnet', after a scandal concerning her tax return.

Leaders make a difference in elections: no one would deny that. But determining exactly how much difference they make is difficult. In fact, harder evidence for the increasing salience of party leaders in determining voting behaviour is rather elusive. Leaders have certainly become more recognized, thanks to television. The proportion of Swedish voters who could put a name to the face of at least four of the five main party leaders jumped from 34 per cent in 1956 to 62 per cent in 1960, 77 per cent in 1964 and 87 per cent in 1968 (Holmberg 2000: 160). There is also a clear correlation between voters' preference for a party and their estimation of its leader.

But which way does the causality run? Is the party supported because the voter likes the leader, or the leader liked because she leads the party? Earlier research by Esaiasson (1985) on leader-influenced voting found some 'coat-tail effects'—that is, popular leaders of parties having beneficial effects on their parties' vote—at the bourgeois end of the spectrum. But, overall, the impact was modest, which he explained largely by the existence of relatively old, institutionalized and internally democratic parties in Sweden, especially on the left. Moreover, those effects that could be identified did little to shape the outcome of the election in terms of government formation. In Sweden, as we have seen, government formation was, and still is, determined by the balance of seats between the socialist and bourgeois blocs; and 'Few voters go for the most popular party leader [if she is] from a political bloc other than the one that their preferred party belongs to' (ibid.: 116).

More recently, analysis of the available survey data led Holmberg to conclude that party-preference rather than leader-preference is still the most important determinant of voting behaviour. When asked directly, for instance, just 3 per cent of voters, unprompted, named the leader as one of the most important factors in party choice in 1988 and 1991. When given the option of a 'good party-leader' as one of their most important motivating factors, fewer than a quarter of respondents picked it in surveys held in 1988 and 1994 (Holmberg 2000: 176). In seeking further evidence about causality, Holmberg compares time-series data on whether party leaders have been more popular than their party among that party's supporters—which,

Holmberg reckons, they would be if voters were being attracted to the party on the basis of its leader. He calls this a 'maximum estimate' of the effect of party leaders on voting behaviour. The average proportion of such leader-influenced voters for each of the five oldest parliamentary parties reached 19 per cent in 1985. But it was stuck on 15 per cent in the four subsequent elections (ibid.: 179).

Something similar can be seen in Table 8.1, which offers a maximum estimate of the proportion of the whole electorate (rather than of each party's supporters) potentially attracted to and put off each party because of its leader. It seems clear, if Holmberg's assumptions hold, that unpopular party leaders may be a greater liability for a party than popular ones are a boon. But two further observations that are particularly relevant to our purpose can be made about these data. First, we see, once more, stability in the average figures for all the parties in each election since 1979, with only a slight upturn in more recent ones. Second, we see outliers—parties for which the leader had an especially positive or negative effect—in various elections: on the plus side, the Moderate leader throughout the 1990s; on the minus side, the Centre's leader from 1979–85, and the Liberals' in 1998. This suggests that party leader effects may be more the product of specific individuals holding a specific position at a specific time, rather than a structural trend.

All this should not be taken as commenting decisively on the effects that party leaders have on voting behaviour, let alone on how 'presidentialized' Swedish elections have become. But we can say that there is as yet no clear

TABLE 8.1. *Potential party-leadership effects in Sweden—maximum gains/losses of votes (per cent)*

Party	1979	1982	1985	1988	1991	1994	1998
Left	1/9	1/9	1/7	1/9	1/11	1/18	2/13
Social Democrats	5/21	8/16	6/19	7/12	4/13	4/11	2/30
Greens	—	—	—	—	0/35	0/34	0/37
Centre Party	2/34	3/29	1/34	2/18	1/31	1/29	1/29
Liberals	2/16	0/28	4/13	2/18	2/21	2/23	0/38
Christian Democrats	—	—	0/20	—	1/17	1/17	2/12
Moderates	5/11	3/10	4/14	1/28	4/20	6/15	8/11
New Democracy	—	—	—	—	1/17	0/19	—
Average	3/18	3/18	3/17	3/17	2/19	3/19	3/24

Notes: The figure before the forward slash is a maximum estimate of the percentage of the electorate that the party won because of its leader, assuming that this constitutes all that party's voters who liked the leader more than they liked the party. The figure after the slash is the percentage that the party lost because of its leader, assuming that this constitutes all the voters for other parties who liked that party's leader less than they liked the party. Missing figures indicate either that a party did not run, or that the survey excluded it. The average is for only the five 'old' parties, that is, excluding the Greens, the Christian Democrats, and New Democracy.

Source: Holmberg 2000: 181.

evidence that Swedish voters are behaving more as if they were in a presidential system, with something approaching a direct accountability relationship with their head of government – even if their suppliers of political information, the mass media, are. Parties, not candidates, are still the most important unit in elections. Indeed, in 2002, to universal surprise, the proportion of voters exploiting their right to vote for individual candidates actually fell, to 26.0 per cent.

CONCLUSIONS

The aim of this chapter has not essentially been to show that a Swedish prime minister is more powerful than the country's parliamentary constitution would seem to indicate, although he very probably is. For sure, the frequency of minority governments means that he cannot be compared to his British counterpart, who, with control of her party and a parliamentary majority for that party, can secure most of the legislation that she wants. Swedish prime ministers have to negotiate with coalition partners or allied parties or, very often, opposition parties if legislative majorities are to be constructed. There is also a long tradition in Sweden of corporatist policy-making, in which major socio-economic groups, particularly those that organize the labour market, are included. That tradition has declined, but it remains (Hermansson, Svensson and Öberg 1997; Svensson and Öberg 2002). One of those group representatives, LO, continues to exercise indirect influence on the political executive when the Social Democrats are in office, through enduring ties at all levels of the labour movement. There are, then, plenty of constraints on the head of a Swedish government. But there is a lot of freedom, too. Institutional veto players (Tsebelis 1995), such as a second parliamentary chamber, a constitutional court or constitutionally protected rights for sub-national government, are few.

The argument here has instead concerned the *nature* of prime ministerial power, and it bears out a fair part of the presidentialization thesis as conceived in this book. Sweden's current prime minister does seem to have become less dependent on parliament and the support of the Social Democratic Party. Rather, it can be argued that his power is derived—at least in part—directly from the electorate itself. So long as a prime minister remains popular among electors, it is likely to be hard for anyone in his party to depose him. Furthermore, even a narrow parliamentary base for his party can, paradoxically, empower a prime minister. As Ruin (1991: 89) argues, 'The fact that it is ultimately the prime minister who, through his negotiations with members of the opposition parties, can create a majority ... for the government's legislation strengthens his position within the government.' Cabinet ministers increasingly owe their appointment solely to the prime minister's patronage, instead of representing some important element within the ruling party (or parties). The resources available to the prime minister in government, particularly in the Prime Minister's Office, have also expanded. In all these senses, he resembles a more presidential figure.

It is also unlikely that the legislature has much real scope, under current circumstances, to exercise one of its defining functions in a parliamentary system—namely, to hold the executive to account by, *in extremis*, bringing it down. Negative parliamentarism in Sweden shores up even narrowly based minority governments and, even when the governing party does not hold the median legislator (as has been the case from 1998 to the present), bloc identity restricts the ability of the party that does hold it—even the Greens, who claim to eschew bloc affiliation—to play the role of genuine swing party, or partisan veto player.

If EU membership, with the decision-making advantages that it accords to governments over parliaments, is added to the equation, the case for identifying a presidentialized executive in Sweden looks rather persuasive. In fact, it is arguable that Sweden, like the other member states, is already presidentialized in the sense that the head of government is part of a collective European presidency, the European Council. This presidency, with its high-profile meetings, seems increasingly to be the institution in which the EU takes its most important decisions. Indeed, at least two Swedish scholars (Algotsson 2001; Bergman 2003) have argued that, notwithstanding its parliamentary constitution, EU membership has brought the nature of Swedish democracy closer to a separation of powers.

Yet there are limits to presidentialization in Sweden. Evidence for it in the electoral face is significantly weaker than it is in the executive and intra-party faces. It may be that the media are devoting more political coverage to party leaders, and that the parties themselves are laying more emphasis than previously on the personalities of their leaders, rather than the content of their programmes and manifestos. But it is not clear—at least, not yet—that voters are more readily swayed, or elections decided, because of the qualities of the prime ministerial candidates, rather than of the parties they represent. There is a deductive logic in the argument that partisan dealignment will give a relatively greater electoral salience to candidates, and that increasingly media-driven politics will privilege the party leader in campaigning (Esaiasson 1985: 119). But, equally, there is the basic logic inherent in a parliamentary system that, if her promises to the electorate are to be credible, a candidate for the legislature must refer to other, like-minded candidates who are making similar promises. Party labels and identities are still very important in Swedish politics.

Even in the intra-party face, a serious conflict with some element in the Social Democrats—with LO, maybe, brought on by some sort of economic crisis, as in 1990 and 1996—would still cause a Social Democratic prime minister real trouble. Powerful as he may be, she is not free of the constraints that the party puts on its primary agent; he cannot entirely govern 'past' it rather than 'through' it. Conversely, it is not *only* Göran Persson's vote-winning qualities that give him such a strong position within his party. The 1998 election saw the Social Democrats' worst performance since the 1920s. Both before and immediately after it, Persson was the subject of some amazingly contemptuous attacks from within his party—although, maybe thanks to its traditions of loyalty, these were often anonymous (Elmbrant 2002: parts 1, 5). Yet his leadership was never seriously threatened. His control of the party was and is firm. This indicates the party organization's enduring political relevance to a prime minister, electorally successful and unsuccessful ones alike.

Some of the factors that have contributed most to the creation of 'President Persson' may, in fact, be less structural than contingent. It is worth remembering that the preferences of Swedish voters and party members are not set in stone. They could change, and thus help to create partisan veto players in parliament. The Greens might act on their threats, made during the post-election negotiations in 2002, to coalesce with the bourgeois parties; alternatively, the Centre or the Liberals might swallow their reluctance to govern with the Social Democrats. This could provide Sweden with proper swing-parties, ready to govern with either right or left, and whose defection from one side to the other could bring down a government. Parliament could then control the executive much more effectively. For good or ill, party and bloc identities and boundaries seem alive and well in Sweden. These constraints do much to create the space for a Swedish prime minister to be 'presidential' within the party and the executive.

NOTES

1. Thanks to the editors of this volume and to colleagues in the Department of Political Science, Umeå University, particularly Svante Ersson, Torbjörn Bergman and Staffan Andersson, for their thoughts on this topic. However, all positions taken in this chapter, and all translations from Swedish-language sources, are my responsibility.
2. The principle was recognized finally by the monarch in 1917.
3. While the monarch's formal executive role had been a constitutional fiction for decades, in 1974 he was deprived of all but a few ceremonial tasks. The responsibility of inviting prime ministerial candidates to form a government passed to the speaker of parliament.
4. If not necessarily *the* party leader. In Scandinavian parties, leadership roles are often divided.

5. The party's presidential candidate may, of course, wish to be renominated to the same role at the next election, and so will naturally want to retain the party's confidence. But, if she wins the first national election, her renomination is very likely; and, if she loses it, she will not be in a strong position to regain the party nomination for subsequent elections. Furthermore, if there are term limits (as in the US), and she has won the last election for which she is eligible, there is no formal mechanism by which the party can exercise control over the candidate. Contrast all this with the position of a party leader in a parliamentary system. Irrespective (at least formally) of election results and the public office that the leader holds, the party can unseat her whenever it likes. It is this that makes the party track so much more substantial in parliamentary than in presidential systems as a chain of delegation and accountability.

6. There is some doubt as to whether this principal–agent approach is really suitable for analyzing parties. Katz (2002), for example, argues that the same intra-party actors can often be equally well conceived as either principals or agents.

7. A journalist's anonymous source suggested, in a nice turn of phrase, that the prime minister, through this centralization of policy-making in the Prime Minister's Office, 'defoliates [*avlövar*] his ministers' (*Svenska Dagbladet,* 29 December 2003).

8. There is a third option for such a party: it could vote against aspiring governments from *both* blocs. If this caused the rejection of the speaker's proposals for prime minister four times, however, a new election would be triggered. Voters would be unlikely then to favour such an obstructive party.

9. The Greens voted for Persson's government in 1998, but after the 2002 election they abstained in the subsequent no-confidence motion, after their leaders had briefly talked to three bourgeois parties about governing with them.

10. The single-party Liberal government at the end of the 1976–9 parliament, which had just thirty-nine seats of its own out of 349 in parliament, was only the most striking case of this pivot in action.

11. This is despite the fact that only the Social Democrats, the Left and the Greens specify any formal connection between the parliamentary group and the party organization, and even then there are no sanctions available to enforce it. Exceptions to this pattern of integration—when, for example, a smaller party has elected a leader who lacks a parliamentary seat—are quite rare and usually short-lived (Hagevi 2000: 153).

12. Chancery is the best translation of *regeringskansliet* (the official one is Government Offices), which includes the cabinet and the ministries (Larsson 1997: 228). Because of the administration of public policy by semi-autonomous agencies, ministries are much smaller than in most other countries (Petersson 1994: 99–100).

13. The most celebrated recent example of such dependence on prime ministerial patronage occurred in October 2000, when Persson's surprise choice as the new minister of justice, Thomas Bodström, rushed immediately to his local Social Democratic association in order to join the party.

14. Apparently, Persson and the then under-secretary in the Prime Minister's Office, Pär Nuder, wrote the Social Democrats' 1998 election manifesto almost alone, with little reference even to the party secretary (*Svenska Dagbladet*, 30 September

1998). Nuder joined the cabinet after the 2002 election as minister for coordination.

15. When Persson became prime minister, proposals for labour-market reform plunged relations between his party and LO into crisis, and he worsened them by pledging to treat the unions like any other interest group. Thereafter, however, and particularly after the 1998 election disaster, he worked hard to repair the relationship.

16. Something similar may now apply to candidates for the European Parliament. Because Sweden comprises a single constituency, candidates are recruited at national-party level, and party leaderships have sometimes encouraged well-known individuals—including some outside the party—to accept nomination.

17. Åsard (2001) exemplifies those critics who dismiss this as another example of Sweden's importing American political techniques, which trivialize politics and thereby short-change voters.

REFERENCES

Algotsson, K.-G. (2001). 'From Majoritarian Democracy to Vertical Separation of Powers: Sweden and the European Union', *Scandinavian Political Studies*, 24: 51–65.
Arter, D. (1990). 'The Swedish Riksdag: The Case of a Strong Policy-Influencing Assembly', *West European Politics*, 13: 120–42.
Åsard, E. (2000). 'Moderatledarens västervridning', *Dagens Nyheter*, 22 May.
—— (2001). 'Väljarna förlorar på politikers tv-mys', *Dagens Nyheter*, 20 February.
Asp, K. and P. Esaiasson (1996). 'The Modernization of Swedish Campaigns: Individualization, Professionalization, and Medialization', in D. L. Swanson and P. Mancini (eds.), *Politics, Media, and Modern Democracy: An International Study of Innovations in Electoral Campaigning and Their Consequences*. Westport, CN: Praeger.
Aylott, N. (2003). 'After the Divorce: Social Democrats and Trade Unions in Sweden', *Party Politics*, 9: 369–90.
Bennulf, M. and P. Hedberg (1993). 'Person och parti i massmediern', in J. Westerståhl (ed.), *Person och parti. Studier i anslutning till Personvals-kommitténs betänkande Ökat personalval*. Stockholm: SOU 1993:21.
Bergman, T. (1993). 'Formation Rules and Minority Governments', *European Journal of Political Research*, 23: 55–66.
—— (1997). 'Utrikes inrikespolitik: riksdagen och EU-nämnden i EU', in I. Mattson and L. Wängnerud (eds.), *Riksdagen på nära håll*. Stockholm: SNS Förlag.
—— (2003). 'From Separation of Power to Parliamentary Supremacy—and Back Again?', in K. Strøm, W. C. Müller, and T. Bergman (eds.), *Delegation and Accountability in Parliamentary Democracies*. Oxford: Oxford University Press.
—— and Aylott, N. (2003). 'Parlamentarism per kontrakt—blir den svenska innovationen långlivad?', *Riksdagens årsbok 2003/03*. Stockholm: Riksdagen.
—— and Erik Damgaard (2000). *Delegation and Accountability in European Integration: The Nordic Parliamentary Democracies and the European Union*. London: Frank Cass.

Dagens Nyheter (2002). 'Minska hans makt' (editorial), 14 November.

Elder, N. C. M. and E. C. Page (2000). 'Sweden: The Quest for Coordination', in B. G. Peters, R. A. W. Rhodes, and V. Wright (eds.), *Administering the Summit: Administration of the Core Executive in Developed Countries*. Basingstoke: Macmillan.

Elmbrant, B. (2002). 'President Persson – hur fick vi honom?'. *Studio Ett*, P1. Stockholm: Sveriges Radio, 22–6 April.

Esaissson, P. (1985). 'Partiledareffekter även i Sverige? Partiledarpopularitetens betydelse för valresultatet i Sverige ur ett jämförande perspektiv', *Statsvetenskaplig Tidskrift*, 88: 105–22.

—— (1990). *Svenska valkampanjer 1866–1988*. Stockholm: Publica.

—— (1991). '120 Years of Swedish Election Campaigns', *Scandinavian Political Studies*, 14: 261–78.

—— and N. Håkansson (2002). 'Tv's maktposition odemokratisk'. *Dagens Nyheter*, 21 May.

Hagevi, M. (2000). 'Parliamentary Party Groups in the Swedish Riksdag', in K. Heidar and R. Koole (eds.), *Parliamentary Groups in Parliamentary Democracies: Political Parties Behind Closed Doors*. London: Routledge.

Hermansson, J., T. Svensson, and PO. Öberg (1997). 'Vad blev det av den svenska korporativismen?', *Politica*, 29: 386–84.

Holmberg, S. (2000). *Välja parti*. Stockholm: Norstedts Juridik.

Katz, R. S. (2002). 'Whose Agent? Principles, Principals, and Party Politics'. Paper prepared for conference on The Cartel Party and Beyond, Pisa, March.

—— and P. Mair (1995). 'Changing Models of Party Organization and Party Democracy: The Emergence of the Cartel Party', *Party Politics*, 1: 5–28.

Kiewiet, D. R. and M. D. McCubbins (1991). *The Logic of Delegation: Congressional Parties and the Appropriations Process*. Chicago: University of Chicago Press.

Larsson, T. (1986). *Regeringen och dess kansli: samordning och byråkrati i maktens centrum*. Lund: Studentlitteratur.

—— (1997). 'Sweden: The New Constitution—An Old Practice Adjusted', in J. Blondel and F. Müller-Rommel (eds.), *Cabinets in Western Europe*, 2nd edn. London: Macmillan.

—— (1999). 'Konflikten som försvann. Hur har det svenska EU-medlemskapet påverkat maktdelningen mellan regering och riksdag?', in E. Amnå (ed.), *Maktutdelning*. Stockholm: SOU 1999:76.

Lewin, L. (1996). *Votera eller förhandla? Om den svenska parlamentarismen*. Stockholm: Norstedts Juridik.

—— (1998). 'Majoritarian and Consensus Democracy: The Swedish Experience', *Scandinavian Political Studies*, 21: 195–206.

Lijphart, A. (1999). *Patterns of Democracy: Government Forms and Performance in Thirty-Six Countries*. New Haven, CT: Yale University Press.

Lindbeck, A., P. Molander, T. Persson, O. Petersson, A. Sandmo, B. Swedenborg, and N. Thygesen (1994). *Turning Sweden Around*. Cambridge, MA: MIT Press.

Lindgren, K. O. (2000). 'EU-medlemskapets inverken på den svenska parlamentarismen', *Statsvetenskaplig Tidskrift*, 103: 133–220.

Müller, W. C. (2000). 'Political Parties in Parliamentary Democracies: Making Delegation and Accountability Work', *European Journal of Political Research*, 37: 309–33.

Oskarsson, M. (1994). *Klassröstning i Sverige: rationalitet, lojalitet eller bara slentrian.* Stockholm: Nernus och Santérus.

Petersson, O. (1994). *Swedish Government and Politics.* Stockholm: Publica.

Pierre, J. and A. Widfeldt (1994). 'Party Organizations in Sweden: Colussuses with Feet of Clay or Flexible Pillars of Government?', in R. S. Katz and P. Mair (eds.), *How Parties Organize: Change and Adaptation in Party Organizations in Western Democracies.* London: Sage.

Pontusson, J. (1992). *The Limits of Social Democracy: Investment Politics in Sweden.* Ithaca, NY: Cornell University Press.

Regeringskansliet (chancery) (2003). *Regeringskansliets årsbok 2002.* Stockholm: Regeringskansliet.

Ruin, O. (1991). 'Three Swedish Prime Ministers: Tage Erlander, Olof Palme and Ingvar Carlsson' *West European Politics*, 14: 58–82.

—— (2004). 'Tvinga statsråden till Riksdagshuset', *Dagens Nyheter*, 19 January.

Sannerstedt, A. and M. Sjölin (1992). 'Sweden: Changing Party Relations in a More Active Parliament', in E. Damgaard (ed.), *Parliamentary Change in the Nordic Countries.* Oslo: Scandinavian University Press.

Strøm, K. (2000). 'Delegation and Accountability in Parliamentary Democracies', *European Journal of Political Research*, 37: 261–89.

Svensson, T. and PO. Öberg (2002). 'Labour Market Organisations' Participation in Swedish Public Policy-Making', *Scandinavian Political Studies*, 25: 295–315.

Tsebelis, G. (1995). 'Decision Making in Political Systems: Veto Players in Presidentialism, Parliamentarism, Bicameralism and Multipartyism', *British Journal of Political Science*, 25: 288–325.

Widfeldt, A. (1999). *Linking Parties with People? Party Membership in Sweden 1960–97.* Aldershot: Ashgate.

Wörlund, I. and D. Hansson (2001). 'Partier och intresseorganisationer i Sverige', in J. Sundberg (ed.), *Partier och intresseorganisationer i Norden.* Copenhagen: Nordic Council of Ministers.

9

Canada: Executive Dominance and Presidentialization

Herman Bakvis and Steven B. Wolinetz

INTRODUCTION

Canadian government and politics is *par excellence* parliamentary politics, yet Canada's eleven governments show distinct signs of presidentialization. The prime minister and the ten provincial premiers dominate their respective governments. Books and articles claiming that power is unduly concentrated in the hands of the political executive (Savoie 1999) or even that the country is run by an elected dictator are common (Greenspon 1999; Simpson 2001). Although claims of prime ministerial dictatorship often ignore the fact of federalism, the Canadian system certainly puts considerable power in the hands of the prime minister, his or her officials, and a handful of cabinet ministers, affording them power and influence which would make many presidents jealous. This concentration of power is more extensive in Canada than in other Westminster systems. Indeed, the most effective opposition comes from the ten provincial governments, where the concentration of power in the executive repeats itself.

The dominance of 'first ministers' reflects diverse factors. Among these are the influence of the Westminster model and its assumptions about where power should lie; the ways in which electoral and party systems manufacture parliamentary majorities; the ways in which parties and the dominant party system have facilitated the concentration of executive power; and the ways in which politicians and parties have coped with the problems of governing a weakly integrated, far-flung federation. Equally important in the 1990s were the centralizing impact of retrenchment and programme review, and after September 11, 2001, the new security agenda thrust upon Western democracies.

THE CANADIAN PARTY AND PARLIAMENTARY SYSTEM

Canada's British-style parliamentary institutions are a useful starting point, but the ways in which they operate can be understood only in their social, economic, and geo-political context. Canada is the second largest country in the world. Most of the population is concentrated within 150 miles of the American border. Differences in language, disparities between centres and peripheries, and a profound sense of regional grievance felt in Quebec and Western Canada divide the country. Goods and people flow north and south more readily than east and west. The pull of the American economy, the penetration of American culture, and the pressures of the American government are factors with which politicians must reckon. Both Canada and the United States have experienced extensive immigration, but Canada is less well integrated. Threats come not only from Quebec separatism but also from a weak sense of national identity and a federation dominated by its stronger provinces, Ontario and Quebec. Many people in the Western provinces feel separate from the rest and alienated by past policies, believed to have favoured the industrial centre to the detriment of the prairies.[1] The four Atlantic provinces share western disaffection but are too dependent on federal transfer payments to give much expression to it.

The institutional setting

Canada is unabashedly federal. Ten strong provincial governments and three territorial governments dominate their own jurisdictions. Each is accountable to a parliament or provincial assembly elected in single-member districts using a plurality decision rule. This tends to produce majorities or, failing that, strong minorities. Nevertheless, Canadian federalism is incomplete. Most federations have some form of regional or provincial representation at the national level. Canada's Senate, like upper chambers in most federations, represents the regions, but the Canadian senate is a chamber of 'sober second thought' whose formal veto powers are never exercised. Senators are appointed by 'the Governor-General in Council'—in effect, the prime minister. Most are designated to reward loyalty and service to the party. Like provincial assemblies, election to the House of Commons (the lower house), is based on the British single-member plurality system (or 'first-past-the-post'), a system that, since 1980, has consistently yielded majority governments, though under the right circumstances it can also produce minority governments, as it did in the 1960s and 1970s and again in 2004 and 2006. Even with majority governments, however, representation tends to be regionally skewed. Thus, following the 2000 election, which the Liberals won with 172 out of 301 seats, 100 seats of that Liberal majority came from the province of Ontario. Indeed, the Liberals captured 100 of the 102 seats in that province, imparting a distinct Ontario flavour to the governing Liberal Party.

The task of representing provincial interests falls to the ten provincial governments. Cooperation on routine matters cannot hide profound disagreement about who should pay, or the proper balance between federal and provincial governments. Provinces like Alberta, British Columbia, and Quebec advance a profoundly decentralized view of confederation.

Canada modelled its institutions after Britain's parliamentary practices; the style of politics, the prerogatives of the institutions, and even the physical layout of the Canadian House of Commons, resemble Westminster. However, there are crucial differences. Fathers of Canadian confederation adapted British institutions to distant territories which contained a significant French minority. While in a formal constitutional sense the federation launched in 1867 was highly centralized, over the years court decisions and practices increased the power of provincial governments. With the rise of the welfare state, areas under provincial jurisdiction such as education, health care, and social welfare became more important. With ownership and control over natural resources vested in the provinces, disparities in these resources have widened the gap between 'have' and 'have-not' provinces. By the 1960s and 1970s, the combined effects of state-building at the federal and provincial levels produced a system which pitted ten centralized, executive-dominated provincial governments, some much larger and richer than others, against a centralized executive-dominated federal government.

When the activities of federal and provincial states were expanding, federal and provincial governments worked with each other, coordinating their activities through 'executive federalism,' federal-provincial first ministers' meetings, and a 'liberal' distribution of booty via regional ministers. This did not prevent serious conflicts among and within levels of government. Tensions arose over regional issues, the balance of power between provinces and the federal government, and the position of Quebec in the confederation. Relations between some provinces and the federal government are at least as adversarial as relations among parties at Ottawa and other Westminster-style parliamentary systems (Tanguay 2002).

The party system

Carty argues that Canada has had three distinct party systems and is on the verge of a fourth (Carty *et al.* 2000). Each represents a different era in which party positions and the coalitions of interests and concerns which they aggregate, and styles of politics, change as well. (1) The first ran from the confederation in 1867 to the First World War; (2) the second from 1919 to the Diefenbaker era (late 1950s and early 1960s); (3) the third from the early

1960s to 1993, when the current system took hold. Up to 1919, Canada had a classic two-party system. The Conservatives under Sir John A. Macdonald, and then the Liberals under Sir Wilfrid Laurier, dominated.

In the second party system, regional demands and prairie discontent produced a series of third parties. The Liberals dominated national politics by accommodating regional and other demands, in good part through so-called regional ministers in the federal Cabinet (Bakvis 1991; Whitaker 1977). Their principal competitors were the Progressive Conservatives (PCs). Deprived of support in Quebec because of the imposition of conscription during the First World War, they were rarely able to displace the Liberals. Among the third parties, only the Cooperative Commonwealth Federation (CCF), later reorganized as the New Democratic Party (NDP), survived.

In the third party system, agrarian discontent was contained in a three-party system, still characterized by the use of federal cabinet and regional ministers and patronage, but now more dependent on pan-Canadian appeals to voters in large urban areas. It is in this era that new campaign technologies based on polling techniques and television advertising were introduced and refined. The Liberals, now under Pierre Elliot Trudeau, remained the dominant party, but were reduced to minority government status from 1972 to 1974, and had to give way to a Progressive Conservative minority government under PC Leader Joe Clark in 1979. Clark's cabinet fell when its budget was defeated. The Liberals returned to power in 1980 and remained in office until 1984. In the interim, Brian Mulroney ousted Joe Clark from the PC leadership. Mulroney's Progressive Conservatives won majorities in 1984 and 1988.

The present party system differs from those which preceded it. There are now four parties—Liberals, New Democrats, the Bloc Quebecois, and the Conservatives (the later formed by the 2003 merger of the Progressive Conservatives and the Canadian Alliance)—in the House of Commons. However, the rules and adversarial style remain those of a two-party system. The current system reflects Canada's cleavages and Brian Mulroney's attempts to forge a PC majority. Mulroney courted Quebec separatists, promising to grant Quebec a veto over constitutional changes and recognize its special status in confederation. In 1987, Mulroney managed to secure agreement on a new constitutional package, the Meech Lake Accord, but changes in provincial governments undermined the unanimity which it required. The failure of the Meech Accord provoked the formation of the *Bloc Quebecois,* (a federal equivalent of the provincial *Parti Quebecois*). This not only deprived the PCs of support in Quebec but also fractured the coalition between western and Quebec interests which Mulroney had forged (Johnston et al. 1992).

Formation of the Bloc was not the only problem which plagued the PCs. Earlier, social and fiscal conservatives in Western Canada, unhappy with the centrist orientation of the PCs, had established the Reform Party. Populist in style, Reform capitalized on western alienation. The 1993 election was earth-shattering. Mulroney's glad-handing style hurt the PCs, and his successor, Kim Campbell, ran an ineffectual campaign. The Liberals, under Jean Chrétien, ended up with 41 per cent of the vote and 177 of the 295 seats in the House of Commons. With fifty-four seats (and 14 per cent of the vote), the *Bloc* was the second largest caucus and the official opposition. Reform took third place, with fifty-two seats (almost all west of Ontario) and 19 per cent of the vote. New Democrats were reduced to nine seats and 7 per cent of the vote. The Progressive Conservatives were reduced from a comfortable majority in 1988 (169 seats, 43 per cent of the vote) to just 16 per cent, losing all but two seats. In 1997, they gained 19 per cent of the vote and twenty seats. In contrast, Reform established a secure base of support in the west. However, they were unable to win support in other parts of Canada. Attempts to broaden their appeal led to the formation of the Canadian Alliance in 2000 and a highly contested merger with the Progressive Conservatives in 2003. It remains to be seen whether the reunited Conservative Party of Canada will be able displace the Liberals as the dominant party. Led by Alliance leader Stephen Harper, the Conservatives were seen by some as a continuation of the Canadian Alliance. In the 2004 elections, the Conservatives won 30 per cent of the vote and 99 seats, while the Liberals, under Paul Martin, were reduced to 37 per cent and 135 seats. The Liberals survived until November 2005, when they lost a vote of confidence. New elections were held in January 2006. Winning 36.3% of the popular vote and 124 seats in the House of Commons (including ten in Quebec), the Conservatives formed a minority government.

THE PARTY FACE

Canadian parties are and have always been cadre parties, with minimal organization outside parliament or provincial legislatures. In Katz and Mair's (1994) terms, there is little party on the ground or in the central office. Constituency organizations are active only at election time or when nomination or leadership contests are underway. In between, constituency organization consists of a handful of politically active people. Skeletal organizations are bolstered by informal networks which candidates and would-be candidates activate when needed. Nominations and leadership positions are won by recruiting friends, neighbours, and anyone else who is willing to vote for candidates or, in the case of leaders selected by conventions, slates of delegates. Memberships are either free or nearly free: fees have been typically $1.00 in the Liberal or Progressive Conservative parties and organizers have sometimes paid the fees for potential recruits. However, both the Conservatives and the Liberals now charge a fee ($10.00) high enough to be considered a barrier. Memberships are at best temporary and imply little obligation. Funds are raised from friends, family, and businesses at the local level and from corporations, businessmen, unions, and other organizations at higher levels. When elections are called or anticipated, candidates and amateur and professional organizers gear up, assembling a bevy of workers to distribute literature, canvass constituents, and ensure that supporters vote on election day. However, the people involved are not necessarily party members or, if they are, the ones previously activated. Campaign teams dissipate as soon as the ballots are counted.

In one sense, the organizational structure at the constituency level is relatively porous and it is not all that difficult to take over any given riding association with a sustained organizational effort. On the other hand, to take over several such associations, as would be required for a leadership selection campaign, requires considerable human and monetary resources and battles between organizers working on behalf of leadership hopefuls have frequently been likened to trench warfare that can stretch out over several months, even years.

Party central offices are equally skeletal but more permanent and more active than constituency associations. At the federal level, each party maintains some kind of extra-parliamentary organization; at the provincial level, governing parties are more likely to maintain central offices than opposition parties, which often use legislative caucus staff. Federal and provincial organizations are disconnected. Some parties compete only in federal or provincial politics, and some federal parties organize in selected parts of the country but not in others. Even in instances in which parties bear the same name—the BC Liberals, the Federal Liberals—federal and provincial parties in most parts of the country are organizationally distinct and typically have little or nothing to do with each other. Only in the smaller Atlantic Provinces and in the New Democratic Party does a degree of interconnectedness endure.

The absence of durable party structures outside parliament and provincial assemblies ensures that power resides in the legislative caucus or, if the party is in government, in the cabinet. There is little or no counterweight to legislative caucuses, which tend to be dominated by party leaders. As in Britain, the prime minister is free to select and shuffle the cabinet at will; provincial premiers enjoy similar prerogatives. Leaders' prerogatives reflect not only British practice but also patterns of recruitment and expertise: parliamentary and provincial legislative careers tend to be short. High turnover reflects the openness of the system and the frustrations of both opposition members and government backbenchers. Neither have much opportunity to influence policy. Members of parliament minimize frustration by specializing in constituency work; those who see little chance to advance get out (Docherty 1997). The net effect is to reinforce the already strong power of party leaders. In office, the leader can control the advancement of caucus members and the distribution of patronage and government projects to members' districts.

The power of the prime minister and provincial leaders is reinforced by the ways in which leaders are selected as well as by the absence of effective de-selection procedures. In the first Canadian party system (1867–1919), leaders were selected by legislative caucuses. However, the experience of the Liberal Party during the First World War—the party split over conscription with primarily anglophone Liberal MPs joining the Conservatives in a national unity (or 'Union') government—led them to adopt a more broad-based leadership selection process in 1919. This included a role for the extra-parliamentary party: each riding association, regardless of whether it had a sitting member, was able to send an equal number of delegates to a national convention. The alternative would have allowed a rump group of Liberal MPs—primarily from Quebec—to determine the leadership. Crafted by the former Liberal prime minister,[2] the new more inclusive procedure was later adopted by the Conservatives (Courtney 1995) and became the norm in both federal and provincial parties.

De-selection was another matter. Only in the 1960s, when the highly erratic leadership of John Diefenbaker caused turmoil in the cabinet and the party generally, did the Progressive Conservatives begin formulating a review procedure. It took more than three years of internecine struggle before the procedure was adopted and Diefenbaker was removed from the leadership. The Canadian leadership convention process and its current variants mean that party leaders typically have few obligations to the parliamentary party: caucus members constitute only a miniscule proportion of those selecting the leader.

Periodic leadership conventions (or in their absence, policy conventions) provide a device to engage party activists and allow them to meet and socialize with each other. Though formulas varied, conventions typically included federal or provincial officials, members of parliament or provincial legislatures, 'riding' or constituency executives, and delegates elected by party members at the riding level. In the 1990s, leadership conventions began to be replaced by every-member vote procedures. Provincial parties began experimenting with telephone balloting and other devices, including setting up polling stations in different regions. Like American primaries, every-member selection procedures put a greater premium on the capacity of the candidates to perform in public and on television. The older convention process, in contrast, put greater emphasis on the organizational abilities of leadership candidates battling to have riding associations select their slate of convention delegates. Bolstered by the populism and *basisme* of the Reform Party and its successor, the Canadian Alliance, every-member vote procedures have become more common in provincial parties, but have not supplanted leadership conventions in the older federal parties (Carty and Blake 1999). The Liberals and the Progressive Conservatives stuck to the traditional format, but with the modification that delegates are bound to the candidate for whom they were initially selected on the first ballot. The new Conservative Party is divided, with some members preferring the populist approach of the Alliance and others the more traditional approach of the Progressive Conservatives.

Neither leadership conventions nor every-member vote procedures give members of legislative caucuses much leverage over party leaders. This pattern is reinforced by the absence of effective de-selection procedures: party rules normally provide for periodic though not necessarily frequent leadership reviews. However, it is difficult to remove sitting party leaders when they are in opposition and virtually impossible to do so if they are in the government. Leaders of opposition parties are more vulnerable but forcing their resignation risks weakening the party. This is an endemic problem: during the long interwar and war time period of federal Liberal dominance, the Liberals remained under the eccentric leadership of William Lyon Mackenzie King.[3] The Progressive Conservatives, being in opposition most of the time, experienced more turnover in leadership. Most leaders left voluntarily after election defeat, however, rather than being forced out. In the late 1960s, it took Herculean efforts to force a recalcitrant John Diefenbaker to relinquish the PC leadership. In contrast, the Canadian Alliance, formed in June 2000, became so divided that its newly elected leader, Stockwell Day, was forced to resign the leadership a few months later. The only instance in which de-selection procedures have worked was in 1983, when Brian Mulroney replaced Joe Clark as Progressive Conservative leader. However, this would not have occurred if Clark had not stated that he would resign if he failed to win 60 per cent in a leadership review. Clark lost to Mulroney in the three-way race which ensued.

The limits of de-selection procedures are amply illustrated by the difficulties which supporters of Paul Martin experienced in trying to replace Jean Chrétien as Liberal Party leader and Prime Minister. Martin, Chrétien's Minister of Finance, had long been regarded as a likely successor. However, Chrétien was deliberately vague about any plans to leave office. He periodically encouraged potential successors to test the waters and begin organizing to contest the leadership, but would clamp down on campaign activity whenever it became too bothersome. By 2002, Martin's supporters had gained control of many constituency parties and were in a position to force a leadership review at an upcoming policy convention in 2003. Had such a convention been held, it was likely that Chrétien would have been ousted. Faced with this prospect, Chrétien announced that he would step down in eighteen months' time, and eventually left office in November 2003. Months earlier, Martin had been forced either to resign from cabinet or abandon the substantial leadership campaign organization constructed on his behalf. He chose the former option. Chrétien's move not only avoided formal de-selection, but also threw the Martin forces off-balance by delaying selection of a new leader and enhancing the prospects of other candidates. This episode suggests that although a sitting prime minister could in the long run not avoid de-selection, he or she could nevertheless delay the process and exert some influence over it. Despite newer parties adopting more open leadership selection procedures, within the Liberal Party, the net effect is that sitting leaders remain strong and almost immune from effective challenge.

In Canada, neither government nor opposition members are strong enough to oust their leaders with any regularity. This weakness is mirrored in another comparison. In contrast to Westminster, where occasional dissent is tolerated in both major parties, Canadian parliamentary caucuses allow minimal tolerance of dissent. Under Jean Chrétien, the rule was zero or near-zero tolerance. The strength of party leaders vis-à-vis their parties reinforces their control over cabinets when they are in government.

THE EXECUTIVE FACE

Let us posit two models of cabinet government. In the first, the prime minister is 'first-among equals'. The prime minister is chair of a board attempting to forge a consensus out of competing and sometimes dissenting views. Typically, the premier cannot move forward unless there is a consensus or, failing that, a clear majority on any given position. In the second, the prime minister is chief executive officer (CEO) and other ministers are equivalent to vice-presidents (Aucoin 1994). Ministers report to the prime minister, and the only collective role which cabinet plays is advisory. The prime minister-as-CEO model is consistent with presidentialization. Labelling the Canadian cabinet as little more than a 'rolling focus group for the prime minister', Donald Savoie (1999) argues strongly that Canada clearly falls in the latter category.

Since the arrival of well organized party machines in the 1870s and 1880s, Canadian prime ministers, within the limits of regional and linguistic considerations, have had considerable discretion about who enters and who leaves cabinet, and who gets what portfolio. The prime minister's appointment prerogative holds true for a wide variety of other appointments, including the top positions in the civil service, judiciary, and Senate. This stands in contrast to the US, where Congress must approve most important presidential nominations (Smith 2000). The prime minister also has exclusive jurisdiction over machinery of government, particularly the design of the cabinet, the number and type of portfolios, and the role of central agencies. The design of the cabinet includes the number and role of cabinet committees and the kind of support these committees will have. This is crucial for prime ministerial power. Both for cabinet as a whole, and most cabinet committees, support is provided by the primary central agency, the Privy Council Office (PCO). The PCO sets the agenda for the cabinet and cabinet committees, and coordinates the proposals which line departments submit to the cabinet for consideration. The Department of Finance supports the budgetary process, but it lacks exclusive control over it. Both PCO and the Prime Minister's Office (PMO) are involved. Moreover, the PCO has been strengthening its capacity in this regard. The treasury board secretariat (TBS) provides support to the treasury board, the cabinet committee responsible for overseeing the expenditure process. The PCO and the senior appointed official, the Clerk of the Privy Council, see themselves coordinating the upper echelons of government. Helping knit things together at the top translates into strong central control. The PMO, composed exclusively of political appointees, includes the prime minister's closest advisers. In most cases, they will have worked with the prime minister for many years. The PMO sets the political agenda on behalf of the prime minister, manages issues, and deals with problems as they arise. Staff in the PMO and PCO increased in the Trudeau era. Numbers have remained strong even when line departments were cut back in the 1990s.

There is close interaction between senior PMO and PCO staff, including the Clerk of the Privy Council and the prime minister's chief-of-staff. The clerk is a career civil servant who is appointed directly by the prime minister. This is true for the appointment of deputy ministers (the highest civil servant in each department) as well. Although ostensibly non-partisan, some clerks of the privy council have been remarkably dedicated to promoting and implementing the prime minister's agenda. This was certainly the case under Brian Mulroney. Paul Tellier, the Clerk, became a close friend and personal confidant of the premier; he was probably closer to Mulroney than the staff in the PMO. During the last years of the Mulroney government, there were pronounced conflicts between PCO and line department officials. Many felt that senior PCO officials had become too involved in overtly political matters and that they had failed to shield less senior civil servants from direct political influence (Sutherland 1991).

The prime minister, along with two or three advisers from the PMO, and the clerk and three or four officials from the PCO, constitute the core executive. Deputy ministers (the top civil servants) of government departments report not only to their ministers but also to the clerk and other central agencies such as the PCO and the TBS. These reporting arrangements enable the centre to exercise considerable influence over line departments and their ministers. This control is bolstered by regular meetings of deputies with (and without) the clerk. These meetings are typically intended to foster a strong 'corporate' identity.

Each minister has half a dozen or so political or 'exempt' staff. Ministers with some seniority and experience choose their own political staff. However, the PMO helps to recruit staff for junior ministers and also vets staff selected by more senior ministers. Furthermore, PMO staff are in constant communication with ministers' staff about the political management of various files. Under Brian Mulroney, ministers had considerable resources to recruit exempt staff. Ministers' chiefs-of-staff enjoyed salaries comparable to those of associate or assistant deputy ministers (Plasse 1994). In 1993 Jean Chrétien's Liberal government restricted the number and remuneration of ministers' exempt staff and asserted greater central control over political appointees.

According to Savoie (1999), the Liberal government's 1995 'Program Review', designed to tackle the rapidly burgeoning deficit, illustrates the power of central agencies. Central agencies, in this case primarily finance and the PCO, orchestrated Canada's version of the New Public Management. Departments such as environment lost more than a third of their budget and staff. Transport was reduced from 16,000 full-time employees to less than 4,000, with activities such air traffic control and airports being transferred to non-profit corporations. When departments or ministers resisted—for example, Human Resource Development Canada (HRDC) and its minister, responsible for most of the federal government's social programmes—the centre would step in and impose its own solution. Although most line departments were cut, some quite substantially, Savoie notes that central agencies, including the PMO, grew in size (see also Aucoin and Savoie 1998). In brief, it is the central agencies—PMO and PCO in particular—that provide the prime minister capacity to direct and coordinate the activities of ministers and their portfolios.

Limitations and constraints

Canada's Westminster-style adversarial system, premised on accountability to parliament and supported by hierarchical command and control systems, is well suited to the concentration of power in the hands of those at the top. Nevertheless, there are limitations and constraints: only so much can be micro-managed. Through necessity, departments retain discretionary authority over operational matters. Astute ministers can use that authority to challenge or bargain with other ministers, including the prime minister. Jean Chrétien was known to tolerate minimal dissent. At the same time, he did give ministers leeway in managing their portfolios and intervened only when something had gone truly amiss in a portfolio. There are a number of examples of this. Thus, former Minister of Finance Paul Martin retained considerable control over the budget; a fiscal conservative, Martin vetoed pet projects of other ministers and the prime minister himself, particularly during the period when the government was battling the deficit. This reflected the centrality of his portfolio and the respect which Martin commanded in party and in financial circles.

Other ministers have also been able to carve out areas of discretion. In 1995, Brian Tobin, then Minister of Fisheries, ordered the arrest of a Spanish trawler off the coast of Newfoundland, launching a fish war with the European Union. While this operation undoubtedly had Chrétien's consent, it was also given rather reluctantly, the Prime Minister being highly cautious by nature. Former Minister of Foreign Affairs, Lloyd Axworthy, carved out a distinctive role by tackling the landmines issue and being more critical of US foreign policy than either the prime minister or other ministers. Nonetheless, while Chrétien rarely criticized or contradicted another minister, if he and his advisers felt that there were problems of ministerial performance that could affect the government's standing, PMO staffers would quickly move in and work with the minister and his or her staff to resolve the problem or rein-in the minister. Typically, at the next cabinet reshuffle the minister would be moved to a lesser portfolio or given a patronage position such as an ambassadorial appointment.

One important constraint on the prime minister is the material that he or she has to work with in constructing a cabinet. Federal cabinets are expected to be representative of Canada's regions and provinces. Convention dictates that each province—even Prince Edward Island with a population of 135,000—should have at least one member in the cabinet. Larger provinces are entitled to more, but here too representation needs to be balanced. In the case of Ontario, for example, there should be ministers from northern and south-western Ontario as well as Toronto. The regional imperative limits the prime minister's capacity to slot people into positions where they can help in implementing or furthering the premier's agenda. As a result, a prime minister may be unable to appoint people who are his or her supporters and/or possess expertise or experience helpful in managing a particular portfolio. Second, the prime minister may be forced to include certain figures in the cabinet because they have strong regional bases of support. Such individuals do not necessarily share the prime minister's agenda and may be in a position to challenge the premier on issues that directly affect their province or region. Under the Mulroney government (1984–93), John Crosbie, the minister from Newfoundland, extracted concessions on offshore resources which benefited the province. Crosbie also forced the prime minister to renounce a treaty between Canada and France on fishing rights off the French islands, St. Pierre and Miquelon. The prime minister also needs to include his or her closest competitors in the leadership race. When Chrétien first came to power, it would have been difficult to exclude his main rival, Paul Martin, or deny him a major portfolio.

Moreover, the prime minister can become beholden to ministers who display considerable competence in their portfolios. The limited experience of Canadian parliamentarians generally, the limited managerial and technical capacity of most MPs, combined with the regional imperative, means that sound judgement, political skills, experience, and substantive expertise are at a premium. A minister who performs well can build up political capital. In the Trudeau era, Allan J. MacEachen was a brilliant strategist and parliamentarian. As the House leader, he kept Trudeau's minority government alive for more than two years in the early 1970s. As a reward, Trudeau assigned MacEachen to the coveted external affairs portfolio and gave him free rein over all matters relating to his province, Nova Scotia. Brian Mulroney came to depend on Donald Mazankowski, a powerful minister from Alberta. Mazankowski became known as minister of everything by virtue of his ability to manage just about any portfolio. As Deputy Prime Minister, Mazankowski headed an expanded office that, among other things, was responsible for the Cabinet's operations committee. For many years, Jean Chrétien was beholden to his main rival, Paul Martin. As Minister of Finance, Martin was regarded as the person responsible for the effective management of the Canadian economy, and Martin's performance translated into electoral support. The Liberals' 1997 election victory followed a campaign based on fiscal responsibility and probity over the preceding four years. It was Martin who could claim credit for taming the deficit (Bakvis 2000).

Even so, although many people argued that Martin's departure would severely undermine the government's standing, Chrétien felt impelled to manoeuvre Martin out of the Cabinet in the spring of 2002. In his place, Chrétien actively promoted younger rising stars who might be able to fill the vacuum. John Manley was advanced to Deputy Prime Minister, given responsibility for national security and crown corporations and then shifted to finance when Martin departed. The press regarded Manley's advance as an astute manoeuvre intended to stifle Martin's leadership aspirations and demonstrate that Martin was not the only competent minister in the cabinet.

As noted earlier, the Canadian prime minister tends to exercise much more control over his parliamentary caucus than his counterparts in the UK, Australia, and New Zealand (Weller 1997). The relative inexperience of MPs generally, the fact that the premier owes very little to the caucus and the fact that most government MPs realize they gained entry to the Commons by virtue of the prime minister's coat-tails, and the heavy stress on the importance of loyalty in the light of the spectre of Quebec sovereignty, all contribute to the high level of control exercised by the prime minister. Within the Commons itself, as Jennifer Smith (2000) notes, the prime minister faces hostile opposition, questioning on a continuing basis when parliament is in session, something to which the American president is not subjected. Question period in the Commons is also the event that is most closely covered by the media. It is in this setting that the prime minister is perhaps the most vulnerable. However, Jean Chrétien had the good fortune to be blessed by a fragmented and inexperienced opposition throughout his tenure.

The press, a key element in ensuring that opposition criticism receives ample publicity, is not as effective as it might be. Most of the press is highly regionalized and for many years only one newspaper, the *Globe and Mail,* based in Toronto, had a national circulation. A second paper, the *National Post,* was launched in 1998 by media baron Conrad Black, and took a distinct, some would say strident, right-wing position, which has subsequently been muted with the sale of the paper and its financial difficulties. The broadcast media, particularly the CBC, provide a modest check on prime ministerial power. Government and government departments' actions can become the target of investigative journalism and media campaigns. This can reinforce and in certain cases stimulate opposition criticism, but not necessarily prevent a determined government or a prime minister from doing what he or she wants.

Finally, the prime minister also controls the timing of elections. Thus in autumn 2000, a little more than three years into the government's mandate and contrary to the wishes of several of his ministers and government MPs, Mr. Chrétien decided the time was ripe for a snap election. The main opposition party, the Alliance, had just selected a new leader and the economy was riding high. His judgement was amply vindicated by an increase in the government's majority and a reversal in the fortune of all the opposition parties, except the Progressive Conservatives. This ensured that the opposition was more fragmented than ever (Bakvis 2001). The Chrétien government's dominance of parliament was due to his unique political skills and the fragmented nature of the opposition.

While there are countervailing sources of power in the form of ministers possessing parliamentary skills or a strong electoral base or support in the party, there are no equivalents to Anthony King's 'big beasts of the jungle', powerful ministers who have their own policy agendas and strong contingents of supporters in the party and the parliament (King 1985). Under Jean Chretien, only former Finance Minister, Paul Martin, could be considered a strong rival to the incumbent Prime Minister. In Canada, ministers with clout are typically more concerned with pork-barrel—government largesse for their constituencies or province. Their ambitions and political horizons are often quite limited. In return for control over government spending in their particular bailiwick they are usually quite happy to leave broader policy issues to the prime minister and his advisers or to those few ministers who have genuine power.

The only genuine structural constraint, therefore, is federalism. Particularly on issues relating to social policy and to a considerable extent economic management, very little can be accomplished by the federal government without cooperation from the provinces. Even in basic areas such as securities regulation, Ottawa is hamstrung because this is under provincial jurisdiction. On the other hand, federalism does put the prime minister into an elevated role as the chief negotiator on behalf of the federal government. Furthermore, the dynamic between Ottawa and provinces may be changing in Ottawa's favour. Since September 11, trans-border issues such as trade and security have become more critical, and Ottawa is still the primary actor in dealings with the US.

THE ELECTORAL FACE: PARTY LEADERS IN CANADIAN ELECTIONS

Canadian elections have always been leader-centred, beginning with Sir John A. Macdonald, leader of a Liberal–Conservative coalition at the time of confederation in 1867. In the nineteenth century Macdonald of the Conservatives and Wilfrid Laurier of the Liberals, both highly skilled orators, dominated not only their parties but also the electoral process. During the interwar period, party leaders depended on regional chieftains to deliver the vote. Examples include Jimmy Gardner, former Premier of Saskatchewan and longtime federal Minister of Agriculture, and Ernest Lapointe and Charles Power in Quebec. This kind of political mobilization was sharply curtailed in 1957 when the Progressive Conservative leader, John Diefenbaker, became Prime Minister. A figure with a decidedly populist mien, Diefenbaker successfully attacked the incumbent Liberal government and its leader, Louis St. Laurent, for being aloof, too beholden to regional power brokers, and out of touch with the grass roots. Diefenbaker was the first leader to make effective use of the new medium of television. In some respects, Pierre Trudeau fitted the Diefenbaker mould, using a strong personal leadership style to emphasize pan-Canadian values.

Other party leaders fared less well electorally. Pearson, a former senior civil servant and winner of the Nobel Peace prize in 1956, was seen as somewhat bumbling and ineffectual and unable to bring order to his Cabinet. He ended up heading minority governments from 1963 to 1968. Trudeau, his successor, was remarkably telegenic and still remembered for iconic performances, many captured on television. Examples include standing his ground in the face of a rock-throwing separatist crowd in Quebec prior to the 1968 election while the rest of his entourage scampered for cover. His Conservative opponent, Robert Stanfield, a thoughtful and well-liked individual, had his own iconic moment when he fumbled a tossed football in front of television cameras. This 'moment' was quickly seized by the press, which used it as a metaphor for what ailed the Conservative election campaign.

These incidents demonstrate both the intense media focus on party leaders, something neither leaders nor their parties discourage, and the way seemingly minor events can become magnified and carry disproportionate weight in electoral outcomes.

The Trudeau era also saw the elevation of the 'leadership tour' as the primary focus of election campaigns. During five-week campaigns party leaders cross the continent in rented aircraft. The leader and his entourage occupy the front of the aircraft while the press fills the rear. The bulk of press coverage, both print and electronic, centres on the leader's tours: all other activities are treated as secondary. The leader's handlers manage press access, and questions from the press tend to be handled in 'scrums'. Questions and answers are short, and leaders pick and choose among the questions fired at them. If the party and the leader are up in the polls, parties cocoon the leader, ensuring that interaction is limited and carefully scripted. Parties now use sophisticated communications technology to keep in touch with campaign headquarters where events and statements relating to the other parties are carefully tracked, responses to possible media questions crafted, and strategy developed. The whole campaign is tightly managed; local candidates follow a well-defined script, for example. Parties have thus far made only limited use of the internet for campaign purposes. Instead, parties have invested more in telephone-based technologies where call-centres appeared to have replaced the more traditional door-to-door campaigning, at least in large urban centres. While the campaign teams of the parties are plugged into the latest technologies and are not averse to bringing in expertise from the US, some of the forays involving the use of US style campaign techniques (such as negative advertising) have not worked well in Canada.[4] Canada's election laws, which limit campaign expenditures by parties and restrict third-party (i.e. soft money) expenditures to negligible amounts, constrain parties further in the range of possible electioneering techniques that could be deployed. Overall, though, leader-centred media campaigns have been a prominent feature of Canadian electoral politics since the Diefenbaker era. Print and electronic journalism focus primarily on party leaders, and most advertising at election time places the leader front and centre. What has changed is the use of polling data to shape campaign messages and target particular social groups, and the capacity of parties to respond almost instantaneously to unfolding events.

Numerous studies show that perceptions and evaluations of leaders' capabilities is a critical consideration in voting decisions. According to Johnston et al. (1992), performance in the televised leadership debates during the 1984 and 1988 election campaigns was among the more crucial determinants of the final outcome. At most, Canadians may recognize the names of two or three other key figures in the cabinet, and would be hard pressed to recognize, let alone name, the rest. The 'personal' vote for most individual parliamentarians is much weaker in Canada than in the US or the UK (Ferejohn and Gaines 1991). Regional and national factors tend to be much stronger, and at the national level party, party policy, and leadership are closely intertwined. If the leader lacks credibility, then neither party nor policy will be sufficiently strong to carry the election. One of the first signs that an election campaign is in trouble is the de-emphasis of the leader's name in favour of the party label.

Studies of the 1997 and 2002 elections assessed the effects of leaders' popularity on electoral outcomes by looking at differences in voter ratings of leaders and how these impacted on party choice. Nevitte et al. (2000: 77) revealed that in 1997 the probability of voting Liberal for someone who ranked Mr. Chrétien ten points higher than the next most highly ranked leader was nine points higher (controlling for all other factors, including partisanship). In a slightly different analysis, they note that Chrétien's popularity relative to that of the other leaders was worth five points outside of Quebec; inside Quebec, Chrétien's relative unpopularity cost the Liberal party three points. In 2000, leadership effects were less clear-cut, in part because voters ranked all five party leaders roughly the same.[5] Furthermore, in the 2000 election Chrétien's popularity dropped by six points relative to 1997. Despite this, the Liberals made slight overall gains.

This last point underscores the fact that, while leadership effects are important, and leaders are typically placed front and centre in campaigns, they are not necessarily the most critical factor in explaining electoral outcomes. As Blais et al. (2002: 166) note: 'On the one hand, [the studies] confirm that leadership has quite a substantial effect on the vote: the party of the most popular leader can typically expect to get a boost of about five points. On the other hand, they suggest that these effects are usually not overwhelming, and seldom important enough to change the outcome of an election.' The same investigators for the 1997 and 2000 Canadian election studies have also noted an overall decline in the relative importance of leadership. As shown in Fig. 9.1, for the Liberal Party there has been a precipitous decline in the importance of leadership relative to party since the 1960s and 1970s. Indeed, it has dropped most sharply in the period covered by Chrétien's tenure as party leader, a period when the putative autocratic proclivities on the part of the prime minister were particularly pronounced. According to this book's analytical framework—and indeed, to other observers such as Michael Foley (1993)—the rise of the presidentialization phenomenon is directly coupled to the increasing focus on personal political leadership both at and between election times. The Chrétien 'presidency' appears to offer a contrast to this development, particularly with respect to garnering voting support at election time. To the extent that the increasing importance of the prime minister and his or her leadership qualities as an electoral force is seen as a hallmark of the presidentialization thesis in Westminster systems, then Canada probably falls somewhat short on this criterion.

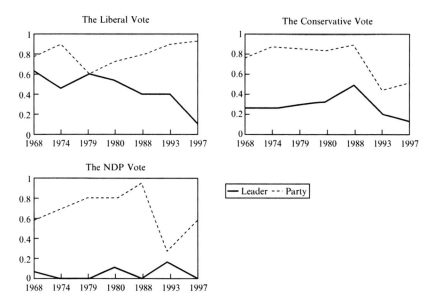

Fig. 9.1. *Leader and party effects by party in Canada*

Note: Vertical scale represents leader and party coefficients derived from simple linear regressions of voter choice on leader and party ratings, estimated separately for each of the three parties under study, with controls for social background characteristics.

Source: Gidengil et al. (2000): 9.

CONCLUSION: CANADA IN COMPARATIVE CONTEXT

In Chapter 1, the editors sketched out three essential characteristics of presidentialism: (1) the political irresponsibility of the executive to the legislature; (2) a popularly elected head of government; and (3) unipersonal executive responsibility. If we apply these three criteria to the Canadian case, we can conclude the following:

First, while the Canadian executive is formally responsible to the House of Commons, in practice it dominates the legislature and does so to a degree that is substantially greater than is the case in the UK and other Westminster systems. Largely due to the nature of the leadership selection process, strict party discipline and a fragmented opposition, this dominance is likely to continue well into the future. Indeed, insofar as the Canadian executive is relatively autonomous from the legislature and at the same time in control of it, it is far more powerful than the American president who, while formally accountable only to the electorate, is subject to the checks of a separately elected legislature. Of course, periods of minority government, such as the one which began in 2004, alter the balance between parliament and prime minister. However, minority governments rarely last more than two years, and the prime minister remains firmly in control of his cabinet.

Second, while in a formal sense the formation of the government is dependent on the number of members elected in individual ridings and the prime minister is selected by the governor general on the basis of the party leader best positioned to form a majority in the House of Commons, in practice, the election campaign and the vote tend to be based in good part on the perceived quality and performance of the leader. Also, the political party and its perceived competence in being able to form a credible government also weighs on the minds of voters, and perhaps more so in recent years. Although in some elections, policy issues can be front and centre—for example, the so-called free-trade election of 1988—perceived leadership and overall party competence are both still significant variables capable of affecting the outcome of elections. Election outcomes are thus seen as verdicts on the party and party leadership. Although considering the Canadian House of Commons to be a functional equivalent of the electoral college in the US would be a gross exaggeration, the power and influence of individual MPs is much more circumscribed than in other Westminster systems. This is even truer of members of provincial legislatures, which meet less frequently and for shorter periods of time.

Third, while the Canadian cabinet is collectively and formally responsible to parliament, in practice the prime minister dominates. It is clear that he or she, and he or she alone, selects and de-selects members of cabinet. In that the president of the United States must have his cabinet nominees ratified by congress, the Canadian prime minister is far more powerful in this respect. Only on rare occasions have the Canadian prime minister and cabinet approximated the first-among-equals model; the prime minister as CEO is far more predominant (Bakvis 2001). Furthermore, the formalities of ministerial responsibility can actually be used by the prime minister to deflect criticism and responsibilities and thereby enhance control. While they are formally responsible to the House, most ministers realize that in practice they are beholden to the prime minister and that their reporting relationship is to him.

In brief, with respect to control over the legislature and cabinet, the Canadian prime minister is more powerful than counterparts in other Westminster systems. When it comes to the personalization and popularization of party leadership, however, the Canadian evidence is somewhat ambiguous. It is an important factor, but not as important as it was two decades ago and currently not as important as voter assessments of the parties. This is especially the case for the Liberals, who have also been the dominant party over the past decade. The basis for labelling the Canadian system as presidentialized, therefore, can be found in the control exercised by the prime minister over his or her party, the Commons and cabinet—that is, in the political rather than the electoral face of the phenomenon.

The presidentialization of Canadian politics, or in other terms, executive dominance in a parliamentary system, is a not a new phenomenon. It dates back to the Diefenbaker and Trudeau eras, and reflects in the first instance the control which leaders exert over their own parties, their caucus, and the cabinet, using levers of power built into the Canadian parliamentary system. The earlier growth of executive dominance reflects the strains of Canadian federalism and the fact that Canadian governments are in continual discussion and bargaining with provincial governments. Executive federalism puts the prime minister and provincial premiers front and centre in the political process and therefore places a premium on these actors having full control over their governments. Factors such as the media and globalization have intensified these presidentialist characteristics, but only slightly, because these characteristics were already present. The prominence of the prime minister and people around him is further reinforced by the configuration of the party system as a one-party dominant system, a state of affairs which became even more pronounced in the decade from 1993 to 2003 with the fragmentation of the opposition into four parties. Merger of the Alliance and the Progressive Conservative Party has reduced but not eliminated this fragmentation. Although minority government has weakened the government vis-à-vis parliament, it is not clear that it has weakened the power of the prime minister over the cabinet or the machinery of government. Complaints about the insularity and heavy-handedness on the part of the current prime minister's office staff continued under Paul Martin. The 2006 federal election has done little to change this. The Conservative Party formed a minority government under their leader, Stephen Harper. Insisting that public statements from government departments and their ministers be vetted with his office, Prime Minister Harper seems determined to assert at least as much control as his Liberal predecessors.

NOTES

1. Many British Columbians, separated from the rest of Canada, identify more with 'Cascadia'—British Columbia, Washington State, and Oregon. Although they now enjoy rents from oil and pay no provincial sales tax, Albertans continue to resent freight rate policies which once favoured the shipment of goods west from the industrial heartland, and the shipment of grain east, but not the reverse, to the detriment of farmers and would-be industrialists. Although it was reversed when the Mulroney government took office in 1984, Albertans remain embittered about Pierre Elliot Trudeau's National Energy Program, which made Albertan oil available at less than market prices. Saskatchewan and Manitoba lack Alberta's oil but share some its alienation.

2. This was Sir Wilfrid Laurier, who had refused to join the Union government, which was composed of the Conservatives and most, though not all, Liberal MPs from outside Quebec.

3. Among other things, King made decisions only when the hands of the clock were in certain positions. With the help of a spiritualist, he regularly consulted his dead mother and dog.

4. A television advert used by the Conservatives in the last weeks of the 1993 election, using an unflattering photograph of the Liberal leader, highlighting a facial deformity, backfired with disastrous results, accelerating the downhill slide in Conservative support.

5. The rankings, on a 100 point scale, ranged from 45 for Stockwell Day to 48 for Chrétien and Duceppe (the Bloc Québecois leader) among those identifying with the party of the leader in question. Among those without party identification, the scores ranged from 45 (Chrétien) to 50 (Duceppe) (Blais et al. 2002: 167).

REFERENCES

Aucoin, P. (1994). 'Prime Ministerial Leadership: Position, Power, and Politics', in M. Mancuso, R. G. Price, and R. H. Wagenburg (eds.), *Leaders and Leadership in Canada*. Toronto: Oxford University Press, 99–117.

—— and D. J. Savoie (1998). *Managing Strategic Change: Learning from Program Review*. Ottawa: Canadian Centre for Management Development.

Bakvis, H. (1991). *Regional Ministers: Power and Influence in the Canadian Cabinet*. Toronto: University of Toronto Press.

—— (1994). 'Cabinet Ministers: Leaders or Followers?', in M. Mancuso, R. G. Price, and R. H. Wagenburg (eds.), *Leaders and Leadership in Canadian Politics*. Toronto: Oxford University Press, 132–53.

—— (2000). 'Rebuilding Policy Capacity in the Era of the Fiscal Dividend', *Governance*, 13: 71–103.

—— (2001). 'Prime Minister and Cabinet: An Autocracy in Need of Reform?', *Journal of Canadian Studies*, 35: 60–79.

Blais, A., E. Gidengil, R. Nadeau, and N. Nevitte (2002). *Anatomy of a Liberal Victory: Making Sense of the Vote in the 2000 Canadian Election*. Peterborough: Broadview.

Carty, R. K. and D. E. Blake (1999). 'The Adoption of Membership Votes for Choosing Party Leaders: The Experience of Canadian Parties', *Party Politics*, 5: 211–24.

—— W. Cross, and L. Young (2000). *Rebuilding Canadian Party Politics*. Vancouver: UBC Press.

Courtney, J. C. (1995). *Do Conventions Matter? Choosing National Party Leaders in Canada*. Montreal: McGill-Queen's University Press.

Docherty, D. C. (1997). *Mr. Smith Goes to Ottawa: Life in the House of Commons*. Vancouver: UBC Press.

Ferejohn, J. and B. Gaines (1991). 'The Personal Vote in Canada', in H. Bakvis (ed.) *Representation and Integration in Canadian Political Parties*. Toronto: Dundurn.

Foley, M. (1993). *The Rise of the British Presidency*. Manchester: Manchester University Press.

Gidengil, E., A. Blais, R. Nadeau, and N. Nevitte (2000). 'Are Party Leaders Becoming More Important to Voter Choice in Canada?'. Delivered at the Annual Meeting of the American Political Science Association, Washington DC, 30 August 3 September.

Greenspon, E. (1999). 'Modern Prime Ministers Growing Ever More Powerful, Liberal Insider Holds: "Court Government" Means Near-total Control Rests in One Pair of Hands, Author Contends', in *Globe and Mail*. Toronto.

Johnston, R., A. Blais, H. E. Brady, and J. Crête (1992). *Letting the People Decide: Dynamics of a Canadian Election*. Montreal: McGill-Queen's University Press.

Katz, R. and P. Mair (1994). *How Parties Organize: Change and Adaptation in Party Organizations in Western Democracies*. London: Sage.

King, A. S. (1985). *The British Prime Minister*. London: Macmillan.

Nevitte, N., A. Blais, E. Gidengil, and R. Nadeau (2000). *Unsteady State: The 1997 Federal Election*. Toronto: Oxford University Press.

Plasse, M. (1994). 'Ministerial Chiefs of Staff in the Federal Government in 1990: Profiles, Recruitment, Duties, and Relations with Senior Public Servants'. Canadian Centre for Management Development.

Savoie, D. J. (1999). *Governing from the Centre: The Concentration of Power in Canadian Politics*. Toronto: University of Toronto Press.

Simpson, J. (2001). *The Friendly Dictatorship*. Toronto: McClelland and Stewart.

Smith, J. (2000). 'The Grass is Always Greener Prime Ministerial vs. Presidential Government', in D. Thomas (ed.), *Canada and the United States: Differences that Count*. Peterborough: Broadview.

Sutherland, S. L. (1991). 'The Al-Mashat Affair: Administrative Responsibility in Parliamentary Institutions', *Canadian Public Administration*, 34: 573–603.

Tanguay, A. B. (2002). 'Political Parties and Canadian Democracies: Making Federalism Do the Heavy Lifting', in H. Bakvis and G. Skogstad (eds.) *Canadian Federalism: Performance, Effectiveness, and Legitimacy*. Toronto: Oxford University Press, 296–316.

Weller, P. (1997). 'Political Parties and the Core Executive', in P. Weller, H. Bakvis, and R. A. W. Rhodes (eds.), *The Hollow Crown: Countervailing Trends in Core Executives*. Basingstoke: Macmillan, 37–57.

Whitaker, R. (1977). *The Government Party*. Toronto: University of Toronto Press.

10

Dyarchic Presidentialization in a Presidentialized Polity: The French Fifth Republic

Ben Clift

The ambiguity inherent in the 1958 constitution as to where power lay within the French 'dual executive', successfully exploited by de Gaulle, established presidential precedents that overstepped the constitutional brief. Having shaped the nature of party competition into a bipolarized pluralism involving electoral blocs on Left and Right, political and electoral presidentialization also changed the nature of the parties themselves, both organizationally, and in their relationship to the state. The leader focus in media coverage of politics, and in political campaigning styles, is here placed in the context, first, of the evolving relationship between the media and the presidency since 1958, and second, of radical deregulation, commercialization, and increased competition within the French audio-visual sector in recent decades.

THE INSTITUTIONAL CONTEXT OF THE FIFTH REPUBLIC AND PRESIDENTIALIZATION

The need to overcome the *immobilisme* which characterized the Fourth Republic's discredited *régime des partis* underpinned the 1958 constitutional project. Constitutional co-designer Michel Debré argued that government had to be accorded supremacy over parliament, and the new constitution was intended to be a blueprint for British-style prime ministerial government (Debré 1981). However, between 1958 and 1962, President de Gaulle emerged as the Fifth Republic's dominant political actor, culminating in his direct election as president in 1965. Precedents set by de Gaulle meant Debré's prime ministerial aspirations went unfulfilled for nearly thirty years.

Sartori identifies the French Fifth Republic as an ideal-type example of a 'semi-presidential' regime, a 'bicephalous system whose heads are *unequal* but also *in oscillation* between themselves'; the 'first head' is by custom (the conventions of the 'living' constitution) the president, but by law (the written text of the constitution) the prime minister. 'The oscillations', Sartori continues, 'reflect the respective majority status of one over the other' (1997: 123). The coexistence of a fixed-term president and a prime minister responsible to a parliament creates a 'finely balanced constitutional dyarchy' (Elgie 1999: 77) at the core of the French executive.

Government pre-eminence was institutionalized through a series of 'structural assets' and 'constitutional weapons': restrictions on censure votes; on areas for parliamentary legislation and amendment; provisions for by-passing parliament altogether by legislating through ordinances; and for transforming bills into 'confidence' issues—passed unless the National Assembly succeeds in passing a censure motion (Elgie 1996a: 38, 57–9; Keeler 1993: 521). However, while categorically establishing the supremacy of the executive over parliament, the Fifth Republic constitution fudges the key question of who has power *within* the executive (Knapp and Wright 2001: 58). A purely textual reading suggests an *apparent* dominance of the prime minister, installed at the head of a government responsible for national policy-making, and able to issue decrees (*règlements*) with the force of law (Elgie 2001: 107).

By comparison, the president's constitutional powers appear clearly defined but limited. Without prime ministerial counter-signature, the president may: nominate (but not dismiss) the prime minister; dissolve the National Assembly (after consultation with the premier); and declare a state of emergency in times of crisis where the president deems the political system is under immediate threat.[1] In addition, the president may resign, provoking a presidential election. Much more ambiguously, the president must 'arbitrate' to ensure respect for the Constitution and the regular functioning of public authorities (Wright 1993). All other presidential powers require a prime ministerial counter-signature, which, in constitutional theory, curtails their autonomous manipulation by the president.

Yet the French head of state has been able to exploit *presidential* structural assets and constitutional weapons, in concert with constitutional ambiguity, to dominate the political system. The best example is provided by Article 5, establishing the president's role as 'arbitrator', which 'can also legitimise almost any intervention that the president might wish to make' (Elgie 1999: 76).

Thus, a purely textual analysis of the new constitution fails to capture its significance, for if the new constitution codified the shift from 'weak' to 'strong' government, it was President de Gaulle (and *not* Prime Minister Debré) who personified that shift. The 1962 parliamentary elections were a 'watershed event' (Ysmal 1998: 14), precipitating an unanticipated revolution within the French party system. Its impact was felt on party structures, on the strategy of key players, the logic and direction of party competition, and on the relationship between president and parliamentary groups.

De Gaulle's dissolution of the hostile assembly, asking for *both* a referendum 'yes' vote on direct presidential election *and* a vote for a parliamentary candidate who would form part of a 'presidential majority' was a master-stroke, heralding an era of secure parliamentary majorities which served as 'sturdy bulwarks' to successive presidents (Avril 1988; Knapp 2002: 108). The rout of the parliamentarist *cartel des non* installed the Gaullist Union pour la Nouvelle Republique (UNR) as dominant party 'at the service' of de Gaulle's 'plebiscitary monocracy' (Duhamel and Grunberg 2001: 533).

Ironically, de Gaulle's most significant extra-constitutional act was to sack Debré in April 1962. Debré's replacement, Pompidou, 'accepted without demur the presidential intervention which Debré had resented as a deviation from the letter of the constitution' (Hayward 1993*a*: 23–5). The finesse achieved by de Gaulle, the self-styled 'arbiter above political circumstances',[2] was to secure the powers associated with the expansive interpretation of that term, and the degree of accountability associated with the minimalist inter-pretation. The Gaullian reinterpretation of Article 5, explicit in the 1946 Bayeux speech, transforms the president, in Massot's (1987) phrase, from referee into team captain (see also Cogan 1996: 183–6 and 210).

However, as Duverger (1974: 188) put it, 'the French republican monarch might be seen as a Protean King, changing shape and power according to the nature of parliamentary forces.' The nature of the parliamentary majority (single party, balanced or imbalanced coalition, supporting or in conflict with the president) explains the varying nature of presidential power. One should be careful not to overstate presidential predominance. The concept of 'shared government' (Elgie 2001: 108–10), leaves significant areas of policy in the prime minister's and the government's hands. Even in the presidential 'reserved domain' of defence and foreign policy, the constitution charges the prime minister with responsibility for national defence, and implies a role for the government in drawing up treaties (ibid.: 108).

This gearing of the political system towards a presidential dominance left its indelible mark on the structure of parties, and the nature of party com-petition. Between 1962 and 1986, when presidential power approximated the Gaullian vision, power distribution and party structure appeared congruent. However, in 1986, Chirac's Rassemblement pour la Republique (RPR) and Giscard's Union pour la Democratie Française (UDF) won a decisive victory in the legislative elections. With the onset of 'cohabitation', the *prime minis-terial* reading of the constitution (Debré 1981) suddenly resurfaced. Prime Minister Chirac, as leader of the parliamentary majority, and recipient of the power accruing from that source of democratic legitimization, exploited the wide-ranging powers the text of the 1958 constitution placed in his hands. Cohabitation thus 'marks the revenge of the prime ministership ... The prime minister becomes the main decision-maker within the dual executive' (Elgie 2001: 120). Furthermore, this began a series of periods of cohabitation

(1986–8, 1993–5, 1997–2002), altering the nature of executive power in France, rendering divided government 'the norm' (Elgie 2001: 112). Bell (2000: 240) claimed the 1997 cohabitation 'showed that France could survive without an executive president'.

The 'neutralized' cohabiting president was confined to the minimalist 'arbiter' role of Article 5. Presidential refusal to sign ordinances—(as Mitterrand did over the privatization programme in 1986) merely delayed the prime minister's programme, forcing him to take the longer, but secure, parliamentary route (Elgie 1996*b*: 57–9). The president was constrained to accept his 'structural submission' to the prime minister, and confined to expressing reservations about government policy (Elgie 2001: 118–20; Parodi 1997: 304).

The post-1986 period illustrated the fluid, changeable nature of executive power in France. Parodi posits a law of diminishing returns for a cohabiting prime minister as he or she becomes further removed from the decisive election which installed them. The fading memory of the legitimacy-conferring mandate, the approach of the next presidential election, and the constant media attention to opinion poll ratings, creates a subtle shift in the balance of forces between powerless president and executive prime minister: 'passing from unequal competition between electoral legitimacies to a more balanced competition between institutional authorities' (Parodi 1997: 304). This characterized Socialist Prime Minister Lionel Jospin's *fin de règne* as, with the main planks of his 1997 programme already enacted, his government began to 'run out of steam' in 2001.

The shift towards 'powerless arbiter' status in 1986, 1993, and 1997, when the prime minister became unambiguously the real head of the executive, was succeeded by presidential reaffirmation in 1988, 1995, and 2002. The last is of 'structural' significance, resulting from the September 2000 constitutional change, aligning the presidential term with the five-year parliamentary term in a bid to reduce (though by no means eradicate) the likelihood of further cohabitation. This attests to the significance of the presidential election process, and the legitimacy it confers, in shaping the contours of executive power in France. This significant constitutional change has been interpreted by many as an attempt to 'stop the rot' undermining the presidential character of the Fifth Republic, an interpretation borne out by the behaviour of President Chirac and Prime Minister Raffarin since May 2002.

Overall, the Fifth Republic constitution induced a very pronounced shift towards a more presidential working mode of the system. Thus, the period in which we are interested starts at a very high level of presidentialization. The remainder of this chapter takes this constitutional presidentialization as a 'given', and explores the ongoing evolution of the political system in which the balance of power has shifted from parties towards executive leaders.

THE PARTY FACE OF PRESIDENTIALIZATION

The advent of the 'presidential majority' precipitated the presidentialization of internal party power relations, heralding the birth of a French constitutional convention which Charlot (1983: 28) describes as 'the principle of presidential initiative'. This subordinates the party to the president in policy formation, personnel selection, policy selection, and electoral campaigning. The centrality of the presidential election cycle to understanding the internal workings of all major French parties has generated a new ideal-type. French specialists thus chart the emergence of 'presidential parties', with shared attributes arising from the structural influences of the semi-presidential Fifth Republic (Cole 1993: 50; Gaffney 1990; Thiebault 1993). Parties are conceived as presidential machines, whose primary function is to act as a springboard for a presidential candidacy, and subsequently to act as an organizational resource for the president ('the president's party').

Thiebault (1993: 287) summarizes the other aspects thus: 'the "president's party" is devoted to playing the part of a "dominated" party. The formal leader of this kind of party is effectively appointed by the president himself with the formal methods of selection only serving to ratify the president's choice. The formal leader's authority and legitimacy depends on the president.' Furthermore, 'the weight of systemic constraints imposed by the Fifth Republic tended to reduce (if not abnegate totally) the capacity of parties to act in a manner autonomous from their *de facto* presidential leaders' (Cole 1993: 63). The nature of the 'presidential majority' (single party majority, coalition, or even presidential minority) provides initial conditions that qualify the operation of this 'law'. It is further contingent upon the electoral success, actual or prospective, of the president or *présidentiable* (prospective presidential candidate). Predictably, a president's supremacy over his party is greatest when the parliamentary majority owes its existence to the president (for instance, Mitterrand 1981–6), and 'the proximity of the presidential and parliamentary elections strengthens [this] dependency' (ibid.: 54–8).

The archetype is the UNR/UDR, which was effectively transformed by party leader Pompidou between 1962 and 1969 into 'both a personalist rally behind a charismatic leader and a vehicle for mobilising support for the Fifth Republic' (ibid.: 50). Paradoxically, for all his disdain of parties, de Gaulle was actively reliant upon the UNR and the *presidential majority* it orchestrated. The publicly aloof de Gaulle, a 'surreptitiously partisan statesman' (Hayward 1993*b*), meticulously vetted parliamentary candidates in 1967 (Knapp 1994). Pompidou's approach to the UDR was more activist and overt as president, and the link between president and party grew closer still: 'in the 1973 general election campaign Pompidou controlled everything through his choice as UDR Secretary-General, Alain Peyrefitte, personally selecting not merely the candidates and the programme but even the slogans and the posters' (Hayward 1993*a*: 25; see also Cole 1993: 51).

Thus the dominant party type within the Fifth Republic swiftly became a presidentialized rally party. The concept of the 'presidential party' is also pertinent to the analysis of the relationship between the undisputed presidential candidate and the party. This personalized leadership of the party is contingent upon power resources continually 'sourced by' public opinion and popularity. The reformulation of the old SFIO into the new Parti Socialiste (PS), culminating in the 1971 Epinay Congress, saw the PS transform into an approximation of the ideal-type under Mitterrand's leadership between 1971 and 1974 (see Cole 1997: 68–83). By dissolving the National Assembly immediately after his presidential victory, Mitterrand took the relationship to its logical conclusion in 1981 and 1988, transforming the party into 'an organized representative of the presidential will' (Cole 1993: 57).

The precise mechanisms of this dominance over the party varied. Within the PS, for example, internal proportional representation fosters presidentialized factionalism (Bell and Criddle 1994*a*). Conventions developed to facilitate smooth party management at times when the next presidential candidate issue was a *fait accompli*. Thus Mitterrand before 1974, and again after the party congress at Metz in 1979, acquired 'leader above faction' status, with all the competing factions synthesizing and compositing their positions, in effect creating a single faction, with Mitterrand as first signatory and leader. A similar internal configuration obtained between 1995 and 2002 during Jospin's unquestioned *présidentiable* and internally hegemonic phase, re-inforced by a newly instated one-member–one-vote leadership election. The ascendancy of Jospin's *dauphin* François Hollande to First Secretary at the 1997 Brest conference was exactly the kind of formality the 'presidential party' model would predict (see Clift 2003*a*).[3]

The successor-party of the Gaullist UNR/UDR, Chirac's RPR, was well organized and funded, and dominated by its President. Chirac's personal power base in the Paris town hall offered material and manpower resources, as well as extensive patronage, to consolidate this dominance. Even after relinquishing formal leadership, he installed the ultra-loyal Juppé as both party president and prime minister in 1995, and continued to conceive of the RPR as an instrument of personal support, closely controlled to ensure it did not become a power base for potential challengers (Knapp 1999: 130–5).

The apparent exception to this rule is Giscard, who won with the support of a partisan base with a distinctly *ancien régime* air about it. His Independent Republicans and a 'loose collection of cadre parties...[which] represented the bulk of the non-Gaullist fraction of the majority' (Cole 1993: 52), were not the single-minded presidential rallies of the new presidentialized partisan order. However, this partial exception is limited by three factors.

First, his ascendancy was facilitated by support from the dominant wing of the Gaullist movement, led by Chirac (who supported Giscard instead of the official Gaullist candidate in 1974, Jacques Chaban-Delmas, and was rewarded with the premiership from 1974 to 1976). Second, in 1978, after he had definitively lost the backing of Chirac's RPR, Giscard did move to create a slightly more structured party—albeit not one conforming to the ideal-type. Finally, the subsequent fate of the Giscardian movement under the Fifth Republic is testament to its partial incompatibility with the institutional logics of the Republic.

The dominance over the party by its presidential candidate extends to 'minor' parties (Colliard 1995: 77). The *Front National* (FN) has always been a highly centralized and autocratically organized party, initially dominated in the 1970s and 1980s by an elite loyal to a small number of foundational faction leaders. After overcoming factional power struggles, and particularly after the death of General Secretary Stirbois in 1988, Party Chairman Jean-Marie Le Pen gained a monopoly of control and authority, determining the membership of the party's elite hierarchy, notably the political bureau and executive bureau. Similar to the cell-like organization of the French Communist Party (PCF), there were no horizontal links between local FN units, only vertical ties to the national leadership, and the national leadership vets all candidacies at every level. The party's political communications strategy, and indeed political agenda, largely arises from Le Pen's media appearances. It operates as a presidential party *par excellence* and, as Ivaldi notes (1998: 55), 'by 1994 ... the major task assigned to the entire FN apparatus was related to Le Pen's candidacy in the forthcoming 1995 presidential election.'

In the case of the PCF, of course, leadership dominance was inspired by Lenin, not de Gaulle. Nevertheless, democratic centralist internal power relations painfully assimilated the 'presidential reality' over three decades (Baudouin 1988). Although never designed with presidentialism in mind, the total lack of accountability of upper echelons, strict party discipline, suppression of minority opinion, and position of the leader at the apex of the hierarchical pyramid (Bell and Criddle 1994*b*: ch. 2) could have served a candidate well. However, ideological hostility to presidentialism and the Fifth Republic apart, the Communists lacked credible and appealing presidential candidates, and their accelerating decline under the Fifth Republic meant they were never realistic presidential contenders.

As one might expect of power in part resourced by public opinion, the dominance of president or *présidentiable* over party is contingent. On the Left, Rocard's position as PS party 'president' became untenable after his 1994 European election rout. In the wake of Jospin's elimination in 2002, Hollande's custodianship of the PS took on a transitional air. The factional non-aggression pact eroded as rival *présidentiables* jockeyed for position within the party and the opinion polls, just as happened after 1988, when the war of Mitterrand's succession began.

On the Right, just as de Gaulle had lost control over the UDR after 1968 (Knapp and Wright 2001: 96–7), so President Chirac effectively lost control of the RPR he had created in 1976 and dominated ever since, after the defeat of Juppé's government in 1997, when Chirac's personal popularity plummeted. The parliamentary group chose Séguin as its president, and an RPR conference echoed this shortly afterwards. Séguin's first act, copying Jospin in 1995, was to introduce internal leadership election (on a one-member–one-vote basis) to bolster the legitimacy of the *de facto* party leader: Seguin enjoyed a 'soviet-style' 95 per cent of the vote (Knapp 1999: 132). Thus one epiphenomenal effect of the spread of internal 'direct' democracy within French parties for leadership selection and endorsement in the 1990s is to facilitate and underline the loss of party control by an unpopular president or *présidentiable*.

Formally, the mode of designation of Fifth Republic presidential candidates has significantly by-passed traditional political formations, breaking the monopoly of parties in determining senior political recruitment under the Fourth Republic (Avril 1995: 51). Party attempts to monopolize presidential candidate selection have never been wholly successful. France lacks 'partified' means of designating presidential candidates. The Right tried and failed to orchestrate internal primaries in 1988 (Colliard 1995), and Prime Minister Edouard Balladur's 'dissident' candidacy in 1995 drew on breakaway support from both RPR and UDF. Jospin's 1995 candidacy was unique in having been preceded by an internal primary, the absence of such a mainstream Left pre-contest process of elimination in 2002 proving extremely costly (Clift 2004). Party institutions (and their dominance by particular sections of the party elite), can also be a barrier to candidacy. Knapp (2002: 135) notes the difficulties experienced by French parties in 'removing their dead candidates from the battlefield: the brooding presence of Giscard after 1981, shattering the hopes of any *présidentiable* from the UDF, is a prime case in point'.

In this context, candidate strategies vary from 'entryism' to external imposition from without (Colliard 1995: 69). Thus Mitterrand in 1965, for example, relying on his Fourth Republic governmental credentials, and his presidential qualities, 'informed' the parties of the Left of his candidacy and demanded that they align themselves accordingly. Subsequently, he joined the PS at the congress of Epinay (on the day he was named First Secretary in 1971) and pursued the 'entryist' strategy to great effect.

The years leading up to the 1995 contest were intriguing. On Right and Left there were effectively two candidates, one with the resources of party organization (Rocard, Chirac), the other 'resourced' by the support of considerably more favourable public opinion (Delors, Balladur). Colliard (1995:

78–9) argues that the lessons arising from that experience were that party organizational resources are indispensable to a successful candidacy. Barre suffered still more from partisan handicap in 1988, and arguably Mitterrand's loose confederation in 1965 provided woefully inadequate party resources compared with de Gaulle's well-oiled UNR machine.

These vital party organizational resources have grown substantially in recent years in part as a result of generous state funding of parties, with the Socialists, Gaullists, and FN all claiming in excess of 100 permanent staff at party headquarters (Knapp 2002: 128). These resources are organized hierarchically under the direction of the party leader. Yet French national-level party leaders by no means dominate all party resources. France's 'presidential' style of local politics is predicated upon personal networks which 'capture' local party organizations and provide office-holders with very extensive resources, making them relatively autonomous from national party authority structures (Frears 1991). Knapp (1999: 112) identifies a 'gravitational pull' of *all* French parties towards 'a loose organization, run by local notables, largely impervious to central discipline and leadership'. However, this loosely structured party may not prevent the presidentialization of national political leadership if other resources are available to the president or the presidential candidate.

All candidates need critical distance from parties, and a distinctly personal dimension to their candidacy, but paradoxically, they also need a secure link to party resources, and its coalition-constructing potential. Thus, the symbiosis between party and candidate is a complex one. Elgie identifies competing logics underpinning the operation of the French party system, and the need to have both presidential (personal or individual) appeal, and at the same time be able to rely on party support (Elgie 1996c: 60). The tension between political parties and individual leaders operates in a curious manner in the French context. It arises not from 'party' resistance to a dominant personal leadership, since all French parties are leader-oriented in terms of structure and behaviour. Rather, the tensions arise when there are numerous pretenders to the throne and a lack of consensus over the 'real' leader, as occurred in the UDR after 1968, the RPR after 1995, and in the PS after 1988 and 2002.

Colliard (1995: 68–70) exaggerates only a little when he notes that the party does not exist without the candidate, and the candidate does not exist without the party. Any candidate's position can only be understood in the context of where they situate themselves within the French party system. The nature of party competition in France means that credible presidential candidacy requires commanding significant personal support (in opinion polls), being leader (*de facto* or actual) of a major 'presidential party', and furthermore, being in a position to extend appeal *beyond* that party, to *ratisser large* (attract support from a wide range of groups) and plausibly construct a 'presidential majority' in parliament (Avril 1995: 57). Overall, then, the major parties are 'presidentialized' to a considerable extent in the Fifth Republic, but leaders are not entirely autonomous of their parties. Since de Gaulle's time, the symbiotic relationship has become more explicitly realized by *présidentiables* and the combination of a strong partisan base and significant personal appeal is today the bedrock of all credible candidacies.

To summarize, since the 1960s, the organizational evolution of French parties has been characterized by personalized leadership, contingent upon power resources continually 'sourced by' public opinion. Candidates have needed both critical distance *from* parties, and a secure link *to* party resources and coalition-constructing potential.

THE EXECUTIVE FACE

As noted above, the 1958 constitution unambiguously established executive dominance over the legislature, specifying in Article 34 the domain of 'laws' requiring parliamentary participation, the assumption being that everything else is subject to executive decree. Furthermore, Article 38 enabled parliament to delegate to the government legislative powers even in those areas reserved for parliament in Article 34. This meant executive encroachment into the legislative domain advanced enormously at the outset of the Fifth Republic. According to Ardant (1991: 10), the prime minister signs, on an average, 1,500 decree laws (*decréts*) and 8,000 ministerial orders (*arrêtés*) each year. The growth of the state has increased the volume, range, and scope of these regulatory executive decrees over the last forty years. One estimate suggested that the 8,000 laws by which France is governed are complemented by 100,000 decrees (Safran 2003: 255).

The organization of the state also provides very significant *structural* assets at the prime minister's disposal, and these resources (administrative support, information flows, policy advice) have grown and expanded since the 1960s. The General Secretariat of the Government (GSG) is responsible directly to the prime minister (Elgie 1993: 12–15), and engages in policy preparation and legal administrative services for the Government. *Chargeés de mission* within the GSG 'provide essential services and generally help the Prime Minister in his capacity as head of government and in his role as an arbitrator between conflicting government departments' (ibid.: 14).

The official membership of the prime ministerial *cabinet*,[4] bringing together senior personal and technocratic advisers and policy experts with close political friends, has fluctuated under the Fifth Republic. In 1959, Debré's *cabinet* was eighteen-strong, and most of his successors appointed between twenty-five and thirty-five *cabinet* members (Elgie 1993: 143). These official memberships have been supplanted in recent decades by large unofficial memberships. Jospin's *cabinet* was fifty-strong, all 'official' (a departure from an earlier trend under which the number expanded to 100 including unofficial advisers). With the GSG and *cabinet*, plus other key bodies, the total number of prime ministerial staff has reached over 5,000, enabling prime ministerial oversight and intervention in *all* policy-making areas (Knapp and Wright 2001: 89). Hence the coordinating capacity of the prime minister has grown very significantly during the Fifth Republic.

This apparent presidentialization of executive power structures requires qualification on two grounds. First, Elgie and Machin (1991) distinguish between 'ownership' and 'control' of these resources. The changing power resources and autonomy of leaders within government hinges on the political context—and specifically, the nature of the parliamentary majority, and the relationship of the president with that parliamentary majority (Duverger 1996: 511). Matignon, the prime minister's official office, 'is at all times the centre of the government machinery. What varies is the president's ability to use his own much smaller staff, as well as his wider networks of support, to penetrate it' (Knapp and Wright 2001: 87). When the president and prime minister are drawn from the same party, in effect presidential loyalists fill these posts and the 'machine' is coordinated and run to deliver the president's interests. However, under cohabitation, the prime minister enjoys both ownership and control of the substantial executive resources, while the president is completely removed from the policy formulation arena (Elgie 1993).

Second, the degree of concentration of power, and the presidentialization of executive policy-making, is hindered by the fragmented nature of the French core executive. This, combined with ministerial autonomy, creates 'veto points' which limit leadership capacity to overcome resistance by others. Indeed Duhamel (1993: 233, 243–9) argues that the government in France *does not exist* as a collective entity. Ministerial autonomy limits dominance of *either* prime minister *or* president. This is demonstrated by the prevailing mode of policy-making within the French core executive, within *réunions interministérielles*. These ad hoc meetings of members of ministerial *cabinets* have increased with the growth of the state, and the expanded scope of legislative activity: 'Their number grew from 142 in 1961 to a peak of 1,836 in 1982, and ran at some 1,400 a year under the Jospin premiership' (Knapp and Wright 2001: 88). The organizational core, which attempts coordination of this fragmented and increasingly complex state activity, is the GSG and the prime minister's *cabinet*.

The prime minister's executive infrastructure has evolved to control and coordinate communications strategy over time. Thus, in the 1970s a prime ministerial 'Information Service' was established. One section reflects the French fixation with opinion polling, dedicated as it is to the analysis (and commissioning) of opinion polls, and content analysis of press reports. Another department is engaged in the coordination, control, and dissemination of information regarding governmental actions to the press and the public. This is the administrative arm of the government's communication strategy, which is usually orchestrated by a trusted ally as 'director of communications'. Both are under prime ministerial control, run under the auspices of the GSG.

Consistent with the concept of political presidentialization, the nature of executive power at the outset of the Fifth Republic was highly personalized. Indeed, after de Gaulle, France was witness to a slight retreat from personalized power and authority as the executive shifted from 'personal' power towards power rooted in both the personal and the partisan. The 'intrusive force of partisan power' (Hayward 1993*b*: 41) was demonstrated by the partified 'colonization' of the French state by first the UDR and then UDF and PS apparatchiks under Giscard and Mitterrand respectively. That said, elements of the executive appointments process show clear evidence of executive presidentialization. Leadership autonomy to select governments primarily according to personal priorities reduced after de Gaulle's time, but it remained considerable, with only limited constraints imposed by partisan context. With a single presidential party majority beholden to 'its' president, as has been the case since 2002, the scope for presidential autonomy in this respect is considerable.

The Gaullian vision of constructing a technocratic government free from party influence has never truly been realized. Even when de Gaulle appointed a non-party technocrat as premier—Couve de Murville—the government had been 'repoliticized', and dominated by Gaullist party figures (Safran 2003: 200). Cabinet formation must take account of the partisan nature of the majority which is its bulwark. Factional leaders tend to get key ministries, and the exigencies of parliamentary coalition politics forced Chirac in 1986–8 into 'la deuxième cohabitation' (with the UDF's Léotard (Elgie 1993: 159)). Mitterrand was similarly constrained, choosing his arch-enemy Michel Rocard as premier in 1988. Within those constraints, however, there is ample scope for either prime minister or president to appoint loyal technocrats or politicians lacking a party base, and Fifth Republic governments have always enjoyed a high degree of independence from 'their' parties. Indeed, the appointment of technocrats and members of 'civil society' have been the feature of *all* Fifth Republic governments. Fifth Republic government composition has consistently involved roughly one-third of those who were *neither* senators *nor* deputies before taking up their ministries (Duhamel 1993: 240), and this is symptomatic of the ability to promote and appoint technocrats or allies without a strong party base.

In summary, the 1958 constitution kick-started an executive encroachment into the legislative domain, which has been further augmented as the growth of the state has increased the volume, range, and scope of government by decree over the last forty years. The corollary of expanded executive attempts to coordinate and control a fragmented core executive has been growth in executive resources formally controlled by the prime minister, whose degree of control ebbs and flows according to the parliamentary majority.

THE ELECTORAL FACE

What of the presidentialization of electoral processes? De Gaulle himself inaugurated and orchestrated the media focus on personality as a characteristic of presidential politics in France, regarding himself 'as the mediator between the people and France', and referring to 'his' regime as a 'popular monarchy' (Hayward 1993a: 14, 22). There was a very personal dimension to his power. Dovetailing with this, de Gaulle's public disdain for parties meant that he carefully constructed his political legitimacy without reference to party.

This must be understood in the context of a Rousseauian branch of French Republican discourse which distrusts intermediaries (parties), preferring a direct engagement with the citizenry to discern the (general) will of the people. Although not a dominant strand of republicanism (discredited as it was by Bonapartism), it was a resource upon which de Gaulle drew with consummate skill. It amounted to 'the confiscation of power by a charismatic figure through plebiscites that both paid homage to and manipulated the principle of popular sovereignty' (Hoffman 1991: 44).

De Gaulle's relationship with the French people was direct—offering a 'contract' between the people and the candidate, excluding parties.[5] In a Gaullian reading of the Fifth Republic, 'presidential power is permanently resourced by public opinion' (Cayrol 1995: 103). The electorate's endorsement of his personal power, whether in referenda which he regarded as plebiscites on his own presidency, or in the 1965 direct presidential election, functioned as national 'confidence votes' in the president.[6] The legislative elections of 1962, 1967, and 1968 also 'counted' although here the direct link was mediated by the notion of the 'presidential majority'. Thus, as Cayrol (1995: 100–1) recalls, 'these elections also functioned as a "confidence vote" mechanism posed directly to French public opinion.' This explains why, having been narrowly defeated (by a margin of 52.6 per cent to 47.6 per cent) on a relatively minor issue of senate and local government reform in the referendum of 1969, the most powerful French leader of the twentieth century summarily resigned (ibid.: 99–100).

Having seen how playing with plebiscitary matches can burn fingers, Pompidou altered the relationship of the referendum to the presidential office. Pompidou carefully distanced himself from the unpredictable 1972 referendum on Britain's EEC membership, so that it was not perceived as a Gaullian style plebiscite on the president's position. With the transition in 1969 'from heroic to humdrum Gaullism' (Hayward 1993a: 26), political legitimacy and power required bolstering by other means. The corollary of the shift away from a direct Gaullian link between the presidency and its support in public opinion was the progressive 'partification' of the presidency.

Both Pompidou and Mitterrand consciously embraced the political resources (in terms of organizational strength, and an alternative source of political legitimacy) which parties could offer. Yet the personal character of elections endured, albeit framed in an explicit partisan context. Decisive elections in the Fifth Republic have always been strongly candidate-centred, both in terms of campaigning and media coverage. At the national level, this owes much to the centrality of presidential elections to national political life. At local level, it is due to the weight and resources of *notables*, particularly mayors of large towns, in local electoral politics.

Leader focus in media coverage

Our model of electoral presidentialization posits an increase in a personal leader focus over time, deriving from various causal factors. In this regard, the big change in France had already occurred by 1965, when direct presidential elections ensured an almost wholly leadership-oriented campaign and media environment; things have remained candidate-dominated ever since. The *non-constitutional* control the president enjoyed over the audio-visual sector (until the 1980s it was entirely state-owned) set the personality-oriented tone of political media coverage in France (Portelli 1994: 60). Until the 1970s close control of state-run TV and radio was orchestrated through two pillars of the Gaullist state, the ministry of information and the *Office de Radiodiffusion Televison Française* (ORTF) (Cayrol 1995: 107–8; Kuhn 1984: 178, 181).[7] Such monopoly control of broadcasting enabled de Gaulle constantly to address public opinion, through press conferences, and reporting of his visits throughout France and abroad, as well as via his formal radio and TV addresses.[8] Pompidou similarly construed his media role as embodying, 'the voice of France' (Hayward 1993*b*: 41–2).

In 1974, Giscard's reforms broke up the Gaullist monolith, creating an 'internal market' within state broadcasting, comprising seven organizationally independent companies, including three TV channels (Cayrol 1995: 111; Kuhn 1984: 180). However, a string of Giscardian placemen were 'an integral part of the Giscardian government's means of controlling the political output of radio and television', allowing Giscard's administration to circumvent its own impartiality regulations (Kuhn 1984: 181–4). With the establishment of an independent regulatory body in 1982, and emergence of commercial channels by 1986 (Cayrol 1995: 113), political influence over broadcasting continued on an informal basis, but arguably at an undiminished level.

Successive presidents ensured broadcasting would serve their interests, 'initially by massive intervention, subsequently by controlling key appointments, and later by creating tame regulatory agencies and assigning networks to friendly private interests' (Harrison 1993: 207).

What has changed is the wider media context of political coverage, and the priority that programmers afford to political programming. The French audio-visual sector underwent the most profound transformation after the 1960s. With the growing centrality of television to French cultural life, television has moved to centre-stage in the conduct and practice of politics—it mediates political reality, and remains the predominant means by which voters receive political information (Machin 1996: 30; Mayer and Perrineau 1992: 105).

Through all this, French political programming has been personality-oriented. Parties, although essential assets to a successful candidacy, do not take centre-stage in presidential elections, and legislative elections are also candidate-centred. The style of French political television journalism tends towards a personal, leader focus, especially given the format of one-on-one interviews and head-to-head debates. As Knapp (2002: 131) notes of political discussion in the televised media, it 'tends to focus more readily on personalities than on parties: flagship interview programmes give hour-long coverage to individuals and to their suitability for presidency or other high office.' Personal approval opinion polling, always a feature of French political TV coverage, became a more prominent part of French political journalism with the advance in polling techniques. The personal dimension was compounded by interviews conducted in political leaders' homes, which paid attention to lifestyle, cultural hinterland, personality, moral values, and interior design(!), as well as political agendas (Neveu 1999: 386).

Although a constant within French political journalism, the personal focus tends to swell in the 'pre-campaign' stage of presidential elections, and then intensifies prior to the first ballot. After the first ballot, when the two best-placed candidates recommence their campaigns, and re-aggregate support from eliminated candidates, the leadership focus reaches fever pitch. The centrepiece and 'symbolic culmination' (Machin 1996: 26–9, 43) of each campaign is the head-to-head televised debate. In 1981, 25 million viewers watched Mitterrand eclipse Giscard.[9] In 1988, 21.7 million viewers watched Mitterrand's head-to-head with Chirac (Mayer and Perrineau 1992: 18).

However, the amount of political programming is declining. The increasing number of TV channels, amount of TV exposure, and levels of TV viewing have generated ever-fiercer competition and commercialization within the French audio-visual sector. Under these conditions, ratings have had a more decisive impact on career paths than presidential favour, and excessively cosy political coverage and commentary would do nothing to improve French political programming's already emaciated viewing figures

(Neveu 1999: 384). The place of political programming in the schedules is thus threatened by a perceived lack of viewer interest. The regulatory authority has recorded 'over many years a tendency towards the diminution of the time accorded to news and to political debate on the majority of generalist channels' (Conseil Supérieure de l'Audiovisuel 2002: 17). Looking at the pre-campaign period (from 1 January to 27 April 2002), there have been significant falls in levels of overall coverage, but what coverage there is remains strongly candidate-focused (ibid.).

Leader focus in campaign styles

In the first direct presidential election campaign in 1965, de Gaulle decreed TV access on an equal (not proportional) time basis for every candidate.[10] No private TV or radio advertising by candidates or parties was permitted. This was not out of concern for a level playing field, since he 'ignored with impunity' regulations, and addressed the nation on TV the Friday before elections, offering other candidates no televised response (Cayrol 1995: 106). A thoroughly candidate-centred campaigning style has remained the norm for presidential elections ever since (Cayrol 1995: 98–9),

The modus operandi of campaigning for presidential election in France has long been candidate-based teams with party support. Both elements are vital. One reason is the 'sponsorship' regulations governing eligibility to stand[11]—a hurdle best overcome with the help of party networks. Second, parties are a very significant source of funds and logistical support, and provide 'the backbone of any serious campaign' (Elgie 1996c: 58). In addition to TV appearances and Paris-based rallies, candidates must campaign *en province*, pressing the flesh and speaking at rallies and events nationwide. This is both expensive and difficult to orchestrate from a Paris 'war room'.[12]

The relationship, as noted above, is symbiotic, since parties need a mouthpiece at election time (Mayer and Perrineau 1992: 101). A presidential candidate's *personal* programme is the key political statement, heavily influencing party election programmes. In the case of an unambiguous *présidentiable* in opposition, a mid-presidential-term parliamentary election serves as a platform to launch a future presidential campaign. The themes of Jospin's 1995 presidential programme, for example, were clearly reprised in the PS's 1997 legislative election manifesto, and reappeared in 2002 (Jospin 1995, 2002a; Parti Socialiste 1997).

Interestingly, leaders and prominent national elite figures also direct campaigns and provide the focus of media coverage in parliamentary elections. However, this national-level personality focus coexists with a local-level personality focus—centring on battles between local *notables* who often combine their parliamentary offices with town or city mayorships. Given their hold over party organizations, established *notables*, will often decide their personal strategies with scant regard for their party's national strategic directives.

TV is where the battle for credibility as a *présidentiable* is won and lost: 'in 1995, Jospin's impressive television performances and calm exchanges in debates with Chirac... contributed to his rise from relative anonymity to widespread popularity' (Machin 2001: 89). Campaign teams focus less on political broadcasts in allotted airtime, than on televised debates, in particular between run-off presidential candidates between first and second ballots. Given the disappointing ratings of, and reduced enthusiasm for, political programming from audiences and schedulers alike noted above, presidential candidates seek invitations to interview, or to secure coverage, on the more popular news bulletins (Kuhn 1984; Neveu 1999: 388). Although the TV is the dominant site of electoral campaigning, the *visite en province* and the structured photo-opportunity have lost little of their political significance, at least for the campaign teams. The vying for front-page coverage on France's regional press is a constant struggle. Furthermore, the real aim of a successful visit or rally *en province* is to 'make the news' (Machin 1996: 30).

The use of private opinion polling of levels of support and public perceptions of candidates swiftly became integral to presidential campaigning. Electoral marketing was seen as an essential preoccupation of candidates and their lieutenants. Those candidates less convinced of its merits (such as Mitterrand in 1974) soon learned their lesson when vanquished by marketing enthusiasts (such as Giscard (Colliard 1995)). Mitterrand's learning curve was steep. His 'official' hiring of professional advertising and public relations experts such as Seguela, to great effect in 1981, and still more in 1988, was a straw in the wind of the professionalization of campaigning in France since the 1970s.

By the 1990s, not only Presidents but all presidential candidates came to rely on the fast-developing industry of private opinion polling as a means of honing their image and gauging public expectations (Machin 2001: 88). Cayrol (1995: 118) charts a shift from a dramatic (Gaullian) to a banalized link between president and public opinion. Ever more frequent public opinion polling replaced referenda as 'votes of confidence', but now without sanction. 'French parties share the national addiction to opinion polls of all kinds, and regularly commission commercial polling firms: for example, the Communist Party has often used the IFOP and SOFRES polling organizations since the 1960s', notes Knapp (2002: 128). Almost all serious French presidential candidates today use public relations consultancies, and 'regularly commission private opinion polls and focus groups... within the main parties, the professions of spin doctoring have proliferated as the demands grew for professional advice on almost every aspect of presentation' (Machin 2001: 88). These resources tend to be controlled directly by the candidate's campaign team, enjoying significant autonomy from party influence, especially during the campaign proper.

Chirac, in 1995, took political marketing to its logical limits, convening his campaign group in 1992, and commissioning extensive private opinion polling research (Machin 1996: 45). The esteemed French political scientist Jean Charlot was hired to conduct a detailed post-mortem of the 1988 defeat, and was charged with identifying themes and issues salient to the public (Machin 2001: 89). As well as researching the electorate, the organization engaged in protracted, professional preparation for the campaign ahead. His 1995 campaign was his longest ever, 169 days (Gerstlé 1995: 24). This was clearly a costly exercise, but Chirac imported American direct mailing techniques, and generated massive personal donations for himself (Machin 1996: 48–9).

Presidentialized political campaigning is a costly business, and concerns about impropriety given the 'legislative vacuum' which had surrounded political finance in France until the 1980s, led to a rolling programme of regulation (Clift and Fisher 2004). The funding issue again highlights the importance of party backing. Balladur's 1995 campaign suffered from a lack of party resources, since the RPR was mobilized primarily behind Chirac. Balladur was endorsed by the UDF, but as an umbrella confederation organization, not a genuine party, the UDF was less helpful. He was, however, able to circumvent the problem. When Prime Minister Balladur promoted an amendment enabling the creation of campaign support committees which would be exempt from restrictions on donations to candidates. Balladur's campaign drew benefit from ninety-eight such 'American style' committees (Doublet 1999: 74). His total declared spending of Fr83.85 million was barely Fr6 million short of the first ballot spending ceiling (Machin 1996: 47). Yet, this was dwarfed by Chirac's spending over the two rounds, which totalled Fr116.62 million. (Machin 1996: 47). Jacques Séguela, Mitterrand's advertising guru, noted of the 1995 contest that 'the campaign of images and clips has replaced the debate of ideas of previous election campaigns. The most "televisual" of the candidates will be elected, which Jacques Chirac has clearly understood' (ibid.: 48).

Leader effects on voting behaviour

The French psephological debate has curiously neglected 'leader effects' on voting behaviour. Little attempt has been made to separate out leader effects from the traditionally assumed determinants of voter choice. Indeed, many studies do not distinguish between candidate and party, or simply substitute the leader for the party as dependent variable, treating these two distinct variables as identical. One reason for this is almost certainly that the distinction between 'president' and 'party' may not be operable in practice in the context of 'presidential parties'.

One way, however, in which we can infer confirmation of leader effects is by comparing levels of candidate support in presidential elections with levels of party support in parliamentary elections. Thus, Goguel estimated 3 million left-wing voters chose de Gaulle in the first presidential ballot in 1965, when he secured the support of 42 per cent of manual workers. By contrast, only 30 per cent voted Gaullist in the parliamentary elections of 1967, or for de Gaulle's successor Pompidou in the 1969 presidential election (Charlot 1971: 63–84; Goguel 1967; Mayer and Perrineau 1992: 99–101). A similar disparity emerged between Mitterrand's presidential election and the Socialists' parliamentary election vote in 1981 and, to a lesser extent, in 1988 (Cole 1988: 91–6). That said, personality ratings alone do not adequately account for these disparities, and it is clear that further research is required which disentangles candidate and party effects in French voting behaviour.[13]

In summary, electoral presidentialization began from a high level in the Fifth Republic, at least in terms of candidate-centred campaigning and leader media focus. The extent of leader effects on voting behaviour cannot be clearly determined, though it can safely be assumed that they are significant, especially in the context of presidential elections; with respect to parliamentary elections, matters are even less clear-cut. The major feature of the electoral face has been the increasing professionalization of leader-centred campaigning and polling, in the context of decreasing interest in political programming and an increasingly pluralistic media environment.

CONCLUSION

The various processes of presidentialization of the French political system were at a relatively advanced stage even in the 1960s, boosted by the constitutional presidentialization of the Fifth Republic, the candidate-centred traditions of French local electoral politics, and a leader-focused media context. All aspects of the French political system, political parties, the party system, and norms of elections and electoral campaigning, have been profoundly affected by the ongoing political and electoral 'presidentialization'.

Under cohabitation, power shifts within the hierarchical 'bicephalous' French executive meant the prime minister benefited from political presidentialization. The fluid, changeable nature of executive power in France has interacted with the international context of hitherto presidentialized French politics. European policy, for example, has presented challenges to the French executive, particularly under recent cohabitations. The executive has been able to dominate policy-making in these areas to the virtual exclusion of Parliament, drawing on constitutional rights for treaty-making and foreign policy. However, *within* the executive, competing political legitimacies under cohabitation have, if anything, partially undermined autonomy. Conceptual distinctions between domestic and foreign policy, and between 'low' and 'high' politics, around which conceptions of the presidential reserved domain cohere, are negated by the reality of advancing European integration; in the face of this, European policy is never 'purely' foreign, and developments in apparently secondary policy areas have profound impacts on French sovereignty. This creates the possibility of policy gridlock, and 'competitive summitry', with both prime minister and president attempting to speak with the authoritative voice of France, each seeing their intervention in the European domain as legitimate, as demonstrated at the 2000 Nice Summit (Cole and Drake 2000; Drake 2001: 461–2; Lequesne 2001).

Moreover, the French executive's powers (whether in the hands of prime minister or president) have been challenged in recent decades in a more profound manner by the changing international context of French politics. The globalization of economic activity undermines the autonomy of the French executive, particularly in macro-economic and industrial policy. In part as a result of developments at the European level, notably the advent of the Single European Market, French capitalism has become increasing 'internationalized' in recent decades. Liberalization of trade in the post-war era, and of financial markets in the 1980s, acting in concert with the neo-liberal bias of EU competition directives and regulations, have powerfully limited autonomous state action in economic and social fields. Thus, French *dirigisme* is under duress in an increasingly internationalized economic context (Clift 2003*a*, *b*; Levy 2000; Wright and Elgie 1996: 174–84).

In the face of such pressures, the inter-governmental nature of many international relationships, affording primacy to president or prime minister and a few key ministers over other actors, may be scant recompense. For example, Prime Minister Jospin carved out a niche in articulating a distinctive critical discourse on globalization, and how it can and should be contested and mediated by nation-states (Jospin 2002*b*). Advancing globalization may afford centre-stage to the French executive to set out the terms of response to the process, but it does little to equip the French executive with the capacity to expand or consolidate threatened state autonomy.

There has been significant recent structural evolution in the political presidentialization of the French polity. The move to a *Quinquennat*, and the inverting of the electoral calendar in 2002 to afford primacy to the presidential election,were attempts to restore presidential dominance to the organization of the state which had been partially undermined after 1986. This in a period when electoral presidentialization continued to shape the media context, campaigning, party organization, and competition. Aligning presidential and parliamentary elections and terms may lead to the closer alignment of the political and electoral dimensions of presidentialization which had become partially disjointed under 'normalized' cohabitation.

The hierarchically superior president becomes more overtly *de facto* head of government, leader of the parliamentary majority, more identified with 'his' or 'her' parliamentary majority. Such closer cooperation between the 'two heads' of the French executive is, some argue, necessary for effective government. However, this has not addressed one of the key causes of cohabitation, namely, electoral volatility and the accelerating swing of the political pendulum in France. The French voter appears a little less anchored to social 'cues' for voting, such as religion and class, although these retain some significance in helping explain voting in France (Boy and Mayer 2000: 153–75).

To summarize, resources are concentrated in the hands of executive leaders (*either* prime minister *or* president), who are relatively autonomous of party constraints, given the 'presidential rally' nature of French parties. Executive autonomy from the legislature is largely constitutionally derived, but has been further enhanced by the growth of the state. However, leadership capacity is limited both by the exogenous features already mentioned, and by the fragmented nature of the executive and administration. Leaders have enjoyed high and rising degrees of autonomy within 'presidential parties', yet this remains contingent upon popular support and electoral success. In terms of electoral presidentialization, candidate-focus, and personality based campaigning and reporting are largely attributable to constitutional presidentialization, but have been further boosted by structural changes, notably to the media environment. Although the erosion of social cleavages further focuses the attention of a volatile electorate on personalities, the evidence for 'leader effects' on voting behaviour (particularly in legislative elections) remains difficult to discern. The 1958 constitution induced a pronounced shift towards a more presidential working mode of the political system. Structural changes since the 1960s have induced further shifts, but the advanced starting point means that subsequent presidentialization has seemed less dramatic than in many other cases.

NOTES

1. It has been invoked only once, by De Gaulle, in April 1961, in the context of the attempted putsch by twelve Army Generals over Algerian independence.
2. A phrase from de Gaulle's infamous 1946 *Bayeux* speech, quoted in Cogan (1996: 187).
3. The choice had to be ratified by the membership, but there were similarities between Jospin's backing of Hollande's candidacy, and Mitterrand's 'monarchical' designation of Jospin in 1981. Opposed only by Melenchon, the *Gauche Socialiste* candidate, who secured only 8.82 per cent of the vote, Hollande was elected with 91.18 per cent of the vote. (*L'Hebdo des Socialistes,* 43 [5 December 1997], 11.)

4. Note that the word *cabinet* is used here in a distinctively French sense, to refer to a team of political advisers that members of political executives gather around them. It should not be confused with the more usual meaning in the Anglo-Saxon world of core members of the government.
5. Here the distinction with the Fourth Republic is stark, where governments often fell due to parliamentary manoeuvrings, rather than to withdrawals of electoral support (see Cayrol 1995: 97–9).
6. Referenda were held in 1961 over Algerian self rule (75 per cent approval); April 1962, over the Evian Accord which settled the Algerian crisis (90 per cent approval); November 1962, over direct election of the president (62 per cent approval). See Bell 2000: 45–64.
7. Alain Peyrefitte, de Gaulle's long-serving Minister for Information, placed many members of his ministerial *cabinet* in top posts at the ORTF.
8. TV addresses averaged six a year during his time as President.
9. This was achieved in part by meticulous conditions imposed by the Mitterrand camp to ensure balance between the two candidates (Kuhn 1984).
10. This contrasts with allocation of audio-visual access in all other French elections, notably legislative elections, where it is proportional (Cayrol 1995: 98–9).
11. These require 500 signatures of elected officials from at least thirty departments, with not more than fifty from any single department. The FN's lack of institutional infrastructure at the time meant Le Pen failed to gain sufficient signatures in 1981, and was thus prevented from standing.
12. Chirac spent Fr10.13 million. on travel alone in his 1995 campaign (Machin 1996: 47).
13. I am grateful to Jocelyn Evans for his help in clarifying these points.

REFERENCES

Ardant, P. (1991). *Le Premier Ministre en France*. Paris: Montchrestien.
Avril, P. (1988). 'Les Chef d'Etat et la Notion de Majorité Presidentielle', in O. Duhamel and J.-L. Parodi (eds.), *La Constitution de la Cinquieme Republique*. Paris: FNSP.
—— (1995). 'La fabrique politique', in N. Wahl and J.-L. Quermonne (eds.), *La France Présidentielle*. Paris: FNSP.
Baudouin, J. (1988). 'L'assimilation Relative de la Constitution de 1958 par le Parti Communiste Francais', in O. Duhamel and J.-L. Parodi (eds.), *La Constitution de la Cinquieme Republique*. Paris: FNSP.
Bell, D. (2000). *Presidential Power in Fifth Republic. France*. Oxford: Berg.
—— and B. Criddle (1994a). 'The French Socialist Party: Presidentialised Factionalism', in D. Bell and E. Shaw (eds.), *Conflict and Cohesion in European Social Democratic Parties*. London: Pinter, 112–32.
—— —— (1994b). *The French Communist Party in the Fifth Republic*. Oxford: Clarendon Press.
Boy, D. and N. Mayer (2000). 'Cleavage Voting and Issue Voting in France', in M. Lewis-Beck (ed.), *How France Votes*. London: Chatham House.

Cayrol, R. (1995). 'La Présidence d'Opinion: Mécanismes Institutionnels et Médiatiques', in N. Wahl and J.-L. Quermonne (eds.), *La France Presidentielle*. Paris: FNSP.

Charlot, J. (1971). *The Gaullist Phenomenon: The Gaullist Movement in the Fifth Republic*. London: Allen & Unwin.

—— (1983). 'Le Président et le Parti Majoritaire', *Revue Politique et Parlementaire*, No. 905: 27–42.

Clift, B. (2003a). *French Socialism in a Global Era*. London: Continuum Books.

—— (2003b). 'The Changing Political Economy of France in the EU: *Dirigisme* under Duress' in M. Ryner and A. Calfruny (eds.), *The Political Economy of the European Union: Critical Studies of a Neo-Liberal Hegemonic Project*. Baltimore: Rowman and Littlefield.

—— (2004). 'Lionel Jospin's Campaign and The Socialist Left: The "Earthquake" and its Aftershocks', in J. Gaffney (ed.), *The French Presidential and Legislative Elections of 2002*. Aldershot: Ashgate, pp. 149–68.

—— and J. Fisher (2004). 'Comparative Party Finance Reform: The Cases of France and Britain', *Party Politics*, 10: 677–99.

Cogan, C. (1996). *Charles de Gaulle: A Brief Biography with Documents*. New York: St. Martin's Press.

Cole, A. (1988). 'La France Unie? Francois Mitterrand', in J. Gaffney (ed.), *The French Presidential Election of 1988*. Aldershot: Dartmouth Publications.

—— (1993). 'The Presidential Party and the Fifth Republic', *West European Politics*, 16: 49–66.

—— (1997). *Francois Mitterrand: A Study in Political Leadership*. London: Routledge.

—— and H. Drake (2000). 'The Europeanisation of the French Polity: Continuity, Change and Adaptation', *Journal of European Public Policy*, 7: 26–43.

Colliard, C. (1995). 'Le Processus de Nomination des Candidates et l'Organisation des Campagnes Électorales', in N. Wahl and J-L. Quermonne (eds.), *La France Presidentielle*. Paris: FNSP.

Conseil Supérieur de l'Audiovisuel (2002). *Rapport sur la campagne électorale a la radio et a la television* (Paris) http://www.csa.fr.

Debré, M. (1981). 'The Constitution of 1958: Its Raison d'Etre and How It Evolved', in W. Andrews and S. Hoffman (eds.), *The Impact of the Fifth Republic on France*. Albany: State University of New York Press.

Doublet, Y. (1999). 'Party Funding in France', in K. D. Ewing (ed.), *The Funding of Political Parties: Europe and Beyond*. Bologna: Cooperativa Libreria Universitaria Editrice.

Drake, H. (2001). 'France on Trial? The Challenge of Change posed by the French Council Presidency of the European Union, July–December 2000', *Modern and Contemporary France*, 9: 453–66.

Duhamel, O. (1993). *Le Pouvoir Politique en France*. Paris: Editions du Seuil.

—— and G. Grunberg (2001). 'Systeme des Partis et V Républiques', *Commentaire* 24: 533–44.

Duverger, M. (1974). *La Monarchie Républicaine*. Paris: Robert Laffont.

—— (1996). *Le Système Politique Français*. Paris: Presses Universitaires Francaise.

Elgie, R. (1993). *The Role of the Prime Minister in France, 1981–91*. London: Macmillan.

—— (1996*a*). *Political Leadership in Liberal Democracies*. Basingstoke: Macmillan.

—— (1996*b*). *Electing The French President*. Basingstoke: Macmillan.

—— (1996*c*). 'The Institutional Logics of French Presidential Elections', in R. Elgie (ed.), *Electing The French President*. Basingstoke: Macmillan.

—— (1999). 'France', in R. Elgie (ed.), *Semi-Presidentialism in Europe*. Oxford: Oxford University Press.

—— (2001). ' "Cohabitation": Divided Government French-style', in R. Elgie (ed.), *Divided Government in Comparative Perspective*. Oxford: Oxford University Press.

—— and H. Machin (1991). 'France: The Limits to Prime-Ministerial Government in a Semi-Presidential System', *West European Politics*, 14: 62–78.

Frears, J. (1991). *Parties and Voters in France*. London: Hurst and Company.

Gaffney, J. (1990). 'The Emergence of a Presidentialised Party: The Socialist Party', in A. Cole (ed.), *French Political Parties in Transition*. Aldershot: Dartmouth Publications, 61–90.

Gerstlé, J. (1995). 'La Dynamique Selective d'une Campagne Décisive', in P. Perrineau and C. Ysmal (eds.), *Le Vote de Crise: L'élection présidentielle de 1995*. Paris: Presses de Sciences Po.

Goguel, F. (1967). 'Combien y a-t-il eu d'électeurs de gauche parmi ceux qui ont voté le 5 décembre 1965 pour le général de Gaulle?' *Revue Française de Science Politique*, 17: 65–9.

Harrison, M. (1993). 'The President, Cultural Projects and Broadcasting Policy', in J. Hayward (ed.), *De Gaulle to Mitterrand: Presidential Power in France*. London: Hurst & Co.

Hayward, J. (1993*a*). 'The President and the Constitution: its Spirit, Articles, and Practice', in J. Hayward (ed.), *De Gaulle to Mitterrand: Presidential Power in France*. London: Hurst & Co.

—— (1993*b*). 'From Republican Sovereign to Partisan Statesman', in J. Hayward (ed.), *De Gaulle to Mitterrand: Presidential Power in France*. London: Hurst & Co.

Hoffmann, S. (1991). 'The Institutions of the Fifth Republic', in J. Hollifield (ed.), *Searching for the New France*. London: Routledge.

Ivaldi, G. (1998). 'The Front National: The Making of an Authoritarian Party', in C. Ysmal and P. Ignazi (eds.), *Changing Party Organisations in Southern Europe*. London: Praeger.

Jospin, L. (1995). *Propositions pour la France 1995–2000*. Paris: PS Presse.

—— (2002*a*). *Je m'engage: présider autrement*. Paris: l'Atelier de Campagne.

—— (2002*b*). *My Vision of Europe and Globalisation*. Cambridge: Polity.

Keeler, J. (1993). 'Executive Power and Policy-Making Patterns in France: Gauging the Impact of Fifth Republic Institutions, *West European Politics*, 16: 518–44.

Knapp, A. (1994). *Gaullism since de Gaulle*. Aldershot: Dartmouth.

—— (1999). 'What's Left of the French Right', *West European Politics*, 22: 109–38.

—— (2002). 'France: Never a Golden Age', in P. Webb, D. M. Farrell, and I. Holliday (eds.), *Political Parties in Advanced Industrial Democracies*. Oxford: Oxford University Press, 107–50.

—— and V. Wright (2001). *The Government and Politics of France*. Basingstoke: Palgrave.

Kuhn, R. (1984). 'The Presidency and the Media 1974–82', in V. Wright (ed.), *French Politics Continuity and Change*. London: Allen & Unwin.

Lequesne, C. (2001). 'The French presidency: the half success of Nice', *Journal of Common Market Studies*, 39: 47–50.

Levy, J. (2000). 'France: Directing Adjustment?', in F. Scharpf and V. Schmidt (eds.), *Welfare and Work in the Open Economy: Volume Two*. Oxford: Oxford University Press, 337–44.

Machin, H. (1996). 'The 1995 Presidential Election Campaign', in R. Elgie (ed.), *Electing The French President*. Basingstoke: Macmillan.

—— (2001). 'Political Leadership', in A. Guyomarch, H. Machin, P. Hall, and J. Hayward (eds.), *Developments in French Politics 2*. Basingstoke: Palgrave.

Massot, J. (1987). *L'arbitre ou le capitaine d'equipe?* Paris: Flammarion.

Mayer, N. and P. Perrineau (1992). *Les Comportements Politiques*. Paris: Armand.

Neveu, E. (1999). 'Politics on French Television', *European Journal of Communication*, 14: 379–409.

Parodi, J.-L. (1997). 'Proportionalisation Périodique, Cohabitation, Atomisation Partisane: un Triple Défi Pour le Régime Semi-presidentiel de la Cinquième République?', *Revue Francaise de Science Politique*, 47: 292–312.

Parti Socialiste (1997). *Changeons L'Avenir: Nos engagements pour la France*. Paris: PS Presse.

Portelli, H. (1994). *La Cinquieme Republique*. Paris: Grasset.

Safran, W. (2003). *The French Polity*. London: Longman.

Sartori, G. (1997). *Comparative Constitutional Engineering*. Basingstoke: Macmillan.

Thiebault, J.-L. (1993). Party Leadership Selection in France, *European Journal of Political Research*, 24: 277–93.

Wright, V. (1993). 'The President and the Prime Minister: Subordination, Conflict, Symbiosis or Reciprocal Parasitism?', in J. Hayward (ed.), *De Gaulle to Mitterrand: Presidential Power in France*. London: Hurst and Co.

—— and R. Elgie (1996). 'The French Presidency: The Changing Public Policy Environment', in R. Elgie (ed.), *Electing The French President*. Basingstoke: Macmillan.

Ysmal, C. (1998). 'The Evolution of the French Party System', in C. Ysmal and P. Ignazi (eds.), *Changing Party Organisations in Southern Europe*. London: Praeger.

11

Finland: Let the Force Be with the Leader—But Who Is the Leader?

Heikki Paloheimo

Since the early 1980s, the regime-type of the Finnish political system has gradually mutated, due to complementary processes of de-presidentialization and re-presidentialization. The former entailed the erosion of the formal prerogatives of the president and a switch from a semi-presidential towards a parliamentary type of executive. This process culminated in the coming into force of a totally new constitution in 2000. Re-presidentialization, in turn, consists of the growing power of the prime minister within the newly parliamentarized political executive.

Changes in the international context and Finland's position within it have been the most important factors behind the regime change. The collapse of the Soviet Union enabled the abandonment of personalized, presidential leadership in foreign policy, while Finnish membership of the European Union has facilitated foreign policy decision-making on a parliamentary basis. While European integration might have served to enhance the personalized power of the prime minister in other countries, in Finland it also strengthened parliamentarism.

In this chapter, I will elaborate on these themes in the course of addressing the following questions:

- To what extent does the Finnish president retain independent political powers? Is Finland still semi-presidential, or are the powers of the president so limited that we can now classify Finland among Europe's other parliamentary regimes?
- Does the shift to parliamentarism in Finland entail a shift from a personalized, presidential leadership towards a more collective, partified form of governance, or is there a trend towards a new kind of presidential leadership in which the prime minister has assumed the role of effective head of the executive?

THE OLD SEMI-PRESIDENTIAL CONSTITUTION:
PRESIDENTIAL LEADERSHIP

The semi-presidential political system in Finland was a result of social and political developments prior to Finnish independence, the desire of conservative politicians to counter the revolutionary pressures of the socialist labour movement, and compromises between conservatives and liberals over the division of power between different state organs. Conservatives wanted a monarchy, or at least an executive vested with strong powers, while Liberals were in favour of parliamentary democracy.

In the semi-presidential regime established in 1919, executive power was divided between the president and the government. The former was elected by an electoral college; every sixth year, voters chose 300 electors to decide who would become president with supreme executive powers. The government—or council of state (*valtioneuvosto*), as it is called in Finland—was headed by the prime minister and was politically responsible to parliament (*eduskunta*).

According to the old constitution (a) the president, appointed governments; (b) presented government bills to parliament; (c) ratified laws passed by parliament; (d) issued decrees; (e) made Finnish foreign policy; (f) appointed judges to the supreme court, the supreme administrative court, and the courts of appeal (on the proposal of the courts concerned); (g) appointed senior civil servants (on the proposal of the government); (h) was head of the armed forces; (i) could grant pardons; (j) had the right to dissolve parliament and call premature general elections; and (h) to convene extraordinary sessions of the parliament. This impressive list of powers and duties incorporated rights over the legislative, executive, and judicial domains. Despite this, a peculiarity of the old constitution was that it provided strong guarantees for minorities within parliament. In effect, one-third of parliamentarians (sixty-seven MPs) could block legislation, or at least delay it for a session, the intention being to prevent the introduction of radical socialist measures by a simple parliamentary majority.

The constitution enacted in 1919 was in force for eighty years, without undergoing any significant changes for the first sixty years. From the early 1980s, however, there were growing pressures to strengthen the parliamentary features of the Finnish political system, and to reduce the powers of the president, as well as the powers of parliamentary minorities to delay legislation.

The changing balance of power in the semi-presidential era

Broadly speaking, Finnish regime history in the semi-presidential era may be divided into four periods (Paloheimo 2001):

- 1917–39, in which the semi-presidential system was constructed;
- 1939–44, the era of centralized war cabinets;
- 1944–82, the age of presidential leadership;
- 1982–2000, which saw the shift towards parliamentarism and greater prime ministerial power.

A fifth period was ushered in during 2000, with the coming into force of the new, 'nearly parliamentary', constitution.

It was typical of the first period (1917–39), often called the *First Republic*, that governments were weak, unstable, and short-lived. In these years, there were twenty-three governments and the average period in office was only 365 days. Governments were mainly minority administrations, and the capacity of political parties to form coalitions was limited. Parliamentary oppositions were effective in overthrowing governments but poor at forming new coalitions. Bargaining over the formation of new coalitions was an almost continuous process. It weakened the power of prime ministers and, combined with the constitutional prerogatives of the president, facilitated the development of a relatively active and strong presidency. Finnish presidents have been active political leaders and decision-makers with their own preferences and policy styles, arbiters of political conflicts, opinion leaders in public life, and representative figureheads of the nation (Nousiainen 1998: 206). In the First Republic and during the First World War, they resembled monarchs in so far as they handed over their party membership cards and did not participate in party activities. They were expected to be above party disputes, and were not publicly criticized in the media (Nousiainen 1985).

The flexibility of the old semi-presidential constitution could easily be seen during the first years after the Second World War. This signalled the start of a period of strong presidency, which endured between 1944 and 1982, and is often referred to as the *Second Republic*. In 1944–6, Prime Minister J. K. Paasikivi was the incontestable leader of Finnish foreign policy, his goal being to improve Finnish relations with the Soviet Union. He retained his dominance over foreign policy when he was elected president in 1946. Paasikivi's successor, President Urho Kekkonen (1956–81) maintained the tradition, and also succeeded in gradually increasing presidential power over domestic affairs. In Kekkonen's era the power of the president was at its zenith (Anckar 1990; Arter 1981; Väyrynen 1994). However, Kekkonen involved himself so actively in party disputes that David Arter refers to this period as one of enlightened despotism (Arter 1981). Moreover, as a result of Kekkonen's engagement in party politics, the president became vulnerable to open criticism in the media, like any other politician. Thus, the presidency lost its monarchical sanctity.

Gradual Parliamentarization of the Semi-presidential Regime

The strong position of the president was eroded in the 1980s and 1990s. As the parliamentary ethos became more prevalent, so the parties, parliament, and Kekkonen's successor, President Mauno Koivisto (1982–94), became willing to reform the Finnish constitution. Various constitutional amendments served to reduce the prerogatives of the president and to strengthen the functioning of the parliamentary system. Thus, the president's right of veto over legislation was weakened in 1987; in 1988 individuals were limited to just two (consecutive) terms of presidential office; and in 1991 the president was formally constrained to consult with the parliamentary speaker and party groups before appointing a new government, or before making major changes to the composition of the government.[1] In the same year, the president lost the right to dismiss a government without a parliamentary vote of no-confidence, and to dissolve parliament and call an early general election except on the initiative of the prime minister.

Finland's entry into the European Union made it further necessary to reconsider the relationship between president and government. New provisions were added to the constitution, making the government responsible for issues decided at EU level. The president remained responsible for taking the lead on other aspects of Finnish foreign policy. This division of responsibility with respect to foreign policy was formally recognized in the new constitution of 2000.

While these changes had the effect of eroding presidential prerogative, it should be noted that parliament also changed the method for electing the president in 1991, though it did so in a way which did not further weaken the office. Since 1994, presidents have been directly elected by a two-ballot system resembling that used in France since 1965. If none of the candidates receives an absolute majority of the votes cast at the first ballot, a further election takes place, contested only by the leading two candidates from the first ballot. Far from weakening the president, this change has probably served to enhance his or her autonomy from parties, by providing a direct personal democratic mandate.

During this period of parliamentarization the coalitional capacity of parties was generally high. Governments were strong and stable: each enjoyed majority status in parliament, and endured for the whole electoral term. Thus, while Finnish governments had been the most unstable in the Nordic area during the 1950s, since the 1980s they have become the most stable.

The balance of power within the Finnish political executive shifted during the semi-presidential era even without formal constitutional changes. The system was, as Dag Anckar (2000: 9–14) put it, like a buffet table: it was up to each president to choose which of constitutional powers vested in him that he wanted to select from the constitutional buffet for active use. Some presidents were quite moderate in indulging themselves, leaving more scope for the prime minister and government, while others took their fill of presidential powers. Kekkonen was, as Anckar says, a gourmand. But no Finnish president has been a real ascetic in this sense, not even those who most obviously exhibited a parliamentary ethos.

During the semi-presidential era, prime ministers were not free to assume the role of national leaders in the manner of their counterparts in pure parliamentary systems. Instead, their role was to supervise the day-to-day detail of domestic politics, taking into consideration the policy preferences of both parliament and the president, while (in the Second Republic) accepting the president's sovereign leadership in foreign policy. Some governments of this era—especially caretaker governments—could justifiably be called president's governments. Not all governments merited such a sobriquet, however. prime ministers of stable majority coalitions secured more independence in relation to the president, and during the period of gradual parliamentarization, Kalevi Sorsa (premier from 1972–5, 1977–9, and 1982–7) even managed to raise the prime minister's profile in the domain of foreign policy. But as late as 1987, President Koivisto appointed a new prime minister (Harri Holkeri) contrary to the wishes of party leaders. As a result, Holkeri lacked autonomy from the president compared to some other prime ministers (though he did survive in office until 1991). It was not until the presidency of Ahtisaari that prime ministers were able to assert themselves as the effective heads of the political executive, reflecting the impact of Finland's membership of the European Union.

THE NEW, NEARLY-PARLIAMENTARY CONSTITUTION: THE PRIME MINISTER TAKES THE LEAD

The gradual process of parliamentarization was formalized with the establishment of a new constitution, passed almost unanimously by parliament in the spring of 1999. This came into force on 1 March 2000, the same day that the eleventh president, Tarja Halonen, took office. With the new constitution began a new phase in the story of the Finnish political executive, since the president was now deprived of most of the prerogatives that were typical of the previous semi-presidential system.

First, the new constitution deprives the president of real powers in respect of government formation. Parliament elects the prime minister, who is thereafter formally appointed to the office by the president. Before the prime minister is chosen, the parliamentary party groups negotiate on the political programme and composition of the government. The president formally appoints other ministers on the proposal of the prime minister (section 61). Rules concerning the resignation of government and the dissolution of parliament (sections 26 and 64) reaffirm the amendments made in 1991.

Second, the president has lost the power to amend government bills. If the president disputes a proposal made by the government, the matter is returned to the government for reconsideration, and the bill is then presented to parliament in a form decided by the government (section 58).

Parliament may now, in effect, override the president's power to delay legislation. If the president does not countersign a law passed by parliament within three months, the bill is returned to the legislature, where it may be readopted without further material amendment; it then becomes law without the president's approval (section 77).

The new constitution retains the dualism with respect to foreign policy leadership that was established when Finland entered the European Union. Thus, while foreign policy is principally the responsibility of the president in cooperation with the government, the latter is responsible for the preparation of decisions relevant to the European Union; parliament also participates in the national preparation of decisions to be made at EU level (section 93).

The president retains the power to appoint some senior civil servants (section 126), is the commander-in-chief of the armed forces, and may grant a full or partial pardon in respect of penalties imposed by a court of law (sections 105 and 128). A comparison of the prerogatives of parliament, government, and president under the old and new constitutions is presented in Table 11.1.

THE EXECUTIVE FACE OF PRESIDENTIALIZATION

Government formation

The new constitution has totally 'parliamentarized' the process of forming new governments, in effect depriving the president of any active role therein. By contrast, the new rules significantly enhance the power of the 'formateur' or prime minister in this respect. In practice, there are five different steps in the formation of a new government:

(1) selecting the formateur;
(2) choosing the parties that will constitute the government;
(3) deciding on the governmental programme;
(4) deciding on the distribution of portfolios between coalition partners; and
(5) selecting the individual ministers.

When a government terminates, due to the intercession of a general election or otherwise, the parliamentary parties negotiate on the formation of a new

TABLE 11.1. *Prerogatives of the parliament, government, and president in the Finnish constitution in three time periods*

	Division of power according to the constitution		
Duty	Old constitution, 1919–80	Old constitution, late 1990s	New constitution since 2000
General authority in executive decision-making	President	President	Government
Appointment of the government	President has autonomous power	President, after hearing parliamentary party groups	Parliament, president's role purely formal
Resignation of the government	Parliament, or prime minister, or President indirectly by dissolving the Parliament	Parliament, or prime minister	Parliament, or prime minister
Dissolution of the Parliament and premature general election	President	President after an initiative by the prime minister	President after an initiative by the prime minister
Government bills	President may change government bills	President may change government bills	Presidential powers to amend government bills largely eroded
Legislation: power of veto	President may postpone to the first session after next general election	President may postpone to the next session	Parliament may immediately override presidential veto
Legislation: decrees	President and government	President and government	Government
Foreign policy: general	President	President	President in cooperation with the government
Foreign policy: EU		Government	Government
Commander-in-chief of the armed forces	President	President	President
Appointment of senior civil servants	President appoints a large section of senior civil servants; remainder appointed by government or ministries	Number of senior civil servants appointed by president was reduced	President appoints only a very limited number of highest civil servants

Source: The Constitution Act of Finland (Act 94/1919) with later amendments. The Constitution of Finland (Act 731/1999).

government. A 'formateur' will be chosen by parliament to take the initiative in this process. According to an informal agreement between parliamentary groups, the leader of the biggest parliamentary party will be the first individual offered the chance of taking on this responsibility. The formateur has considerable power to decide which parties will participate in government; he or she may call some parties to the negotiating table, while overlooking others. Since the 1980s, it has been the Finnish practice to include two big parties and a couple of smaller ones in governing coalitions, while leaving a further 'big' party in opposition. The key question of the process is usually which of the three big parties will be excluded from the coalition, and the answer is generally policy-dependent. If questions of European integration are particularly high on the agenda of negotiation, it is likely that the Social Democrats and Conservatives will be relatively close to each other, and a left–right coalition will be formed, leaving the Centre Party in opposition. If traditional issues of income distribution and welfare are more prominent, however, the probable outcome will be either a centre–left (Social Democrat plus Centre Party) or centre–right (Conservative plus Centre Party) coalition.[2]

The construction of governmental programmes is an institutionalized process in Finland, and leads to the production of detailed, specific and binding documents (Nousiainen 1991). Parties contribute position papers, and the work of negotiation is divided into several sub-groups. In effect, this largely affirms the partified nature of governance. On the other hand, the final decision on coalition partners will not have been made while negotiations remain in progress, and this makes the formateur an important veto player in bargaining process. Interestingly, since 1991, a new feature of programme negotiations has emerged. In the cases of several ministries, senior civil servants have introduced their own programmatic proposals into the negotiations, a move which probably enhances the power of public administration. However, politicians supply the main principles of programmatic ideas, while bureaucrats are important in drafting the details.

The distribution of portfolios is a task in which the formateur has limited power, since the bargaining is essentially an inter-party affair in which the bigger parties take the most important portfolios. Neither does the formateur have an entirely free hand in choosing ministers. While quite free to select ministers from his or her own party, other coalition parties nominate their own ministers. In summary, then, the process of government formation in Finland is one in which the leader-formateur is an influential player with the power to take initiatives and sometimes impose vetos, but in which he or she nevertheless remains significantly constrained by the power of the parties.

Division of power between president and cabinet

Within the Finnish divided executive there are two kinds of sessions: *Presidential Sessions of Government*, where the president takes the chair and makes his or her decisions on the proposal of the government; and *General Meetings of Government*, headed by the prime minister. When a bill is presented to parliament, when a law approved by parliament is ratified, and when the president issues a decree, or appoints a civil servant, he or she acts in the context of a *Presidential Session*. Each issue on the agenda is presented by the minister concerned, but there is no voting in these sessions. As in a pure presidential system, the president has the sole right to make the decision in these cases, and is not tied to the opinion of the government. However, the contrary is the case in respect of *General Meetings of Government*. Here, decisions are made collegially, with issues sometimes put to the vote, but more typically through the pursuit of inter-party consensus.

The new constitution strengthens the prerogatives of the government at the expense of the president. The latter still formally presents government bills to parliament, but if there is a disagreement between government and president, the former may consider the bill anew, and re-present it to parliament without the president's counter-signature. The process of presenting government bills has thus been parliamentarized.

In foreign policy, both president and government enjoy their own prerogatives, which suggests that Finland has still not evolved into a fully parliamentary model in this policy domain. Thus, of the member states, only France and Finland send both president and prime minister to EU summits (though in the French case, the former alone may represent his country, when he has the support of a parliamentary majority). In the Finnish case, the division of power in international affairs might be regarded as the Achilles' heel of the constitution. The principle seems clear enough: the government should take the lead in EU matters, while the president should take the lead in other international affairs. But the borderline between the two is becoming increasingly blurred as the EU develops. This gives rise to the prospect of a constitutional crisis should the Finnish president and government ever disagree on certain foreign policy matters, with both parts of the executive claiming the right to have the last word (Jyränki 2000). Not surprisingly, as European integration proceeds further, there are pressures to remove semi-presidentialism in foreign affairs.

Finally, it should be noted that the president may assert himself or herself over the government in one other respect—the power of appointment: senior civil servants remain within the presidential prerogative. Indeed, in two cases, President Halonen has appointed managers of the Bank of Finland against the express wishes of the cabinet. Overall, then, although there has certainly been some erosion of presidential power in respect of setting the legislative agenda and foreign policy, the president retains a significant degree of autonomy from the government in some decision-making matters.

Division of power between parliament and cabinet

The Finnish parliament has mainly been a policy-influencing assembly, in common with most parliamentary systems. Up to the 1950s, governments were mostly weak and unstable; indeed, as recently as 1991, one-third of parliamentarians could effectively veto legislation, which strengthened the power of the opposition in relation to government. However, with the stabilization of majority governments and the concomitant loss of opposition power to delay legislation, the Finnish parliament has effectively become an executive-dominated assembly, which exerts marginal influence on most issues. About 99 per cent of the legislation is based on government bills, and ministers' supporters in parliament are active in supervising the legislative timetable. Virtually all private legislative initiatives taken by MPs fail. The high tide of parliament's power vis-à-vis the executive now occurs during the formation of new governments. During such periods, parliamentary party groups can make policy proposals, which, if included in the programme of the new government, become politically binding.

Indicative of the developing 'fusion' of executive and legislature in Finland is the extraordinary growth of prime ministerial presence in parliament. In the 1970s and 1980s, some prime ministers appeared in plenary sessions of parliament only a couple of times a year. Since 1990, it has become the norm for premiers to address plenary sessions more than 100 times a year (Aula 2003: 96–8). This reflects the developing management of the parliamentary agenda by the government, and the particular importance of the prime minister to this process.

Division of power within the cabinet

Decisions by the Finnish government are either made collegially at *General Meetings of Government* or, on minor departmental issues, by individual ministers. Traditionally, most governmental decision-making in Finland was of the former, collegial, variety (Nousiainen 1975), but in the mid-1990s, decision-making was decentralized and the scope for individual ministerial governance expanded correspondingly. Thus, whereas in the late 1980s, about 2,000 decisions a year were made at *General Meetings of Government*, since the late 1990s, this number has fallen to between 500 and 700 (Statistics Finland 2002: 555). In any case, as the number of issues on the agenda has risen continuously since the 1960s, informal arenas of decision-making have become more important, while *General Meetings* have been left as an arena of formal decision-making.

In Finland today, government committees and special ministerial groups play an important role in the preparation of government policy. There are four permanent ministerial committees (foreign and security policy; state finance; economic policy; EU affairs) and several ministerial working groups on special policy areas. Typically, each coalition party is represented on each government committee and in most of the special ministerial groups. The latter function as watchdogs of multiparty cohabitation by monitoring individual ministers' policy development: their brief is to ensure that individual ministerial power does not endanger the carefully constructed political balance that was crafted during the formation of the governing coalition and negotiation of a detailed programme of government. The prime minister also plays a vital part, since he heads all the permanent ministerial committees, and his role has become increasingly like that of the managing director of a major corporation; he or she coordinates government activity and seeks to ensure that the spirit of the coalition agreement is adhered to.

Since 2000, the prime minister and his or her office have also gained power by taking on responsibility for coordinating the preparation of policy relevant to the EU, a task inherited from the ministry of foreign affairs. This role tends to increase bilateral connections between the prime minister's office and specific ministries, but EU membership also underlines the importance of those ministers enjoying the biggest responsibilities in the EU council of ministers, such as the minister of finance.

The increased coordinating responsibility of the prime minister is reflected in the growing capacity afforded through the resources available in his or her office. Thus, in 1990 there were approximately 150 civil servants working in the Prime Minister's Office, while this number had grown to 227 by 2000—a growth rate of 50 per cent in a decade.

It should be borne in mind that a kind of informal inner cabinet operates in Finland today (Murto 1994, 1997). This inner cabinet consists largely of the leaders of the coalition parties. They occupy the most important government committees and ministerial working groups and in this way supervise the functioning of the ministerial governance. The core of this inner circle consists of the prime minister and the leader of the other major coalition partner. These are the two 'biggest hitters' in Finnish government, and any informal understandings they might reach can seriously restrict the bargaining power of smaller coalition parties.

In summary, the Finnish style of governance is a mixture of eroded formal presidential rule, weakened cabinet government, and increased ministerial governance, supervised by a growing network of government committees and ministerial working groups. The prime minister lies at the centre of this network and, in the increasing realm of EU matters, he or she is also the key actor in a new set of bilateral relationships with other decision-makers. Finnish government remains strongly partified in many ways, but there is no doubt that the prime minister enjoys significantly greater power resources and autonomy than hitherto. The rising power of prime ministers within the executive is based on their new-found autonomy from presidents, their leadership in setting the daily agenda of government, their importance in settling disputes within government (a job previously often done by the president), and their role as the conductor of Finnish policy towards the EU.

THE PARTY FACE OF PRESIDENTIALIZATION

Interviews with elite politicians tend to confirm the views of academic observers that trends towards electoralist organizations like the catch-all party (Kirchheimer 1966), electoral-professional party (Panebianco 1988) or cartel party (Katz and Mair 1995) are well established in Finland (Nousiainen 1996). Parties increasingly appeal to floating voters; membership in party organizations is declining;[3] the vertical ties between party leaders and members have become weaker; and the relationship between party leaders and supporters in the electorate is increasingly mediated by the national mass media—especially television—at the expense of the local party organizations (Sundberg 1994, 2002). These trends strengthen the position of party leaders, and make them more autonomous of their extra-parliamentary organizations, and to a certain extent of their own parliamentary parties. Now, more than ever, the opinions and statements of various party leaders are publicized in the media on a daily basis.

Party leaders' prominence has increasingly come to reflect their position in government rather than their position within the party. Previously, during the semi-presidential era, a president could quite easily choose to exclude party leaders from the government, but since the 1980s, it has become the rule that leaders of the parties in office should also be ministers. For these politicians, their role as minister in a coalition government is at least as important as their role as party leader. The need for consensus in a coalition government increases their autonomy from the party. For prime ministers, their role as prime minister clearly predominates over their role as party leader. It is widely, though not universally, accepted by their followers that, if a government succeeds, then the prime minister's party will succeed. Only the most militant ideologues in a prime minister's party complain loudly about the compromises made in the government.

In addition, there are a number of other factors, some of which we have already touched upon, which serve to enhance the autonomy of prime ministers from their parties.

- First, as we have seen, the parliamentarization of the Finnish constitution means that the prime minister has become the effective head of the political executive.
- Second, the prime minister is highly involved in international cooperation and summitry, and gains considerable decision-making power from this.
- Third, prime ministers in contemporary Finland enjoy the benefits of stable majority coalitions that in most cases survive in office for the whole electoral term.
- Fourth, Finnish prime ministers are nowadays quite free in their choice of ministers from their own parties, although, unlike their British counterparts, they cannot usually reshuffle ministers in mid-term without very good reasons.

Meetings of extra-parliamentary party executives are often meetings in which the prime minister and other ministers do little more than report on the current activities of government. Thus, in day-to-day politics, the party executive is largely subordinate to the ministerial group of the party. That said, the prime minister does not have an entirely free hand. He or she still has to take some care to monitor, via the party executive, the limits of his or her autonomy. The executive not only serves as a communication channel for party members, but will also reflect, and anticipate the reactions of, various other actors who can limit the autonomy of the prime minister, including the media, the public, and coalition partners.

If leaders of modern electoral-professional parties are generally given more power within their organizations, they can, however, also be more vulnerable to rebellion brought on by perceived electoral weaknesses. Between 1950 and 1979 none of the three major parties' (Social Democrats, Centre Party, Conservative Party) leaders resigned or were dismissed because of their personal unpopularity among voters, or because of the poor electoral performance of their parties. Since 1980, however, six out of ten changes of party leader have been provoked by disappointing electoral results or the low personal standings of leaders in the eyes of the electorate (see Table 11.2). The choice of party leaders now clearly turns on their real or supposed effects on voting behaviour.

THE ELECTORAL FACE OF PRESIDENTIALIZATION

Personalization of electoral competition

Since the 1980s, there has been a growing tendency to emphasize the personal role of leaders as figureheads of their party's electoral campaign. As ideological differences between political parties have eroded, and election manifestos have become general and cursory, so parties have come to compete

TABLE 11.2. *Changes of major party leaders, Finland 1980–2003*

Party leaders	Years as a party leader	Reason for resignation	
Social Democratic Party			
Mr. Emil Skog	1946–57	power struggle in the party	
Dr. Väinö Tanner	1957–63	power struggle in the party, defeat in general election	*
Mr. Rafael Paasio	1963–75	natural rotation	
Mr. Kalevi Sorsa	1975–87	electoral defeat	*
Mr. Pertti Paasio	1987–91	electoral defeat	*
Mr. Ulf Sundqvist	1991–93	poor personal image	*
Mr. Paavo Lipponen	1993–2005	natural rotation	
Mr. Eero Heinäluoma	2005–		
Centre Party			
Dr. V. J. Sukselainen	1945–64	power struggle in the party	
Dr. Johannes Virolainen	1965–80	power struggle in the party	
Dr. Paavo Väyrynen	1980–90	natural rotation	
Mr. Esko Aho	1990–2002	poor personal image, 'insufficient' electoral victory	*
Mrs. Anneli Jäätteenmäki	2002–3	poor personal image	*
Mr. Matti Vanhanen	2003–		
Conservative Party			
Mr. Arvo Salminen	1945–55	natural rotation	
Mr. Jussi Saukkonen	1955–65	natural rotation	
Mr. Juha Rihtniemi	1965–71	death of the party leader	
Mr. Harri Holkeri	1971–79	natural rotation	
Mr. Ilkka Suominen	1979–91	natural rotation	
Mr. Pertti Salolainen	1991–94	poor personal image	*
Mr. Sauli Niinistö	1994–2001	natural rotation	
Mr. Ville Itälä	2001–2004	poor personal image, defeat in general election	
Mr. Jyrki Katainen	2004–		

* Party leader resigned or was dismissed as a result of electoral defeat of the party, or poor personal image of the party leader.

more and more on the basis of leaders' images (Carlson 2000; Isotalus 1998; Moring and Himmelstein 1993; Pekonen 1989).

This process has been facilitated by the advent, in the early 1990s, of political advertising on radio and television. Hitherto, this had been prohibited. The introduction of political advertising was part and parcel of the general commercialization of the mass media in the country, with a growing role for commercial TV channels and a growing number of local commercial radio stations. In the general elections in 1995, 1999, and 2003 some political parties focused their television adverts and posters on their leaders. Previously, this kind of imagery had been reserved for presidential elections. Now it seems that even parliamentary elections are 'presidentializing'.

This reflects the fact that electoral competition between the three biggest parties—the Social Democrats, the Centre Party, and the Conservative Party—is increasingly also a competition for the next prime minister. Each party seeks to present its leader as the most suitable formateur-prime minister. This constrains such leaders from adopting militant political stances, privileging instead the quality of 'statesmanship' and the (perceived) ability to manage a coalition government. Debate about the relative merits of rival candidates for the prime ministership is thus an important new feature of Finnish election campaigns. When it was up to the president to choose the government formateur, the name of the next prime minister rarely featured as an open issue in electoral campaiging. By the time of the 2003 general election, discussion and speculation about the next premier had become one of the key issues of the campaign.

Personalization of Voting Behaviour

It is to be expected that personal candidate effects should become more influential as partisan loyalties erode. In the 1970s, about 80 per cent of voters claimed to remain loyal to the same party across two consecutive elections, but only two-thirds did by the 1990s. And indeed, there is some evidence to suggest that leadership effects have generally become more important for Finnish voters. Finnish Election Studies reveal that in 1991, 21 per cent of those who voted claimed that a positive evaluation of the party leader had a big effect on their party choice, while the corresponding figure stood at 33 per cent in 1999, and at 39 per cent in 2003.[4]

A more systematic examination of the changing impact of leadership evaluations at the individual level can be provided by conducting a multivariate analysis of Finnish Voter Barometer survey data.[5] In these surveys, respondents are asked to evaluate various qualities of political parties, including that of 'skilful party leadership'. Using data gathered during the election campaigns of 1975, 1978, 1990, 1995, 1999, and 2003, we can attempt to assess the changing influence of leadership evaluations on those voting for the three biggest political parties in Finland, the Social Democratic Party (SDP), the Centre Party (Cent), and the Conservative Party (Cons). Logistic regression is used, which is appropriate for situations in which the dependent variable is dichotomous and the independent variables may be categorical (Hosmer and Lemeshow 2000). Party vote is the dependent variable, with respondents intending to vote for (or, in 2003, actually having voted for) the party concerned coded 1, and all others coded 0.

A simple model based on two independent variables is tested: 'party loyalty' is a dichotomous variable measuring whether or not a respondent voted for the same party at the previous election; the other independent variable gauges (negative) leadership evaluations, scoring 1 for those respondents judging the party to have an incompetent leadership, and 0 for other respondents.[6] By controlling for party choice in the previous election, we can estimate the independent effect of leadership evaluations on party choice. The results of this logistic regression analysis are presented in Table 11.3.

It can be seen that leadership evaluations explain more of the variance in party choice in 1995, 1999, and 2003 than at earlier elections. For all three parties, leadership evaluations are statistically significant predictors of party choice in 1995; prior to then, however, leadership effects are not statistically significant, except in the case of the SDP in 1975. The overall goodness of fit of the models is indicated by the Nagelkerke R^2 coefficient, which may be interpreted similarly to R^2 in a linear regression model (Norusis 1999: 45–7). It is no surprise that the overall goodness of fit of each model is mainly accounted for by respondent's party choice in the previous election, even at the three most recent elections: however, leadership evaluation does improve the goodness of fit of the models in these years, while failing to do so prior to 1995.

There is cross-national evidence from democratic states around the world that parties in office are more prone to lose votes than parties in opposition. This is the cost of ruling (Bengtsson 2002; Paldam and Scott 1995). But in the context of coalition government, this raises the questions as to whether or not the costs of ruling are particularly high for the prime minister's party, compared to other governing parties. If so, this would suggest that voters attribute a particular responsibility for government to the individual who heads the political executive. Table 11.4 presents figures on the electoral performance of the prime minister's party, other governing parties, and the biggest opposition party at Finnish general elections from 1966 to 2003. With the exception of 1983 and 2003, the share of the vote cast for the prime minister's party has always decreased. The result in 1983 is due to a Finnish version of the 'Mitterrand effect'—a political euphoria induced by the victory of the Social Democratic candidate for the presidency in 1982, the first victory for the party at this level. The result in 2003 is explained by the exceptional impact of the incumbent prime minister. The Finnish Election Study reveals that 50 per cent of new Social Democratic Party voters said that an important reason for their party choice was the incumbent prime minister and SDP leader, Paavo Lipponen, whom they felt would be the best prime minister for the next government.

The reverse side of the cost of ruling is that the share of votes cast for the biggest party in opposition has increased at all general elections except in 1972. (On that occasion the Conservative opposition was in some disarray following the death of the party leader a year before the election). However, the key point, from our perspective, is that with the growth of prime

TABLE 11.3. *Logistic regression analysis of electoral support for the major parties in Finland, 1975–99*

	Social Democratic Party						Centre Party						Conservative Party					
	1975	1979	1991	1995	1999	2003	1975	1979	1991	1995	1999	2003	1975	1979	1991	1995	1999	2003
Party loyalty	45.53***	89.66***	46.19***	33.95***	48.45***	39.18***	198.62***	128.77***	60.93***	41.05***	36.49***	72.2***	95.64***	165.35***	28.71***	50.01***	50.69***	51.5***
Negative evaluation of party leadership	0.37**	0.58	0.78	0.16***	0.11***	0.25***	0.25(*)	0.32	0.54	0.08***	0.36***	0.23***	0.97	0.47	0.88	0.21***	0.05***	0.37**
Constant	0.12***	0.06***	0.07***	0.12***	0.06***	0.11***	0.04***	0.05***	0.08***	0.06***	0.07***	0.13***	0.03***	0.05***	0.07***	0.04***	0.07***	0.03***
−2 log likelihood	815.1	631.3	539.5	819.2	561.8	419.6	419.8	505.5	515.3	591.4	619.1	372.2	415.1	478.1	559.0	605.6	622.2	349.1
Nagelkerke R²	0.53	0.63	0.50	0.52	0.56	0.54	0.63	0.62	0.50	0.53	0.48	0.61	0.53	0.63	0.39	0.53	0.53	0.57
Increase in the Nagelkerke R² contributed by the leadership evaluation variable	0.00	0.00	0.00	0.05	0.07	0.04	0.00	0.00	0.00	0.05	0.01	0.04	0.00	0.00	0.00	0.04	0.02	0.02
Number of cases	1,143	1,196	940	1,388	1,222	753	1,143	1,196	940	1,388	1,222	753	1,143	1,196	940	1,388	1,222	753

Notes: The dependent variable is coded 1 for respondents intending to vote for party concerned and 0 for other respondents. The independent variables are coded as follows:

Party loyalty: 1 — respondent voted for the party concerned at previous election; 0 — voted for other party or no party at all.

Evaluation of party leadership: 1 — respondent evaluates party leader negatively (incompetent leadership); 0 — respondent evaluates party leader positively or has no clear opinion on this matter.

Regression coefficients in the table are e^B coefficients, which can be interpreted as odds ratios. Significance of the regression coefficient is tested with Wald statistics. *** p < 0.001; ** p < 0.01; * p < 0.05; (*) p < 0.10. Overall goodness of fit of the model is measured by −2 log likelihood coefficient and the Nagelkerke R² coefficient (see Norusis 1999).

Source: Finnish Voter Barometer Surveys FSD1002 (1975), FSD1005 (1978), FSD1016 (1990), FSD1031 (1995), FSD1038 (1999), and Finnish Election Study 2003 FSD1260 (2003).

TABLE 11.4. *Electoral performance of prime minister's party, other governing parties, and the biggest opposition party in general elections, 1966–99*

	1966	1970	1972	1975	1979	1983	1987	1991	1995	1999	2003
Prime minister's party	−1.7	−3.8	−0.7	−0.9	−1.0	2.8	−2.6	−3.8	−5.0	−5.4	1.6
Other governing parties	−2.1	−10.2	1.8	−0.1	−2.2	−3.0	−2.7	−3.3	−1.9	3.6	−4.0
All governing parties	−3.8	−14.0	1.1	−1.0	−3.2	−0.2	−5.3	−7.1	−6.9	−1.8	−2.4
Biggest opposition party	7.7	4.2	−0.4	0.8	3.3	0.4	1.0	7.2	6.2	2.6	2.3

Note: All figures are changes in the percentage share of votes won.

Source: Statistics Finland, *Statistics on General Elections.*

ministerial power under the newly parliamentarized polity of the 1990s, the prime minister's party has in most general elections lost more support than the other coalition parties in combination. If people are dissatisfied with the coalition government in office, they are prone to punish the prime minister's party. This has been the electoral cost of presidentialization for the premier's party.

Prime minister and party leaders in the media

The structure of the mass media in Finland has altered radically in recent decades. Notable features of change include the declining role of the party-linked press, the growing predominance of television, and the advent of commercial mass media. There are three changes in the relationship between politics and the media which are of particular significance for the question of presidentialization.[7]

1. Contemporary politics *enters the public domain in real time*. Previously, it was possible for politicians to make decisions, and subsequently make them public. Nowadays, the gap between the stages in this two-step process has been greatly reduced as the media monitors and broadcasts political news every hour of the day. The daily agenda of politics is much more closely connected to the daily agenda of the media.
2. Political decisions and statements are increasingly *made in the media*. The real time connection between political and media agendas encourages politicians to issue many of the most important political statements through the media rather than in parliament. The attempt to shape the media's agenda is a continuous and important part of contemporary politics.
3. The media *personalize politics*. There are several reasons for this. Ideological differences between political parties have diminished; political

issues are often technical and arcane; national decisions are often made in the complex framework of European or global developments; and the agenda of political decision-making is increasingly crowded. By focusing on the current opinions, conflicts, and traits of political leaders, the media avoids the challenging complexity of issues. Moreover, in the commercial sector, it is often more rewarding (that is, profitable) for the media to focus on the personalities of politicians.

All these changes have contributed to the rising visibility of the prime minister in the media. Up to the 1960s, the activities of the Finnish parliament were quite extensively reported in the Finnish mass media; indeed, parliament was more central to the focus of the media than the government. The president and even the speaker of parliament received as much, or more, media attention than the prime minister. From the 1960s, however, this began to change. The government became more prominent in the media, and the publicity accorded to the prime minister began to grow inexorably (Murto 1994: 364–5). In 1967, the prime minister was mentioned on 115 days on the editorial or front pages of *Helsingin Sanomat*, the biggest daily newspaper in Finland—that is, in 32 per cent of all issues that year. By 1986, this had risen to 145 issues (40 per cent), and to half of all issues by 2002 (Nousiainen 1992: 74–5; Puoskari 2002). The parliamentarization of the political system, Finnish membership of the European Union, and the internationalization of political decision-making have been the most important factors driving the growing media visibility of the prime minister during the last decade. Indeed, it is no exaggeration to say that the prime minister is now a far more visible figure in the media than the president.

CONCLUSION

Since the 1980s, the Finnish political system has gradually changed from a semi-presidential to a parliamentary one. The prerogatives of the president have to a large extent been removed, while those of the cabinet have been strengthened, and the prime minister has become the effective head of the executive. That said, the president still retains some prerogatives, especially in foreign policy, and in appointing senior civil servants, which serves to differentiate Finland from 'normal' parliamentary systems.

Several factors underlie these changes, the most important of which is the collapse of the Soviet Union. This eliminated the legitimacy of an authoritarian form of presidential rule in the foreign policy domain. Indeed, discussion of the excessive powers of the president in this respect started after the retirement of President Kekkonen in 1981. Finland's membership in the European Union from 1995 increased the need to have a broader parliamentary basis for national decision-making in international affairs. Furthermore, the improved coalitional capability of political parties in contemporary Finland has facilitated the shift towards governmental power at the expense of the president. The growing predictability of processes of coalition-formation and the enhanced stability of government have both reduced the need or space for presidential intervention in day-to-day politics.

In conjunction with the formal de-presidentialization of Finnish politics, however, there has been a *de facto* 're-presidentialization' in the sense of the general model set out in this book. That is, since the time of the Ahtisaari presidency (1994–2000), Finnish prime ministers have become much more 'presidential' figures in their own right, although this should be understood in the context of the limits imposed by multiparty governance and collaboration with the president in foreign affairs.

Most of the causes of the *de facto* 're-presidentialization' of Finnish politics are structural rather than contingent. The internal activities of political parties have declined as they have transformed themselves into modern electoralist organizations, and the autonomy of the leaders from their parties has increased. Government formateurs are no longer dependent on the close involvement of presidents in the process of making new governments. The new constitution radically increases the power of the cabinet relative to the president. And the power and status of the prime minister inside the cabinet has grown with a changing model of executive rule in which he or she has become the key coordinating figure in a centre of network of decision-making processes and structures.

In addition, the electoral face of presidentialization in Finland also depends largely on structural causes of change. Thus, partisan dealignment and ideological convergence between the parties has made space for the personalization of politics. Leadership image matters far more now, both to party competition and voting behaviour. The personalization of politics, in combination with the declining role of party organizations, enhances the autonomy of party leaders within their own parties. Thus, among the parties in office, meetings of the extra-parliamentary party executives are not so much decision-making arenas, as opportunities for the leader and other government ministers to report on current governmental policy developments. Parties in opposition are more autonomous in setting the agenda of the extra-parliamentary party.

The growing presidentialization of electoral processes can benefit and impose costs on the major parties competing for national governmental office. At most general elections during the last two decades, the prime minister's party has generally been a big loser. If people are dissatisfied with the incumbent government—and it seems they often are—then they are prone to blame the prime minister's party.

Under the semi-presidential system, contingent factors largely conditioned shifts in the balance of power between president and prime minister. Presidents are now doomed to be the weaker partners, though personal factors remain important to the relationship and can affect the authority and autonomy of the premier. In a multiparty system with coalition governments, *de facto* presidentialization operates somewhat differently from the way it does in a two-party system. It always takes time for party leaders to 'presidentialize' themselves, for they must have a long career in politics, and must be accepted and respected by several parties, not just their own. In contemporary Finland, the leaders with the strongest presidential capacities contest the premiership rather than the presidency, but in the context of multiparty government, the personal authority of the prime minister tends to develop gradually during the period in office. Thus, while there are certainly very real constraints on *de facto* presidentialization, and it does not operate quite as it would in a majoritarian democracy with a two-party system, it is nonetheless tangible.

NOTES

1. In fact, this practice had been followed as an informal convention for several decades, but it is not insignificant that it was now transformed into a formal constitutional requirement.
2. Much of this section of the chapter is based on the following expert interviews conducted by the author in 2002:
   Aho, Esko. Prime Minister, 1991–5. Centre Party. 27 May 2002.
   Heikkinen, Ari. Secretary General of Green League. 4 January 2002.
   Holkeri, Harri. Prime Minister, 1987–91. Conservative Party. 7 January 2002.
   Kankare, Matti. Secretary General of the Conservative Party. 4 January 2002.
   Lankia, Eero. Secretary General of the Centre Party. 4 January 2002.
   Linna, Markku. Secretary of State in the ministry of education. 7 January 2002.
   Sorsa, Kalevi. Prime Minister, 1972–5, 1977–9, 1982–7. Social Democratic Party. 7 January 2002.
3. In 1980, there were in total approximately 750,000 members of Finnish political parties (18 per cent of the adult population). In 2003, there were about 400,000 members (10 per cent of the adult population).
4. These data sets are archived by the Finnish Social Science Data Archive. Finnish Election Study 1991 (FSD1018); Finnish Election Study 1999 (FSD1042); Finnish Election Study 2003 (FSD1260).
5. The Finnish Voter Barometer data are also supplied by the Finnish Social Science Data Archive, with the following archive reference numbers: FSD1002 (1975), FSD1005 (1978), FSD1016 (1990), FSD1031 (1995), FSD1038 (1999).
6. In the 2003 election study, there was a barometer question asking respondents to express their like or disike for each party leader on a scale running from 0 to 10. For this chapter, a dummy variable was created from this attitudinal barometer.
7. Again, this section draws on the sources listed in note 2.

REFERENCES

Act 94/1919. *The Constitution Act of Finland*, with later amendments.

Act 731/1999. *The Constitution of Finland* (see http://www.om.fi/constitution/ 3340.htm).

Anckar, D. (1990). 'Democracy in Finland: The Constitutional Framework', in J. Sundberg and S. Berglund (eds.), *Finnish Democracy*. Jyväskylä: Finnish Political Science Association.

—— (2000). 'Jäähyväiset semipresidentialismille', *Politiikka*, 42: 9–14.

Arter, D. (1981). 'Kekkonen's Finland: Enlighted Despotism or Consensual Democracy', *West European Politics*, 4: 219–34.

Aula, M. K. (2003). 'Eduskunta Suomen poliittisessa järjestelmässä', in P. Saukkonen (ed.), Paikkana politiikka, University of Helsinki, Department of Political Science, *Acta Politica*, 26.

Bentsson, Å. (2002). *Ekonomisk röstning och politisk kontext. En studie av 266 val i parlamentariska demokratier*. Åbo: Åbo Akademi University Press.

Carlson, T. (2000). *Partier och kandidater på väljarmarknaden: Studier i finländsk politisk reklam*. Åbo: Åbo Akademis förlag.

Hosmer, D. and S. Lemeshow (2000). *Applied Logistic Regression*. New York: John Wiley and Sons.

Isotalus, P. (1998). *Kaveri vai peluri. Poliitikko mediassa*. Jyväskylä: Atena.

Jyränki, A. (2000). *Uusi perustuslakimme*. Turku: Iura nova.

Katz, R. and P. Mair (1995). 'Changing Models of Party Organization and Party Democracy: The Emergence of the Cartel Party', *Party Politics*, 1: 5–28.

Kirchheimer, O. (1966). 'The Transformation of the Western European Party Systems', in J. LaPalombara and M. Weiner (eds.), *Political Parties and Political Development*. Princeton: Princeton University Press.

Moring, T. and H. Himmelstein (1993). *Politiikkaa riisuttuna. Kampanjakulttuuri murroksessa televisioidun politiikan aikaan*. Helsinki: Oy Yleisradio Ab.

Murto, E. (1994). *Pääministeri. Hallintohistoriallisia tutkimuksia No. 13*. Helsinki: Painatuskeskus.

—— (1997). 'Sisäpiirit valtioneuvoston toiminnan yhteensovittajana', in J. Selovuori (ed.), *Hallinnon historiasta hallinnon kehittämiseen*, Valtioneuvoston kanslian julkaisusarja No. 23.

Norusis, M. (1999). *SPSS Regression Models 10.0*. Chicago: SPSS Inc.

Nousiainen, J. (1975). 'Valtioneuvoston järjestysmuoto ja sisäinen toiminta', in *Valtioneuvoston historia 1917–1966, vol. III*. Helsinki: Valtion painatuskeskus, 217–390.

—— (1985). *Suomen Presidentit valtiollisina johtajina K. J. Ståhlbergista Mauno Koivistoon*. Porvoo, Helsinki: WSOY.

—— (1991). 'Ministers, Parties and Coalition Policies', *University of Turku, Department of Political Science, Studies on Political Science No. 10*.

—— (1992). *Politiikan huipulla. Ministerit ja ministeristöt Suomen parlamentaarisessa järjestelmässä*. Porvoo, Helsinki: WSOY.

—— (1996). 'Finland: Ministerial Autonomy, Constitutional Collectivism, and Party Oligarchy', in M. Laver and K. A. Shepsle (eds.), *Cabinet Ministers and Parliamentary Government*. Cambridge: Cambridge University Press, 88–105.

Nousiainen, J. (1998). *Suomen poliittinen järjestelmä. Kymmenes, uudistettu laitos.* Porvoo, Helsinki: WSOY.

Paldam, M. and P. Scott (1995). 'A Rational-Voter Explanation of the Cost of Ruling', *Public Choice*, 83: 159–73.

Paloheimo, H. (2001). 'Divided Government in Finland: From a Semi-Presidential to a Parliamentary Democracy', in R. Elgie (ed.), *Divided Government in Comparative Perspective*. Oxford: Oxford University Press.

Panebianco, A. (1988). *Political Parties. Organization and Power*. Cambridge: Cambridge University Press.

Pekonen, K. (1989). *Charismatic Leadership and the Role of Image in Modern Politics. The Case of Finland in the 1980s*. Jyväskylä: University of Jyväskylä.

Puoskari, M. (2002). *Unpublished Data Set on the Visibility of Ministers in Helsingin Sanomat in 2002*.

Statistics Finland (2002). *Statistical Yearbook of Finland 2002*.

Sundberg, J. (1994). 'Finland: Nationalized Parties, Professionalized Organizations', in R. S. Katz and P. Mair (eds.), *How Parties Organize: Change and Adaptation in Party Organizations in Western Democracies*. London: Sage, 158–84.

—— (2002). 'The Scandinavian Party Model at the Crossroads', in P. Webb, D. Farrell, and I. Holliday (eds.), *Political Parties in Advanced Industrial Democracies*. Oxford: Oxford University Press, 181–216.

Väyrynen, R. (1994). *Tasavalta kasvaa ja kansainvälistyy 1956–1981. Tasavallan Presidentit: Kekkonen*. Porvoo: Weilin + Göös.

12

The Presidentialization of Portuguese Democracy?

Marina Costa Lobo[1]

The future points to a personalization of politics. When ideological barriers break, leaders emerge to lead the parties and politics. I am a prime ministerial candidate precisely in a time of dilution of ideological barriers—a time when leaders have become the main point of reference. . . . For democracy to gain credibility, it is important that the population is able to hold someone accountable for what was and what was not accomplished. I don't think it is negative for politics to have a human face.[2]

INTRODUCTION

This chapter seeks to explain the extent to which Portuguese democracy has become presidentialized in the sense outlined in Chapter 1, and to discuss possible causes. Presidentialization has been identified as a trend in several advanced industrial democracies, regardless of their constitutional framework (see, for instance, Foley 1993; Jones 1991). According to our analytical framework, it is possible to distinguish three faces of presidentialization—the executive, the party, and the electoral. Before we analyse the empirical detail of these aspects of the phenomenon, it is first necessary to consider how the framework can be applied to the case of a semi-presidential regime such as Portugal's. It is also important to explain why the discussion of presidentialization in Portugal refers to increased autonomy and power resouces of the prime minister, and not the president of the Republic.

THE EVOLVING SEMI-PRESIDENTIAL CONTEXT

In his classic article on semi-presidentialism, Duverger included Portugal among the list of countries he designated 'semi-presidential'. According to him, there were three defining characteristics of such a regime: first, a president elected by direct universal suffrage; second, a president with considerable political powers; third, a prime minister and ministers possessing considerable executive and governmental powers and responsible to parliament (Duverger 1980: 166). This system does not amount to an alternation between a parliamentary form of government and a presidential one. In a semi-presidential system, even when faced with a hostile parliamentary majority, the president still has considerable autonomy; however, a president in a semi-presidential system is never the sole executive, since the prime minister is responsible to parliament for the government. From these constitutional rules very different political systems may emerge, depending on the constitutional detail and the workings of the party system. In Portugal, constitutional and party system changes since 1976 have altered the functioning of the political system, and bear upon the theme of presidentialization since the mid-1980s.

According to the Portuguese constitution of 1976, the government was accountable not only to parliament, as in other parliamentary democracies, but also to the President of the Republic (Article 193). This meant that the president could withdraw his political confidence in a government (that is, force it to resign), even if it enjoyed the support of the assembly. Moreover, the president had the power to nominate the prime minister (Article 136), after considering an election result: if no majority could be found in parliament, the president could try to engineer a majority himself, as was the case in 1978. In fact, until 1982, the government lay at the intersection between the two sources of legitimacy laid down by the constitution: the military-revolutionary and the party-pluralistic, represented respectively by the President of the Republic and the Council of the Revolution on one hand, and the assembly on the other (Canotilho and Moreira 1991: 27).[3] The government's difficulty in asserting its power reflected the tension between these two sources of legitimacy, especially when there was no majority in the assembly. The president was attributed particular powers in the conduct of foreign policy (Article 139), although he needed the countersignature of the prime minister to declare war, to ratify treaties once they had been approved by parliament, and to appoint ambassadors. More importantly, the president had a suspensive veto[4] over any laws that had been submitted to him by the assembly for promulgation, and was able to veto any government decree-laws submitted to him (Article 278).

The 1976 constitution also states that the government conducts the general policy of the country, is the highest body of public administration (Article 185), and attributes to the prime minister a clear ascendancy within government. First, it is the prime minister's function to direct, coordinate and guide all ministerial actions, and to direct the workings of government, establishing the general relations between it and other institutions (Article 204); second, ministers are nominated by the president on the proposal of the prime minister (Article 190); third, Article 189 underlines the primacy of the latter within the executive by stating that the resignation of the prime minister implies the resignation of the entire government. Thus, within the semi-presidential framework set out in 1976, the prime minister was effectively the head of government.

In 1982, the constitution was revised: the powers of the president in policy terms were reduced, and his control over the government 'in normal circumstances' was also curtailed (Araújo 2003). With that revision, the government became politically responsible only to the assembly. This meant that in contrast to the original draft, the president could now no longer dismiss the government by invoking a lack of political trust, although he could still do so in 'exceptional' political circumstances (that is, in order 'to ensure the regular functioning of democratic institutions' [Article 136]). Moreover, even though the president retained the power to veto any law, the suspensive veto was abolished, with respect to both assembly laws and government decree-laws. Even more fundamentally, the 1982 constitutional revision dissolved the council of the revolution, a military body that functioned as a constitutional court; for some analysts this move signalled the final step in the consolidation of democracy in Portugal, removing the tension in the 1976 constitution between the military-revolutionary and party-pluralist sources of legitimacy (see, for instance, Linz and Stepan 1996).

Subsequent changes in the party system have ensured that the government has been the great beneficiary of these constitutional changes. Between 1976 and 1987, the party system was characterized by the existence of four relatively strong parties—one of which was anti-system—and a high degree of government instability. During that first decade of democracy, governments proved quite vulnerable: none survived a full term, each lasting on an average for eleven months. In contrast, between 1987 and 2002, the two centre parties have alternated in government. In 1987, the centre-right (*Partido Social Democrata*—PSD) led by Cavaco Silva, won an absolute majority, and governed alone for the full term. In the 1991 elections, Cavaco Silva and the PSD were returned to power, their majority reinforced. In 1995, the Socialists (*Partido Socialista*—PS), led by António Guterres, won a comfortable working minority on a 'Third Way' platform. Thus, for the first time there was alternation in government, with the PS government lasting a full term. In 1999, the PS renewed its mandate, but was unable to complete a full parliamentary term in office. Prime Minister Guterres resigned on the night of the local elections, and new legislative elections were held in March 2002 (Freire and Lobo 2002). No party emerged with an absolute majority, but the PSD formed a coalition with the conservative right-wing (*Centro Democrático Social-Partido Popular*—CDS-PP).

An analysis of the effective number of parliamentary parties in Portugal shows that it has decreased substantially since 1987, largely due to the concentration of votes in the two largest centre parties, the PS and the PSD.[5] This trend continues, with the combined PS and the PSD vote share climbing to 77.7 per cent in 2002. Thus, since 1976 the party system has evolved from a relatively polarized and fragmented system to a bipolar and majoritarian one.

The constitutional revisions of 1982, which sought to curtail presidential power, coupled with the party system changes described, have led to claims that the system has become presidentialized. According to Moreira (1989: 36):

> The [1987 legislative] elections must be understood as a triumph for the prime minister, who broke party barriers, and not as a triumph of the party which served as a platform for him. So, we must consider that these elections provoked a regime change, without a constitutional reform [...] we suggest calling it presidentialism of the prime minister.

This opinion was not readily accepted in presidential quarters, with President Soares vehemently refuting such a regime characterization (Soares 1992: 37). However, the Portuguese public seem to perceive the growing power of the prime minister. Successive opinion polls, carried out in 1978, 1983, and 1993, asked the Portuguese to list the most powerful national institutions and found that the prime minister has always been perceived as more powerful than the council of ministers (Bacalhau 1993). And although the prime minister was not considered as important as the president in 1978 or 1983, perceptions of the relative power of these two actors had clearly changed a decade later, by which time Cavaco Silva had held the premiership for eight years. Thus, in 1993, 50.3 per cent of those interviewed considered the prime minister to be the most powerful political office, whereas the council of ministers maintained its perceived share of importance, and the president's decreased. Evidently, the combined impact of constitutional and party system changes was not lost on the Portuguese people. This provides a cue for the remainder of this chapter.

THE PARTY FACE OF PRESIDENTIALIZATION[6]

Leaders in Portugal have generally been considered pre-eminent within their parties, as a result of the conditions in which the major parties were created, and the rules governing the internal distribution of power (Lobo 2002). The real questions here, however, are whether leadership power has increased within the parties since democratization, and whether parties and leaders have become more autonomous of each other.

An analysis of modes of election of national executive bodies of the four main Portuguese parties reveals some differences. The Communist Party

(*Partido Comunista Português*—PCP) is the most centralized party from this perspective,[7] and the centre-right PSD and the conservative CDS/PP the most decentralized, in that their national congresses elect the national executive bodies.[8] The PS (*Partido Socialista*) is an intermediate case in which there have been successive statutory changes, sometimes centralizing, other times decentralizing, the process of electing the national executive (Lobo 2002: 261–3). That said, one can discern a creeping trend of presidentialization in the two largest parties, the PS and the PSD. In 1998, the Socialist Party introduced direct election of the secretary-general by the rank-and-file members; candidates must have gathered the signatures of at least 1,000 members.[9] In effect, this innovatory process, while democratizing, serves to enhance the leader's autonomy of party activists. In the PSD, there have also been recent calls for direct election of the party leader. At the party congresses in 1999 and 2001, a growing faction declared itself in favour of this change, but did not manage to gather enough votes to carry the motion. Once again, the objective seems to be the sidelining of party activists, who in the PSD have traditionally held powers with respect to the election of national bodies and the choice of parliamentary candidates.

Candidate-selection in Portugal is orientated towards the needs of the list PR electoral system. Apart from the PSD, which has a *de jure* decentralized process, all other parties can be considered relatively centralized in respect of this function (Freire 2001b: 45–55). Yet it is necessary to distinguish between official party statutes and actual practice. Thus, during the period when Cavaco Silva was prime minister and PSD leader, it seems that his *de facto* power was even greater than the statutes suggested, and moreover was contingent on the electoral success of the party; this suggests a degree of intra-party presidentialization (Lobo 2002: 264). Cavaco Silva (2002: 278) explained thus his growing role in parliamentary candidate selection by 1987: 'On the one hand my authority in the party had grown [after two years as prime minister]. On the other, the chances of a large rise in PSD voting in the upcoming elections increased the number of seats to distribute.'

With regard to party election programmes, analysis of the statutes shows that, where it is regulated, the process is relatively centralized. In the PSD, the party's national council has to approve the general outline of the programme. Only the PSD and the CDS-PP formally regulate the formation of coalition governments; in both cases, it is the national council which deliberates on coalition with other parties. Regarding the composition of government, only the PSD states that its national political committee has to approve it. Despite this power, from a constitutional perspective, it is the prime minister who proposes the members of government. Thus, Cavaco Silva (2002: 103) recalls that 'I had total freedom from the party to choose the members of government, for the entirety of my time as prime minister.' In coalition governments, it is necessary to discuss the composition with other parties. Even then, however, the prime minister has a veto power over the rest of the parties in government.[10]

Despite the statutory obligations of the PSD, and the agreement needed when there are coalition governments, there is evidence that in matters of government formation the Portuguese prime minister has been able to 'govern past parties' through the use of independent nominees in government. This phenomenon is not recent to Portugal, but stems from the implantation of democracy. Both the centre-right PSD governments and the centre-left PS governments have included a substantial number of individuals who were not affiliated to the governing party. In the case of the PSD, in 1985, 40 per cent of junior ministers were independents, with the proportion decreasing to 30 per cent in 1987 and 15 per cent in 1991. In the Guterres governments, 31 per cent of ministers were independents in 1995, and 28 per cent in 1999 (Lobo 2002: 266). The two parties thus have somewhat different patterns of recruitment to government, with independents more likely to be appointed as ministers by the left, and as junior ministers by the right. Still, both patterns evidence the capacity of the prime minister to ignore the party in constructing cabinets. However, it is striking that the number of independent members of the PSD governments (1985–95) decreased over time. This trend points to a 'partification' of government rather than its presidentialization.

Finally, have leaders become more dependent on electoral results? Again, there is variation among parties. Looking only at legislative elections, the PCP's leader is clearly immune to poor party results. Carlos Carvalhas presided over the collapse of the Communists' vote in the 1990s, and yet his unrivalled leadership of the party endured. However, other party leaders have apparently become more dependent on election results. The small CDS/PP brought in three leaders between 1991 and 1995 in an attempt to prevent the party's continued electoral decline. In the PSD, party resignations up to 1985 were largely motivated by struggles over intra-party factionalism, rather than election results. In 1995, however, Cavaco Silva resigned as party leader, partly in anticipation of poor electoral results at the following elections.

On the left, whereas the Socialists' 'historic leader' Mário Soares suffered a series of electoral defeats in 1979 and 1980 without any consequence for his power, António Guterres resigned as prime minister and party leader in December 2001, largely because of expectations of poor performance at the forthcoming elections. That said, the current incumbents as PSD and PS leaders, Durão Barroso and Ferro Rodrigues, have withstood legislative election defeats, in 1999 and in 2001 respectively. Overall, the power of party leaders now seems more contingent upon electoral results, though this is obviously not the only significant factor.

Overall, we might say that, in the Portuguese case, the circumstances of democratization helped generate a high degree of personalization of party politics from the outset, a feature since overlaid by the tendency of major party leaders to enhance their intra-party power resources and autonomy in various ways. What of leadership power within government?

THE EXECUTIVE FACE

The growth of prime ministerial power in Portugal can be understood from an analysis of the policy-making instruments the head of government has at his disposal. In essence, the resources available to the prime minister have been strengthened since 1987 through the reorganization of the prime minister's office and support structures, and through the nomination of ministers without portfolio to oversee other ministers' work.

Analysis of the resources of the Presidency of the Council of Ministers (PCM)—in effect, the Portuguese Cabinet Office—reveals an increase in spending on prime ministerial support structures from 1989 onwards. Interestingly, this increase in resources has been geared towards the PCM's political bodies—that is, those freely nominated by the PM—rather than its bureaucratic structures: with the exception of 1992, it is the former which has predominated in expenditure terms.[11] The increased expenditure on political support has been shared almost equally between the prime minister's *cabinet*[12] and his ministers without portfolio (respectively enjoying growth of 53 per cent and 55 per cent). By 1995, the prime minister's *cabinet* absorbed 58.2 per cent of the political support budget. Clearly, then, since the late 1980s there has been a conscious effort to direct resources towards the prime minister's critical support structures.

Within the PCM, the prime minister's *cabinet* is the only body specifically responsible for providing support for prime ministerial action.[13] Initially, it should be said, its size and purpose was quite limited compared to similar bodies elsewhere in Western Europe. A decree-law of 1977 stipulated the number of advisers allotted to each governmental post, entitling the prime minister to a maximum of ten advisers and four secretaries.[14] A report issued in 1985 on the functions of the prime minister's *cabinet* observed:

Given the information available, it is estimated that the prime minister's *cabinet* has very scant intervention in the legislative process. We do not know what kind of support the *cabinet* provides for the purpose of preparing Council of Ministers' meetings; everything suggests, however, that the *cabinet* provides essential personal and political support to the prime minister (Bragança 1985: 23).

Thus, in the mid-1980s, the *cabinet* did not seem to fulfil the function of providing policy advice to the prime minister.

However, from 1985 onwards (under Cavaco Silva), the number of personnel and the competencies attributed to the *cabinet* increased. Thus, the *cabinet* came to include an extra twenty expert policy advisers, each with his or her own own portfolio.[15] In addition to these policy specialists, there were three people employed to deal exclusively with the prime minister's relationship with the media. Interestingly, Cavaco Silva's chosen advisers were generally not senior PSD members because, the prime minister did not want to bring the 'party' into his *cabinet*. It is important to stress that even under Cavaco Silva, prime minister's *cabinets* were hardly formidable structures of policy support: they were relatively small, were not partisan, and functioned at the margins of governmental activity. Still, the reinforcing of *cabinet* structures since 1985 can reasonably be seen as an attempt by the prime minister to increase his autonomy from the party and from other members of government. To this extent, it is consistent with the concept of presidentialization which we are investigating in this book.

Ministers without portfolio have also been used by Portuguese prime ministers to further their political power. They are seen as trouble-shooters and progress-chasers for the prime minister, and are thus a reflection of his power to influence others and control government. Those nominated have been loyal party supporters of each prime minister, and in two cases replaced them as party leaders, with the premier's blessing. When Mário Soares resigned as PS leader to run for the presidency in 1985, he supported António Almeida Santos to take his place. A decade later, in 1995, Fernando Nogueira was chosen as PSD leader, to facilitate Cavaco Silva's (unsuccessful) presidential bid. In short, the growing number of ministers without portfolio can be regarded as a measure of the personalization of government leadership.

Whereas ministers without portfolio have been a tool for Portuguese prime ministers throughout the democratic era, Cavaco Silva resuscitated and exploited an office created during the dictatorship, namely that of Minister of the Presidency. This may have contributed to the presidentialization of the executive by insulating the prime minister from certain procedural and political matters: that is, by removing the need for the prime minister to take direct responsibility for these mundane issues he is left more free to concentrate on a strategic, coordinating role. The incumbent is a loyal facilitator of the prime ministerial will, which affords the prime minister simultaneously greater power resources and autonomy from the rest of government. Again, this is consistent with the general impact of the overall increase in resources available to the Portuguese prime minister since the 1980s.

Moving beyond the question of the resources at the disposal of the prime minister vis-à-vis other members of government, it is important to enquire whether the working methods in government tend towards the collective or the individual, and whether there have been changes in this respect. Our model of presidentialized government places greater emphasis on bilateral decision-making methods (involving the head of the executive and individual ministers) and less emphasis on collegial decision-making in the Council of Ministers.

Qualitative research conducted on Portuguese government ministers[16] reveals a distinction between policy and 'political' issues.[17] With respect to the former, ministers concurred that the council of ministers was central to decision-making. Until 1985, the lack of preparatory work in committees meant that the Council was overwhelmed by the detail of policy issues, leading to very long and tedious meetings, and leaving no time for political debate. Ministers from all governments between 1976 and 1985 complained about council of ministers meetings for these reasons. From 1987 onwards, Cavaco Silva instituted a weekly junior ministers' meeting, chaired by the minister of the presidency, at which technical matters would be discussed, with the objective of decreasing the number of unresolved issues facing the council of ministers. Parallel to this, Cavaco Silva institutionalized regular bilateral meetings with ministers in which the latter were obliged to account for their actions and the extent to which the government programme was being fulfilled. These occasions presented the premier with an opportunity to provide feedback and direction to individual members of the government: the coordinating potential of this is self-evident (Silva 2002: 124–5).

The council of ministers has generally not been the preferred venue for strategic political coordination. Until 1987 such matters were rarely on the agenda of the council of ministers, primarily because the meeting was over-burdened with concrete policy issues; discussion of the main political issues of the day was secondary (Lobo, 2005: 247). Although it was the practice of some prime ministers, such as Sá Carneiro, Balsemão, and Cavaco Silva, to start council of ministers meetings by making a summary of political events, this was essentially a monologue rather than a discussion.

Instead, political decision-making occurred increasingly in an inner cab-inet, formed around the prime minister and including mostly senior party members (see Table 12.1). The Sá Carneiro government, a right-wing coali-tion which lasted from 1979 to 1980,[18] was the first to institute an inner cabinet, which met weekly. According to Freitas do Amaral, Minister of Foreign Affairs in that government, this meeting was 'an informal gathering each Friday, where political action for the following week was planned, including a discussion on the most delicate political issues, such as the relationship with the president and the political image of the government. This was one of the secrets of success of the first AD (*Aliança Democrática*) government, for it gave a clear political guidance to the government.'[19] Between 1983 and 1985, during the PS–PSD coalition, there were also meetings to coordinate political issues, although according to Rui Machete, Minister of Justice at the time, they were ad hoc.[20] On the contrary, ministers interviewed who belonged to Cavaco Silva's governments, attributed great importance to the 'inner' cabinet. Thus, a common trait of Portuguese governments' decision-making both before and after the 1987 electoral watershed has been the formation of inner cabinets to decide on political issues. These inner cabinets are one of the preferred working methods of Portuguese prime ministers, and constitute evidence that political decisions are collective even though they do not include the whole of the government. This has to be taken into account when assessing the degree to which there is a trend of intra-governmental presidentialization in Portugal. That said, note that whereas in the AD coalition government the inner cabinet included ministers from different parties, under Cavaco Silva it included mostly the premier's most fervent supporters. Thus, it is possible to conclude that the inner cabinet itself gradually came to act as a structure which empowered the prime minister, rather than as a collective decision-making body.

Table 12.1 shows the party and ministerial positions of the members of inner cabinets since 1979. It is clear from this that most inner cabinet members were also senior party members. It may perhaps seem obvious that in a coalition, such as the Sá Carneiro or Soares governments, there should be restricted meetings for political coordination consisting essentially of coalition party leaders. However, that they are also used under single-party governments attests to the enduring importance of parties and party links in political decision-making. Under Cavaco Silva's successive executives the composition of the inner cabinet did not change substantially, but its members' positioning within the PSD became more firmly entrenched: thus, in 1985 two members of the inner cabinet did not belong to the National Political Committee, the highest PSD body, but by 1991 they were all members of that body. It is not the party as an organization which is important, or the party in parliament, but the members of the National Political Committee who are also ministers. The message of Table 12.1 is that political decisions remain collective in Portuguese government, even if they are not open to the entire Council of Ministers; that is, parties continue to be central to political decisions, since practically all members of inner cabinets are senior party members.

Thus, it is clear that after 1985 there was a concerted effort to improve the working of the core executive by reinforcing the position of the prime minister. However, not all of the innovations discussed in this section can be considered to constitute the presidentialization of government. Bilateral meetings and the strengthening of the prime minster's cabinet are clear signs of this tendency, but the centrality of inner cabinets composed of senior party members is not. The evidence on presidentialization is thus mixed concerning the intra-governmental sphere: in certain respects the power resources and the autonomy of the prime minister have undeniably been enhanced, but parties continue to play a significant role.

TABLE 12.1. *The party positions of inner cabinet members in Portugal*

Government	Inner cabinet members	Government portfolio	Senior party position
AD 1979–80 (PSD-CDS-PPM)	Sá Carneiro	PM	President PSD
	Balsemão	Minister Adjoint to PM	National Political Committee (NPC)—PSD
	Freitas do Amaral	Foreign Minister	President CDS
	Amaro Costa	Defence Minister	President of Political Committee—CDS
	Pulido Valente	State Secretary to PM	None
PS-PSD 1983–5	Mário Soares	PM	Secretary General PS
	Mota Pinto	Vice PM	Leader of PSD
	Rui Machete	Minister of Defence (then Vice PM)	Vice President of NPC—PSD (1983–4)
	Ernâni Lopes	Finance Minister	Independent
	Jaime Gama	Foreign Minister	Permanent Council PS
	Almeida Santos	State and Parliamentary Affairs	Permanent Council PS
PSD minority 1985–7	Cavaco Silva	PM	Leader of PSD
	Fernando Nogueira	Minister Adjoint and Parliamentary Affairs	Member of NPC—PSD
	Eurico de Melo	Minister of Interior	Member of NPC—PSD
	Santana Lopes	Junior Minister for PCM	Member of National Council PSD
	Marques Mendes	Junior Minister to Minister Adjoint	Member of NPC—PSD
	Durão Barroso	Junior Minister to Minister of Interior	Member of NPC—PSD
PSD majority 1987–91	Cavaco Silva	PM	Leader of PSD
	Eurico de Melo	Vice PM and Defence, until 1990	Member of NPC—PSD
	Fernando Nogueira	Minister of Presidency and Justice until 1990, then Presidency and Defence	Member of NPC—PSD
	Dias Loureiro	Minister for Parliamentary Affairs	Member of NPC—PSD
	Santana Lopes	Junior Minister Culture from 1990	Member of NPC—PSD
	Marques Mendes	Junior Minister for PCM	Member of NPC—PSD
	Durão Barroso	Junior Minister Foreign affairs	Member of National Council PSD
PSD majority 1991–5	Cavaco Silva	PM	Leader of PSD
	Fernando Nogueira	Presidency and Defence	Member of NPC—PSD
	Dias Loureiro	Minister of Interior	Member of NPC—PSD
	Marques Mendes	Minister Adjoint to PM	Member of NPC—PSD
	Durão Barroso	Minister of Foreign Affairs 1992–5	Member of NPC—PSD

Note: The politician is considered a senior party member if he was elected to a national body at the previous party congress. In the PS, membership of the political committee, or the permanent committee of the political committee, as well as secretary-general, are considered senior party positions. In the PSD, membership of the National Political Committee (NPC), the Permanent Committee of the NPC, or of the National Council, are considered senior party positions.

THE ELECTORAL FACE

Concerning the electoral face of the presidentialization thesis, there are two lines of investigation which can be pursued: first, the growing personalization of electoral campaigns, including the degree to which the media focus on party leaders (McAllister 1996) and parties concentrate their campaign efforts on their leaders; and second, the influence of party leaders on electoral behaviour. Research in Portugal on these matters is relatively limited, but here we can attempt to review available evidence in order to present a picture of certain observable trends.

The 'old campaign politics' was fundamentally the product of party decisions, party organizations, and party activists (McAllister 1996: 185). The party controlled not only the message but in many cases the medium through which the message was conveyed due to wide circulation of party newspapers and the importance of grass roots campaigning. By contrast, the 'new' campaign politics has at its core the displacement of parties as the monopolizers of the channels through which their message is conveyed to electors. There is a widespread consensus that campaigning has undergone a modernization process in the past few decades (Schmitt-Beck and Farrell 2002: 9). This process is a complex phenomenon which imparts a marketing logic to political campaigns. This logic has been the cause and consequence of the professionalization of campaigning, often through the outsourcing of what used to be party activities, namely marketing and the commissioning of opinion polls.

As Pasquino has argued (2001: 184), given the timing of democratization in southern Europe, one ought to expect campaign politics to be a mixture of old and new techniques. Parties had from the outset access to direct means of communication such as television, which may have served as an additional factor in the personalization of party politics, and as an inhibitor of the full development of more traditional campaign styles such as door-to-door campaigning by local party activists. Expert analyses of successive elections concur that campaign politics is relatively personalized in Portugal.

In two elections in particular, namely those in which Cavaco Silva and the centre-right PSD obtained parliamentary majorities in 1987 and 1991, there was consensus on the importance of the leader in the election result. In 1987 the PSD victory was largely unexpected. According to Goldey (1992: 172), those who had supported a motion of censure that precipitated these elections 'underestimated Cavaco and his popularity': the prime minister, 'with the help of a compliant state television, campaigned hard and effectively for a majority'. On a similar note, and for the same election, Corkill (1988: 249) noted that 'The party [PSD] had a clear objective—to obtain a majority—and a strong personality as its leader [who] attracted the vote which was regarded as crucial in the quest for a "historic majority".' In 1991, the PSD retained its parliamentary majority. Here the result seemed to be even more dependent on the personality of the prime minister, especially given the party's poor results in the local elections of 1989. According to Calder (1992: 168), the parliamentary majority 'must be credited to Social Democratic leader, Cavaco Silva': indeed, his campaign was personalized to the extent that it 'was presented by the PSD as a referendum on its leader's personal abilities'. When Cavaco Silva resigned as prime minister and leader of his party shortly before the 1995 elections, Corkill argues that 'the PSD was deprived of a major electoral asset' (Corkill 1996: 403). In the elections of 2002, the governing PS was obliged to find a new leader at the beginning of the campaign since António Guterres had resigned after the local elections of December 2001, as explained above. Perhaps because neither of the main contenders for the post of prime minister had any previous experience of the job, the campaign was less personalized and rather more centred on programmes (Freire and Lobo 2002). Even so, this campaign had a discernibly 'presidential' aspect. Whereas access to public television is strictly regulated by law and ensures equal access to all parties who are running in the election, the private television channels (which have existed since 1992 in Portugal) have more room for manouevre. In 2002 one of the private channels staged a debate between the leaders of the PS and the PSD, Ferro Rodrigues and Durão Barroso. This adversarial confrontation between the two men most likely to become prime minister was heavily criticized by both the CDS-PP and the PCP, who argued that the private media were presidentializing a campaign which should have been about the election of parliamentarians, rather than a prime minister and his team of government ministers.

In summary, some leaders, due to their government experience or historic role in democratization, have been perceived as major electoral assets for their parties: Soares, Sá Carneiro, Cavaco Silva, and Guterres, for a certain period, all fall into such a category. To be sure, not all leaders are so regarded, but even so, private television channels have tried to presidentialize legislative elections by focusing on the confrontation between the main parties' leaders, thereby reinforcing the growing bipolar and majoritarian tendency of the Portuguese party system described above.

It is also necessary to bear in mind the way in which the semi-presidential nature of the regime—especially the direct election of the president—serves to personalize and presidentialize all elections (Pasquino 2001: 192). Periodically, a senior party member, often a leader and ex-prime minister, has to position himself above his party, in order to have a real chance of becoming the president of the republic. This is due to the fact that the winner needs to build a broad coalition of support in order to win an absolute majority of the valid votes which are cast. As in France, if this is not achieved by any candidate in the first round of elections, a second round is held, at which only the two best supported candidates from the first round run off against each other. The presidential election is by its very nature a candidate-centred affair and it has consequences for other elections in that it periodically serves to place parties in the background and leaders at the centre of media attention.

Two factors are symptomatic of the importance of party leaders in determining electoral behaviour in Portugal: the declining level of party identification (Katz 1996), and the relatively high level of electoral volatility from one election to the next. Both of these reflect the comparative weakness of social cleavages as structural determinants of the vote in the country, which leaves the way clear for more contingent and short-term influences, including leader effects.

Unfortunately, data on partisanship in Portugal are very limited, but Eurobarometer surveys provide some indication of this aspect of the country's political life between 1985 and 1994. During these years the percentage of respondents who identified with a party was actually slightly above the EC average. Thus, in the 'EC9' (that is, the states that were EC members prior to the accession of Portugal, Spain, and Greece) between 1985 and 1992 the average percentage claiming a partisan attachment was 58.3 per cent; in Portugal, the corresponding figure between 1985 and 1994 was 60.6 per cent (Schmitt and Holmberg 1995: 126–7). At that point, then, Portugal fared well compared to other West European democracies (and was experiencing an upward trajectory). However, a post-election survey carried out in Portugal after the March 2002 elections revealed that there had been a significant decline in party identification since 1994.[21] In this survey only 52 per cent of respondents admitted to any kind of identification with a political party. Therefore, the last decade seems to have coincided with a significant erosion of partisanship among Portuguese voters.

Portugal experienced two of the ten most volatile European elections between 1945 and 2000 (Gunther and Montero 2001: 87). This is an indicator that social cleavages are not very strong, especially since much of that volatility is inter-bloc, that is, involves voters switching allegiance between parties of left and right (ibid.: 124).[22] The relative insignificance of social cleavages in explaining voting behaviour suggests that short-term factors, such as voter evaluations of party leaders, could play a strong part in determining the outcome of elections, and Gunther and Montero have demonstrated that this is indeed the case. In fact, they discovered this to be so even in 1993—when partisan identification had not yet started to erode in Portugal. Specifically, evaluations of party leaders explained little of the electoral support for parties on the extremes of the left-right spectrum (the Communists and the Popular Party), but were significant in accounting for the vote achieved by the two centrist parties, explaining 13 per cent and 14 per cent of the variance in support for Social Democrats and Socialists, respectively. This confirms that, as we might expect, the more deeply anchored the voters are in cleavage-based party blocs, the less of an independent contribution the 'party leadership' factor makes to electoral choice. Conversely, the more weakly rooted a party's electoral support is in distinct social or ideological blocs, the greater the extent to which voters' attitudes towards individual party leaders can affect electoral behaviour (ibid.: 130–1).

More recently, the Gunther and Montero model of voting behaviour has been used to test the importance of party leader evaluations for voter choice in the 2002 legislative elections. This study found that such evaluations remain a very important explanatory factor in Portugal, second only to ideology in respect of the five main parties (Lobo, 2006). But interesting differences between parties of Left and Right emerged: whereas left-wing voters chose between the PCP and the PS mainly on ideological grounds, right-wingers, probably due to the greater ideological proximity to the CDS and the PSD, relied far more heavily on leader evaluations in deciding which to support.

Thus, the decline of partisan attachment and the relative weakness of cleavage politics ensure high levels of electoral availability in Portugal, making way for the presidentialization of electoral politics. Research into the importance of party leadership for voting behaviour indicates that it matters considerably in explaining support for the two largest parties. These developments are all consistent with the phenomenon of presidentialization as defined in this book, and are perhaps to be expected in view of the catch-all nature of the PS and the PSD.

CONCLUSION

In this chapter we have reviewed the extent to which presidentialization is discernible in Portugal. Intra-party developments and the growing concentration of intra-executive power around the prime minister tend to confirm the thesis. Governing parties—especially the two centre parties—have traditionally been relatively personalized. This historic trait is due in part to the late democratization of politics and to the turbulent context in which these parties were founded. This existing personalization has been enhanced by changes in the mode of election of party leaders in the PS. Moreover, it is evident that party leaders have considerable autonomy from their parties when it comes to choosing the members of government. Indeed, in Portugal it is common for leaders to appoint non-party figures to control policy portfolios. At the same time, there is some evidence to suggest that PS and PSD leaders' power is now more contingent on electoral success than hitherto.

It is very clear that, since 1985 a considerable effort has been made in financial and organizational terms to ensure that the prime minister is in a better position to control and coordinate decision-making in government. However, not all of the changes effected have served to presidentialize the executive. It is useful to distinguish between policy and political coordination in government: whereas the prime minster may have enhanced his power in the former domain through greater recourse to bilateral decision-making with specific ministers, strategic political decisions are generally taken by a core group of ministers who are also senior party members. This indicates that parties remain central to key governmental processes in Portugal, thus serving to mitigate the notion of a presidentialized prime minister.

As regards electoral presidentialization, there are signs of eroding partisanship and weakly structured voting behaviour, which imply greater scope for the influence of more contingent short-term factors such as leader evaluations. Recent research confirms the importance of such evaluations in explaining voter choice.

Therefore, there are trends that indicate presidentialization is at work, although the evidence is not unequivocal. In particular, the importance given to parties in government decision-making is a strong indicator of their enduring importance in Portuguese politics. Still, it is undeniable that there has been a strengthening of the position of prime minister, as well as an increase in his autonomy vis-à-vis the party, so long as the electoral results are positive. At the root of these developments are the constitutional, party system, and media changes, in a context of deepening European integration. The impact of the latter process, although hard to quantify, should not be overlooked. It has been argued that Portugal's entry into the EC in 1986 has diminished the capacity of the national parliament to hold the government accountable for its decisions (Barreto 1999). The transfer of decision-making from national to supra-national arenas has undoubtedly helped to increase autonomy of the government vis-à-vis other national institutions, which may reinforce the presidentialization process. Beyond this, the 1982 constitutional reform allowed for the civilianization of the regime, and decreased the powers of the president in 'normal' circumstances. Subsequently, the concentration of electoral support around the two major parties guaranteed governmental stability, a stronger premier, and more candidate-centred electoral processes, fuelled by the private media's pressure to presidentialize electoral contests.

NOTES

1. The author would like to thank all project participants for their input at the meetings in Copenhagen (2000) and Sussex (2002). Particular thanks are due to Paul Webb, Thomas Poguntke, and António Araújo. Any remaining faults are my responsibility.

2. Cavaco Silva (Portuguese Prime Minister, 1985–95) in *Expresso*, 18 January 1992.
3. Following the military involvement in the transition to democracy, the first president of the Republic was a General, and the council of the revolution was a body with oversight powers composed exclusively of military officers.
4. This enabled the president to delay the promulgation of laws.
5. For detailed analysis of recent changes in the Portuguese party system, see Bruneau (1997); Magone (1998); Manuel (1996); Morlino (1998); and Nataf (1995).
6. In addition to the references listed in the text, this section draws on the following party document: 'Acordo Político, Parlamentar e de Governo celebrado entre o PS e o PSD', in *Fontes para a história do Partido Socialista*, cd-rom, Lisboa: Fundação Mário Soares, Section IV.
7. PCP Statutes (1992); see www.pcp.pt.
8. PSD statutes (2000) and CDS/PP statutes (2000).
9. PS Statutes (1998), Article 59.
10. In the coalition government between 1983 and 1985, however, the parties concerned agreed that all ministers should be chosen by the prime minister and the vice prime minister together.
11. The large increase in bureaucratic support expenditure in 1992 was due to the creation of a legislative database centre within the PCM, the *CEGER*, which computerized all existing Portuguese legislation in order to assist policy-makers. This extraordinary expenditure does not negate the trend of growing preponderance of political structures within the PCM.
12. The term cabinet is used here to denote the prime minister's staff of personal advisers, rather than the body of senior governmental ministers.
13. This section draws on interviews with two prime ministerial *chefs de cabinet*, Alfredo Barroso (11 November 1998) and Honorato Ferreira (11 May 1999), who served Mário Soares and Cavaco Silva, respectively. Barroso was Soares' *chef de cabinet* in the first constitutional government, and Ferreira served Cavaco both as economic adviser (1985 to 1991) and *chef de cabinet* (1991 to 1995).
14. Decree Law No. 267, of 2 July 1977, Article 10. Ministers could employ up to three advisers and two secretaries; junior ministers could employ two advisers and two secretaries; ministers of state, ministers without portfolio, and ministers for Madeira and the Azores, were entitled to eight advisers each, and four secretaries, with the prime minister's permission. In addition, ministers and secretaries of state could employ an extra three people.
15. There were nine portfolios in the *cabinet* between 1991 and 1995: Diplomatic, European Affairs, Economics, Social Affairs, Press and Media, Administrative, Military, and Political. Each portfolio had two or three advisers, producing a total of twenty-two advisers for Cavaco Silva.
16. This section draws on interviews conducted with government ministers. Between 1998 and 2000, two prime ministers, twenty-five ministers, nine junior ministers, and three civil servants in the PCM were interviewed. Since many ministers had held office more than once, the total ministerial experiences amounted to forty-nine, and the number of junior ministerial experiences to nineteen. The partisan breakdown was as follows: ten PS members (including three junior ministers); twelve PSD members (including one junior minister); four CDS members

(including two junior ministers); one PPM member (no junior ministers); and six independents (including two junior ministers).

17. In this context, 'political' refers to relations with other institutions, namely parliament, parliamentary groups, and the president of the Republic, as well as to matters of inter-party relations in coalitional situations. Policy issues are of course also political, but it is necessary to take into account the instability of the first decade of democracy, and the sometimes difficult relationship between prime minister and president, to appreciate the importance of this distinction.

18. This coalition included the centre-right PSD, the conservative CDS-PP and the monarchist party PPM (*Partido Popular Monárquico*). It was a pre-electoral alliance (known as *Aliança Democrática*) which won the 1979 and 1980 elections. It eventually collapsed in 1982 with the resignation of the prime minister due to intra-party conflict.

19. Interview with Freitas do Amaral, 11 November 1999.

20. Interview with Rui Machete, 5 June 2000.

21. The survey was part of a project entitled 'Portuguese Electoral Behaviour and Political Attitudes in Comparative Perspective'. This applied the questionnaire designed by the Comparative Research on Election Systems network, a group of national election studies coordinated by a team at the University of Michigan.

22. For an account of the various measures of electoral volatility, see Bartolini and Mair (1990). For further detail on levels of volatility in Portugal, see Lobo (1996) and Freire (2001a).

REFERENCES

Araújo, A. (2003). 'El Presidente de la República en la evolución del sistema político de Portugal', in B. Gómez, A. Barreto, and P. Magalhães (eds.), *El Sistema Político de Portugal*. Madrid: Siglo XXI.

Bacalhau, M. (1993). *Atitudes, opiniões e comportamentos políticos dos portugueses: 1973–1993*. Lisboa: FLAD.

Barreto, A. (1999). 'Portugal: Democracy through Europe', in J. J. Anderson (ed.), *Democracy and Regional Integration*. New York: Rowman and Littlefield.

Bartolini, S. and P. Mair (1990). *Identity, Competition and Electoral Availability*. Cambridge: Cambridge University Press.

Bragança, J. V. (1985). *Reorganização da Presidencia do Conselho de Ministros*. Lisboa: PCM.

Bruneau, T. (1997). *Political Parties and Democracy in Portugal: Organizations, Elections and Public Opinion*. Oxford: Westview Press.

Calder, C. (1992). 'An Orange sweep: The Portuguese General Election of 1991', *West European Politics*, 15: 2.

Canotilho, J. G. and V. Moreira (1991). *Fundamentos da Constituição*. Coimbra: Coimbra.

Corkill, D. (1988). 'Portugal's Political Transformation: the Election of July 1988', *Parliamentary Affairs*, 41: 246–57.

—— (1996). 'Portugal Votes for Change and Stability: the Elections of 1995', *West European Politics*, 14: 4.

Duverger, M. (1980). 'A New Political System Model: Semi-presidential Government', *European Journal of Political Research*, 8: 165–87.

Freire, A. (2001*a*). *Mudança Eleitoral em Portugal Continental, 1983–1999: Clivagens, Economia e Voto nas Legislativas*. Oeiras: Celta.

—— (2001*b*). *Recrutamento Parlamentar—Os Deputados Portugueses da Constituinte à VIII Legislatura*. Lisboa: STAPE.

—— and M. C. Lobo (2002). 'Portuguese Election Report', *West European Politics*, 25: 221–8.

Foley, M. (1993). *The Rise of the British Presidency*. Manchester: Manchester University Press.

Gunther, R. and J. R. Montero (2001). 'The Anchors of Partisanship', in N. Diamandouros and R. Gunther (eds.), *Parties, Politics and Democracy in the New Europe*. Baltimore: Johns Hopkins University Press.

Goldey, D. (1992). 'The Portuguese Elections of 1987 and 1991 and the Presidential Election of 1991', *Electoral Studies*, 11: 171–6.

Jones, G. W. (1991). 'Presidentialization in a Parliamentary System?', in C. Campbell and M. J. Wyszomirski (eds.), *Executive Leadership in Anglo-Saxon Systems*. Pittsburgh: Pittsburgh University Press.

Katz, R. S. (1996). 'Party Organizations and Finance', in L. LeDuc, P. Norris, and R. Niemi (eds.), *Comparing Democracies*. London: Sage Publications.

Linz, J. and A. Stepan (1996). *The Politics of Democratic Consolidation*. Baltimore: Johns Hopkins University Press.

Lobo, M. C. (1996). 'A evolução do sistema partidário Português à luz de mudanças económicas e políticas (1976–1991)', *Análise Social*, 139: 1085–116.

—— (2002). 'A elite partidária em Portugal: dirigentes, deputados e membros do governo', in A. Freire and A. C. Pinto (eds.), *Elites, Sociedade e Mudança Política*. Oeiras: Celta.

——, (2005), *Governar em Democracia*. Lisbon, ICS.

——, (2006), 'Short-term Voting Determinants in a Young Democracy: Leader Effects in Portugal in the 2002 Legislative Elections', in *Electoral Studies*, 25, pp. 270–286.

Magone, J. (1998). 'Portugal: Party System Installation and Consolidation', in M. Donovan and D. Broughton (eds.), *Changing Party Systems in Western Europe*. London: Pinter, 232–54.

Manuel, P. C. (1996). *The Challenges of Democratic Consolidation in Portugal: Political, Economic and Military Issues, 1976–1999*. London: Praeger.

McAllister, I. (1996). 'Leaders', in L. LeDuc, P. Norris, and R. Niemi (eds.), *Comparing Democracies*. London: Sage Publications.

Moreira, A. (1989). 'O Presidencialismo do Primeiro-Ministro', in M. B. Coelho (ed.), *Portugal, o Sistema Político*. Lisboa: ICS.

Morlino, L. (1998). *Democracy Between Consolidation and Crisis: Parties, Groups and Citizens in Southern Europe*. Oxford: Oxford University Press.

Nataf, D. (1995). *Democratization and Social Settlements: The Politics of Change in Contemporary Portugal*. Albany: SUNY Press.

Pasquino, G. (2001). 'The New Campaign Politics in Southern Europe', in N. Diamandouros and R. Gunther (eds.), *Parties, Politics and Democracy in the New Europe*. Baltimore: Johns Hopkins Press, 183–223.

Schmitt, H. and S. Holmberg (1995). 'Political Parties in Decline?', in H-D. Klingemann and D. Fuchs (eds.), *Citizens and the State*. Oxford: Oxford University Press.

Schmitt-Beck, R. and D. Farrell (2002). *Do Political Campaigns Matter?* London: Routledge.

Silva, A., Cavaco (2002). *Autobiografia Política*. Lisboa: Bertrand.

Soares, M. (1992). *Intervenções (vol. 4)*. Lisboa: INCM.

Sousa, M. R. (2000). *A Revolução e o Nascimento do PPD*. Lisboa: Bertrand.

13

The Failure of Presidential Parliamentarism: Constitutional versus Structural Presidentialization in Israel's Parliamentary Democracy

Reuven Y. Hazan

In no parliamentary democracy has the presidentialization of politics achieved such magnitude as in Israel, where in the 1990s it took the form of constitutional change. Yet the consequences of this phenomenon were so negative that the change was abolished less than five years after it was first implemented.

In 1992, the Israeli parliament, the Knesset, adopted a law that altered not only the electoral system, but also Israel's constitutional framework.[1] According to this law, Israel would become the first parliamentary democracy in which the prime minister was directly and popularly elected. However, after taking office, the prime minister could be removed by a no-confidence vote supported by a bare majority of the Knesset (61 of the 120 members). This development produced a unique constitutional system in which a 'presidentialized' prime minister was grafted onto an essentially parliamentary democracy. In the light of these developments, this chapter addresses the following questions:

- First, did the constitutional reform in the 1990s reflect a *de facto* change that had already taken place? In other words, is it appropriate to speak of a phenomenon of presidentialization occurring within Israel's parliamentary democracy prior to the 1990s? Did the constitutional reform simply make the implicit explicit, or was it a radical departure from the brand of parliamentarism which had hitherto obtained?
- Second, what were the causes and consequences of constitutional presidentialization? What structural factors acted as constraints on the constitutionally presidentialized prime minister? How did these outcomes affect the political parties, electoral competition, political

representation, legislative behaviour, legislative-executive relations, and
other associated factors?

- Third, how does Israel's experience of the presidentialization of politics
  compare with other modern democracies? Were the political and electoral attributes of leadership powers amplified by factors flowing from
  the formal constitutional change?
- Fourth, how does Israel's rather extreme experience of the presidentialization of parliamentary democracy contribute to the assessment of this
  phenomenon?

FROM *DE FACTO* TO CONSTITUTIONAL PRESIDENTIALIZATION

Structural and contingent sources of change across the three faces

From the late 1940s, when Israel achieved independence, until the early
1990s, the political system in Israel was purely parliamentary, inspired by
the British model. The Knesset was elected according to the most proportional system in existence.[2] The electoral system in Israel consisted of one
national constituency, with fixed party lists and a legal threshold set at only
1 per cent of the valid vote. The Hare quota was used for seat allocation until
1973, and after that the Hagenbach-Bischoff quota (with results identical to
d'Hondt). The outcome was a multiparty system, with no less than ten parties
represented in the Knesset, and usually at least a dozen. No party ever won
a majority, leaving the government in the hands of coalitions that often
included five or more parties and were based on a political culture of
power-sharing (Hazan 1999*b*).

During this period, the office of the prime minister was strengthened over
time, at the expense of the parliament, the parties, and the ministers. This
happened for two main reasons: first, structural-institutional provisions;
second, the contingent personalities of the prime ministers. Institutional
provisions changed over the years from the objectives first outlined in the
Government Yearbook of 1949. The formal institutional definition of the
prime minister's office at that time was minimalist—coordination and organization of the government. Since then, the scope of the prime minister's
office has increased significantly. For example, ministerial committees, which
have the delegated authority to make policy decisions in place of the government, were formed in the prime minister's office. These committees expanded
over time, starting with four established by Israel's first prime minister, and
currently numbering approximately fifty. These committees deal with issues
relating to the jurisdiction of several ministries, and together they oversee all
areas of government involvement. The institutionalization of the ministerial

committee system enhances the power of the prime minister for several reasons: (i) appointments to ministerial committees are decided in a closed circle, where the prime minister is most influential; (ii) the prime minister can participate in, and even chair, any committee meeting; (iii) the work of ministerial committees is secret; and (iv) the committee system allows the prime minister to deal with only the committee members, rather than with the full government.

By the early 1960s, the Government Yearbook had already redefined the prime minister's office to reflect a more activist role, entrusted now with agenda-setting and policy-initiation. At times, the prime minister's office concentrated mainly on formulating guidelines and initiatives for the ministries to carry out, and at other times, it was directly involved in their implementation as well. By the late 1970s, the prime minister's office evolved into an increasingly centralized organ, with the formation of sub-cabinets on many salient issues that were headed by ministers without portfolio under the prime minister and entrusted with policy-making, evaluation, and implementation of special programmes. Occasionally, a team or staff within the prime minister's office was formed in order to constrain, or even counter, the activities of particular ministries.[3]

The prime minister's institutional powers have also been strengthened statutorily. The initial version of the 'Basic Law: The Government,' enacted in 1968, established the authority of the prime minister over all aspects of government activity, including its rules of procedure—decisions on which the ministers could only appeal. The revised 1992 version of this law subjected all the rules and procedures of the government to the prime minister's discretionary authority. For example, the prime minister determines the agenda of government meetings. Ministers can propose that items be included on the agenda, but cannot force a discussion.

In 1981, a new law was passed that allowed the prime minister to dismiss a minister—a power that until then he was not *legally* able to wield. By the early 1990s, the increased executive functions of the prime minister's office, and the diminishing role of the individual ministers, were manifested by the creation of the 'prime minister's staff', which fostered a phase of clear personalization. For example, this staff helped the prime minister and his director-general carry out government policy according to the prime minister's priorities. It also at times coordinated with, and took control of the ministries, and intervened heavily in policy-making, to the extent that several ministers complained of the infringement of their authority and responsibility. The 1992 reform even revoked the collective responsibility of the government, and made the individual ministers directly responsible to the prime minister alone.

The cumulative effect of these institutional provisions was a continuous transformation of the position of prime minister and a formalization of his dominant position. As Arian and his colleagues (2002: 48, 147) argue: 'While by design the prime minister...has been *primus inter pares*, in practice all Israeli prime ministers have been *primus*...The twin trends of executive governance in Israel since the establishment of the state are expansion and consolidation.' Yet the sources of *de facto* changes in the working mode of the Israeli parliamentary system were not just structural. While the structural factors pushed Israel towards a presidentialized working mode, they were amplified by contingent changes.

The clear leadership role played by Israel's first prime minister, David Ben-Gurion, is an example for the impact of the contingent factors which include personal attributes. Being one of the nation's 'founding fathers', he dominated the Mapai Party, which led all Israeli governments until the late 1970s and was the predominant party in the party system (Hazan 1998). Ministerial appointments—at least in those important offices that the main party controlled—and continued tenure in office became increasingly dependent on the prime minister. By the late 1970s, when Menachem Begin—the undisputed leader of the Likud party—became prime minister, the office became even more active in dealing directly with the most pressing issues, including those that the prime minister personally addressed and those of great national importance.

In contrast to the highly fragmented Knesset, the executive has traditionally been highly unified, and policy-making has been firmly in the hands of the prime minister. Party discipline, a dominant party, and unchallenged party leadership during Israel's first three decades culminated not only in executive encroachment on the legislature, but outright defiance of the latter by the former. The legislature can attempt to influence the substance of policies, primarily through coalition politics and a strong committee system, but it rarely initiates them. Moreover, within the executive we see prime ministerial encroachment on the government. Indeed, Israeli politicians and the Israeli public expect the prime minister to be the predominant figure and to play a leadership role. Prime ministers who have emphasized consensual, collegial decision-making have been criticized for being weak and indecisive. The most important policy initiatives, in terms of both domestic and foreign policy issues, have by and large been initiated by the prime minister.

In order to assess personal leadership styles, it is important to look at Israeli politics after 1977, when the first rotation in government took place. Between then and the implementation of the electoral reform in 1996, Israel had four prime ministers, three of whom embarked on personal policy initiatives that changed long-standing commitments of the government and the political parties involved: in the 1970s, Menachem Begin introduced the land-for-peace formula in the peace agreement with Egypt; in the 1980s, Shimon Peres instituted the stringent economic stabilization plan that reined in hyper-inflation; and, in the 1990s, Yitzhak Rabin started the peace process with the Palestinians. All three cases are characterized by the central role of the prime minister.[4]

The managerial style of each prime minister was quite different. Begin was a clear leader who allowed only a few trusted advisers to affect his policies. Peres was a manager who preferred consensus to conflict. Rabin was removed from political intricacies, but did not allow any major policy decision without his approval. Regardless, all three practically ignored the political parties, the legislature, the government ministers, the media, and the public until a decision was all but made.

During Begin's negotiations with Egypt, only Foreign Minister Moshe Dayan knew of the preparations and the details. One must remember that Dayan was not a member of Begin's party. The Defence Minister, who was from Begin's Likud Party, was not informed of developments and subsequently resigned. When the outlines of the agreement were reached, Begin reported to his ministers that a meeting had occurred with Egypt's President Anwar Sadat, but not the content of the talks. When the proposal of autonomy for the Palestinians was discussed, which was eventually included in the peace agreement and was much more far-reaching than either the Likud party platform or the coalition agreement, Begin decided to bring it neither to the government nor to the party central committee. As the negotiations became more intense, the circle of those whom Begin consulted grew smaller. To Camp David, Begin took a team of top civil servants, as if they were the prime minister's staff, and kept most of his veteran political colleagues at home. Despite this blatant bypassing, the latter supported his proposals when they were finally put before the government, with minor reservations. Dayan (1976: 173) wrote, 'I served in the governments of Ben-Gurion, Eshkol, and Golda Meir. But never had I seen ministers bending so completely to the will of the prime minister.'

Peres, on the other hand, combined centralization with coordination, keeping many ministers ignorant of policy initiatives while co-opting as many as needed in order to advance his desired policies. He relied heavily on experts, rather than politicians. He worked in stages, exploring alternatives with experts, providing the chosen ministers with extensive briefings by policy specialists, steering decisions to different forums, mediating, and delaying until he felt the moment was right. The full details were decided in complete secrecy, outside the party, parliament, government, and media. For example, when the economic stabilization plan was to be approved, the government meeting was called immediately after a regular cabinet meeting adjourned, to avoid any political or public input; and it was finally approved after a 19-hour marathon session—the longest in Israeli history.

Rabin, unlike Begin and Peres, was not a politician, but entered politics after a distinguished military career. He was private and intent on maintaining control. When secret negotiations began between Israel and the

Palestinians, only a handful knew of them. As the process progressed, Rabin kept most of the relevant information from the parliament and even his government. He was just as reticent with his closest colleagues, who considered resigning when they realized what had transpired. For example, the Declaration of Principles between Israel and the Palestinians (the 'Oslo Agreement') was signed on 20 August 1993, nine days before the Israeli government knew anything about it. However, once the policy initiative was unveiled, the ministers supported it overwhelmingly.[5]

Begin, Peres, and Rabin, like dominant leaders before them, made extensive use of the growing powers that the office of prime minister afforded them. Indeed, they exploited the possibilities presented to them. By relying on personal advisers and keeping most of their colleagues in the dark, they qualitatively shifted the locus of power to the prime minister, and changed the way power was exercised.

One consequence of the earlier structural presidentialization was a gradual shift from collective to individual control over the formulation of governmental programmes. This process was accompanied by—and also encouraged—parallel shifts within the political parties, such as the growth of the leader's power and a greater emphasis on the leader during election campaigns. There were other structural factors that played an important role as well, such as the international nature of Israel's most pressing political problem, foreign affairs, and security—which would become its dominant dimension of electoral competition—and helped pave the way toward structural presidentialization.[6] The gradual, *de facto* shift toward greater personal visibility, accountability, and power subsequently led to formal changes in institutional arrangements. The Israeli prime minister, during the era of pure parliamentarism and in spite of the multiparty nature of both the Knesset and the governing coalitions, continually reinforced and consolidated his power. The trend of formal strengthening resulted in the clear predominance of the prime minister over the government, and of the government over the parliament.

The *de facto* presidentialization of Israel's parliamentary democracy was therefore in effect long before the direct election of the prime minister was adopted. In other words, the definition of the prime minister's position as *primus inter pares* gradually eroded. Thus, it is quite appropriate to speak of a phenomenon of presidentialization occurring within Israel's parliamentary democracy prior to the 1990s, and it entailed both structural and contingent sources of change.

The electoral-constitutional reform in the mid-1990s, however, did not simply make the implicit explicit, but was quite a radical departure. Moreover, as will be shown below, the electoral reform strengthened the prime minister *constitutionally*, but undermined much of the prior *de facto* concentration of power in his hands.

Constitutional presidentialization

The monumental reform of the 'Basic Law: The Government' changed the electoral, political, and constitutional systems in Israel.[7] This law—originally enacted in 1968, amended in 1992, and completely overhauled in 1996—made Israel the first country to elect its prime minister directly, concurrently with the parliamentary elections (see Fig. 13.1). The prime minister was elected using the two-ballot system—similar to French and Russian presidential elections—thus requiring an absolute majority. However, each of the three direct elections of the prime minister featured only two candidates, as Table 13.1 shows. The Israeli Knesset continued to be elected by an extreme form of proportional representation on the same day as the first round of the prime ministerial election.

The electoral reform had a profound effect on the constitutional form of the government itself. The directly elected prime minister had the power to nominate the government, but a parliamentary vote of investiture was required before the government could take office and begin to function.[8] At any time during the prime minister's tenure, he could be ousted by a parliamentary vote of no-confidence, carried by a bare majority of 61 out of the 120 Members of Knesset (MKs). However, removal of the prime minister in this fashion would have brought about the dissolution of the Knesset as well, heralding new elections for both.[9] By the same token, the prime minister had the power to dissolve the Knesset, though this would have ended his tenure as well, and once again forced new elections for both.

The main constitutional effect of the new law was that Israel ceased to be a purely parliamentary democracy, thanks to its direct election of the prime

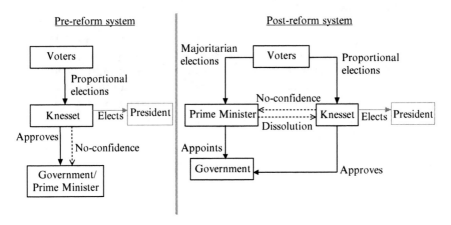

FIG. 13.1. *The pre- (1948–96) and the post-reform (1996–2003) electoral and political systems in Israel*

TABLE 13.1. *Prime ministerial election results*

29 MAY 1996			17 MAY 1999			6 FEB 2001		
Candidate	# Votes	%	Candidate	# Votes	%	Candidate	# Votes	%
Benjamin Netanyahu	1,501,023	50.5	Ehud Barak	1,791,020	56.1	Ariel Sharon	1,698,077	62.4
Shimon Peres	1,471,566	49.5	Benjamin Netanyahu	1,402,474	43.9	Ehud Barak	1,023,944	37.6

minister. Under parliamentarism, the executive emerges from and is responsible to the legislature—a fusion of powers—whereas under presidentialism, there is a separation of executive origin and survival from the legislature. As of 1996, with the direct election of the prime minister, the head of the executive branch no longer emerged from the legislature but was separately elected. The direct popular election of the prime minister dismantled the parliamentary system that Israel had used since its creation. Israel thus no longer belonged to the parliamentary regimes category, yet, neither did it cross into the presidential category, because while the prime minister was elected separately, he continued to be responsible to the Knesset and was a member of it—an apparent violation of the separation of powers principle.

Israel moved closer to being 'semi-presidential', like the French Fifth Republic. Semi-presidentialism (Duverger 1980), or premier-presidentialism (Shugart and Carey 1992), is a regime in which a directly elected president coexists with a government headed by a premier who rests on parliamentary confidence. In semi-presidentialism, a dual executive serves to apportion power between the executive and the legislature. When the directly elected president has the support of the legislature, power rests in the hands of the president. However, when the president is faced with a hostile legislative majority, the prime minister can take control of the reins of power. As Aron (1982: 8) wrote, 'the President of the Republic is the supreme authority as long as he has a majority in the National Assembly; but he must abandon the reality of power to the prime minister if ever a party other than his own has a majority in the Assembly.' This is also true for other semi-presidential systems, such as Finland and post-1982 Portugal, which have experienced opposing executive and legislative majorities.

This flexible and intermediate type of regime was not exactly the case in Israel, though. When the legislative and executive majorities coincided—the results of the 1996 and 1999 elections—Israel's political system functioned much like the French system does when the president has a supportive legislature. But, when the legislative and executive majorities did not coincide, there was no parliamentary-supported premier in Israel to lead a government backed by the legislature. In Israel, it was the directly elected prime minister himself who headed the government and rested on parliamentary confidence. So in this case, the Israeli prime minister, and the entire executive branch, found themselves confronting a hostile legislature, akin to the situation of divided majorities in a presidential regime—with the important difference that presidents cannot be removed from power by a hostile legislature. In the event when the directly elected prime ministers saw their legislative majorities collapse, their response was not to continue governing in a presidential manner—for example, by building ad hoc legislative coalitions on particular issues—but either to support early elections for both prime minister and parliament (as Netanyahu did in 1998) or to resign and hold new elections for only the prime minister (as Barak did in 2000).

THE CAUSES AND CONSEQUENCES OF CONSTITUTIONAL PRESIDENTIALIZATION

The implementation of direct elections for the prime minister had consequences for each of the faces of presidentialization outlined by Poguntke and Webb in Chapter 1. While this was largely expected in respect of the electoral and party faces, the changes experienced in respect of the executive were not only unexpected, they were also responsible for the subsequent abolition of direct elections.

Consequences for the electoral and party faces

In order to win the necessary absolute majority, the main parties understood that their prime ministerial candidates would have to attract voters from other parties. The race for the prime minister thus had to be 'above' parties. Their candidates, therefore, conducted campaigns that were practically devoid of any party connection. The major parties, for their part, not only accepted this clear priority and allowed the campaign to focus on the prime ministerial race, but held back from competing with the smaller parties, fearing that a challenge in the Knesset race would mean that the smaller parties would not support their candidate for prime minister. Both Labour and Likud were thus willing to sacrifice seats in the proportional Knesset election in order to win the majoritarian prime ministerial race.

Moreover, prior to both the 1996 and 1999 elections, Israel's two major parties created two separate election headquarters, one for the prime ministerial election and one for the Knesset election. Despite a series of struggles within each party concerning the prevalence of one campaign over the other, the result was the same in both parties: there was only one comprehensive campaign, not two, and the race for prime minister came first. Moreover, the

Knesset race was not only relegated to a position of secondary importance, it was largely *absent* from the campaigns of the two largest parties. Both parties thought, correctly, that whoever won the contest for prime minister would be able to form a supporting majority coalition in the Knesset. In short, it is plain to see that the prime ministerial candidates were able to usurp attention, finances, and organizational resources from their parties: the separate and predominant prime ministerial election thus increased the intra-party power of leaders.

The all-embracing focus in terms of party funds, campaign time, and organizational effort on the election of the prime minister culminated in the creation of cross-party alliances by the party leaders. These alliances, aimed at winning the necessary absolute majority in the prime ministerial contest, were not accepted with enthusiasm by the main parties. For example, in 1996, Netanyahu created a formal alliance between three parties to advance a single candidate for prime minister and a single list for the Knesset election. In exchange for the two smaller parties removing their prime ministerial candidates, they were allotted one-third of the seats on the joint Likud-led parliamentary list—a much higher percentage than any poll suggested they would obtain on their own. In 1999, it was Barak's turn to mould a joint list of three parties, with positions allocated to the minor partners on the Labour-led list in exchange for their support of his prime ministerial candidacy. In other words, the two main parties not only had most of their financial, electoral, and organizational efforts usurped by their leaders—who had but a single goal of winning the executive contest—but these same leaders were also willing to decapitate their own parties by paying a high price to the small parties in exchange for their support in the prime ministerial race: that price was paid in terms of their own parties' representation in parliament.

There were other elements as well that characterized this presidentialization of the electoral process in the Israeli case. When the Knesset adopted the direct election of the prime minister in March 1992, it also decided that this reform would not come into effect in the forthcoming elections that year, but only in subsequent elections. Regardless, the parties immediately started to gear up for the new system. Labour, for example, already adopted party primaries for choosing its prime ministerial candidate for the 1992 election. After selecting Rabin, the party then officially changed its name to 'Labour Headed by Rabin'—even though this was still a single-ballot, fixed-list national parliamentary election. Likud followed suit, and adopted party primaries after the 1992 election.

The kind of candidates the two main parties selected also changed dramatically. Instead of seasoned parliamentary veterans, who slowly and painfully climbed the party ladder, the electoral reform brought an entirely new type of candidate to the head of the party. Netanyahu was selected as leader of Likud at the start of only his second term in parliament, due to the personal characteristics he possessed that were now appropriate in a candidate-centred contest. Barak was chosen to lead Labour less than a year after being elected to parliament for the first time. The main parties in Israel thus entered a new era in which they were forced to 'accept' leaders who were thrust upon them—similar to the parties in the US—by the exigencies of the new electoral and political system that created a direct relationship between the head of the executive branch and the voters. Moreover, since the parties accepted their new leaders due to their electoral potential, once they lost an election they were immediately replaced: both Netanyahu and Barak announced their resignation from the party leadership as soon as the exit polls showed that they had lost.

Consequences for the executive face

Beyond their desire to strengthen the head of the executive, and thereby enhance governability, the reformers hoped that the direct election of the prime minister would also reduce the size, number, and influence of the smaller parties in the Knesset, without changing the proportional nature of the electoral system used to elect it. These smaller parties granted disproportionate influence to sub-groups in Israeli society, which resulted in governing coalitions that became more and more difficult to maintain. That is, the proponents of reform hoped that a separate ballot for the prime minister, with its requirement of an absolute majority, would reduce the prime ministerial race to the two main parties and encourage 'straight-ticket' voting in the second ballot for the Knesset, as well.[10] The results of the 1996 and 1999 Knesset elections were, however, quite the opposite. The availability of 'split-ticket' voting actually increased the multiparty composition of the Knesset, while the two main parties were decimated.[11] In other words, the electoral reform not only failed to attack the problem for which it was designed, but actually made it worse.[12]

Ballot-splitting—a hitherto unavailable option in Israeli elections—decreased the combined strength of the two major parties (Labour and Likud) from 76 to 66 seats in the 1996 elections, a reduction of 13 per cent, and then to 45 seats in the 1999 elections, a further reduction of 32 per cent. The sectarian parties—those representing a particular sub-group in society—increased their representation from 21 to 39 seats in the 1996 elections, a growth of 86 per cent, and to 47 seats in the 1999 elections, a total increase of 224 per cent. These included the religious parties, who represent the orthodox Jewish minority and whose seats increased from 16 to 23 in the 1996 elections, and to 27 in the 1999 elections; the Arab parties, who represent the national minority in Israel and whose seats rose from 5 to 9 in 1996, and to 10 in 1999; and the immigrants' parties, who represent the Russian ethnic minority, and won 7 seats for the first time in 1996, and 10 in 1999 (see Table 13.2).

Not only did ballot-splitting increase fragmentation in the Israeli party system, it reduced the strength of all of the main ideological and aggregating parties while it exacerbated sectarian tensions along the three main contentious cleavages in Israeli society: between religious and secular Jews; Arabs and Jews; and natives and immigrants. In other words, while the social

TABLE 13.2. *Pre- (1992) and post-reform (1996 and 1999) election results for the Israeli Knesset [number of seats]*

BLOC	PARTY	1992	1996	1999
Arab	Democratic Front for Peace and Equality	3	5	3
	United Arab List	2	4	5
	National Democratic Alliance[a]	—	—	2
Left	One Nation ▲	—	—	2
	Meretz ♥♣	12	9	10
	Labour[b] ♥♣▲	44	34	26
Middle	Shinui[c]	—	—	6
	Centre ♣	—	—	6
	Yisrael B'aliyah ♦♣▲	—	7	6
	Third Way ♦	—	4	—
Religious	Sephardi Torah Guardiansc ♥♦♣▲	6	10	17
	United Torah Judaism ♦♣▲	4	4	5
	National Religious Party ♦♣	6	9	5
Right	Likud[d] ♦▲	32	32	19
	Tsomet[e]	8	—	—
	Yisrael Beitenu ▲	—	—	4
	National Unity[f] ▲	—	—	4
	Moledet[g]	3	2	—
Total seats		120	120	120

♥   Parties (3) forming the 1992 coalition government headed by Prime Minister Yitzhak Rabin.
♦   Parties (6) forming the 1996 coalition government headed by Prime Minister Benjamin Netanyahu.
♣   Parties (7) forming the 1999 coalition government headed by Prime Minister Ehud Barak.
▲   Parties (8) forming the 2001 coalition government headed by Prime Minister Ariel Sharon.

[a] In 1996, the newly formed National Democratic Alliance ran together with the Democratic Front for Peace and Equality.
[b] In 1999, Labour joined with Gesher and Meimad to form a joint list called One Israel.
[c] In 1992 and 1996, Shinui was part of the Meretz alliance.
[d] In 1992, Likud ran alone and won 32 seats. In 1996, the joint Likud-Gesher-Tsomet list won 32 seats, of which 22 were Likud and 5 each were for Gesher and Tsomet. In 1999, Likud ran alone and won 19 seats.
[e] In 1996, Tsomet ran with Likud and won 5 seats (see note *d* above).
[f] In 1999, the newly formed National Unity party was based on splits from the Likud and the National Religious Party, and incorporated the Moledet party.
[g] In 1999, Moledet ran as part of the National Unity party (see note *f* above).

cleavages in Israeli society were kept at bay by a single-ballot electoral system and existential security issues which dominated politics, the adoption of a second ballot allowed these social cleavages to gain a substantial foothold in the party system (Lijphart et al. 2000).

The results of the only two instances of separate executive and legislative elections were, therefore, dramatic. The largest party list in the Knesset was reduced to its lowest point ever, while the parties representing the three sub-cultural minorities in Israeli society—religious Jews, Arabs, and immigrants—together gained more seats than the two largest parties in the Israeli party system. The increase in representation of the sectarian parties, compared to the two main parties, is presented in Fig. 13.2.

After the 1999 elections, the two largest parties together held only 45 seats—38 per cent of the total number of seats—which is the lowest number of seats they have ever won. The main party on the right, Likud, and the main party on the left, Labour, each won their lowest number of seats ever. While the reformers had hoped to strengthen the incipient bipolarization in Israeli politics, which resulted from the development of a competitive two-bloc structure from the mid-1970s, they instead brought about its breakdown and Balkanization.

The implications for governability in light of this decline, and the concurrent upsurge in sectarian representation, are clear. With direct elections, the

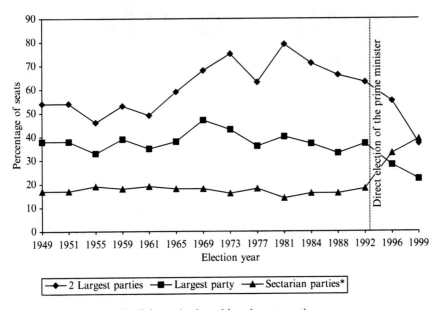

*Religious, Arab and immigrant parties.
Fig. 13.2. *Party seats in the Israeli Knesset, 1949–99 (total = 120)*

decision of who would be prime minister was no longer in the hands of party leaders, and no longer the result of extensive horse-trading in the process of creating a coalition government. Yet, while the directly elected prime ministers were able to create a supportive legislative majority coalition relatively easily—since the smaller parties could no longer act as king-makers but faced a simple decision of being in or out—they each confronted the increasingly difficult tasks of keeping the coalition intact and sustaining its legislative discipline. Ballot-splitting had eroded the size of the two major parties and increased the size and number of necessary coalition partners, thereby undermining the nucleus of automatic support for either prime ministerial candidate. The Likud Party in 1996 and the Labour Party in 1999, whose candidates won the first two directly elected prime ministerial contests and who headed the two subsequent coalition governments, did hold the largest number of seats in their respective coalitions, but they only constituted minorities within these coalitions (22 of 66 legislators in 1996, and 26 of 75 in 1999)—the only two times this had occurred in Israel's history.[13] The dominance of the prime ministerial race thus, paradoxically, served to weaken the governing capabilities of the directly elected prime minister.

The consequences of adopting a new electoral system in Israel, and the resulting presidentialized political system, are thus quite reminiscent of presidential systems that use proportional representation for their legislative elections, both empirically and theoretically (Shugart and Carey 1992: Ch. 11). However, the extent of divergence in electoral outcomes for the two branches was greater in Israel than in any of the other cases that use concurrent elections.

The need to include an ever growing number of parties, who were continuously increasing their share of parliamentary seats, forced the constitutionally presidentialized prime minister to allocate more government ministries and more of the national budget to his coalition partners, thereby further constraining his ability to govern and to control the agenda of government. For example, the average percentage of ministers from the prime minister's party in the twenty-six governments during the era of pure parliamentarism (1949–96) was about two-thirds, and never below 50 per cent.[14] In contrast, the governments formed by directly elected prime ministers had an average of just over 40 per cent of the ministers coming from their party, and never over 50 per cent. Moreover, the distribution of the national budget—measured by the budget-weighted portfolio allocations that each coalition partner obtained, divided by the number of seats the party had in parliament—shows that the smaller coalition partners did better than the larger (that is, the prime minister's) ones, particularly after the electoral reform (Nachmias and Sened 1999).

As regards voting behaviour, the availability of two ballots allowed each voter not only to split the ballot, but also to create a hierarchy of voting intentions for each ballot based on different motivations. Since the two prime ministerial candidates competed primarily on the dominant dimension in Israeli politics, that is, foreign affairs and security, the voters adopted this dimension as the main criterion for choosing a candidate. For Knesset elections, however, parties presented much more specific appeals as some of them correctly realized that, with more than one ballot available, it was now possible to compete on an entirely different dimension while remaining neutral on that of foreign policy and security. As a result, voters could now express a more particular identity. Voters were thus able to express both a national interest and a rather narrow social or ideological identity, by selecting from a multidimensional menu of parties on two distinct ballots. This is, again, precisely what one sees in presidential systems (Shugart and Carey 1992: Chapters 1, 2, and 9). The prime ministerial elections became the arena for general ideas—the 'representation of ideas' in Pitkin's (1976) words— while the Knesset became the arena for more precise ideas—the 'representation of presence' according to Phillips (1995). The political parties in the Knesset that either gained entrance or enlarged their representation—with the single exception of the Centre party in 1999—were the less aggregative ones which sought a more specific social or ideological voter base. Instead of social groups being represented *within* parties, they became represented *by* parties. Incentives for negotiation and compromise between social groups also decreased, due to the increased reflection of social cleavages in the party system.

The loss of almost one-half of the two main parties' seats, and the dramatic increase in the representation of sectarian parties, thus created a multidimensional party system with centrifugal social pressures. The two main parties did not try to preclude the possibility of vote-splitting by the electorate, but actually supported and even augmented this new phenomenon, which resulted in their own decline. The new, mixed electoral system did not produce the best of two worlds, but instead what Sartori (2000) calls a bastard parliament that served no purpose. The already overloaded Israeli political system (Horowitz and Lissak 1989) thus became even more burdened after the 1996 and 1999 elections.

The direct election of the head of the executive—constitutional presidentialization—thus failed to achieve its goal of enhancing the prime minister's powers of governing. On the contrary, effective prime ministerial governing capability was undermined due to the production of a sectarian-centrifugal Knesset via ballot-splitting (Hazan and Rahat 2000). In other words, the constitutional presidentialization of Israel's essentially parliamentary democracy served to undermine the structural presidentialization that had been in place before.

Moreover, the electoral reforms influenced legislative behaviour. During the 14th Knesset (1996–9), and the first two years of the 15th Knesset, the prime minister's coalition was defeated on numerous issues. Decisions taken by the government were overturned by the legislature due to the abstention of key partners, both in the coalition and within the prime minister's own party, who were holding out for increased pay-offs. The decline of the major parties and the rise of the sectarian ones made coalition maintenance a full-time, if practically impossible, task. The efforts of the government to pass its own legislation, or to thwart the opposition's popular and costly bills, largely failed. The annual budgets, for example, were revised by the coalition members in the finance committee, at times with the cooperation of the opposition, to an extent that was previously unknown in Israel.

The directly elected prime minister was unable to reign in the anarchy within both his coalition and his party, and repeatedly castigated his partners for their unruly behaviour. However, the reform should not have been expected to lead to increased executive control over the legislature because, indeed, the direct election of the head of government in democratic presidential systems expands the independence, not the compliance, of the legislature (Laver and Shepsle 1994).

Thus, the governing coalitions in Israel, after the implementation of direct election of the prime minister, exhibited behavioural characteristics that were significantly different from those that preceded it (Hazan 1997). The constitutional presidentialization actually made the prime minister's control of the legislative agenda and output an extremely difficult task, because it became institutionally easy for the evermore socially and politically fragmented Knesset to diminish both the prime minister's legitimacy and his effectiveness. Executive control over the legislature, another one of the electoral reform's goals, was not strengthened but rather weakened. So, while one of the major goals of direct elections was to increase governing capability, by enhancing the *de facto* presidentialization that had developed earlier, the actual result was constitutional presidentialization alone, 'virtual' dominance resulting from the electoral reform, at the expense of *de facto* presidentialization. That is, as both the popular source of legitimacy and the formal authority of the presidentialized prime minister expanded, so did his dependence on an increasingly fragmented and policy-incoherent coalition. The constitutionally more powerful prime minister was forced to spend more time and effort than ever before on maintaining, rather than on heading, the government.

One of the results of the increasingly apparent negative consequences of the electoral reform was that public support for the new system deteriorated decisively during the years it was applied, as shown in Fig. 13.3. In a 1992 survey, before it was implemented, three out of four Israelis thought the direct election of the prime minister would be a better system of government. By the time it was repealed in 2001, only one out of four thought it was a better system of government.[15]

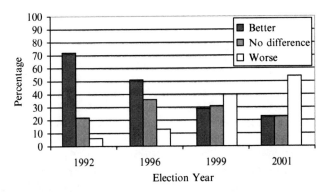

Fig. 13.3. *Assessing the direct election of the prime minister*

Question: 'Does the direct election of the prime minister make for a better system of government, a worse one, or does it not make any difference?'

Source: Israel Election Study 2001.

CONCLUSION: PRESIDENTIALIZATION, SEMI-PRESIDENTIALISM, AND PRESIDENTIAL PARLIAMENTARISM

In Chapter 1, Poguntke and Webb outline a model of presidentialization as a process by which regimes become more presidential in their actual practice, without necessarily changing their formal regime structure. Thus, the presidentialization of parliamentary democracy entails increasing leadership power resources and autonomy within the party and the executive, and increasingly leadership-centred electoral processes. Presidentialization flows across these three faces largely from structural and contingent, rather than constitutional, factors.

The formal-constitutional patterns are differentiated between distinct regime types: parliamentary, semi-presidential, and presidential. This is not a continuum, but a categorization based on three rigidly partitioned regime types. Thus, semi-presidentialism is not a half-way point between the two polar alternatives, but rather a constitutionally distinct regime.

The Israeli case, from 1996 to 2003, fell into the semi-presidential category, in so far as the executive leader was both separately elected and responsible to parliament. Despite the differences between Israel and other semi-presidential cases, such as France, Finland, and Portugal, it is clear that Israel no longer belonged to the parliamentary category, but neither did it enter the presidential type. The question that remains is how this rare form of constitutional innovation relates to the political and electoral aspects of *de facto* presidentialization outlined by Poguntke and Webb.

In terms of leadership power within the party, it is quite clear that the prime ministerial candidates were able to usurp attention, finances, and organizational resources from their parties, with little or no objection. The separate and predominant prime ministerial election thus increased the power of the leader within the party. Both Netanyahu and Barak, prior to their election victories, were able to solidify control of their respective parties by, for example, changing the composition of the central committees to include a majority of their supporters. After the election victory, the direct mandate gave the prime minister even more legitimacy and control over his party. For example, the allocation of ministerial portfolios was left completely to his discretion, which had hitherto not been the case.[16] However, while the prime minister had the power to organize his party's cabinet representatives without significant interference, he was forced to accept the dictates of those parties, ever increasing in number and size, that he would need in order to form a parliamentary majority and assume office. Moreover, the demise of his own party's parliamentary strength made his ability to head the executive and govern more difficult, rather than less, compared to the period before the constitutional reform. In short, the directly elected prime minister had a legitimate mandate and increased power within his party, but this did not translate into enhanced executive power and governing capability.

Of course, in other fragmented multiparty systems (such as Belgium and the Netherlands) we sometimes find this does not preclude the development of strong, 'presidentialized' prime ministers. However, in the Israeli case, the main effect of constitutional presidentialization was not only a further fragmentation of the party system, but a specific kind of breakdown based on sectarian issues that escalated centrifugal social pressures (Hazan and Rahat 2000). Such fragmentation, at the expense of the two main parties, made it practically impossible for the constitutionally strong prime minister to handle the situation by establishing himself as chief negotiator. While the directly elected prime minister could claim popular legitimacy, he became increasingly dependent on an extremely partified and socially centrifugal parliament that made any coalition tenuous at best.

Thus, although the directly elected prime minister was protected from pressures to oust him from both inside and outside his party, because the price for bringing him down was the dissolution of parliament,[17] this did not mean that he was protected from the daily pressures of running an increasingly heterogeneous and conflictual coalition. While his own party stood behind him, he lacked a majority in the governing coalition, due to the voters' tendency to split their ballots. Leadership autonomy for the directly elected prime minister in Israel was based on both electoral appeal and organizational control, rather than just on the former, due to the parliamentary aspects of Israel's transformed regime. In short, despite having leadership autonomy within the party, the prime minister did not have protection from political pressures, nor was his survival assured—the terms in office of all three directly elected premiers ended prematurely.

The electoral aspect of presidentialization, manifested in the personaliza-tion of the electoral process, has been the most evident that Israel has exhibited. Indeed, practically all aspects of the electoral contest were moulded by the personalities of the leading candidates during the period of direct election, and the predominance of this contest had significant spillover effects on the parliamentary elections as well (Hazan 1999*a*, 2001).

The repeal of the direct election of the prime minister prior to the parlia-mentary elections of 2003 has already reversed many of the developments evident during the period of reform, thus making an impact on each face of presidentialization (Kenig, Rahat and Hazan 2005). The power resources and the autonomy of the party leader within the party have diminished once again, since the leader no longer receives a separate and direct mandate from the electorate at large, but merely heads the party list. Prime ministers are once again elected because of and together with their party, rather than individually, and at times despite, their party.

Conversely, power resources and autonomy of the prime minister within the executive has been augmented by the repeal of direct elections. The simple fact that the prime minister's party was able to reverse its decline in 2003—it actually doubled its parliamentary strength—allowed the party not only to regain a majority within the coalition but also to reduce the number of necessary coalition partners. Governing stability and capability returned, permitting the prime minister once again to devote more time to heading, rather than maintaining, the government. Moreover, the weakening of the sectarian parties, which crippled the three directly elected prime ministers and their governments, diminished not only the centrifugal social tendencies in the party system but also the policy-incoherence of the coalition.

The electoral attributes of presidentialization have also been weakened by the repeal of direct prime ministerial election, but not to such a great extent. Despite the fact that there was no longer an individual ballot in the 2003 elections, the media remained largely candidate-centred in its coverage. The parties, which were practically absent in the two previous elections, returned to the forefront of the campaign but still took a secondary position to the leaders. The premature collapse of the government, and the 'snap' election, could help explain why the media did not internalize the full significance of the return to a single-ballot fixed party list electoral system and a purely parliamentary political system.

The conclusion from the Israeli case is that the various attributes of *de facto* presidentialization need not go hand-in-hand. The presidentialization of the electoral process does not necessarily lead to the presidentialization of executive or party power; they are thus not causally linked. While the electoral face of presidentialization might be amplified by factors that are contingent and structural as well as constitutionally formal, the executive face might be pushed closer to the 'partified' pole of the continuum rather than the presidentialized pole, and could actually be undermined by the unexpected and reciprocal consequences of electoral presidentialization. Although the directly elected prime ministers in Israel inferred that their personal mandate justified a more dominant role within the executive, the Knesset taught each of them that Israel had retained an essentially parliamentary form of government.

Israel was, after 1996, no longer purely parliamentary nor purely presidential, but was closest to being semi-presidential. However, since the Israeli case needed to be placed at two points simultaneously within the semi-presidential category—the electoral and party faces closer to presidentialized government and the executive face nearer to partified government—it might be fitting to distinguish it from the other semi-presidential cases. Therefore, when attempting to describe the institutionally unique and hybrid type of political regime in Israel between 1996 and 2003, it may be best, and most appropriate, to call it presidential parliamentarism (Hazan 1996).

Is the Israeli version of presidential parliamentarism the best of both worlds? Sartori (1994: 135; italics in original) declared, 'I believe that the case *against* the two extremes, pure presidentialism and pure parliamentarism, is a strong one. By the same token, I believe that the positive case *for* "mixed systems" is equally strong.' Regretfully, the Israeli version of a mixed system was not the best of both worlds, and might actually have been the worst (Hazan 2001). As Sartori (1994: 153) warned:

Presidentialism and parliamentarism are single-engine mechanisms. In the first system the engine is the president, in the second the engine is parliament . . . Semi-presidentialism is, instead, a double-engine system. However, since its two engines operate simultaneously, what if they start pulling in opposite directions and work against one another? While the French system is able to handle divided government, still the risk of having two counter-pulling engines cannot be ruled out.

The Israeli modification of semi-presidentialism allowed neither the principles of parliamentarism nor those of presidentialism to dominate, but rather created incongruous operating principles. The result was a presidentialized prime minister who, in order to govern and survive, relied on an increasingly polarized, fragmented, fractionalized, and sectarian parliament. This combination was dangerous, not only for the effectiveness of Israel's government, but also for the stability of its democracy.

The primary lesson to be learned from the Israeli case is that if presidentialization is not a result of structural developments in the sense outlined in the opening chapter of this book, such as the erosion of social cleavages, the changing structure of mass communication or the internationalization of politics, or derived from contingent factors such as prime ministerial personality, but flows from constitutional reform, then the latter must be properly designed in order not to undermine the efficiency and stability of the entire democratic system. Moreover, the Israeli case teaches us that long-term structurally derived developments can be undermined, or even reversed, by constitutional changes.

The Israeli decision to graft a majoritarian, presidentialized prime minister onto a proportional parliamentary infrastructure resulted in a unique constellation, and an extreme manifestation, of the presidentialization of politics in democratic societies. In the form that it took in Israel, it produced more negative consequences than positive results. Other countries have discussed the possibility of adopting such a system, but in light of the Israeli experience they should clearly think twice before embarking on such a perilous journey. Israel was able to extricate itself rather quickly from this debacle—others might not be as fortunate.

NOTES

1. The term 'constitutional' must be used with reservation in Israel, because the country lacks a codified constitution. Instead, a series of Basic Laws have been formulated and adopted over time. These Basic Laws, of which there are eleven, are the building blocks of the Israeli constitution-in-the-making. The term constitutional throughout this chapter refers to the formal legal framework of Israeli democracy.
2. Israel's proportionality was surpassed in 1956 by the Netherlands, when the Tweede Kamer was enlarged from 100 to 150 representatives.
3. Arian et al. 2002 (Chapter 3) describe the growth in prime ministerial power according to four distinct phases: 1949–66, characterized by the definition and specification of the office's functions and structures; 1967–77, marked by reorganization and concentration of power in the office; 1977–92, which was concerned with refining the organizational structures of the office; since 1992, the phase of personalization of the office (due to the direct election of the prime minister).
4. This section draws heavily on Chapter 6 of Arian et al. 2002.
5. Rabin's dominant leadership role in this process is partially responsible for his being singled out and subsequently assassinated by a person who wanted to terminate this policy.
6. It is fascinating to observe that, in *The Federalist Papers*, Alexander Hamilton pointed out that war naturally increases the power of the executive at the expense of the legislative authority, explaining that, 'the direction of war most peculiarly demands those qualities which distinguish the exercise of power by a single hand.' This phenomenon has recently manifested itself even in a presidential regime, for, after the attacks on New York and Washington on September 11, 2001, the United States is witnessing the most dramatic expansion in presidential power in a generation.
7. For a discussion of the politics leading to the electoral reform, see Diskin and Diskin (1995). For a description and analysis of the new system, see Hazan (1996, 1997). For contrasting opinions concerning this kind of system, see Bogdanor (1993), Lijphart (1993), and Sartori (1994).

8. If the Knesset did not approve the prime minister's government, the result would have been new elections for both the Knesset and the prime minister. It is interesting to note that this vote of investiture was not part of the original bill, but was added later during the committee phase. One of the proponents of the electoral-constitutional reform, who opposed the inclusion of such a vote of investiture, explained why it did not belong: 'The moment that one enables the Knesset, or that one says that the Knesset ought to express a vote of confidence in the prime minister, the meaning is that the Knesset is given the power to annul the mandate that the prime minister received from the people.' Uriel Lynn, Chairman of the Constitution, Law and Justice Committee, 21 November 1990. Quoted in Ottolenghi (2001: 122).

9. It is interesting to note that according to the original bill, in order for the Knesset to oust the prime minister it would have needed the support of at least 70 MKs, and not 61. This, along with the lack of a vote of investiture (see note 8), made the original bill more 'presidential' than the one that was eventually adopted, in that there would have been greater separation of powers.

10. It is rather striking that there was an expectation by the reformers that the prime ministerial race would be limited to only two candidates, even if they did prove to be right. After all, one would expect the two-round system to promote a first round with several candidates, which almost happened in 1999; see Shugart and Taagepera (1994). For a discussion of the expectations versus the results of the direct election of the prime minister, see Ottolenghi (2001).

11. Literature on divided government in the United States (Jacobson 1991; Fiorina 1992) is instructive on how this possibility could have been foreseen. Moreover, some of the political scientists in Israel warned of this danger while the electoral reforms were still under deliberation.

12. It is interesting to note that some of the smaller parties did not oppose the electoral reforms when they were deliberated and adopted. Maybe they were more confident of the 'rationality' of the Israeli voters, of their ability to split their votes, and of the unique opportunity the electoral reform would give them not only to survive, but to thrive.

13. This does not include the deviant cases of national unity (grand) coalitions, where neither of the two major parties comprised, by themselves, majorities within the coalition.

14. Again, this does not include the deviant cases of national unity (grand) coalitions, where the prime minister's party did not, by itself, comprise a majority within the government.

15. The return to a single-ballot parliamentary election, according to the 2001 version of *The Basic Law: The Government*, went into effect with the parliamentary elections of 2003.

16. Prospective ministers, and thereby members of the party leadership, lined up outside the prime minister elect's office—under the lights of the television cameras—and were each asked to enter for a few minutes to find out if and what portfolio they would be given.

17. This was the case unless those opposed to the prime minister could muster two-thirds of the parliament to oust him from office—a rare occurrence which was never achieved during the era of presidential parliamentarism in Israel.

REFERENCES

Aron, R. (1982). 'Alternation in Government in the Industrialized Countries', *Government and Opposition*, 17: 1.

Arian, A., D. Nachmias, and R. Amir (2002). *Executive Governance in Israel*. New York: Palgrave.

Bogdanor, V. (1993). 'The Electoral System, Government, and Democracy', in L. Diamond and E. Sprinzak (eds.). *Israeli Democracy Under Stress*. Boulder: Lynne Rienner.

Dayan, M. (1976). *The Story of My Life*. New York: Morrow.

Diskin, H. and A. Diskin (1995). 'The Politics of Electoral Reform in Israel', *International Political Science Review*, 16: 1.

Duverger, M. (1980). 'A New Political System Model: Semi-Presidential Government', *European Journal of Political Research*, 8: 2.

Fiorina, M. P. (1992). *Divided Government*. New York: Macmillan.

Hazan, R. Y. (1996). 'Presidential Parliamentarism: Direct Popular Election of the Prime Minister, Israel's New Electoral and Political System', *Electoral Studies*, 15: 1.

—— (1997). 'Executive-Legislative Relations in an Era of Accelerated Reform: Reshaping Government in Israel', *Legislative Studies Quarterly*, 22: 3.

—— (1998). 'Party System Change in Israel, 1948–1998', in P. Pennings and J.-E. Lane (eds.), *Comparing Party System Change*. Routledge: London.

—— (1999*a*). 'Israel and the Consociational Model: Religion and Class in the Israeli Party System, from Consociationalism to Consensualism to Majoritarianism', in R. K. Luther and K. Deschouwer (eds.), *Party Elites in Divided Societies: Political Parties in Consociational Democracy*. London: Routledge.

—— (1999*b*). 'The Electoral Consequences of Political Reform: In Search of the Center of the Israeli Party System', in A. Arian and M. Shamir (eds.), *The Elections in Israel 1996*. Albany: State University of New York Press.

—— and G. Rahat (2000). 'Representation, Electoral Reform and Democracy: Theoretical and Empirical Lessons from the 1996 Elections in Israel', *Comparative Political Studies*, 33: 8.

—— (2001). 'The Israeli Mixed Electoral System: Unexpected Reciprocal and Cumulative Consequences', in M. S. Shugart and M. P. Wattenberg (eds.), *Mixed-Member Electoral Systems: The Best of Both Worlds?* New York: Oxford University Press.

Horowitz, D. and M. Lissak (1989). *Trouble in Utopia: The Overburdened Polity of Israel*. Albany: State University of New York Press.

Jacobson, G. C. (1991). *The Politics of Divided Government*. Boulder: Westview.

Kenig, O., G. Rahat and R. Y. Hazan (2005). 'The Political Consequences of the Introduction and the Repeal of the Direct Elections for the Prime Minister', in A. Arian and M. Shamir (eds.), *The Elections in Israel 2003*. New Brunswick, NJ: Transaction Publishers.

Laver, M. and K. A. Shepsle (1994). *Cabinet Ministers and Parliamentary Government*. New York: Cambridge University Press.

Lijphart, A. (1993). 'Israeli Democracy and Democratic Reform in Comparative Perspective', in L. Diamond and E. Sprinzak (eds.), *Israeli Democracy Under Stress*. Boulder: Lynne Rienner.

Lijphart, A., P. J. Bowman, and R. Y. Hazan (2000). 'Party Systems and Issue Dimensions: Israel and Thirty-Five Other Old and New Democracies Compared', in R. Y. Hazan and M. Maor (eds.), *Parties, Elections and Cleavages: Israel in Comparative and Theoretical Perspective*. London: Frank Cass.

Nachmias, D. and I. Sened (1999). 'The Bias of Pluralism: The Redistributive Effects of the New Electoral Law in Israel's 1996 Election', in A. Arian and M. Shamir (eds.), *The Elections in Israel 1996*. Albany: State University of New York Press.

Ottolenghi, E. (2001). 'Why Direct Elections Failed in Israel', *Journal of Democracy*, 12: 4.

Phillips, A. (1995). *The Politics of Presence*. Oxford: Clarendon.

Pitkin, H. (1976). *The Concept of Representation*. Berkeley: University of California Press.

Sartori, G. (1994). *Comparative Constitutional Engineering: An Inquiry into Structures, Incentives and Outcomes*. New York: New York University Press.

—— (2000). 'The Party Effects of Electoral Systems', in R. Y. Hazan and M. Maor (eds.), *Parties, Elections and Cleavages: Israel in Comparative and Theoretical Perspective*. London: Frank Cass.

Shugart, M. S. and J. M. Carey (1992). *Presidents and Assemblies: Constitutional Design and Electoral Dynamics*. New York: Cambridge University Press.

—— and R. Taagepera (1994). 'Plurality Versus Majority Elections of Presidents: A Proposal for a 'Double Complement Rule', *Comparative Political Studies*, 27: 3.

14

The Semi-Sovereign American Prince: The Dilemma of an Independent President in a Presidential Government[1]

Sergio Fabbrini

INTRODUCTION

Since the 1960s, the electoral process in America has undergone a pronounced process of personalization. Candidates for the presidency have grown increasingly independent of the traditional party organizations. There has arisen a highly personalized process of selecting the presidential candidate: so personalized, indeed, that it has given rise to outright candidate-parties. However, this personalization of the electoral process has not been matched by an equivalent personalization of the system of government. There are both structural and contingent reasons for this circumstance. The structural ones reflect the nature of the American system of government, which is a system of *separated government* (Fabbrini 1998a; Jones 1994; Rockman 1984)—the arrangement by which the executive (the president) and the legislature (the congress) each enjoys its own electoral legitimacy, even if they are then obliged to share the same powers of government. As Neustadt (1990: 29), the most influential scholar of the American presidency of the past generation, puts it: 'The Constitutional Convention of 1787 is supposed to have created a government of "separated powers". It did nothing of the sort. Rather it created a government of separated institutions *sharing* power.'

Of course this sharing does not come about on equal terms; for in the nineteenth century it was Congress that held governmental pre-eminence, whereas in the twentieth century that pre-eminence has shifted to the president. Only when viewed in this light can the American system be termed a presidential system. The contingent reasons have to do with the progressive institutionalization—especially since the 1980s—of a practice of *divided government* within the system of separated government. Divided government occurs when opposing parties control congress and presidency (Fiorina 1992). Thus, having conquered the presidency on the basis of his personal resources, the president finds that he lacks the instrument essential for him to exercise that office to the fullest extent, namely a party able to link him with congress.

The difficulty of governing with a divided government was exacerbated by the end of the Cold War, because it deprived the president of a crucial reason for asserting his leadership. However, the dramatic terrorist attacks of September 11, 2001 reaffirmed the need for presidential leadership, but it could not resolve the problems that had led to the institutional weakening of the presidency. Thus, after the attacks, America found its *democratic prince*[2] again, but he was still a prince with only half his powers.

THE ELECTORAL AND PARTY FACES

Selecting the presidential candidate: The direct primary

Any study of presidential leadership in the United States must be linked with the analysis of its political parties, particularly in respect of their role in selecting presidential candidates. At the beginning of the nineteenth century, the United States saw the formation of the first modern party system, the purpose of which was that of organizing electoral competition for the several elective offices of the federal government. Given the separated nature of the system of government, the political parties historically performed the function of connecting congress and presidency, thereby making governmental action possible, albeit within the constraints imposed by a constitution designed to restrict such action (Schramm and Wilson 1993).

The ascent of the president (and therefore of the presidency) during the 1930s and 1940s reduced significantly the political role of the parties in American democracy. Parties were strong organizations as long as congress retained the central role in the federal decision-making process. As Milkis (1993: 5) has argued 'the Democratic Party became during the late 1930s the party to end all parties. Under Roosevelt's leadership, it was dedicated to a program that eventually lessened the importance of the two-party system and established a modern executive as the principal focus of representative government in the United States.' Nevertheless, although their importance was lessened, the parties continued to keep their strategic function in the first decades of the presidential era. That is, they continued to connect office-holders of the various governmental branches, or better, to organize the president's support within congress. The party-in-government (comprising the president and his party supporters in the congressional caucus) continued to be an effective organization, although its leadership was (at this time) clearly presidential. Moreover, presidential ascendancy helped to nationalize the parties' perspective, in conjunction with the nationalization of federal government (Lunch 1987).

This institutional equilibrium was seriously challenged in the 1960s. In the second half of the 1960s, as the country split over the military intervention in Vietnam, a deeply-rooted tangle of contradictions and conflicts came to the surface. The violence that exploded at the 1968 Democratic National Convention in Chicago imposed on the public agenda—with an urgency unprecedented even by the progressive experiences of the beginning of the century—the issue of democratizing the political parties, given that these, together with the country's other governing institutions, were now held in extremely low public esteem. As the reform of the political parties got under way in the 1960s it was not shaped by a specific party model (Crotty 1982). The reform process stemmed from a diversity of pressures and political cultures, but one of its main components was indubitably the anti-party tradition that drew its inspiration from the more populist variant of the Progressivism of the early 1900s (Crotty 1980). This inspired a democratization of political parties, especially in respect of the selection of presidential candidates; the outcome was the adoption of a selection process based on *direct primaries*.

Thus, America became the first, and to date, the only country to adopt the direct primary as a system for candidate-selection (specifically in respect of *presidential* candidates). In fact, for one of the foremost scholars in the field (Ranney 1990: 182), 'perhaps the sharpest contrast between nominating procedures in the United States and those in other democratic countries is provided by the U.S. use of direct primary.' Even in those European countries where primaries are used, they can be more properly defined as *party* primaries rather than *direct* primaries (Fabbrini 1998b: 76–104), in that the candidate is selected by the members of the party (and no longer exclusively by its leaders), but not by a variegated group of supporters. According to Ranney (1990), the direct primary is 'a procedure in which candidates are selected directly by the voters in government-supervised elections rather than indirectly by party leaders in caucuses or conventions'.

The first direct primary was held in Wisconsin in 1903 (Merriam 1908), but only in the last three decades of the twentieth century did it become the predominant system for selecting presidential candidates (Fabbrini 1993). After the *self-nomination* procedure adopted at the end of the eighteenth century, for the first two decades of the nineteenth century presidential candidates were selected by the *congressional caucus*, known as 'King Caucus', or rather, by the elite that had created the new constitutional republic. But the populist wind very soon began to blow against the elitist equilibria, and in the 1830s the introduction of the *national convention* system assigned the power of selection to the party leaders of the states and counties, removing it from the country's narrow federal oligarchy. After 1908, there was experimentation with a *mixed system* in which selection was still centred on the national convention but was influenced by the results of selected direct primaries. This system was scrapped at the end of the 1960s and replaced, in 1972, by a selection system based exclusively on *direct primaries*.

Thereafter, the primary system *de facto* superseded the national convention. It is true that in 1916, 53.5 per cent of delegates to the Democratic national convention and 58.9 per cent of delegates to the Republican national convention were selected by means of primaries, but by 1968 only seventeen states held direct primaries, and the delegates elected through them represented just 37.5 per cent of votes at the national conventions. Since 1972, more than two-thirds of convention delegates have been selected by direct primaries on the basis of their support for a particular presidential candidate. Indeed, by 2000, 84 per cent of Democrats and 89 per cent of Republican delegates to their respective national conventions were chosen in this manner (across forty states in both parties' cases: the remaining states organized caucuses). And by 2004, 86 per cent of the delegates to the Democratic Convention were chosen through the primaries (of course, the Republicans, having an incumbent president, didn't need to select their candidate). This is why the convention now does no more than formalize a decision—the choice of candidate—already made during the direct primaries (Ware 1988). In effect, the deliberative capacity of party conventions, and the decision-making power of the party elites which was traditionally emphasized by the conventions, have been neutralized.

The growth of candidate-centred politics

Of course, there are differences within the direct primary system with regard to exactly *who* is entitled to vote. Nevertheless, none of the primaries draws a clear distinction between the supporter and the voter; indeed, as far as possible, the direct primary system has entirely eliminated the distinction. Consequently, by being selected by those who then vote for them, candidates have been able to leapfrog the traditional party intermediation (Polsby 1983) between voters and themselves.

Reforms have institutionalized this in two ways: first, through changes to the composition and functioning of national conventions, and second, through new rules on campaign finance. With the elections of 1972, restrictive criteria were imposed on the representation of the so-called *unpledged delegates* not directly chosen in the primaries (or caucuses). In 1972 no more than 10 per cent of the delegates could be unpledged, simply representing the party organization or its legislative caucus in the state and federal legislatures. The percentage of unpledged delegates was reduced to 8 per cent in 1984 and then settled at 11 per cent during the 1990s. Furthermore, measures were introduced to ensure a more open debate at the convention (i.e., the abolition of the so-called 'unity rule' under which the local and state delegations were obliged to vote as an undifferentiated bloc), and to protect the decision-making autonomy of individual delegates (by putting an end to the last-minute *bandwaggoning* that had marked previous conventions). Although the constraints introduced in 1972 were subsequently relaxed, they continue to characterize the organizational set-up of the major parties' national conventions. The operational effect of this reform is clear: the candidate does not have (nor does he need to have) any form of dependence on the party in government (i.e., on the members of 'his' party in congress). But this also means that the latter feel no obligation to support a president chosen by others.

The second concerns the reform centred on the rules governing the funding of electoral campaigns (Malbin 1984; Sorauf 1992). Approved in 1971, and subsequently amended in 1976, the Federal Election Campaign Act (FECA) imposed tight controls on private financial contributions to electoral campaigns, and regulated public funding on a radically new basis. As regards private funding, the law stipulated that individuals and interest groups could contribute no more than $1,000 or $5,000 respectively, to a candidate's election campaign. As regards public funding, it determined that federal contributions to election campaigns should be directed to the candidates and no longer paid to the party's electoral committee. Both provisions were evidently intended to deprive the parties of control over resources of crucial importance. It is thus now the candidates who receive funds and support, and no longer the parties. Moreover, this candidate-centred process of running for office has become an extremely expensive activity (Donnelly et al. 2001).

The combined effect of these two directions of reform was a drastic cutback in the parties' electoral role. Since the 1970s the electoral process has undergone progressive and almost ineluctable change which works in favour of the candidate (Wattenberg 1991). The candidate has become the crucial actor of the electoral process, although that does not imply that electoral competition is a game based exclusively on personal qualities. With respect to the 2000 presidential elections, Bartels (2002: 69) remarked that 'what is surprising is not that the electoral impact of candidate traits was modest . . . (but that) the modest effect of candidate traits was . . . large enough to be decisive.' Thus, party politics still matters. Yet, in the context of declining levels of partisan identification among voters, evaluations of candidates' personal qualities generally count for more. And with regard to the presidential election in particular, the personalization of competition has become the most distinctive feature of the entire electoral process. Candidates now use their own resources, not those of their parties, to fund their campaigns: their reputations, their networks of campaign contributors and supporters, their policy preferences and their communication skills matter more than support from their parties.

Hence there no longer exists in America, at the federal level, the party— understood as a collective organization able to generate a relatively stable identification among voters. This is not to imply that the United States has become a democracy without parties. The American parties, in fact, have transformed themselves into support structures—equipped with formidable technologies—for individual candidates. It is as if the parties are now identified with their candidates in the sense that the latter connote the former and not vice versa. America is today a democracy of *candidate parties*. As Aldrich (1995: 288) remarks, 'by the 1960s an alternative means to office became a viable alternative to the older form of parties-in-the-electorate. It became technologically feasible for a candidate—to be sure, almost invariably a major party's affiliate—to substitute his or her own campaign organization for the party's. This became possible first at the presidential level.' Of course, the media coverage of the campaign adapted quite easily to this transformation, thus focusing more and more on the candidates rather than the parties. Although it seems implausible to detect a cause–effect relationship between the transformation of electoral campaign and the commercial evolution of political communication within the media, the personalization of electoral campaigning suited the media's growing preference for communicating over-simplified political messages.

In sum, parties have turned into highly efficient support organizations for candidates. That is, they are politically empty vessels (Katz and Kolodny 1994), even if they are endowed with technical and financial resources at the disposal of the chief (the candidate) who is able to take possession of them. Thus, after the reforms of the late 1960s, the party came to be 'designed around the ambitions of effectively autonomous politicians, responsible for their own electoral fates and therefore responsive to the concerns of their individual electoral constituencies' (Aldrich 1995: 289; see also Aldrich and Niemi 1996: 101).

THE EXECUTIVE FACE: THE PERSONALIZATION OF SEPARATED GOVERNMENT

The birth of the modern presidency: The domestic sources

If it is true that the electoral process has grown increasingly personalized, can one say that there has been an equivalent personalization of the separated government? In other words, has the *autonomy* which presidential candidates have acquired in the electoral process translated into increased *power* once in office, with respect to the other institutions of the separated government (and Congress in particular)?

It is well known that for a long period of time the presidency performed a role anything but central to the American political system (Pious 1996). Indeed, it was a prime concern of the founding fathers to give the presidency an exclusively executive function, while simultaneously protecting it against pressures imposed by the legislature (considered to be the more important institution, but one with the potential to impose a 'tyranny of the majority') and by public opinion. Throughout the nineteenth century, congress was able to preserve its place at the centre of governmental power as the main arena for defining the policy issues of concern to the country, or to sections of it. After all, the candidate for the presidency was selected by a method which guaranteed the pre-eminence of the congress.[3] And once the national party convention was adopted with 1830s, the congressional leaders were able to influence its outcome through their connections with the organizations and leaders of the local and state parties. Similarly, once the presidential candidates were selected by the parties, the congressional party leaders were able to influence the behaviour of the presidential electoral college through connections with state legislatures. Even when the college electors started to be chosen by popular vote, their election took place on the basis of party lists controlled by the leaders of the state legislatures in accordance with the leaders of the federal legislature. One way or another, then, presidents were conditioned by the congressional parties. In short, for almost the whole of the nineteenth century, congress had resources with which to control the behaviour and policies of the president, thereby celebrating the pre-eminence of state and local interests over national ones. In terms of this book's analytical framework, we might say that, though formally a presidential regime, the American executive was strongly 'partified'.

Not even authoritative presidential leaderships like those of Andrew Jackson (1829–36) and Abraham Lincoln (1861–5) were able to change this constitutional equilibrium, although they had extremely important effects on the party system and on relationships between public and private powers. Not surprisingly, therefore, this system of government was called a 'congressional government' (Wilson 1973 [1884]), or in other words, a system in which Congress was able to secure its decision-making pre-eminence over the other institutions of government (and the president in particular). This was because Congress appeared to be the only body whose legitimacy resided in the popular will, whereas the president was forced to resort to the constitution to legitimize his actions and claims. And, indeed, throughout that century, it was customary to talk of a 'constitutional presidency'.

This institutional equilibrium was severely undermined by the complex processes of economic and social change that traversed the country between the 1880s and the middle of the twentieth century. Internally, it was in particular the turmoil provoked by the Great Depression that imposed the need for urgent transformation of separated government into presidential government. The first two presidencies of F. D. Roosevelt (1933–40) are generally considered by scholars to be the ones that introduced the basic institutional and political innovations on which the modern presidency was founded (Rozzel and Pederson 1997). The creator of a new political order (or a 'regime builder'), Roosevelt was able to utilize the dramatic conditions of his time, and the climate of national emergency created by them, to impose an unprecedented presidential initiative on the country (and also on the other separated institutions) (Skowroneck 1997). Thus, the leadership of the modern presidency was recast in terms of both its popular component (i.e., the ability to mobilize citizens and public opinion) and its governmental one (i.e., the ability to lead the government by imposing the presidential will on his party's members of congress).

Thanks to the radio, Roosevelt made constant appeals to citizens, urging them to mobilize against individual members of Congress, or against the constitutional judges who defended the previous equilibrium of the congressional government. Indeed, Roosevelt's first two presidencies were characterized by constant institutional conflict. Such was the nature of that conflict that he was forced to find different inspirational criteria for his political action, and hence for the exercise of his leadership. From this conflict sprang what has been called (Tulis 1987) the 'rhetorical presidency': namely an institution of government that founded its legitimacy on direct communication (rhetorical but not necessarily demagogic) between the president and citizens. Since then, all presidents 'go public' (Kernell 1992) as popular support has become crucial for winning the upper hand in conflicts with rival institutional actors (such as congress or state legislatures).

By means of this particular exercise of presidential leadership, it was possible for the post-Second World War presidents to consolidate the main innovations introduced by the 'Roosevelt revolution', viz.: (a) at constitutional level, the strengthening of the federal government at the expense of the state governments; (b) at institutional level, a shift in the gravitational centre of governmental activity from congress to the presidency; (c) at political level, a scaling down of the parties' role as agents of political support to the president; and (d) at organizational level, a reinforcement of the executive's structure, so that it could undertake the new tasks to which it laid claim (Lowi 1985: ch. 3).

The ascent of the presidency: The external source

However, while it is true that the transition in the United States from congressional to presidential government has been driven mainly by domestic factors, it is equally true that the president's primacy in the system of separated government was consolidated because of the role the country came to perform in international politics from the 1940s onwards (Fabbrini 1995). First, with its decisive role in the Second World War, and then with its role as leader of the Western world during the Cold War—a role officialized at the end of that decade (1948) as the United States definitively abandoned an isolationism from world affairs which had lasted for almost a century and a half. Of course, 'isolationism' really means isolation from European affairs, with the major exception of America's intervention in the First World War, given that the United States had regularly intervened in the affairs of the American continent on the basis of the well-known doctrine propounded by President Monroe in 1824, which brought that continent (in its entirety) within the United States' sphere of security and influence.

Competition and conflict with a rival superpower reinforced and accelerated the process, already begun for domestic reasons, of rebalancing the relationship between congress and presidency. Although the pre-eminence of the president was challenged in the 1970s as a result of the conflict in Vietnam, and as a result of the more or less contemporaneous neo-liberal critique of domestic policy, the Cold War order nevertheless continued to provide formidable support for the hierarchy now established in the decision-making process. One may say that, whereas isolationism had furnished scant justification for the exercise of presidential leadership, such justification was substantial in the context of post-Second World War internationalism.

The gigantic international role assumed by the United States in the period after 1945 reinforced the president's popular leadership, in that he was the sole representative of the country in the system of world conflicts. The more a country is internationally exposed, the more its population needs a domestic leader with whom to identify—and even more so if the country is engaged in what is perceived to be a life-or-death international conflict with an intrinsically antagonistic power like the Soviet Union. External threat generated a formidable pressure for rationalizing domestic authority structures.

Thus, each president found himself having to direct an executive of extreme and increasing complexity—a 'stratified presidency' (Fabbrini 1993; Hart 1995; Warshaw 1996) comprising diverse organizational levels:

- the *administrative presidency* represented by independent establishments and government corporations, which now consist of sixty-odd agencies formally controlled jointly by the president and congress but in fact, highly sensitive to the president's interests and programmes;
- the *departmental presidency,* now comprising the fourteen federal departments headed by president's secretaries and further administrative agencies charged with managing specific policy problems;
- the *personal presidency,* consisting of the White House Office (WHO) and the Executive Office of the President (EOP), the latter including agencies of strategic importance to the president like the Office of Management and Budget (OMB) and the National Security Council

(NSC), the former responsible for coordinating budget policy and the latter for monitoring security policy.

In particular, the Cold War stimulated (and justified) the formation within the presidency of a sort of 'informal regime of crisis management' (Gaddis 1991: 117). In other words, it gave rise—especially since the 1960s and 1970s—to a closed personal presidency standing at the head of an enormous military and intelligence apparatus necessarily in contrast with the open character of the institutions (from congress to the political parties) of domestic policy (Preston 2001). It also contrasted with the constitutionally controllable nature of the departmental presidency (Warshaw 1996), in that although the heads of the latter—secretaries, under-secretaries, and high-level political functionaries—are appointed by the president. They are then subject to approval by the senate under the constitutional clause which requires the latter's 'advice and consent' before such appointments are ratified; such a provision does not apply to many members of the personal presidency, whose legal status differs from that of public officials.

Moreover, the personalization of the presidency has enabled the president to surround himself with personal supporters rather than professional politicians of party provenance. Presidents have brought with them the people who helped them to win the electoral campaign. But campaigning is not governing. In fact, not only have many of these electoral experts proved to be governmental amateurs (Campbell 1998), but they have sought to transform governing into a sort of 'permanent campaign' (Blumenthal 1982). As the president's responsibilities increased after the Second World War, so did his need to equip himself with the means to exert direct control over the activities of his presidency, both departmental and administrative.[4] Hence, the growth of the personal presidency as a structure personally at the president's disposal. The more the presidential apparatus expanded, the more the president extended his personal presidency to control it, in an ever-increasing spiral, but with the outcome that he came to control it less and less. If the total executive staff (inclusive of all the people working in the EOP) averaged some 1,269 across the second Truman presidency (1949–52), that number increased to 5,142 during the Nixon presidencies (1969–73), but scaled back to 1,683 during the two Clinton presidencies, to increase again during the George W. Bush presidency (between 2,000 and 2,500 units). The WHO (within the EOP) doubled from Truman (256 individuals, on an average, between 1949 and 1952) to Clinton (415 individuals, 1993 to 2000) (Ragsdale 1996: 257–61). In sum, the 'size, complexity, and organizational capacity of the modern Presidency has grown dramatically. Presidential behaviour can no longer be understood, if it ever was, in mainly personal terms' (Jacobs and Shapiro 2000: 492).

PERSONALIZED PRESIDENTIAL LEADERSHIP IN THE ERA OF THE DIVIDED GOVERNMENT

Reagan and Bush between popular and governmental leadership

All the presidents since the Second World War have interpreted their role in the light of the 'Rooseveltian revolution' (Shapiro et al. 2000). Moreover, from the Democrat Harry S. Truman (President from 1949 to 1952) to the Republicans Richard Nixon and Gerald Ford (1969 to 1976), presidential primacy was underpinned by the support of a party linking the presidency with congress (the 'party-in-government'). However, with Jimmy Carter's presidency (1977–80) this political order started to crumble, although it was Ronald Reagan's two terms of office (1981–8) which opened a new chapter in the history of the modern presidency (Rockman 1988). In fact, since the late 1970s, presidents have frequently had to govern without the support of a party-in-government, thus having to rely only on their own organization.

When analysing the Reagan presidencies, one notes their twofold character. On the one hand, they displayed a continuity with the previous history of the modern presidency: as Greenstein (2000:147) notes, 'Reagan took Roosevelt's use of the presidential pulpit as the prototype for his own political leadership.' On the other, they introduced novel features because Reagan, in exercising his leadership, had to deal with a series of problems unknown (at least of such magnitude) to previous presidencies. These problems were largely related to the decline of the political parties, both as agencies for the mobilization of electoral support and as political links between institutions. It was this decline which had fostered the era of divided government, as the parties lost the ability to promote uniform political majorities in the various institutions of the separated government.

The Reagan administration's answer to this new context was the personalization of presidential action: but this enormously increased public expectations of the president. The president made more and more promises while becoming increasingly unable to fulfil them—not least because he was prevented from doing so by politically hostile congresses. To cope with this incongruence, Reagan fuelled a constant climate of tension, governing as if he were in the middle of a permanent election campaign (King 1997). After the initial policy success of the period 1981–3, Reagan relied increasingly on his popular leadership, to the detriment of the governmental one. He constantly went public, mobilizing symbolic issues rather than substantive ones (Hinckley 1990). A personalized political process became permanently installed during Reagan's two presidencies. Presidential leadership was exercised in order to accentuate the features of that process, heightening the visibility of the president's position and bolstering his role as the nation's only leader.

The net result of Reagan's rhetorical presidency was to accentuate the separation of the institutional system, further fragmenting the political process. An unprecedented neo-factional regime (Heclo 1989) took place, because of the impossibility of finding effective ways to aggregate interests and opinions. Such a fragmented political process (and behind it, the social organization which post-industrialization had balkanized and divided into interest groups no longer relatable to larger social aggregations) guaranteed periodic gridlocks between president and congress in crucial areas of domestic and foreign policy. In sum, Reagan sought to project his leadership as uniquely able to offer an overall identity to this fragmented political process, while simultaneously seeking to gain any possible advantage (in terms of freedom of action) from the fragmented situation. But, devoid of institutional support and entrapped by several scandals (such as the *Iran-Contra* Affair) he ended up, during his second term, as a congressional hostage. Thus, even a 'presidency by plebiscite' (Rimmermann 1993) was unable to escape the logic of the institutional system.

The election of George Bush in 1988 came about in similar circumstances. In fact, Bush's victory was offset by the defeat of his party: the Republicans lost further ground in the House (three seats fewer), in the Senate (one less) and also among governors and in the state legislatures. In short, the election of 1988 greatly reinforced the divided government, and Bush's only option was to avoid conflict with congress. Scholars almost unanimously agree that the Bush presidency took largely the form of what Mullins and Wildavsky (1991) have called a 'procedural presidency'. While Reagan was distinguished by his ability to politicize every dispute with congress and turn it into an opportunity to mobilize public opinion, Bush was able to keep disputes out of the public domain as far as possible. For example, he rarely used press conferences to apply pressure on the rival institution. He much preferred to resolve conflict by setting up *ad hoc* committees consisting of members from the two branches of government, holding informal meetings sheltered from the media with the leaders of congress, and by making personal telephone calls to his political adversaries. Campbell and Rockman (1991) have called Bush the 'let's deal president'— the president who, when confronted by a problem, prefers to negotiate, to find an accommodation or exchange of favours with opponents.

Bush's willingness to 'do a deal' reflected his personal characteristics; indeed, from the beginning of his political career in 1964 he displayed the features of a public functionary rather than those of a political leader. As Greenstein (2000: 160) has written, 'it is necessary to go back to Franklin Roosevelt to find a chief executive with the rich governmental experience of George Bush.' Nevertheless, in Bush's case those characteristics were intensified by the historical conditions (the divided government) in which he had to act. With the virtuous relationship between popular and governmental leadership severed, when Bush found that he had to forego the former, he concentrated on the latter. This was exactly the opposite of what Reagan had done: on finding it impossible to utilize governmental leadership, after his initial successes he sought to rely on popular leadership. Bush's presidency was so reactive in its nature that he decided to concentrate more on foreign policy than on domestic policy, both out of personal preference and in order to assert his presidential role. However, although the Gulf War of 1991 enabled him to do this, in order to wage the war he had to obtain the approval of the Democratic Congress, which it only granted after long and fierce debate.

CLINTON AND 'POLITICS BY OTHER MEANS'

Although Bill Clinton was able to act in the context of a government which enjoyed almost complete party unity during his first two years as president, the circumstances of his electoral victory certainly did not allow him to claim supremacy over the legislature. Clinton had been able to beat Bush more because of the presence of a third candidate (the Independent Ross Perot) in direct competition with the latter than because of the electoral consensus that he enjoyed. In fact, Clinton emerged victorious even though he had obtained only 43.3 per cent of votes, compared to Bush's 37.7 per cent and Perot's 19 per cent.

Clinton's victory was accompanied by the success of Democratic candidates in congressional elections. Those of 1992 resulted in Democrat majorities in both houses of congress. Nevertheless, Clinton found it extremely difficult to obtain the approval of this 'friendly' congress for many of his proposals; indeed, the most important of them (to set up a national health system) was 'sanded' down by the congressional Democrats. At the mid-term elections of 1994, the Republicans regained the majority in both houses of congress, doing so on the basis of a radical neo-conservative programme ('Contract with America') unprecedented in the party's history. Moreover, the promoter of the programme, Newt Gingrich, was elected Speaker of the House of Representatives. This, therefore, was a return to divided government, but now interpreted as a Republican government conditioned by a Democratic president.

In fact, the Republicans transformed divided government into a formidable tool with which to weaken or even call into question the legitimacy of the Clinton presidency. A tremendous assault on the presidency was launched from Republican quarters with the aim of impeaching the president. This assault grew even fiercer after Clinton's re-election in 1996. From 1994 to 1998 the new Republican majority in congress acted as if it were the only legitimate governmental majority of the country, Gingrich portraying 'himself as a prime minister with more influence over policy than President Clinton' (Schickler 2002: 99). However, the assault on Clinton was so dubious constitutionally (Ackerman 1999) that it backfired. The Republicans performed poorly in the mid-term elections of 1998: while the overall partisan balance remained the same, for the first time since 1934 the President's party gained five seats in the House. This unexpected outcome led to Gingrich's resignation as Speaker although, even under his successor Danny Hastert, the impeachment strategy was maintained, ending in a formal vote of the senate in 1999 which failed to achieve the qualified majority of two-thirds necessary to dismiss the president.

The threat of impeachment that dogged both Clinton administrations was part of a new political practice which spread with divided government and was used by both parties to define their relative power relationships. Dramatic falls in electoral participation—just over one-third of voters visiting the polling stations in congressional elections, and around half doing so for presidential contests—weakened the representativeness of both parties, and in the absence of any intention to rectify this (incumbents had no interest in mobilizing the electorate since any change in the *status quo* might have jeopardized their re-election), each used the governmental institution it controlled to attack its rival (thereby also delegitimizing the institution controlled by the latter). Thus the conflict between the parties came to assume the features of an outright battle between institutions.

What Ginsberg and Shefter (1991) called 'politics by other means' at the beginning of the 1990s had grown even more blatant by the end of the decade. The Republican congress used its institutional instruments of control and supervision over the president for partisan ends. Inquiries by various committees and sub-committees followed each other relentlessly, their purpose being to reveal the personal weaknesses of the president or of his closest aides, the covert conditioning exerted on them during the electoral campaign by real or presumed funders, or decision-making confusion in one or other of the presidential departments. The Democratic president, for his part, had no qualms about using the intelligence agencies under his control—the CIA especially (Draper 1997)—to delve into the private lives of congressional leaders. It was a battle that had judicial implications, for congress deliberately used its right to stage hearings under oath of members of the presidency, or called for intervention by the department of justice's special prosecutor,[5] to place the president and his policies in difficulty.

Since the resignation of the Republican Nixon in 1974 under threat of impeachment by a Democratic senate, a new constraint has been imposed on presidential action—that of the president's *personal credibility*. Electoral victory is now no longer enough to give the president personal legitimacy: the threat to his reputation is constant, but so too is the threat to the reputation of the presidential institution itself. Revelations, investigations, prosecutions (or RIPs as Ginsberg and Shefter (1995) have synthetized them[6]) are the new weapons of inter-party competition. RIPs have taken the place of door-to-door canvassing, meetings, rallies, marches, and demonstrations. Indeed, the former have increased dramatically since 1974, while the latter have almost disappeared from the political scene. The greatest price has been paid by the presidency. While Reagan and Bush strove to restore power to the institution after its dramatic fall following the Vietnam defeat and the Watergate scandal, Clinton's entrapment brought a serious reversal to the work previously done. David Calleo writes (2000: 72):

[O]ver the past three decades, the Congress, the courts and the states have frequently combined to cut the presidency down to size. Nothing illustrates this trend more than Clinton's ordeal. Despite the president's continuing popularity with the electorate and his impressive achievements in the economic field, his presidency has been subjected to the most savage constitutional attack since Nixon's time.

Not surprisingly, therefore, the Clinton presidency, too, was reactive. Clinton had to cope with the most aggressive Republican congressional caucus since the Second World War, and with an assault of unprecedented proportions waged on his presidential credibility by his adversaries. Thus, he was forced to prioritize the domain of specific public policies. It became, that is to say, a micro-management leadership. Perhaps, as Bennet and Pear (1997) have written, Bill Clinton was obliged to be an incremental president, who tried to achieve piece by piece what he was unable to achieve through a grand public policy design. His was a government of individual problem-solving—what we may call potluck government.[7] Nevertheless, this piecemeal approach suited Clinton's qualities: 'No American president has exceeded Clinton in his grasp of policy specifics, especially in the domestic sphere, but his was a mastery that did not translate into a clearly defined point of view' (Greestein 2000: 187). The presidential leadership was consequently deployed to form specific and limited majorities, to reach agreements, and administratively to reformulate each of the agreements proposed so that it gained maximum consensus. Of course, when a president governs problem by problem, when he becomes 'an *aficionado* of policy *qua* policy' (Greenstein 1998: 179), it is difficult for him to steer any sort of consistent course.

The fact of the matter is, however, that the Clinton presidency (especially in the period 1995–8) saw the advent of a leadership consisting of 'parliamentarism with minority government'—one, as Schier (2000: 265) puts it, with 'narrow agendas, limited governmental possibilities, and flexible post-modern personal style'. It is noteworthy, however, that the divided government and the attack on his reputation notwithstanding, Clinton was able to 'achieve popularity despite the low public regard for his character and morality' (ibid.). Of course, the president, unlike the prime minister of a minority government, was able to exploit the legitimacy accruing from his personal election (while the latter only has the legitimacy stemming from a 'lack of anything better'), and he also benefited from the resources (primarily communicative) deriving from his monocratic office (though he had to use them prudently). However, while Clinton was able to save his presidential role from a parliamentarist drift, he could not change the American electoral and institutional order of the 1990s: 'he merely accommodate(d) himself to it' (Rae 2000: 184).

THE PRESIDENCY OF GEORGE W. BUSH
AND THE TERRORIST THREAT

The controversial victory of the Republican candidate George W. Bush in the elections of 2000 over the Clinton's vice-president and Democratic candidate Albert Gore (Dershowitz 2001) was accompanied by a partial abatement of divided government. The Republicans retained their majority in the house, although they lost their majority in the senate, albeit by a single seat. Faced with the dissipation of presidential leadership and the disappearance of the Soviet menace, on his election George W. Bush chose to distance himself from any serious international engagement and sought to build more co-operative relations with the congress. Because the president knew that he did not enjoy full legitimacy, he behaved like a parliamentary prime minister, rather than a president. Domestically, he endorsed the congressional agenda of the second half of the 1990s which focused essentially on tax reduction. Internationally, he endorsed the unilateral perspective previously pursued by the (Republican) congress. Thus, prior to September 11, 2001, American criticism of international agreements and organizations reached an unexpected degree of severity.

September 11 changed the presidential role dramatically. Faced with the terrorist threat, the American people discovered the need for a president, and they found one. Bush met popular expectations by behaving as a true 'commander-in-chief', and foreign policy became the first priority of his administration. Of course, Bush had to abandon his doctrine of selective engagement (which was widely and erroneously confused with isolationism) to embrace a more active global perspective. In order to create the conditions for intervention in Afghanistan, the administration engaged in an extensive diplomatic campaign of coalition-building, which successfully pulled together friends and foes in support of the American military operation. To obtain international legitimacy necessary for the intervention, congress was finally persuaded to pay the American dues to the UN. A spirit favourable to more international cooperation seemed to emerge from the public statements of the president and his team.

Moreover, diplomatic overtures notwithstanding, Bush continued to pursue the unilateral approach envisaged by the Republican congress since 1994.

This unilateralism has been justified on the basis of a new grand strategy defined by the president and made public on 20 September 2002 (Bush 2002), a strategy that many dubbed as 'American national sovereignty comes first'—or rather, 'a willingness to go along with international accords, but only so far as they suit America, which is prepared to conduct policy outside their constraints' (*The Economist* 2001: 24). Thus, a radical transformation of the international environment created the conditions for presidential leadership to re-emerge domestically. Nevertheless, it had to re-emerge from a now largely de-legitimized institution (Neustadt 2001). In order to impose his leadership, Bush had to separate himself from the White House and re-invent himself as a popular leader. The mid-term elections of 2002 presented a great opportunity to work for the future of his governmental leadership by sponsoring and supporting candidates close to him and his team. In fact, the surprising success of Republican candidates in those elections (the Republicans increased their majority in the house and regained the majority in the senate) was widely perceived as a personal success for the president.

Thus, between September 2001 and November 2002, the decline of the American presidency seems to have been arrested: the threat of terrorism reinvigorated the popular leadership of the president, while electoral success created the conditions for the re-launching of his governmental leadership. The new strategy gave the presidency ideological justification to claim a renewed primacy within the separated governmental system. America was under siege and it had to protect itself. To do so it had to free itself from all external multi-lateral constraints, but from domestic institutional constraints as well. As happened during the Cold War, the new war on international terrorism facilitated a reordering of domestic relations. Nevertheless, if it can be questioned whether the war on international terrorism can replicate the Cold War as a disciplining strategy with which to fuse American interests with those of other democratic countries (Nye 2002), it is also questionable to assume that the war will be sufficient to impose presidential power over congress. In fact, the separated governmental system will make it difficult for anyone (even a president fighting a vicious terrorist enemy) to reduce its internal pluralism. After September 2001, President George W. Bush tried forcefully to re-impose presidential pre-eminence in the domestic decision-making process. The new foreign policy strategy of American unilateralism (celebrated with the war in Iraq in spring 2003) carried with it domestic implications, in the form of renewed presidential power vis-à-vis other governmental institutions. Again, in America, foreign policy is a crucial determinant of presidential leadership. To be sure, after the mid-term elections of November 2002, President George W. Bush increased his prospects of governing, with the electoral success of Republican candidates in both the house and the senate. Nevertheless, given the inevitability of periodic recourse to divided government, presidential leadership will continue to be based on the fragile foundations of candidate-centred politics (Cain 2002; Peele et al. 2002). As the assertion of American predominance will elicit countervailing strategies abroad, so it will elicit countervailing forces at home. Thus, we can assume that the American political (dis)order (Dahl 1994) will reappear as soon as the drama of the war on terrorism lessens.

CONCLUSION

It is true that 'the highly personalized nature of the modern American presidency makes the strengths and weaknesses of the White House incumbents of the utmost importance' (Greenstein 2000: 189), but it also true that the individual incumbents have to cope with the structural constraints of their position. In a separated government, exposed to periods of divided government, presidential primacy can never be taken for granted. Indeed, devoid of party linkages with the other governmental institutions, presidential primacy looks like 'a castle in the sand'.

In fact, through the personalization of the electoral process, the president has become highly autonomous of his party and a legislative majority, although this does not necessarily imply that he is able to get his way in the policy process. Indeed, the president appears to be more constrained by the legislature than a prime minister in a parliamentary system, because he does not control his legislative party to the same extent. The enormous personal power of the president does not necessarily enable him to achieve his desired policy outcomes, unless external factors, like a national or international crisis, furnish an opportunity to impose his own agenda and leadership on the other domestic institutions (and congress in particular). But the transfer of preeminence in foreign policy to domestic policy cannot be taken for granted. Indeed, increased presidential power may coincide with a declining steering capacity of the state altogether. Thus, the increased autonomy acquired by the presidential candidate in the electoral process has not translated into increased governmental power. If anything, the contrary appears to have been the case.

Presidents have found it difficult to govern with a hostile congress and an extremely complex presidency. Candidate-centred politics, weakening the party-in-the-electorate, made mutually reinforcing electoral majorities less likely. The candidate's party, at presidential as well as congressional levels, has made the party-in-government impossible. Hence, in America, the presidentialization process has brought into existence presidents who can govern only through ad hoc coalitions or by using their public appeal to force their will upon congress. Presidentialized prime ministers, in fact, while achieving greater autonomy from and power over their parties, still have to govern with their support, and cannot survive substantial dissent from their own parties. This is not the case for the presidentialized president of the American system.

Nevertheless, in both presidentialized parliamentary systems and the presidentialized American separated system, a common transformation of the governmental process seems to have taken place: the legislature and the chief executive have moved apart. Of course, the different institutional structures of the two systems offer different opportunities to presidentialized leaders to promote their own pre-eminence. Drawing on the theoretical framework of this book, one can conclude that the American system of separated government has gradually presidentialized in the last three decades, in the sense that the chief executive has had to rely on his own personal mandate and resources in order to negotiate his way through the political agenda. But this process has not altered his status as a semi-sovereign prince within a fragmented governmental system.

NOTES

1. The author wishes to thank the editors of the volume for their helpful comments to the previous version of the chapter and for their valuable suggestions in drafting the Conclusion.
2. On the features and roles of 'democratic princes', that is prime ministers and presidents in democratic government, see Fabbrini (1999).
3. According to Article II, section 1 of the Constitution, the President of the United States 'shall remain in office for a period of four years'. The election of the president is not direct but is instead mediated by the electoral college. The electors of each state choose the members of the electoral college of that state, the number of whom is equivalent to the number of representatives and senators pertaining to that state in the federal congress. The system by which the members of the electoral college are elected is established by the ordinary law of the respective state legislatures (although the Constitution stipulates that persons already holding public office may not be elected members of the electoral college). Today, almost all the states use the so-called 'winner takes all' method whereby the presidential candidate who wins most votes in a particular state has the right to the support of all that state's electoral college votes. The law of 1934 stipulated that this election must be held on 'the first Tuesday after the first Monday of November', naturally at four-yearly intervals, although the electoral college of each state meets to formalize the victor (again on the basis of the 1934 law) on 'the first Monday after the second Wednesday of December following the November election'. Each electoral college meets in the capital of its state, and therefore separately from the other state electoral colleges. The results are sent to the President of the Senate, who authenticates them in the presence of the Senate and the House of Representatives. Finally, on the basis of the twentieth constitutional amendment of 1933, the candidate elected president takes (presidential) office at the stroke of 'midday on the 20th of January' following the November election and the December formalization of its result. The twenty-second constitutional amendment of 1951 established that 'no person shall be elected to the office of the President more than twice.'

4. Although Clinton scaled down the size of each of these by approximately a quarter, some 1,628,000 individuals were still employed within the fourteen departments in 2002 (compared to 2,060,387 in 1993). The Department of Defense alone enlisted 1,184,000 units on active duty in 2002 (Stanley and Niemi 2003: 344–5).

5. The special prosecutor (later renamed 'independent counsel' by the Ethics Act of 1978) is an interim member of the presidency. S/he is appointed by the Secretary of Justice and then confirmed by one of the federal courts. S/he should enjoy a certain amount of independence in investigating allegations of wrongdoing by members of the presidency, if not (as in Nixon's case between 1973 and 1974 or in the Clinton's case between 1993 and 1999) by the president himself. In reality, his/her independence from the Secretary of Justice (or even from the president himself) continues to be a matter of fierce constitutional conflict between congress, the presidency, and the supreme court (Fisher 1991: 25, 77–8).

6. These activities are favoured by congressional hearings so that they come to interact with the interests of the media and the dispositions of the courts of justice. Ginsberg and Shefter (1995) argue that, between 1974 and 1992, a sort of alliance (against the Republican control of the presidency) arose among members of the Democratic Congress, a number of leading Democratic newspapers and television editors, and liberal sectors of the investigative judiciary.

7. In American usage a 'potluck meal' is one at which each guest brings food which is then shared by all present, so that the meal consists of a haphazard mix of dishes. Likewise, 'potluck government' consists of a mix of not necessarily congruent policies.

REFERENCES

Ackerman, B. (1999). *The Case Against Lameduck Impeachment*. New York: Seven Stories Press.

Aldrich J. H. (1995). *Why Parties? The Origin and Transformation of Political Parties in America*. Chicago: University of Chicago Press.

—— and R. G. Niemi (1996). *The Sixth American Party System: Electoral Change 1952–1992*, in S. C. Craig (ed.), *Broken Contract? Changing Relationships between Americans and their Government*. Boulder: Westview Press, 87–109.

Bartels, L. M. (2002). *The Impact of Candidates Traits in American Presidential Elections*, in A. King (ed.), *Leader's Personalities and the Outcome of Democratic Elections*. Oxford: Oxford University Press, 44–69.

Bennet, J. and R. Pear (1997). 'A Presidency Largely Defined by the Many Parts of Its Sum', *The New York Times*, 8 December.

Blumenthal, S. (1982). *The Permanent Campaign*. New York: Touchstone Books.

Bush, G. W. (2002). *The National Security Strategy of the United States*, Washington D.C., 20 September.

Cain, B. (2002). *The United States in Evolution: Majoritarian Reforms in a Madisonian System*, in G. Peele, C. J. Bailey, B. Cain, and B. G. Peters (eds.), *Developments in American Politics*. New York: Palgrave, 300–316.

Calleo, D. P. (2000). 'The US Post-Imperial Presidency and Transatlantic Relations', *The International Spectator*, XXXV, 69–79.

Campbell, C. (1998). *The U.S. Presidency in Crisis: A Comparative Perspective*. Oxford: Oxford University Press.

—— and B. Rockman (1991). *The Bush Presidency: First Appraisals*. Chatham, NJ: Chatham House.

Crotty, W. J. (1980). *Political Reform and the American Experiment*. New York: Thomas Y. Crowell.

—— (1982). *Party Reform*. New York: Longman.

Dahl, R. A. (1994). *The New American Political (Dis)order*. Berkeley: IGS Publishers.

Dershowitz, A. M. (2001). *Supreme Injustice: How the High Court Hijacked Election 2000*. Oxford: Oxford University Press.

Donnelly, D., J. Fine, and E. S. Miller (2001). *Are Elections For Sale?* Boston: Beacon Press.

Draper, T. (1997). 'Is the CIA Necessary?', *The New York Review of Books*, XLIV, 13: 18–22.

Economist, The (2001). 'Working Out the World'. London: *The Economist*.

Fabbrini, S. (1993). *Il presidenzialismo degli Stati Uniti*. Roma-Bari: Laterza.

—— (1995). 'Challenges to the American Political System: The United States in the Post-Cold War Era', in A. M. Mastellone (ed.), *Towards a New American Nation? Redefinitions and Reconstruction*. Keele: Keele University Press, 45–58.

—— (1998a). 'The American System of Separated Government: An Historical-Institutional Interpretation', *International Political Science Review*, 19: 95–116.

—— (1998b). *Quale democrazia. L'Italia e gli altri*. Roma-Bari: Laterza, 2nd edn.

—— (1999). *Il Principe democratico. La leadership nelle democrazie contemporanee*. Rome-Bari: Laterza.

Fiorina, M. (1992). *Divided Government*. New York: Macmillan.

Fisher, L. (1991). *Constitutional Conflicts Between Congress and the President*. Lawrence: University Press of Kansas, 3rd edn.

Gaddis, J. L. (1991). 'Toward the Post-Cold War World', *'Foreign Affairs'*, 70: 1–19.

Ginsberg, B. E. and M. Shefter (1991). *Politics by Other Means: the Declining Significance of Elections in America*. Basic Books: New York.

—— —— (1995). 'Ethic Probes as Political Weapons', *Journal of Law and Politics*, XI: 497–511.

Greenstein, F. I. (1998). 'There He Goes Again: the Alternating Political Style of Bill Clinton', *PS: Political Science and Politics*, XXXI: 179–181.

—— (2000). *The Presidential Difference: Leadership Style from FDR to Clinton*. Princeton: Princeton University Press.

Hart, J. (1995). *The Presidential Branch: From Washington to Clinton*. Chatham: Chatham House, 2nd edn.

Heclo, H. (1989). 'The Emerging Regime', in R. A. Harris and S. M. Milkis (eds.), *Remaking American Politics*. Boulder: Westview Press, 289–320.

Hinckley, B. (1990). *The Symbolic Presidency: How Presidents Portray Themselves*. London: Routledge.

Jacobs, L. R. and R. Y. Shapiro (2000). 'Conclusion: Presidential Power, Institutions and Democracy', in R. Y. Shapiro, M. J. Kumar, and L. R. Jacobs (eds.), *Presidential Power: Forging the Presidency for the Twenty-first Century*. New York: Columbia University Press, 489–508.

Jones, C. O. (1994). *The Presidency in a Separated System.* Washington D.C.: The Brookings Institution.

Katz, R. S. and R. Kolodny (1994). *Party Organization as an Empty Vessel: Parties in American Politics,* in R. S. Katz and P. Mair (eds.), *How Parties Organize.* London: Sage, 23–50.

Kernell, S. (1992). *Going Public: New Strategies of Presidential Leadership.* Washington D.C.: C.Q. Press, 2nd edn.

King, A. (1997). *Running Scared: Why America's Politicians Campaign Too Much and Govern Too Little.* New York: The Free Press.

Lowi, T. (1985). *The Personal President: Power Invested Promise Unfulfilled.* Ithaca: Cornell University Press.

Lunch, W. M. (1987). *The Nationalization of American Politics.* Berkeley: University of California Press.

Malbin, M. J. (1984). *Money and Politics in United States: Financing Elections in the 1980s.* Chatham: Chatham House.

Merriam, C. (1908). *Primary Elections.* Chicago: University of Chicago Press.

Milkis, S. M. (1993). *The President and the Parties: The Transformation of the American Party System Since the New Deal.* Oxford: Oxford University Press.

Mullins, K. and A. Wildavsky (1991). 'The Procedural Presidency of George Bush', *Society,* 28: 49–59.

Neustadt, R. E. (1990). *Presidential Power and Modern President: The Politics of Leadership from Roosevelt to Reagan.* New York: The Free Press, 3rd edn.

—— (2001). 'The Weakening White House', *British Journal of Political Science,* 31: 1–12.

Nye, J. (2002). *The Paradox of American Power.* Oxford: Oxford University Press.

Peele, G., C. J. Bailey, B. Cain, and B. G. Peters (2002). 'Introduction: The United States in the Twenty-First Century', in G. Peele, C. J. Bailey, B. Cain, and B. G. Peters (eds.), *Developments in American Politics.* New York: Palgrave, 1–14.

Pious, R. (1996). *The Presidency,* Boston: Allyn and Bacon.

Polsby, N. W. (1983). *Consequences of Party Reform.* New York: Oxford University Press.

Preston, T. (2001). *The President and His Inner Circle: Leadership Styles and the Advisory Process in Foreign Affairs.* New York: Columbia University Press.

Rae, N. C. (2000). 'Clinton and the Democrats: The President as a Party Leader', in S. E. Schier (ed.), *The Postmodern Presidency: Bill Clinton's Legacy in U.S. Politics.* Pittsburgh: Pittsburgh University Press, 183–200.

Ragsdale, L. (1996). *Vital Statistics on the Presidency.* Washington DC: Congressional Quarterly.

Ranney, A. (1990). *Governing: An Introduction to Political Science.* Englewood Cliffs: Prentice Hall.

Rimmerman, C. A. (1993). *Presidency by Plebiscite: The Reagan-Bush Era in Institutional Perspective.* Boulder: Westview Press.

Rockman, B. A. (1984). *The Leadership Question: The Presidency and the American System.* New York: Praeger.

—— (1988). 'The Style and Organization of the Reagan Presidency', in C. O. Jones (ed.), *The Reagan Legacy: Promise and Performance*. Chatham, NJ: Chatham House, 3–29.

Rozzel, M. J. and W. D. Pederson (1997). *FDR and the Modern Presidency: Leadership and Legacy*. Westport: Praeger.

Schickler, E. (2002). 'Congress', in G. Peele, C. J. Bailey, B. Cain, and B. G. Peters (eds.), *Developments in American Politics*. Basingstoke: Palgrave, 97–114.

Schier, S. E. (2000). 'Conclusion: American Politics After Clinton', in S. E. Schier (ed.), *The Postmodern Presidency: Bill Clinton's Legacy in U.S. Politics*. Pittsburgh: Pittsburgh University Press, 255–265.

Schramm, P. W. and B. P. Wilson (1993). *American Political Parties and Constitutional Politics*. Lanham: Rowman and Littlefield.

Shapiro, R. Y., M. J. Kumar, and L. R. Jacobs (2000). *Presidential Power: Forging the Presidency for the Twenty-first Century*. New York: Columbia University Press.

Skowroneck, S. (1997). *The Politics Presidents Make: Leadership from John Adams to Bill Clinton*, Cambridge, MA, Harvard University Press, 2nd edn.

Sorauf, F. J. (1992). *Inside Campaign Finance: Myths and Realities*. New Haven: Yale University Press.

Stanley, H. W. and R. G. Niemi (2003). *Vital Statistics on American Politics, 2003–2004*. Washington DC: CQ Press.

Tulis, J. K. (1987). *The Rhetorical Presidency*. Princeton: Princeton University Press.

Ware, A. (1988). *The Breakdown of Democratic Party Organization, 1940–1980*. Oxford: Clarendon Press.

Warshaw, S. A. (1996). *Powersharing: White House-Cabinet Relations in the Modern Presidency*. New York: State of New York Press.

Wattenberg, M. P. (1991). *The Rise of Candidate-Centered Politics: Presidential Election in the 1980s*. Cambridge, MA, Harvard University Press.

Wilson, W. (1973 [1884]). *Congressional Government: A Study in American Politics*. Gloucester, MA, Peter Smith.

15

The Presidentialization of Contemporary Democratic Politics: Evidence, Causes and Consequences

Paul Webb and Thomas Poguntke

The point of departure for this volume was the observation that a variety of academic and non-academic commentators have referred to the alleged 'presidentialization' of politics in the world's advanced industrial democracies. While these observers have rarely moved beyond using the term as a loose analogy to the way in which the political system of the United States operates, we set ourselves the task of systematically and rigorously investigating the following issues:

- In so far as the term 'presidentialization' might have a substantial meaning at all, what is it?
- To what extent does it really exist?
- Under what circumstances does it occur?
- How far is its occurrence affected and constrained by formal constitutional features such as regime-type (presidentialism, parliamentarism, or semi-presidentialism), federalism, or consensus/majoritarian forms of democracy?
- Where presidentialization can meaningfully be said to exist, what are its causes?
- What are its implications for modern democracies?

In Chapter 1 we offered an answer to the first of these questions by setting out a three-dimensional concept of '*de facto* presidentialization', which threw into relief the growth of leadership power and autonomy within parties and political executives, and the greater prominence of leaders in electoral processes. Each of these developments represents an erosion of more collective, 'partified' forms of politics, though we do not suggest that they entirely supplant them. We also discussed the ways in which presidentialization can occur in consensual and majoritarian systems. Having applied this model of presidentialized politics to a variety of advanced industrial democracies, this chapter summarizes the evidence and addresses the remaining questions.

THE EMPIRICAL EVIDENCE

Table 15.1 précises the wealth of material uncovered and discussed in the earlier chapters. Let us consider the various faces of presidentialization in turn.

The executive face

Here, in general terms, we have sought evidence of a shift in intra-executive power to the benefit of the head of government (whether a prime minister or a president), accompanied by signs of growing executive autonomy from his or her party. Note that the latter development should not be confused with the leader's growing autonomy from intra-party power-holders in respect of issues of *party management and policy-making*: the latter should properly be considered an aspect of the party face, to which we will come in due course. Here, however, we are concerned with the leader's autonomy from the party in respect of *the business of the executive of the state* (for instance, over government formation and portfolio allocation); thus, it only refers to the leaders of governing parties. (For a reminder of the differences between these analytical dimensions in terms of specific indicators, see Chapter 1.) This is one of the most common ways in which the adjective 'presidential' is used as a loose analogy in the context of parliamentary regimes, and is well illustrated by references to the 'presidential leadership styles' of premiers such as Thatcher, Blair, or Berlusconi.

Several of our country experts stress that presidential-style domination of the political executive by leaders such as these is often explained by short-term contingent factors, such as the size and cohesion of the parliamentary support on which they can draw, their current standing with the electorate, their personalities, and the sheer and inevitably unpredictable impact of what Harold Macmillan once inscrutably and memorably referred to as 'events'. This comes out, for instance, in a reading of the chapters on Spain, Sweden, and the UK. Indeed, no observer of British politics since 1979 could reasonably deny that each of these contingent factors hugely conditioned the nature of prime ministerial leadership offered by Margaret Thatcher, John Major, and Tony Blair. Contingent factors of this nature constrain and shape executive leadership in all types of democratic regime, even presidential and semi-presidential ones. True, the US President cannot be fatally weakened by rebellious members of the cabinet, and neither can he be deprived of his office

TABLE 15.1. *Trends towards presidentialization: Evidence from fourteen nations*

Indicators of presidentialization	The Executive Face		The Party Face	
	Shift in intra-executive power to benefit of leader	Increasing autonomy of executive leader vis-à-vis party	Shift in intra-party power to benefit of leader	Increasing autonomy of party leader from intra-party power holders
Belgium	+	+	+	+
Canada	+[i]	0 (always high)	0 (always high)	+
Denmark	+	+	+	+
Finland	+	+	+	+
France[ii]	+	0 (always high)	+	+
Germany	+	+	+	+
Israel (pre-1996)	+	+	+	+
Israel (1996–2003)[iii]	0	–	+[iv]	+
Italy	+	+	+	+[v]
Netherlands	+[vii]	+	+	+[vi]
Portugal	+	+	+	+
Spain	+	+	+	+
Sweden	+	+	+	+
United Kingdom	+	+	+[viii]	+[ix]
United States	+	+	n/a	n/a

Indicators of presidentialization	The Electoral Face			Summary
	Growth of media coverage of leaders	Increasingly leadership-centred campaign strategy	Growing leader effects on voting behaviour	
Belgium	+	+	+	moderate change
Canada	+	0 (always high)	−	small change, high level of presidentialization throughout
Denmark	+	+	u	moderate change; strong party constraints
Finland	+ (but high)	+	+	moderate change
France	0 (but high)	0 (but high)	0 (but high)	small change; high level of presidentialization throughout 5th Republic
Germany	+	+	+	strong change
Israel (pre-1996)	+	+	+	strong change
Israel (1996–2003)[x]	+	+	+	strong change
Italy	+	+	+	strong change
Netherlands	+	+	+	moderate change
Portugal	+	+	0 (always high)	moderate change
Spain	0 (always high)	0 (always high)	0 (always high)	moderate change
Sweden	+	+	u	moderate change
United Kingdom	+	+	+	moderate change
United States	+	+	+	moderate change

Notes:

+: change in the expected direction; 0: no change;   −: change against the expected direction; u: uncertain/contradictory evidence.
[i] Starting from a low level.   [ii] Refers to both chief executives (i.e. president and prime minister).
[iii] Post 2003: tendency to revert to pre-1996 pattern.   [iv] Mainly Alleanza Nazionale, Forza Italia.
[v] Mainly Alleanza Nazionale, Forza Italia.   [vi] Mainly PvdA.
[vii] Starting from a low level.   [viii] Mainly Labour.
[ix] Always high in the Conservative Party.   [x] Only weak reversal of trend after 2003.

through losing a majority in the congress, but the power to realize his legislative programme can be seriously undermined. Sergio Fabbrini (p. 330) reports that 'the enormous personal power of the president does not necessarily enable him to achieve his desired policy outcomes, unless external factors, like a national or international crisis, furnish an opportunity to impose his own agenda and leadership on the other domestic institutions (and congress in particular)'. Thus, presidents can be forced by circumstance to govern through ad hoc coalitions in the congress or by using their public appeal to 'force their will' upon the legislature, the latter being a favoured tactic of 'the Great Communicator', Ronald Reagan. In a similar vein, Ben Clift reminds us that the relative powers of president and prime minister under the French semi-presidential system can be influenced by considerations such as which of them has the most recent electoral mandate.

These examples illustrate that the presidentialization of the executive face does not always coincide with increased legislative power. First and foremost, it implies a reduction of a party's political influence on executive leadership. Presidentialized chief executives, whether presidents or prime ministers, tend to govern past their parties rather than through them—even if this undermines their chances of realizing their legislative agenda.

Thus, we may usefully speak of 'contingent presidentialization' of the executive—the leader's domination of the political executive through the impact of short-term factors. This phenomenon should certainly not be underestimated, but as we emphasized in Chapter 1, we are more interested in the underlying long-term developments which enhance the potential of the chief executive office of the state for strong leadership, even if contingent influences do not necessarily enable an incumbent to fully realize it in the short-term. Such enduring developments we have referred to as 'structural presidentialization', and these are indicated by a number of variables. Such variables in turn reflect the adaptation to underlying structural causes of presidentialization, and include: attempts to reorganize government so as to enhance the resources or strategic coordinating capacity available to the leader; signs of reduced opportunities for collective decision-making within the executive (for instance, reduced frequency or length of cabinet meetings); the growth of bilateral decision-making processes involving the chief executive and individual ministers, to the exclusion of the cabinet collectively; a tendency to promote non-party technocrats or politicians lacking distinctive party power bases, and so on.

Overall, Table 15.1 reveals that, in almost every case, leaders' power resources and autonomy within national political executives have increased and/or were already at a high level (compared to the ideal-type of collegial government that one associates with parliamentarism) at the outset of the period analysed. This is not to deny that parties and parliaments remain important actors, especially in traditionally partified parliamentary systems, such as Sweden's. But even in multiparty systems where coalitional and consensus models of politics are the norm, it is fascinating to observe that premiers have apparently often become more 'presidential'. The Low Countries offer a good example: Stefaan Fiers and André Krouwel tell us that 'within the last two decades, party leaders and prime ministers alike, both in Belgium and the Netherlands, acquired more prominent and powerful positions, transforming these consensus democracies into a kind of 'presidentialized' parliamentary system' (p. 128). In short, while parties remain significant constraints in most countries, personal authority, if not to say dominance, over the executive by premiers and presidents has become more prevalent. In majoritarian systems, such as the UK, the growth of the prime minister's underlying structural power within the executive has been even more notable. Indeed, this trend has been steadily growing over several decades, if not longer, but has been particularly associated with the premierships of Margaret Thatcher and Tony Blair, as Heffernan and Webb demonstrate in Chapter 2.

The only apparent exceptions to the rule of structural presidentialization of the executive occur in the Israeli and American cases, which simply represent, upon closer inspection, special cases of the general pattern. Reuven Hazan provides a fascinating insight into Israel's experiment with a directly elected prime minister. The unintended and seemingly paradoxical outcome of this short-lived flirtation with (partial) constitutional presidentialization was that it actually served to undermine the prime minister's control over both his executive and the Knesset. By divorcing the prime minister's mandate from his party's, the constitutional presidentialization of elections facilitated ticket-splitting by voters, which in turn served to further fragment the party system, and rendered governing coalitions still less manageable than had been the case. Israel's peculiar achievement was to enhance the electoral and party faces of presidentialization while undermining the executive face. Furthermore, the prime minister could still be removed by a hostile majority in the Knesset—which, if anything, had become more likely as a result of the separation of electoral contests to decide on the composition of the legislature and the identity of the premier. Interestingly, however, Hazan reports clear evidence of a structural evolution towards executive presidentialization *prior* to the introduction of direct election of the prime minister: 'The Israeli prime minister, during the era of pure parliamentarism, and in spite of the multiparty nature of both the Knesset and the governing coalitions, continually reinforced and consolidated his power. The trend of formal strengthening resulted in the clear predominance of the prime minister over the government, and of the government over the parliament' (p. 294). Prime ministerial power within the executive was immediately enhanced again following the repeal of the constitutional reform. This strongly suggests that, apart from the aberration occasioned by the ill-fated constitutional reform, Israel's experience is in fact consistent with that of most of the other countries in our sample.

The case of the USA presents a remarkable parallel with Israel during the era of directly elected prime ministers. As in Israel, the direct election of the chief executive does not require mutually reinforcing majorities. During recent decades, the increasingly candidate-centred nature of elections has made divided government more likely and, in consequence, presidents have found it difficult to govern with a hostile congress. There is, of course, an important difference between formally presidential USA and Israel in the era of directly elected prime ministers: US presidents remain dominant within the executive, and do not have to worry about keeping fragile coalition governments intact. However, Sergio Fabbrini argues that 'the American system of separated government has gradually presidentialized in the last three decades, in the sense that the chief executive has had to rely on his own personal mandate and resources in order to negotiate his way through the political agenda' (p. 331). Moreover, the structural basis of presidentialized politics is ever-present (and growing) in the USA, given the phenomenal resources open to the chief executive of the world's most powerful nation.

It is interesting to reflect on the position of semi-presidential systems in this context. It is striking that, in France, Finland, and Portugal, the prime ministerial side of their bicephalous executives has become more prominent with the passage of time. In every case, this seems to coincide with the waning of national insecurities about the normal workings of democratic governance: The French Fifth Republic was forged out of de Gaulle's idiosyncratic but powerful brand of leadership at a time when the menace of a military coup hung heavily over a country struggling to cope with the crisis in Algeria; Portugal's new constitution of 1976 was constructed after long years of dictatorship, and reflected military-revolutionary, as well as party-pluralistic, sources of legitimacy; and Finland's semi-presidentialism reflected the peculiar geo-political sensitivity of a country profoundly aware of the immense Soviet neighbour on its eastern border. Yet as France survived the process of de-colonization in Algeria and an eventual transfer of national power, first to the non-Gaullist Right, and subsequently to the Left; as Portugal's new democracy survived transition and consolidated in a new era of European Community membership; and as Finland's sense of national security grew with the demise of the USSR and her own membership of the European Union, so the parliamentary aspect of each country's political systems emerged. In France, this took the form of frequent outbreaks of political cohabitation between presidents and prime ministers of different partisan hue, though one might argue this should more properly be regarded as contingent than structural presidentialization of the prime ministerial office. In Portugal and Finland, however, it was associated with formal constitutional amendments which significantly reduced the powers of the presidency (in 1982 and 2000, respectively). But here's the rub: in each and every case, the shift towards more parliamentary modes of politics has been accompanied by the growth of prime ministerial power within the executive. In common with the other parliamentary systems in our sample, then, Finland and Portugal have experienced a structural presidentialization of executive power, while France has experienced frequent bouts of contingent presidentialization of the executive: all such developments have benefited prime ministers rather than presidents.

The party face

Clearly, presidential leadership styles also leave their mark on the way chief executives interact with their parties. Short-term contingent factors permitting, strong leaders with electoral appeal will not only be able to assert themselves within the executive, they will also be able to dominate their own parties. Undoubtedly, much of this trend towards leadership-centred intra-party politics is driven by the modern mass media and facilitated by loosening party loyalties (see below), which is why we see the same phenomenon within opposition parties. The way Gerhard Schröder imposed himself on the German SPD as Chancellor-candidate in 1998 is a conspicuous, but not atypical, example of the growing tendency of leaders to by-pass regular procedures and 'govern' their parties 'presidentially'. Much of this is, however, facilitated by underlying structural changes, which provide the resources and levers necessary for leaders to act in such way.

Table 15.1 reveals an equally clear-cut trend towards the growth of leaders' power within, and autonomy from, their parties. Whereas power within the party might be thought of as the capacity of leaders to get the party to do as they want, autonomy from the party can be thought of as the ability to ignore or bypass the party altogether. With respect to the former (power), we asked the country experts to look for evidence of party rule changes which give leaders more formal power, and the growth of the leaders' offices in terms of staff or other resources. With respect to the latter (autonomy), we have looked for signs that leaders have developed their capacities to forge programmes independently of their parties, or made use of plebiscitary modes of political communication and mobilization vis-à-vis the grassroots, thereby bypassing party activists.

Developments in the party face of presidentialization can be reported very straightforwardly: none of the country experts doubts that the leaders of (potentially) governing parties have enjoyed a growth in intra-party power and/or autonomy, or these were already comparatively high at the start of the period analysed and have remained so, in each and every case. This, it should be noted, holds even for parties where reforms have been introduced in the name of democratization. This follows from Peter Mair's well-known paradox that empowering the grass roots in matters of candidate-selection can be an effective way of by-passing the activist office-holders in parties. As he puts it:

[I]t is not the party congress or the middle-level elite, or the activists, who are being empowered, but rather the 'ordinary' members, who are at once more docile and more likely to endorse the policies (and candidates) proposed by the party leadership . . . the activist layer inside the party, the traditionally more troublesome layer, becomes marginalized . . . in contrast to the activists, these ordinary and often disaggregated members are not very likely to mount a serious challenge against the positions adopted by the leadership. (Mair 1994: 16)

One of the country experts most equivocal about the parties' loss of place to leaders is Nicholas Aylott, yet he concedes that even in Sweden, 'as elsewhere in Europe, party elites have grown increasingly dominant' (p. 184). This is reflected above all, perhaps, in what Aylott calls the notable 'departification' of the cabinet under prime minister Göran Persson (strictly speaking, an indicator relevant to the executive rather than party face), and the weakening of the traditional link between the dominant Social Democrats and the trade unions. This organic link lay at the heart of party power in Sweden, but its partial erosion has created greater scope for the autonomy of the individual leader. Indeed, the Swedish Social Democrats are not unique in loosening their ties to external collateral organizations in order to expand their leaders' room for manoeuvre (Poguntke 2000: 51). Apart from such (relatively rare) formal changes, the social anchorage of political parties has been eroded across the board. As a result, party leaders are less constrained when (re)positioning their parties in order to remain electorally competitive.

Arguably, an equally strong push towards more power and autonomy for party leaders is often associated with parties entering national governments. The example of the German Greens is instructive here: As they moved into national government a series of organizational reforms were implemented which were aimed at improving the steering capacity of the party leadership (Poguntke 2001; Rüdig 2002). Yet, the most significant development was quite unrelated to party rules and regulations. The 'unofficial' party leader and Foreign Secretary, Joschka Fischer, gained paramount influence over the party and could almost single-handedly push through major policy changes, most notably the decision to approve German military involvement in Kosovo.

The relevance of governing potential warns us, however, against assuming a uniform trend. In countries with highly fragmented party systems (like Denmark), large parties will experience stronger presidentializing tendencies than smaller parties, and our country experts have alluded to these differences. The presidentialization of party politics is a competitive phenomenon and the success of highly presidentialized parties such as Silvio Berlusconi's Forza Italia puts all major competitors under pressure to adapt. Moreover it is clear from Mauro Calise's analysis of the Italian case that the presidentialization of party politics there has been more pronounced on the Right.

The electoral face

With respect to the electoral face of presidentialization, we have examined three components. First, we have looked for evidence of a growing emphasis on leadership appeals in election campaigning. Here our country experts have trawled through work on political marketing and communication to see if parties have become more inclined to emphasize their leaders than hitherto. Although one could easily imagine that such evidence might be strongly contingent on the personalities and leadership styles of particular leaders, we were particularly interested to see if candidate-centred campaigning has become too widespread and enduring in parliamentary regimes to be explained entirely in these terms. Relatedly, we have sought evidence that media coverage of politics focuses more on leaders than hitherto (through a review of such material studies of media agendas during election campaigns). Finally, if party campaigns and media coverage are now more leader-centred, we might reasonably expect such developments to resonate with the electorate, so we have looked for signs that leader effects have become more significant influences on voting behaviour.

The country experts agree that leader-centred election campaigning and media coverage have generally both been increasing, or started from comparatively high levels in most cases. Once again, Sweden probably represents the most 'partified' exception, but even here Aylott confirms that the media focus more on party leaders, and that the parties have responded by increasing the leadership emphasis in their campaign strategies. Very similar findings are reported in these candidate-centred times across the range of our cases. However, it is less certain that voters are behaving more as if they were in a presidential system, with something approaching a direct accountability relationship with the head of their government. Parties still preponderate in voter assessments when it comes to parliamentary elections, though this is clearly not so true of presidential elections or in the case of Israel's directly elected premiers. This, then, is probably the least convincing aspect of the presidentialization thesis. Even so, leader effects on voters do appear to be significant and/or increasing in eleven of the fourteen cases we have examined; significant and declining in one case (Canada); and we could find no clear evidence either way in two cases (Denmark and Sweden). While none of our cases reveals evidence that direct effects on voters are strong, where change has occurred it has been mainly in the direction of growing leadership effects, and a number of our authors have suggested that leaders are sometimes responsible for 'indirect' (but unmeasurable) effects on party support via their ability to shape overall party images.

We would add that, in an age of increasingly competitive elections, electorally appealing leaders may make all the difference. Undoubtedly, a large (and growing) number of voters in modern societies are less constrained by stable party loyalties, and are thus likely to be freer to base their voting decisions on the personal and political qualities of the leading candidates; this perception encourages party strategists to respond by focusing their campaigns increasingly on leaders. Indeed, one might say that this perception of the importance of leaders is what really matters: even if leaders actually only have a modest direct effect on voting behaviour, the fact that the strategists tend to be convinced of their importance nevertheless results in campaigns which are increasingly centred on party leaders. This, in turn, furnishes leaders with additional legitimacy (and hence power), as they are increasingly able to claim a personalized mandate to lead their party. Thus, as we hypothesized in Chapter 1, the party leadership rests less on a dominant coalition within the party than it does on the claim that it delivers the votes necessary to govern. Its increased power and autonomy is based on electoral appeal (or the promise of it), and this is a relatively precarious power base: presidentialized party leaders are less likely to survive electoral defeats than their precursors, who were more safely entrenched in their parties. Germany provides a clear example of this (see Chapter 3).

Overall, this review suggests that the overwhelming weight of evidence lies in favour of the presidentialization thesis, as set out in this book. To be clear about this, we have suggested that, if the term, when used as a *de facto* analogy, is to be meaningful, it should be understood as a shift in the direction of the typical presidential mode of operation—implying greater executive and party power resources and autonomy for leaders, and more personalized electoral processes. Note that this is not the same thing as presidentialism per se: we clearly recognize that a parliamentary system is a parliamentary system, with all the constraints that it imposes. Thus, there is no doubt that even a 'presidential' prime minister in a majoritarian system like the UK's can be hauled back by the countervailing forces of cabinet and parliamentary party, as demonstrated by the exit of Margaret Thatcher. We recognize too that the power and autonomy of apparently 'presidential' leaders can rest on shallow and sometimes unsustainable contingencies. So we are not simplistically proposing that parties and parliaments no longer matter, and that everything now revolves around dominant leaders. Indeed, in our different ways, we have both spent a good many years researching the operation of modern party politics and arguing that it is in the main an exaggeration to speak of 'the decline', or the 'crisis', of party (Poguntke 1996, 2002; Webb 2000, 2002). Parties continue to fulfil a number of important functions in representative democracies and remain central mechanisms for the delivery of democracy. However, it is widely recognized that the mass party of old is largely obsolete in advanced industrial democracies, and that today's major parties have adapted in various ways.

Notwithstanding the continuing relevance of party politics, though, it seems clear that under certain circumstances (for instance, when enjoying a 'personalized' electoral mandate), leaders can act with such power and/or autonomy within party or executive, and the electoral focus on them can be so considerable, that their position can be in some ways akin to that of presidents. Furthermore, we believe that there is now indisputable evidence of a steady shift in various underlying structural factors which generate greater potential for, and likelihood of, this 'presidential' working mode. This seems to hold across different formal constitutional regime-types, across consensus and majoritarian democracies, and across both federal and unitary states. It even holds where parties are most strongly institutionalized, although the absolute level of presidentialization will vary from face to face, and will certainly be constrained by institutional settings. But overall we feel confident, in view of the evidence set out in this book, that it is reasonable to talk of the 'presidentialization' of contemporary democracy. This begs an obvious question: what are the sources of this remarkable phenomenon?

THE CAUSES OF PRESIDENTIALIZATION

Verifying the causal processes behind the presidentialization phenomenon is a very challenging undertaking. We suggested a range of plausible explanatory factors in Chapter 1 and asked our country experts to evaluate their relevance to the specific cases. Clearly, such an approach stops short of rigorous quantitative modelling, but this would have been beyond the scope of the present (and perhaps any) study, for a number of reasons. One concerns the difficulties inherent in operationalizing most of the variables relevant to this study of presidentialization. How, indeed, might one quantify presidentialization itself in a precise and meaningful way? For example, when Stefaan Fiers and André Krouwel report that membership of the EU has enhanced the capacity of Belgian and Dutch prime ministers to act autonomously of other cabinet members in respect of certain policy matters, how should we interpret such information in terms of quantitative scales of measurement? It is not readily apparent how one could calibrate the concept of intra-executive autonomy in a precise way. A second issue is the classic problem of the mismatch between a relatively limited number of cases and a large number of variables with potential explanatory power (Lijphart 1971: 686): 'there are a huge number of sources of extraneous variance, but only a few cases in which to attempt to discover the manner in which all those variables operate' (Peters 1998: 65). As a result, some researchers have drawn the conclusion that the statistical and comparative methods are fundamentally different, and should not be confounded with each other (Ragin 1994). From this perspective, comparative research is a kind of half-way house between qualitative case-studies and quantitative rigour, the basic goal of which is to uncover patterns of diversity within a limited range of cases, rather than to seek out general patterns of statistical covariation across a large number of cases. Thus, it has been an important objective of this study to explore the various paths to presidentialization which have been followed within very different regime settings—parliamentary, (semi-)presidential, majoritarian, consensual, and so on. This investigation of diversity under the broad aegis of 'presidentialization' has, we hope, served to advance empirical political theory.

In this light, we asked our country experts to embark on largely qualitative studies of the extent and nature of presidentialization and the relative impact of its multiple underlying causes. On this basis, we feel able to offer some judgements about the status of our hypotheses regarding the causes of presidentialization. We can do this with reasonable confidence, though we would accept that they remain plausible hypotheses rather than incontrovertible generalizations. Nevertheless, they are supported by a good number of detailed contextual country studies, each of which draws on existing literature and circumstantial evidence.

Presidentialization, as we conceive it, is not a single process, but a set of parallel and interrelated processes, which in their different ways serve to enhance the centrality of national political leaders (see Figure 1.3). Notwithstanding the fact that we have not sought to test a general statistical model here, it is apparent from the case-studies that there is considerable support for what is essentially a parsimonious explanation. The causal inferences outlined draw heavily on secondary research, and four major factors stand out, as outlined in Chapter 1: one is a macro-societal factor (the erosion of cleavage politics) which particularly accounts for electoral presidentialization, while two others bear more heavily on the changing the nature of the state (the internationalization of decision-making and the growth of the state), and impact chiefly on executive presidentialization. The presidentialization of parties is explained by a combination of all these factors, which reflects their status as the central linkage between state and society (Lawson 1980; Poguntke 2002). Finally, we believe that one other macro-societal factor, the changing structure of mass communications, has a causal impact on all three faces of presidentialization.

Explanations of Electoral Presidentialization

(1) The erosion of traditional social cleavage politics.
As we saw in the book's opening chapter, there is a vast literature dealing with the alleged decline of traditional social cleavages like religion and class,

and its impact on party and electoral politics. While national and comparative debates have been longstanding and sometimes heated (see, for instance, Evans 1999; Franklin et al. 1992), we believe that there is simply too much smoke for there to be no fire behind it. It seems logical that where such social group identities no longer dictate voter loyalties and related ideological conflicts have become less acute, a range of other factors—including the personal qualities of party leaders and, particularly, of actual or prospective heads of governments—will become more important in guiding election campaign strategies and voting behaviour. This is not to suggest that leadership has only recently become significant: it has most probably always had some bearing on campaigning, media coverage, and voting behaviour. In part this might be because leaders sometimes represent a kind of shorthand for significant policy or ideological differences between parties or political factions. In part too, leadership evaluations have always had an important, though often overlooked, role to play in rationalistic accounts of party competition and voting behaviour. That is, pure policy preferences alone are only part of the calculation that rational utility-maximizing voters are assumed to make: they must also discount their policy evaluations of parties or candidates by estimations of the capacity of these actors to implement the promises they make. A key element of such an assessment is the view that voters take of (prospective) national leaders: are they competent or honest enough for us to believe that they will redeem their policy pledges? (Webb 2000: Ch. 3). Thus, the question of leadership has always been a rational and non-trivial part of the democratic electoral process. However, we hypothesized that it had become more prominent with the erosion of the politics of group identity in many Western democracies, and this view is certainly confirmed by the case-studies in this book. Of the fourteen countries covered, authors affirm the significance of weakening socio-political cleavages in ten cases (UK, Germany, Denmark, Finland, France, Italy, Netherlands, Portugal, Spain, Sweden).

(2) The changing structure of mass communication.
The second major societal change which would seem to be an obvious candidate in accounting for electoral presidentialization is the growing and changing role of the electronic media, which by their very nature tend to focus on personalities rather than programmes. In Chapter 1 we argued that a two-way process operates whereby the media focus on personality factors partly in order to reduce the complexity of policy issues, while politicians respond by concentrating on personal image in order to cater for the media's approach. This idea receives overwhelming support from our country experts: all bar Reuven Hazan (Israel) explicitly endorse the explanatory power of the changing structure of mass communication in relation to their countries, and Hazan does not directly deny it; rather, the focus of his chapter is a

little different to most of the others in that its primary purpose is to consider
the impact of a rare example of constitutional presidentialization. This gives
us considerable confidence about the likelihood of the media playing a
significant part in the process of electoral presidentialization.

Explanations of executive presidentialization

(1) Internationalization of political decision-making

The first major explanation of executive presidentialization which we
proposed in Chapter 1 was that the internationalization of decision-making
in certain policy domains tended to shift power towards heads of governments and their coteries of key colleagues and advisers. This has particular
relevance for the European Union member states in our sample, since European integration means that a substantial part of domestic politics is decided
like international politics, traditionally a domain of leaders rather than
parties. Eleven of our country experts give credence to this argument, including one non-EU case (UK, Germany, Canada, Denmark, Finland, Italy,
Netherlands, Belgium, Portugal, Spain, and Sweden). It is no contradiction
to our argument that so many see it this way even though the internationalization of politics can also be said to undermine the power of national
executives: that is, with more decision-making power supposedly in the
hands of supra-national non-state bodies like the IMF or the European
Central Bank, national political executives are apparently losing the power
and autonomy to decide about preferred paths of action without (potential)
interference by other political actors (Cerny 1996; Garrett and Lange 1996;
Held and McGrew 1993; Hirst and Thompson 1996; McGrew 1998). Nevertheless, from our point of view, this does not alter the fact that leaders are still
required to negotiate directly with supranational agents on behalf of their
governments. Moreover, the very fact that many domestic decisions are now
constrained by supra-national governance provides national chief executives
with additional power resources and autonomy vis-à-vis potential sources of
domestic political dissent (including their own cabinet or parties) precisely
because they can argue that their freedom of action is constrained by international or supra-national governance.

(2) Growth and complexity of the state

In Chapter 1, we drew attention to the long-term growth of state responsibility, which had rendered it increasingly fragmented and complex. This
in turn creates a pressing need for greater strategic coordination from the
centre, which might logically be expected to generate, among other things,
attempts to enhance the power and autonomy of the state's 'chief executive'.
We pointed out that this might go hand in hand with a 'hollowing-out' process

which leaves these more centralized executives in direct control of smaller domains, as the hiving-off of routine functions to new agencies or the private sector combines with other developments like growing supra-nationalism and/or the devolution of powers to sub-national political units. There is perhaps more equivocation about this as a cause of executive presidentialization among our country experts, notwithstanding the existence of authoritative secondary research which is consistent with the theory (see, for instance, Peters et al. 2000). Nevertheless, in seven cases (UK, Denmark, France, Italy, Netherlands, Belgium, and USA) our contributors offer support for this interpretation.

Explanations of intra-party presidentialization

Given the function of parties as essential linkage between the institutions of democratic governance and society, we hypothesized that the presidentialization of parties would flow from a mixture of the other explanatory processes. That is, the causes of electoral presidentialization are relevant to intra-party change in so far as they drive the leadership's desire to maximize strategic autonomy in order to play the game of party competition. Furthermore, the very fact that party leaders have assumed a paramount role in campaign strategies and media coverage alike enhances their control over all aspects of internal party life. To the extent that the party becomes identified with its leaders, it is the leader who decides what the party is and what it stands for. In addition, the process of executive presidentialization plays a part because, once in government, it becomes inconceivable that a leader who dominates the executive should be dictated to by his or her party. While the effects of the growth of the state are more indirect, the internationalization of politics immediately strengthens leaders' ability to achieve desired policy outcomes: as nation states are increasingly constrained by international and supra-national governance structures, party leaders can (and have to) use these constraints in internal disputes. Note that the same processes which strengthen chief executives work in favour of leaders of opposition parties with governing potential.

To summarize, it is clear that the model we outlined at the beginning of the book has received a wide degree of endorsement from our country experts, which in turn reflects their knowledge of the secondary literature and primary source material relevant to their countries. To reiterate, we acknowledge that this does not in itself constitute a truly systematic and independent quantitative test of the model portrayed in Fig. 1.1. Nevertheless, we believe that we have set out a persuasive interpretation for which there is considerable prima facie evidence. Ideally, further, more systematic verification would follow from our study, though we feel that there may be too many problems of operationalization for this to be feasible; this is precisely why we have chosen to rely on a combination of theoretical reasoning and expert judgements.

IMPLICATIONS FOR MODERN DEMOCRACY

This volume has assembled strong evidence that presidentialization is clearly more than a mere catchword used by journalists and political analysts alike to capture the leadership style of specific ('strong') leaders. Instead, we have argued that a meaningful concept of presidentialization needs to look at changes in the working mode of modern democracies which, in a nutshell, implies a shift from collective (or organizational) to individual power and accountability. These changes manifest themselves in three interrelated faces, that is, within the executive, within political parties, and within the electoral process. Normally, such changes are not induced or sustained by formal legal-constitutional modifications. Rather, they tend to occur within the unaltered institutional frameworks of parliamentary, semi-presidential, and presidential systems. They make parliamentary and semi-presidential systems function more according to the inherent logic of presidential regimes, while they take the working mode of presidential regimes closer to their logical conclusion.

First and foremost, this means a weakening of party as a collective actor in modern democracies. This is not to be confounded with the widely discussed 'decline of party' (see, for example Cotter and Bibby 1980; Daalder 1992; Reiter 1989). On the contrary, there is widespread evidence that parties continue to perform tasks that are critical to the operation of modern democracy (Webb 2002: 444–50). Most notably, they have maintained their central role as a mechanism for elite selection. Even within the European multi-level system of governance, widely criticized for its 'democratic deficit' (Boyce 1993; Hayward 1995; Schmitter 2000), parties have a central role as gatekeepers controlling access to virtually all important positions (Hix 1999: 168; Mair 2000: 38). However, they have been substantially challenged as actors aggregating interests (Lawson and Poguntke 2004), shaping policy outcomes or controlling political communications. This is in keeping with the dominant interpretation of party theory, which has maintained that political parties in modern democracies have changed from vehicles of mass integration to organizations which are increasingly providing democracy as a service by the state for its citizens.

Since the early 1960s commentators have been suggesting the transformation of western political parties away from the classic mass party model into something inherently less concerned with the functions of mass integration or the articulation of specific social group interests. Major parties, at least, since Otto Kirchheimer (1966) have generally been regarded as motivated primarily by vote-winning and office-seeking goals, a change which requires, *inter alia*, the downgrading of narrow group ties and softening of class ideologies in favour of broadly aggregative programmatic appeals. This conception of party change lies at the heart of Kirchheimer's own model of the 'catch-all' party, but is equally central to later conceptions, which have added further layers of analysis, such as Angelo Panebianco's 'electoral-professional' party (1988) and Katz and Mair's 'cartel party' (1995). Central to each of these models is the claim that the power of party leaders relative to that of members has been enhanced. Why? Primarily because leaders and their closest advisers require maximum autonomy to adjust party strategy in order to more effectively win the support of the key swing voters who decide election outcomes, and who lack close ties or loyalties to particular parties. Thus, the presidentialization of politics in advanced industrial democracies might be seen as a logical component and vindication of these models of party development.

It may seem counter-intuitive but chief executives and party leaders in an age of presidentialization have become more vulnerable than they were in the era of partified politics. As they rely less on the support of a dominant coalition within their party and base their claim to political leadership more exclusively on their personal mandate, they become more susceptible to the fickle mood swings of public opinion. The credibility of this mandate is continuously monitored by opinion polls, and any serious downturn undermines the legitimacy of their claim to leadership. To be sure, this is more immediately relevant for leaders of a government responsible to parliament who need to maintain the re-election prospects of those MPs keeping them in office, but the prospects of a US president to push desired legislation through Congress are also directly related to his public opinion approval ratings. While a president's survival in office will, of course, not be threatened by negative public opinion, prime ministers are highly vulnerable. The more they have based their leadership on a personalized mandate rather than on anchorage in a dominant intra-party coalition, the more they will be vulnerable as soon as their claim to power erodes. While Helmut Kohl could survive a string of defeats and poor publicity because he could count on the solid loyalty of most relevant party actors, Gerhard Schröder could not endure a similar set of circumstances for long: his decision to renounce the party leadership in early 2004 was a clear indication of his precarious power base within his own party.

Clearly, while presidentialization does not necessarily imply durable leadership, it is associated with strong leadership—while it lasts: as long as presidentialized leaders can count on robust public support they may be able to impose their will upon their party (and the legislature) quite unilaterally. Felipe González's U-turn on Spanish NATO membership, Tony Blair's engagement in Iraq or Gerhard Schröder's decision to initiate neo-liberal reforms in 2003 are but three conspicuous examples—the latter illus-trating both the ability of presidentialized leaders to push through policy changes and their vulnerability if their poll ratings slump.

In one sense, presidentialization seems to hark back to elitist models of representative democracy. For instance, Schumpeter's classic *Capitalism, Socialism and Democracy* (1942) emphasizes several features which resonate with the political phenomenon described in these pages, including the com-petitive struggle for power between rival political elites, the centrality of political leadership to this struggle and to government, and the prescription of a relatively limited political role for citizens, as voters who periodically choose leaders, but are largely passive beyond this. Schumpeter felt that this situation was both inevitable and desirable in view of most citizens' poor cognitive capacities in respect of public affairs: it was imperative that there was 'democratic self-control', as he put it—that is, broad agreement about the undesirability of voters and politicians confusing their respective roles, and of excessive criticism of leaders on all issues. Of course, democratic elitism is also compatible with parliamentarism and competition between parties, but the shift to greater leadership power and autonomy within parties and the executive of the state further reduces the body of actors who shape and define key strategic political decision-making. Principles of collegiality and accountability to cabinet colleagues, party sub-leaders or grass roots take a further step into the background.

However, the fit between this elitist model of democracy and the modern presidentialization phenomenon is far from exact. While Schumpeter strongly favoured maximum autonomy for political elites after having as-sumed office, modern media democracy means that democratic legitimacy is more frequently reasserted nowadays via membership ballots, referenda, and the continuous tracking of leadership popularity through opinion polls. Furthermore, Schumpeter's prescription for a limited political role for a largely ignorant citizenry has clearly become unsustainable in an age of cognitive mobilization and more differentiated participatory aspirations (Barnes et al. 1979; Dalton 1984; Jennings et al. 1990).

From this perspective, it could be argued that modern democracies are moving towards a fusion of elitist and plebiscitary models of democracy. While leadership power grows, it is supposedly legitimated and checked through the plebiscitary elements of modern media democracy, including polling and the increasing use of methods of direct democracy. However, these are highly imperfect forms of democratic accountability, since they are at least partly susceptible to being elite-driven. Membership ballots and referenda, for example, are more often than not initiated and controlled by leaders, and opinion research can hardly be regarded as a tool of the public at large to control elite action (though it can be a means by which the media may set the political agenda). In a nutshell, the plebiscitary features of modern democratic politics tend to enhance, rather than limit, elite autonomy by providing leaders with an additional power resource through which to bypass collective decision-making bodies. Yet, the plebiscitary element of what might be called a 'neo-elitist' model of democracy is a double-edged sword: deprived of their previously relatively stable power bases that were built on alliances within political parties, leaders are left stronger in victory, but weaker in defeat.

REFERENCES

Barnes, S. H. and M. Kaase (1979). *Political Action: Mass Participation in Five Western Democracies*. London/Beverly Hills: Sage Publications.

Boyce, B. (1993). The Democratic Deficit of the European Community, *Parliamentary Affairs*, 46: 458–477.

Cerny, P. (1996). 'International finance and the erosion of state policy capacity', in P. Gummett (ed.), *Globalization and Public Policy*. Cheltenham: Edward Elgar, 83–104.

Cotter, C. and J. Bibby (1980). 'Institutional Development of Parties and the Thesis of Party Decline', *Political Science Quarterly*, 95: 1–27.

Daalder, H. (1992). 'A Crisis of Party?', *Scandinavian Political Studies*, 15: 269–287.

Dalton, R. J. (1984). 'Cognitive Mobilization and Partisan Dealignment in Advanced Industrial Democracies', *Journal of Politics*, 46: 264–284.

Franklin, M. N., T. T. Mackie, and H. Valen (1992). *Electoral Change: Responses to Evolving Social and Attitudinal Structures in Western Countries*. Cambridge: Cambridge University Press.

Garrett, G. and P. Lange (1996). 'Internationalisation, institutions and political change', in R. Keohane and H. Milner (eds.), *Internationalisation and Domestic Politics*. London: Cambridge University Press, 48–75.

Hayward, Jack E. S. (1995). *The Crisis of Representation in Europe*. London: Frank Cass.

Held, D. and A. McGrew (1993). 'Globalisation and the Liberal Democratic State', *Government and Opposition*, 28: 261–285.

Hirst, P. and G. Thompson (1996). *Globalisation in Question*. Cambridge: Polity Press.

Hix, S. (1999). *The Political System of the European Union*. New York: St. Martin's Press.

Jennings, M. K. and J. van Deth (1990). *Continuities in Political Action: A Longitudinal Study of Political Orientations in Three Western Democracies*. Berlin/New York: de Gruyter.

Katz, R. S. and P. Mair (1995). 'Changing Models of Party Organization and Party Democracy: The Emergence of the Cartel Party', *Party Politics*, 1: 5–28.

Kirchheimer, O. (1966). 'The Transformation of the Western European Party System', in J. LaPalombara and W. Myron (eds.), *Political Parties and Political Development*. Princeton, NJ: Princeton University Press, 177–200.

Lawson, K. (1980). 'Political Parties and Linkage', in K. Lawson (ed.), *Political Parties and Linkage. A Comparative Perspective.* New Haven/London: Yale University Press, 3–24.

—— and T. Poguntke (ed.) (2004). *How Political Parties Respond: Interest Aggregation Revisited.* London/New York: Routledge.

Lijphart, A. (1971). 'Comparative Politics and the Comparative Method', *American Political Science Review*, 65: 682–93.

Mair, P. (1994). 'Party organizations: from civil society to state', in R. S. Katz and P. Mair (eds.), *How Parties Organize: Change and Adaptation in Party Organizations in Western Democracies.* London: Sage Publications, pp. 1–22.

—— (2000). 'The Limited Impact of Europe on National Party Systems', *West European Politics*, 23: 27–51.

McGrew, A. G. (1998). 'Globalisation: conceptualising a moving target', in J. Eatwell et al. (eds.), *Understanding Globalisation.* Stockholm: Almqvist and Wicksell, 7–30.

Panebianco, A. (1988). *Political Parties: Organization and Power.* Cambridge: Cambridge University Press.

Peters, B. G. (1998). *Comparative Politics: Theory and Methods.* Basingstoke: Macmillan.

—— R. A. W. Rhodes, and V. Wright (2000). 'Staffing the Summit—the Administration of the Core Executive: Convergent Trends and National Specificities', in B. G. Peters, R. A. W. Rhodes, and V. Wright (eds.), *Administering the Summit: Administration of the Core Executive in Developed Countries.* Basingstoke: Macmillan.

Poguntke, T. (1996). 'Anti-Party Sentiment—Conceptual Thoughts and Empirical Evidence: Explorations into a Minefield', *European Journal of Political Research*, 29: 319–344.

—— (2000). *Parteiorganisation im Wandel. Gesellschaftliche Verankerung und organisatorische Anpassung im europäischen Vergleich.* Wiesbaden: Westdeutscher Verlag.

—— (2001). *From Nuclear Building Sites to Cabinet: The Career of the German Green Party*, Keele: Keele European Parties Research Unit (KEPRU), Working Paper No. 6.

—— (2002). 'Parties without Firm Social Roots? Party Organisational Linkage', in K. R. Luther and F. Müller-Rommel (eds.), *Political Parties in the New Europe: Political and Analytical Challenges.* Oxford: Oxford University Press, 43–62.

Ragin, C. (1994). *Constructing Social Research.* Thousand Oaks: Pine Forge Press.

Reiter, H. L. (1989). 'Party Decline in the West: A Sceptic's View', *Journal of Theoretical Politics*, 1: 325–348.

Rüdig, W. (2002). 'Germany', in F. Müller-Rommel and T. Poguntke (eds.), *Green Parties in National Governments.* London/Portland, Or: Frank Cass, 78–111.

Schmitter, P. C. (2000). *How to Democratize the European Union . . . and Why Bother.* Lanham, MD: Rowman and Littlefield.

Webb, P. D. (2000). *The Modern British Party System.* London: Sage Publications.

—— (2002). 'Conclusion: Political parties and democratic control in advanced industrial societies', in P. Webb, D. Farrell, and I. Hollidays (eds.), *Political Parties in Advanced Industrial Societies.* Oxford: Oxford University Press, 438–460.

Index

CPSIA information can be obtained at www.ICGtesting.com
Printed in the USA
LVOW09s1310120416

483225LV00001B/1/P

9 780199 218493